Charleston Syllabus

Charleston Syllabus

READINGS ON RACE, RACISM,
AND RACIAL VIOLENCE

EDITED BY

**CHAD WILLIAMS,
KIDADA E. WILLIAMS,
AND KEISHA N. BLAIN**

THE UNIVERSITY OF GEORGIA PRESS
Athens

A Sarah Mills Hodge Fund Publication
This publication is made possible in part through a grant from the Hodge
Foundation in memory of its founder, Sarah Mills Hodge, who devoted her
life to the relief and education of African Americans in Savannah, Georgia.

A portion of the royalties from the sales of the book will go to The
Lowcountry Ministries Fund, an initiative of the Palmetto Project and
the City of Charleston.

Library of Congress Cataloging-in-Publication Data
Names: Williams, Chad Louis, 1976– editor. | Williams, Kidada E., editor.
| Blain, Keisha N., 1985– editor.
Title: Charleston syllabus : readings on race, racism, and racial violence /
edited by Chad Williams, Kidada E. Williams, and Keisha N. Blain.
Description: Athens : The University of Georgia Press, 2016. | Includes
bibliographical references.
Identifiers: LCCN 2015048921| ISBN 9780820349565 (hardcover : alk.
paper) | ISBN 9780820349572 (pbk. : alk. paper)
Subjects: LCSH: United States—Race relations—History. | Racism—
United States—History. | African Americans—History.
Classification: LCC E184.A1 .C4445 2016 | DDC 305.800973—dc23
LC record available at http://lccn.loc.gov/2015048921

CONTENTS

Charleston Syllabus

INTRODUCTION

CHAD WILLIAMS, KIDADA E. WILLIAMS,
AND KEISHA N. BLAIN

The June 17, 2015, evening bible study at the Emanuel African Methodist Episcopal (AME) Church in Charleston, South Carolina, began innocently enough. Twelve regular parishioners and church members gathered in the basement fellowship hall, including pastor and South Carolina state senator Rev. Clementa Pinckney. A new participant joined them on this night, a twenty-one-year-old white man named Dylann Roof, who arrived just after eight. The group welcomed Roof, who made a point to sit next to Rev. Pinckney, into their circle. They prayed and read verses from the Gospel according to Mark, with Roof occasionally disagreeing about certain passages. Then, after an hour had passed, he stood and calmly announced, "I'm here to kill black people."

At that point, he pulled a Glock 41 .45-caliber handgun from his fanny pack and began to unload. Rev. Pinckney was his first victim, shot at point-blank range. Roof continued to fire and, equipped with eight magazines of hollow-point bullets, reload as he methodically executed eight other men and women, ranging in age from twenty-six to eighty-seven, some of whom pled with him before their lives were taken. When asked by one victim why he was doing this, Roof responded, "You are raping our women and taking over the country." Roof last approached seventy-year-old church trustee Polly Sheppard. "I'm going to let you live so you can tell what happened," he told her before exiting the church and driving away, leaving a scene of bloodshed and horror in his wake. As the full magnitude of the shooting unfolded overnight, it became clear that the Charleston Emanuel AME shooting would stand as one of the worst incidents of racial terrorism in American history.[1]

Law enforcement apprehended Dylann Roof the following day. Details about his life and beliefs soon emerged, revealing Roof to be a committed white supremacist. Pictures surfaced of Roof posing with the Confederate battle flag and wearing a jacket adorned with apartheid-era South African and Rhodesian flags. In a manifesto posted on a personal website, Roof mused on a range of topics, including his racial enlightenment as a result of the Trayvon Martin case; the inherent inferiority of African Americans, Jews, and Latinos; and the fallacy of American patriotism. Explaining his murderous actions and desire to start a race war, Roof wrote:

> I have no choice. I am not in the position to, alone, go into the ghetto and fight. I
> chose Charleston because it is most historic city in my state, and at one time had

the highest ratio of black to Whites in the country. We have no skinheads, no real KKK, no one doing anything but talking on the internet. Well someone has to have the bravery to take it to the real world, and I guess that has to be me.

In his iconography and words, Roof proudly presented himself as a soldier in the cause of white supremacy and racial nationalism, all underlined by a distorted interpretation of history.

Certain narratives began to coalesce in the immediate aftermath of the massacre that revealed a widespread lack of historical understanding and willingness to engage with the substance of what took place in Charleston. Dylann Roof was quickly painted as a lone, troubled young man with views far outside the bounds of mainstream white opinions about race. Media outlets questioned if the shooting truly qualified as an act of terrorism. The soon all-consuming debate about the Confederate flag presented its supporters as honest adherents of southern "pride" and "heritage." Politicians praised the willingness of the victims' families to forgive Dylann Roof, using their actions to convey the message that the nation as a whole must also move on from its troubled racial past. This was offered as the basis for a renewed "conversation" about race in America.

The Charleston massacre, however, revealed the need for a different type of conversation, one that as historians we knew had to be grounded in an honest appraisal of the past. Dylann Roof was not an anomaly but, in fact, a product of American history, a history shaped by a legacy of white supremacist thought dating back to the founding of the country. His actions carried on a long tradition of white terrorist violence against African Americans stretching through much of the nineteenth and twentieth centuries. The "heritage" of the Confederate States of America was of unabashed commitment to white supremacy and the perpetuation of chattel slavery. Dylann Roof had a clear understanding about what the flag represented and the "pride" it engendered as the basis for a particular type of white identity. Talk of forgiveness could not be understood without knowledge of the history of African American religion and the specific role of the black church as a site of both salvation and resistance.

As educators committed to engaging with a larger public, we also realized the significance of the Charleston shooting as a learning opportunity and knew we had a unique responsibility. Indeed, we asked ourselves, what exact role were we to play at this moment as historians? What resources could we bring to light for people to understand the meaning of the Charleston shooting and its both historical and contemporary relevance? How could we help educators teach about Charleston when classes resumed in the fall? Perhaps most important, in what ways could we empower people who were hungry to learn and eager to do something—anything—in the wake of the tragedy but did not know where to turn?

Social media has become a vital tool for communal learning and the spread of knowledge beyond traditional sources. Twitter, in particular, has emerged as an important democratic space for challenging mainstream media narratives and engaging in critical dialogue. Use of the hashtag has proven remarkably effective in shaping conversations about race, connecting people across time and space, and mobilizing new social, political, and intellectual movements. It can also, if employed conscientiously, serve as a bibliographic marker and tool for historical literacy.

In thinking about events in Charleston and our frustration surrounding their portrayal, the #FergusonSyllabus immediately came to mind. On August 9, 2014, in the St. Louis suburb of Ferguson, Missouri, white police officer Darren Wilson shot and killed unarmed African American teenager Michael Brown following a confrontation between the two men. Protests erupted in the aftermath of the shooting, to which local police responded with militarized force. The governor of Missouri declared a state of emergency. Everyday life for Ferguson's black community came to a halt. Marcia Chatelain, professor of history and African American studies at Georgetown University, recognizing this also meant an interruption to the start of the new school year, took to Twitter and, using the hashtag #FergusonSyllabus, began soliciting resources to help teachers and parents assist their children in understanding the events surrounding the Ferguson uprising. Professor Chatelain's #FergusonSyllabus proved remarkably successful and demonstrated the potential of hashtag education to address moments of racial trauma in ways that connected the public and the classroom.

Inspired by the #FergusonSyllabus and eager to create a constructive space to channel these frustrations, Professor Chad Williams took to Twitter on the evening of June 19, 2015, and introduced the hashtag #CharlestonSyllabus. "Lots of ignorance running rampant," Williams wrote. "Folks need a #CharlestonSyllabus." Shortly thereafter, the three of us began tweeting book and article titles and links to primary sources related to the Charleston shooting and its much longer historical context. We were joined by dozens of other scholars, librarians, teachers, and students of history who suggested a range of sources, including art and creative fiction. They even recommended museums and galleries to visit and documentaries to view. Within the span of an hour, #CharlestonSyllabus became a trending topic. With people tweeting in from across the nation and the world, the hashtag represented the very best of crowdsourcing and collaboration between educators and the larger public.

The magnitude of what we had initiated quickly set in. Professor Keisha Blain worked to keep track of the flood of recommended readings and began to compile the reading list on the website of the African American Intellectual History Society (AAIHS). Librarians Cecily Walker, Ryan P. Randall, and Melissa Morrone volunteered to assist in organizing the titles and linking them to the WorldCat Library database. Elliot Brandow, a librarian at Boston College, provided additional assistance by tagging all the books and resources on Worldcat—making it easy for scholars and members of the general public to scroll through the selections and determine which were available at their local libraries. By midweek, over ten thousand tweets had been posted under the hashtag, and #CharlestonSyllabus had gone from one tweet to a major library resource.

In just a few days, we had compiled a remarkable list of resources. The list consisted of texts that offered extensive historical contextualization across a broad range of time periods, including the antebellum period and its accompanying concerns regarding slavery, the Civil War and Reconstruction, the late nineteenth- and early twentieth-century Jim Crow era, and the mid- to late twentieth-century civil rights and Black Power movements. Within this periodization the #CharlestonSyllabus highlighted specific themes and issues, such as race and religion, the Confederate flag, global white supremacy, and the particular histories of South Carolina and the city of Charleston. As a resource for more than just historians, the #CharlestonSyllabus also included contemporary editorials about the Charleston shooting, novels and poetry, children's literature, musical selections, key primary source documents, and links to educational websites and curriculum materials.

A challenge we soon faced was what to do with the #CharlestonSyllabus and how best to use this remarkably rich collection of resources. Some people commented that the #CharlestonSyllabus was not really a true syllabus in the sense that it neither articulated a pedagogical objective nor provided a clear road map for translating the various books, essays, songs, and documents into use in the classroom. This was true. The issue of accessibility also loomed large. We never envisioned the #CharlestonSyllabus solely for scholars or individuals familiar with how to locate the materials on the #CharlestonSyllabus, whether in a library or elsewhere. Could we move the #CharlestonSyllabus from a web page and Twitter conversation into people's hands as an actual physical resource?

These questions were still being discussed when Lisa Bayer and Walter Biggins of the University of Georgia Press approached us about producing a book for both educators as well as a general or nonacademic audience. Despite the wealth of scholarship and resources at our disposal, teachers at the college and university level remain challenged when it comes to issues of race and African American history specifically. The black experience, in all its pain and beauty, is still too often treated as tangential to the larger narrative of American history.

As such, issues related to the legacies of white supremacy, such as racial violence, are not seriously confronted in the classroom. For those professors willing to commit the time and energy necessary to an honest engagement with the American past, just what sources to utilize and how best to structure their pedagogical approaches can be vexing.

The barriers to critical learning about the black experience outside academia remain even more acute. So much academic history is published in journals with paywalls or written in jargon for other academics that it is virtually inaccessible to nonspecialists. Textbooks published for K–12 schools have certainly improved in terms of providing more inclusive histories involving African Americans, but they still sidestep larger, more complex issues such as white identity and institutional racism. On issues such as the Civil War, pressure from interest groups to tell a more "positive" U.S. history, one that elides slavery's centrality to the conflict, has resulted in some of today's students receiving watered-down or whitewashed histories. People educated before the histories of gender, religion, class, and race and ethnicity were included in U.S. history curriculums are less familiar with the advances in historical knowledge. State divestment from higher education has resulted in higher and higher tuition, making college unaffordable to larger numbers of the public. Is it no wonder then that some Americans who were attempting to make sense of the massacre could not connect the dots between slavery, white terror organizations such as the Ku Klux Klan, the Confederate battle flag, and Dylann Roof's decision to walk into an African American religious sanctuary and shoot down nine of its members?

This book addresses these concerns. It brings together a condensed version of the #CharlestonSyllabus. Knowing that we could not reasonably choose every text, our pedagogical objective here is to provide some of the best works from the reading list so that educators and people invested in expanding their knowledge can obtain a better understanding of the histories feeding into the massacre or the reactions. We hope readers will see this book as a gateway into the never-ending process of historical enlightenment and empowerment. For existing students of history who are disconnected from institutions of higher education, we hope the book serves as a ramp onto another, higher level of U.S. and global history.

The structure of the book is based largely on the #CharlestonSyllabus resource list. Many of the readings are from the list itself, but we have added readings to address gaps and omissions. This reader incorporates a combination of primary and secondary sources, including op-eds, speeches, song lyrics, and excerpts from books and journal articles. Each section contains historical context for various issues that informed the Charleston shooting and its aftermath. We pay particular attention to the history of South Carolina and Charleston and place this history in conversation with related national and international historical developments.

From its inception as a hashtag, we envisioned the #CharlestonSyllabus as a work of historical scholarship and as a reflection of the breadth of the black intellectual tradition. Indeed, #CharlestonSyllabus is a testament to the generations of remarkable scholarship to which we as professional historians owe our existence. The texts, novels, poems, films, songs, and primary source documents selected for the #CharlestonSyllabus are foundational to the study of black people's experiences and the meaning of race in modern history. While by no means exhaustive, the #CharlestonSyllabus offers a useful starting point for immersion into the richness of African American history.

The reader is arranged thematically and chronologically. The first section examines the histories of the transatlantic slave trade and the rise of chattel slavery and antiblack racism in the United States and the Atlantic World. Rather than simply focusing on the institution and how it functioned, this section also illuminates African and African-descended peoples' efforts to resist slavery's dehumanizing effects. In Charleston, South Carolina, and beyond, the legacies of slavery remain etched into nearly every aspect of American society and continue to inform the value placed on black life today.

Confronted with daily physical and spiritual assaults on their lives and very humanity, enslaved Africans and their descendants turned to religion as a source for resistance and salvation. Section 2 shows how Africans, and then African Americans, fought to navigate a world in which their traditional religious heritage was not always tolerated and how they nevertheless found ways to create a spiritual center that affirmed their individual and collective self-worth. Black men and women forged religious practices, identities, and institutions, such as Charleston's Emanuel African Methodist Episcopal Church, that helped them cope with and fight against the various incarnations of white supremacy. African Americans, through their varying relationships to God, also developed understandings about the meaning of faith, justice, freedom, and forgiveness that have been shaped by their unique historical experiences from slavery to the present.

The third section addresses the misconceptions many Americans continue to hold about the Civil War and Reconstruction. Documents reveal the true basis of the Confederate nation-building project, as well as the actions of enslaved people to transform the war into a battle for their freedom. The legacy of political and religious leaders such as Clementa Pinckney can be traced back to the Reconstruction era, a period of democratic promise that came to an abrupt end, due in no small part to white racial terrorism. Understanding debates about the Confederate flag cannot be separated from attempts to forget the history of Reconstruction, as well as the causes of the Civil War and the central role of race and slavery in it.

Section 4 shifts to slavery's political and social afterlife and the rise of domestic and global white supremacy. The idea of white supremacy constituted the foundation of a global color line and the imperial exploitation of African peoples. In the United States, this took the form of a racial caste system that segregated Americans in most areas of life and that was backed with the brutal violence of lynching coupled with systemic economic subjugation and the beginnings of mass incarceration. The texts here show how African Americans fought back using lawsuits, armed self-defense, and a coordinated effort to expose the logics behind Jim Crow and their contradictions to the nation's professed values.

African Americans' fight against white supremacy reached a high point in the 1950s and 1960s. The fifth section showcases the maturation of two interconnected social movements designed to dismantle Jim Crow and undo its effects. The texts here demonstrate the regional and ideological diversity of the civil rights and Black Power movements and their participants. From Charleston across the nation to Oakland or up the coast to Philadelphia, African Americans committed to transforming the nation and themselves. These readings reveal the national and international scope of activists' efforts into the 1970s, which laid the foundation for twenty-first-century black politics.

The final section offers perspectives on race and racial violence from the 1980s to the present. The readings challenge commonly held perceptions about the emergence of a "postracial" society since the passage of the Civil Rights Act (1964) and Voting Rights Act (1965). Despite the political gains of the modern civil rights–Black Power movement, the readings in this section capture the continued struggles for racial justice and equality and reflect on the significance of the presidential election of Barack Obama. They highlight a new generation's fight against racial violence by vigilantes and the state as well as mass incarceration. The texts here close the circle, bringing us back to the massacre at Mother Emanuel on June 17 and the national and international reaction to it.

It is impossible to measure the full devastation of the Charleston massacre. The lives of Sharonda Coleman-Singleton, Cynthia Hurd, Susie Jackson, Ethel Lance, Depayne Middleton-Doctor, Clementa Pinckney, Tywanza Sanders, Daniel Simmons, and Myra Thompson can never be replaced. The scars on the collective psyches of black people in Charleston, throughout the United States, and indeed across the globe will remain. The history of American racial violence will now forever include the tragic events of June 17, 2015. It is our responsibility to confront this history, understand it, learn from it, and do our part, however small, to ensure that what took place in Charleston never happens again. We hope that the *Charleston Syllabus* provides knowledge, strength, and inspiration in this cause.

NOTE

1. "3 Survivors of the Charleston Church Shooting Grapple with Their Grief," *Washington Post*, June 24, 2015; "Church Massacre Suspect Held as Charleston Grieves," *New York Times*, June 18, 2015.

PART 1

Slavery, Survival, and Community Building

KIDADA E. WILLIAMS

Historian Ira Berlin has described the transatlantic slave trade and chattel slavery as being the "ground zero" of race relations in the United States, shaping ideas about white racial superiority and black inferiority that continue to resonate today.[1] After slavery ended, these histories were erased. Or they were sanitized, as seen in the all too common beliefs that slavery simply involved working without pay. Views such as these overlook the sheer terror and brutality associated with slavery and deemphasize its dehumanizing aspects. Where violence is acknowledged in portrayals of the institution, enslaved men and women are typically rendered helpless victims—entirely stripped of their agency. Contrary to the image of submissive and faithful slaves, enslaved men and women devised a range of strategies to challenge slavery. African captives and their descendants did not simply surrender their freedom; enslavers had to take it using extreme amounts of violence.

Historical records indicate that the trade in African captives across the Atlantic began circa the early 1500s and lasted until the late 1880s. Over the trade's time span, European powers transported roughly 10 million men, women, and children from West and Central Africa to the Americas, where they enslaved them for life. The majority of these captives were sent to Brazil (roughly 4.8 million), the Caribbean (4 million), and Central America (1.3 million). Only about 650,000 were transported to what became the United States. Roughly 1–2 million died or were killed before they arrived in the Americas. Statistics such as these, while useful, fail to embody the horror such people faced being kidnapped and forcibly transported to a strange land.

Statistics also do not help us understand worlds thrown into chaos by the trade. The excerpt from Stephanie Smallwood's *Saltwater Slavery* illuminates the social landscapes of the West African coastal cities exporting slaves. Close attention to the particulars of the trade allow us to understand who was taken and when, where, and how those things shaped the communities to which these men, women, and children were delivered on the other side of the Atlantic.

Slavery in the most basic terms was an economic and labor system focused on maximizing wealth in the production of cash crops, extraction of natural resources, or use of domestic or urban laborers. The economic benefits that the subjects of Europe, citizens of the United States, and all levels of the state from both sides of the Atlantic gained from the slave trade and slavery were significant. Even having one or two slaves could make an owner wealthy and set dependents on course for prosperity. Chasing profit by extracting the most work possible out of laborers while providing them with the least amount of food, shelter, and medical care constituted a greater priority for slaveholders and the industries that helped the institution function than the well-being of the slaves themselves. As a result, enslaved people were treated primarily as property, without social, political, or economic rights.

Chattel slavery in the Americas was a more vicious institution than other types of unfree labor, including European indentured servitude, Russian serfdom, or domestic slavery in West and Central Africa. Indentured servitude was mostly voluntary, while chattel slavery was always compulsory. Servants were bonded for an established tenure, but chattel slaves were held for life. Although English servants were bound, they maintained many of their rights and privileges as English subjects, which was a vital check on their masters' abuse of power. Enslaved Africans only enjoyed the rights enslavers granted. Domestic slaves in West and Central Africa did not acquire their legal status at birth, as American slaves did. Indentured servants, serfs, and domestic slaves could improve their societal and economic status over time and anticipate a life of freedom, unlike chattel slaves.

Enslavers extorted compliance using extreme amounts of physical violence—ranging from threats of bodily harm to actual whipping, rape, torture, and mutilation. In the selections from her memoir, *Incidents in the Life of a Slave Girl*, Harriet Jacobs recounts the continual physical and sexual abuse she endured while enslaved in North Carolina. While slaveholding men stand out in the popular imagination as the perpetrators of violence in slavery, Jacobss's memoir shows how slaveholding women embraced violence too.

Between 1808 and 1859, a brisk trade in slaves continued as Americans moved west and south. Two million enslaved people were sold, and traders made millions of dollars annually. About six hundred thousand of these men, women, and children were transported from places such as Virginia and Maryland to locales such as Mississippi and Louisiana. The rest were traded within their respective states. As Walter Johnson's piece shows, the buyers and sellers of slaves brought to the marketplace ideas about the inferiority of blackness and the supremacy of whiteness that were strengthened by what enslavers saw in the antebellum market.

The domestic slave trade devastated families. Charles Ball was one of the souls violently uprooted from people he loved and who loved him and from the world to which his family belonged. The excerpt from his narrative reveals the heartbreaking horrors and uncertainties of forced relocation.

When enslavers took bondspeople's freedom, the bondspeople fought back. Even as chattel slavery became more entrenched in the nation, enslaved people ran away, killed, destroyed property, and planned and participated in revolts to destroy the institution. Unlike parts of the Caribbean where black majorities and slaves' military service gave a critical edge to rebels seeking to destroy slavery (even succeeding in the case of Haiti), the black minority and a near universal ban on blacks having access to guns or serving in militias undermined enslaved Americans' chances to destroy slavery via a peacetime revolution in the United States. Leslie Harris's work shows that enslaved people resisted northern slavery too. Interracial coalitions led to northern abolition in states such as New York.

The majority of Africans and African Americans remained enslaved for life, but as a result of self-purchase, military service in the American Revolution and the War of 1812, the destruction of slavery in the northern colonies and then states, and flight, the free black population grew. After the United States was formed, these men and women fought to enjoy rights as citizens. They petitioned legislators for the right to vote based on the taxes they paid. They even withheld their taxes, risking jail. In the American urban centers where free blacks lived, they created schools and churches and formed benevolent societies and businesses to address their various needs. Some abandoned the United States altogether, heading to Sierra Leone, Liberia, or Haiti. Others decided to fight for social and political rights in America.

With relatives who were still enslaved, and knowing that as long as slavery existed, they would never enjoy equal rights, free blacks worked tirelessly to destroy the institution. As the op-ed from Maurie McInnis shows, black northerners weren't the only ones trying to destroy slavery. Outraged by the proslavery teachings of Charleston's Christian churches, free blacks established the African Church to provide religious instruction suitable to their antislavery interests. City officials saw this as a threat to their slaveholding concerns and launched numerous attacks, which was the likely catalyst for some members of Emanuel, including Denmark Vesey, to launch a plot to destroy slavery once and for all. The plot failed, and white Charlestonians retaliated, but they never extinguished African Americans' desire for freedom and their determination to attain it.

Henry Highland Garnet's "Address to the Slaves" shows the links between black communities across the line of slave and free. But enslaved people did not need urging. They were always fighting in ways that made sense to them. For many of them, this meant preserving their lives and those of their loved ones so that they could enjoy freedom together.

Black Americans celebrated freedom wherever it occurred in the Americas. They fled slavery and aided freedom seekers. Blacks joined forces with white abolitionists and formed organizations to destroy slavery once and for all. By 1860, all enslaved Americans and their allies needed to strike at the heart of slavery was a civil war.

NOTES

1. Ira Berlin, "Coming to Terms with Slavery in the Twenty-First Century," in *Slavery and Public History: The Tough Stuff of American Memory*, ed. James Oliver Horton and Lois E. Horton (Chapel Hill: University of North Carolina Press, 2008), 3.

An Address to the Slaves
of the United States

(1843)

Brethren and Fellow Citizens:—Your brethren of the North, East, and West have been accustomed to meet together in National Conventions, to sympathize with each other, and to weep over your unhappy condition. In these meetings we have addressed all classes of the free, but we have never, until this time, sent a word of consolation and advice to you. . . .

Slavery has fixed a deep gulf between you and us, and while it shuts out from you the relief and consolation which your friends would willingly render, it affects and persecutes you with a fierceness which we might not expect to see in the fiends of hell. But still the Almighty Father of mercies has left to us a glimmering ray of hope, which shines out like a lone star in a cloudy sky. Mankind are becoming wiser, and better—the oppressor's power is fading, and you, every day, are becoming better informed, and more numerous. Your grievances, brethren, are many. We shall not attempt, in this short address, to present to the world all the dark catalogue of this nation's sins, which have been committed upon an innocent people. Nor is it indeed necessary, for you feel them from day to day, and all the civilized world look upon them with amazement.

Two hundred and twenty seven years ago, the first of our injured race were brought to the shores of America. They came not with glad spirits to select their homes in the New World. They came not with their own consent, to find an unmolested enjoyment of the blessings of this fruitful soil. The first dealings they had with men calling themselves Christians, exhibited to them the worst features of corrupt and sordid hearts; and convinced them that no cruelty is too great, no villainy and no robbery too abhorrent for even enlightened men to perform, when influenced by avarice and lust. Neither did they come flying upon the wings of Liberty, to a land of freedom. But they came with broken hearts, from their beloved native land, and were doomed to unrequited toil and deep degradation. Nor did the evil of their bondage end at their emancipation by death. Succeeding generations inherited their chains, and millions have come from eternity into time, and have returned again to the world of spirits, cursed and ruined by American slavery. . . .

Nearly three millions of your fellow citizens are prohibited by law and public opinion, (which in this country is stronger than law,) from reading the Book of Life. Your intellect has been destroyed as much as possible, and every ray of light they have attempted to shut out from your minds. The oppressors themselves have become involved in the ruin. They have become weak, sensual, and rapacious—they have cursed you—they have cursed themselves—they have cursed the earth which they have trod. . . .

. . . In every man's mind the good seeds of liberty are planted, and he who brings his fellow down so low, as to make him contented with a condition of slavery, commits the highest crime against God and man. Brethren, your oppressors aim to do this. They endeavor to make you as much like brutes as possible. When they have blinded the eyes of your mind when they have embittered the sweet waters of life then, and not till then, has American slavery done its perfect work.

TO SUCH DEGREDATION IT IS SINFUL IN THE EXTREME FOR YOU TO MAKE VOLUNTARY SUBMISSION. The divine commandments you are in duty bound to reverence and obey. If you do not obey them, you will surely meet with the displeasure of the Almighty. He requires you to love him supremely, and your neighbor as yourself—to keep the Sabbath day holy—to search the Scriptures— and bring up your children with respect for his laws, and to worship no other God but him. But slavery sets all these at nought, and hurls defiance in the face of Jehovah. The forlorn condition in which you are placed, does not destroy your moral obligation to God. You are not certain of heaven, because you suffer yourselves to remain in a state of slavery, where you cannot obey the commandments of the Sovereign of the universe. If the ignorance of slavery is a passport to heaven, then it is a blessing, and no curse, and you should rather desire its perpetuity than its abolition. God will not receive slavery, nor ignorance, nor any other state of mind, for love and obedience to him. Your condition does not absolve you from your moral obligation. The diabolical injustice by which your liberties are cloven down, NEITHER GOD, NOR ANGELS, OR JUST MEN, COMMAND YOU TO SUFFER FOR A SINGLE MOMENT. THEREFORE IT IS YOUR SOLEMN AND IMPERATIVE DUTY TO USE EVERY MEANS, BOTH MORAL, INTELLECTUAL, AND PHYSICAL THAT PROMISES SUCCESS. If a band of heathen men should attempt to enslave a race of Christians, and to place their children under the influence of some false religion, surely Heaven would frown upon the men who would not resist such aggression, even to death. If, on the other hand, a band of Christians should attempt to enslave [the] race of heathen men, and to entail slavery upon them, and to keep them in heathenism in the midst of Christianity, the God of heaven would smile upon every effort which the injured might make to disenthral themselves.

Brethren, it is as wrong for your lordly oppressors to keep you in slavery, as it was for the man thief to steal our ancestors from the coast of Africa. You should therefore now use the same manner of resistance, as would have been just in our ancestors when the bloody foot prints of the first remorseless soul thief was placed upon the shores of our fatherland. The humblest peasant is as free in the sight of God as the proudest monarch that ever swayed a sceptre. Liberty is a spirit sent out from God, and like its great Author, is no respecter of persons.

Brethren, the time has come when you must act for yourselves. It is an old and true saying that, "if hereditary bondmen would be free, they must themselves strike the blow." You can plead your own cause, and do the work of emancipation better than any others. The nations of the world are moving in the great cause of universal freedom, and some of them at least will, ere long, do you justice. The combined powers of Europe have placed their broad seal of disapprobation upon the African slave trade. But in the slaveholding parts of the United States, the trade is as brisk as ever. They buy and sell you as though you were brute beasts. The North has done much—her opinion of slavery in the abstract is known. But in regard to the South, we adopt the opinion of the New York Evangelist—We have advanced so far, that the cause apparently waits for a more effectual door to be thrown open than has been yet. We are about to point out that more effectual door. Look around you, and behold the bosoms of your loving wives heaving with untold agonies! Hear the cries of your poor children! Remember the stripes your fathers bore. Think of the torture and disgrace of your noble mothers. Think of your wretched sisters, loving virtue and purity, as they are driven into concubinage and are exposed to the unbridled lusts of incarnate devils. Think of the undying glory that hangs around the ancient name of Africa—and forget not that you are native born American citizens, and as such, you are justly entitled to all the rights that are granted to the freest. Think how many tears you have poured out upon the soil which you have cultivated with unrequited toil and enriched with your blood; and then go to your lordly enslavers and tell them plainly, that you are determined to be free. Appeal to their sense of justice, and tell them that they have no more right to oppress you, than you have to enslave them. Entreat them to remove the grievous burdens which they have imposed upon you, and to remunerate you for your labor. Promise them renewed diligence in the cultivation of the soil, if they will render to you an equivalent for your services. Point them to the increase of happiness and prosperity in the British West Indies since the Act of Emancipation. Tell them in language which they cannot misunderstand, of the exceeding sinfulness of slavery, and of a future judgment, and of the righteous retributions of an indignant God. Inform them that all you desire is FREEDOM, and that nothing else will suffice. Do this, and for ever after cease to toil for the heartless tyrants, who give you no other reward but stripes and abuse. If they then commence the work of death, they, and not you, will be responsible for the consequences.

You had better all die immediately, than live slaves and entail your wretchedness upon your posterity. If you would be free in this generation, here is your only hope. However much you and all of us may desire it, there is not much hope of redemption without the shedding of blood. If you must bleed, let it all come at once—rather die freemen, than live to be slaves. . . .

Fellow men! Patient sufferers! behold your dearest rights crushed to the earth! See your sons murdered, and your wives, mothers and sisters doomed to prostitution. In the name of the merciful God, and by all that life is worth, let it no longer be a debatable question whether it is better to choose Liberty or death.

In 1822, Denmark Veazie [Vesey], of South Carolina, formed a plan for the liberation of his fellow men. In the whole history of human efforts to overthrow slavery, a more complicated and tremendous plan was never formed. He was betrayed by the treachery of his own people, and died a martyr to freedom. Many a brave hero fell, but history, faithful to her high trust, will transcribe his name on the same monument with Moses, Hampden, Tell, Bruce and Wallace, Toussaint L'Ouverture, Lafayette and Washington. That tremendous movement shook the whole empire of slavery. The guilty soul thieves were overwhelmed with fear. It is a matter of fact, that at that time, and in consequence of the threatened revolution, the slave States talked strongly of emancipation. But they blew but one blast of the trumpet of freedom and then laid it aside. As these men became quiet, the slaveholders ceased to talk about emancipation; and now behold your condition today! Angels sigh over it, and humanity has long since exhausted her tears in weeping on your account!

The patriotic Nathaniel Turner followed Denmark Veazie [Vesey]. He was goaded to desperation by wrong and injustice. By despotism, his name has been recorded on the list of infamy, and future generations will remember him among the noble and brave.

Next arose the immortal Joseph Cinque, the hero of the Amistad. He was a native African, and by the help of God he emancipated a whole ship load of his fellow men on the high seas. And he now sings of liberty on the sunny hills of Africa and beneath his native palm trees, where he hears the lion roar and feels himself as free as that king of the forest.

Next arose Madison Washington that bright star of freedom, and took his station in the constellation of true heroism. He was a slave on board the brig Creole, of Richmond, bound to New Orleans, that great slave mart, with a hundred and four others. Nineteen struck for liberty or death. But one life was taken, and the whole were emancipated, and the vessel was carried into Nassau, New Providence.

Noble men! Those who have fallen in freedom's conflict, their memories will be cherished by the true hearted and the God fearing in all future generations; those who are living, their names are surrounded by a halo of glory.

Brethren, arise, arise! Strike for your lives and liberties. Now is the day and the hour. Let every slave throughout the land do this, and the days of slavery are numbered. You cannot be more oppressed than you have been—you cannot suffer greater cruelties than you have already. Rather die freemen than live to be slaves. Remember that you are FOUR MILLIONS!

It is in your power so to torment the God cursed slaveholders that they will be glad to let you go free. If the scale was turned, and black men were the masters and white men the slaves, every destructive agent and element would be employed to lay the oppressor low. Danger and death would hang over their heads day and night. Yes, the tyrants would meet with plagues more terrible than those of Pharaoh. But you are a patient people. You act as though, you were made for the special use of these devils. You act as though your daughters were born to pamper the lusts of your masters and overseers. And worse than all, you tamely submit while your lords tear your wives from your embraces and defile them before your eyes. In the name of God, we ask, are you men? Where is the blood of your fathers? Has it all run out of your veins? Awake, awake; millions of voices are calling you! Your dead fathers speak to you from their graves. Heaven, as with a voice of thunder, calls on you to arise from the dust.

Let your motto be resistance! resistance! RESISTANCE! No oppressed people have ever secured their liberty without resistance. What kind of resistance you had better make, you must decide by the circumstances that surround you, and according to the suggestion of expediency. Brethren, adieu! Trust in the living God. Labor for the peace of the human race, and remember that you are FOUR MILLIONS.

From *Life and Adventures of Charles Ball*

(1837)

. . . From my earliest recollections, the name of South Carolina had been little less terrible to me than that of the bottomless pit. In Maryland, it had always been the practice of masters and mistresses, who wished to terrify their slaves, to threaten to sell them to South Carolina; where, it was represented, that their condition would be a hundred fold worse than it was in Maryland. I had regarded such a sale of myself, as the greatest of evils that could befall me, and had striven to demean myself in such manner, to my owners, as to preclude them from all excuse for transporting me to so horrid a place. At length I found myself, without having committed any crime, or even the slightest transgression, in the place and condition, of which I had, through life, entertained the greatest dread. I slept but little this night, and for the first time felt weary of life. It appeared to me that the cup of my misery was full—that there was no hope of release from my present chains, unless it might be to exchange them for the long lash of the [overseers] of the cotton plantations; in each of whose hands I observed such a whip as I saw in possession of Mr. Randolph's slave driver in Virginia. I seriously meditated on self-destruction, and had I been at liberty to get a rope, I believe I should have hanged myself at Lancaster. It appeared to me that such an act, done by a man in my situation, could not be a violation of the precepts of religion, nor of the laws of God.

I had now no hope of ever again seeing my wife and children, or of revisiting the scenes of my youth. I apprehended that I should, if I lived, suffer the most excruciating pangs that extreme and long continued hunger could inflict; for I had often heard, that in South Carolina, the slaves were compelled in times of scarcity, to live on cotton seeds.

From the dreadful apprehensions of future evil, which [harassed] and harrowed my mind that night, I do not marvel, that the slaves who are driven to the south often destroy themselves. Self-destruction is much more frequent among the slaves in the cotton region than is generally supposed. When a [Negro] kills himself, the master is unwilling to let it be known, lest the deed should be attributed to his own cruelty. A certain degree of disgrace falls upon the master whose slave has committed suicide—and the same man, who would stand by, and see his overseer give his slave a hundred lashes, with the long whip, on his bare back, without manifesting the least pity for the sufferings of the poor tortured wretch, will express very profound regret if the same slave terminates his own life, to avoid a repetition of the horrid flogging. Suicide amongst the slaves is regarded as a matter of dangerous example, and one which it is the business and the interest of all proprietors to discountenance and prevent. All the arguments which can be devised against it are used to deter the negroes from the perpetration of it; and such as take this dreadful means of freeing themselves from their miseries, are always branded in reputation after death, as the worst of criminals; and their bodies are not allowed the small portion of Christian rites which are awarded to the corpses of other slaves.

Surely if [anything] can justify a man in taking his life into his own hands, and terminating his existence, no one can attach blame to the slaves on many of the cotton plantations of the south, when they cut short their breath, and the agonies of the present being, by a single stroke. What is life worth, amidst hunger, nakedness and excessive toil, under the continually uplifted lash?

HARRIET JACOBS

From *Incidents in the Life of a Slave Girl*

(1861)

During the first years of my service in Dr. Flint's family, I was accustomed to share some indulgences with the children of my mistress. Though this seemed to me no more than right, I was grateful for it, and tried to merit the kindness by the faithful discharge of my duties. But I now entered on my fifteenth year—a sad epoch in the life of a slave girl. My master began to whisper foul words in my ear. Young as I was, I could not remain ignorant of their import. I tried to treat them with indifference or contempt. The master's age, my extreme youth, and the fear that his conduct would be reported to my grandmother, made him bear this treatment for many months. He was a crafty man, and resorted to many means to accomplish his purposes. Sometimes he had stormy, terrific ways, that made his victims tremble; sometimes he assumed a gentleness that he thought must surely subdue. Of the two, I preferred his stormy moods, although they left me trembling. He tried his utmost to corrupt the pure principles my grand-mother had instilled. He peopled my young mind with unclean images, such as only a vile monster could think of. I turned from him with disgust and ha-tred. But he was my master. I was compelled to live under the same roof with him—where I saw a man forty years my senior daily violating the most sacred commandments of nature. He told me I was his property; that I must be subject to his will in all things. My soul revolted against the mean tyranny. But where could I turn for protection? No matter whether the slave girl be as black as eb-ony or as fair as her mistress. In either case, there is no shadow of law to protect her from insult, from violence, or even from death; all these are inflicted by fiends who bear the shape of men. The mistress, who ought to protect the help-less victim, has no other feelings towards her but those of jealousy and rage. The degradation, the wrongs, the vices, that grow out of slavery, are more than I can describe. They are greater than you would willingly believe. Surely, if you credited one half the truths that are told you concerning the helpless millions suffering in this cruel bondage, you at the north would not help to tighten the yoke. You surely would refuse to do for the master, on your own soil, the mean and cruel work which trained bloodhounds and the lowest class of whites do for him at the south.

Every where the years bring to all enough of sin and sorrow; but in slavery the very dawn of life is darkened by these shadows. Even the little child, who is accustomed to wait on her mistress and her children, will learn, before she is twelve years old, why it is that her mistress hates such and such a one among the slaves. Perhaps the child's own mother is among those hated ones. She listens to violent outbreaks of jealous passion, and cannot help understanding what is the cause. She will become prematurely knowing in evil things. Soon she will learn to tremble when she hears her master's footfall. She will be compelled to realize that she is no longer a child. If God has bestowed beauty upon her, it will prove her greatest curse. That which commands admiration in the white woman only hastens the degradation of the female slave. I know that some are too much brutalized by slavery to feel the humiliation of their position; but many slaves feel it most acutely, and shrink from the memory of it. I cannot tell how much I suffered in the presence of these wrongs, nor how I am still pained by the retrospect. My master met me at every turn, reminding me that I belonged to him, and swearing by heaven and earth that he would compel me to submit to him. If I went out for a breath of fresh air, after a day of unwearied toil, his footsteps dogged me. If I knelt by my mother's grave, his dark shadow fell on me even there. The light heart which nature had given me became heavy with sad forebodings. The other slaves in my master's house noticed the change. Many of them pitied me; but none dared to ask the cause. They had no need to inquire. They knew too well the guilty practices under that roof; and they were aware that to speak of them was an offence that never went unpunished.

Mrs. Flint possessed the key to her husband's character before I was born. She might have used this knowledge to counsel and to screen the young and the innocent among her slaves; but for them she had no sympathy. They were the objects of her constant suspicion and malevolence. She watched her husband with unceasing vigilance; but he was well practiced in means to evade it. . . .

I had entered my sixteenth year, and every day it became more apparent that my presence was intolerable to Mrs. Flint. Angry words frequently passed between her and her husband. He had never punished me himself, and he would not allow any body else to punish me. In that respect, she was never satisfied; but, in her angry moods, no terms were too vile for her to bestow upon me. Yet I, whom she detested so bitterly, had far more pity for her than he had, whose duty it was to make her life happy. I never wronged her, or wished to wrong her; and one word of kindness from her would have brought me to her feet.

The secrets of slavery are concealed like those of the Inquisition. My master was, to my knowledge, the father of eleven slaves. But did the mothers dare to tell who was the father of their children? Did the other slaves dare to allude to it, except in whispers among themselves? No, indeed! They knew too well the terrible consequences.

. . . Dr. Flint contrived a new plan. He seemed to have an idea that my fear of my mistress was his greatest obstacle. In the blandest tones, he told me that he was going to build a small house for me, in a secluded place, four miles away from the town. I shuddered; but I was constrained to listen, while he talked of his intention to give me a home of my own, and to make a lady of me. . . . I vowed before my Maker that I would never enter it. I had rather toil on the plantation from dawn till dark; I had rather live and die in jail, than drag on, from day to day, through such a living death. I was determined that the master, whom I so hated and loathed, who had blighted the prospects of my youth, and made my life a desert, should not, after my long struggle with him, succeed at last in trampling his victim under his feet. I would do any thing, every thing, for the sake of defeating him. What *could* I do? I thought and thought, till I became desperate, and made a plunge into the abyss.

Roll Jordan Roll

Adapted by Nicholas Britell

Verse 1

Went down to the river Jordan,
where John baptized three.
Well I woke the devil in hell
sayin John ain't baptize me
I say;

Chorus

Roll, Jordan, roll.
Roll, Jordan, roll.
My soul arise in heaven, Lord,
for the year when Jordan roll.

Verse 2

Well, some say John was a Baptist;
some say John was a Jew.
But I say John was a preacher of God,
and my bible says so too.

Chorus

Roll, Jordan, roll.
Roll, Jordan, roll.
My soul arise in heaven, Lord,
for the year when Jordan roll.
(Repeat)

I've Been in the Storm So Long

I've been in the storm so long,
I've been in the storm so long, children,
I've been in the storm so long,
Oh, give me little time to pray.

Oh, let me tell my mother
How I come along,
Oh, give me little time to pray,
With a hung down head and a aching heart,
Oh, give me little time to pray.

Oh, when I get to heaven,
I'll walk all about,
Oh, give me little time to pray,
There'll be nobody there to turn me out,
Oh, give me little time to pray.

I've been in the storm so long,
I've been in the storm so long, children,
I've been in the storm so long,
Oh, give me little time to pray.

DOUGLAS R. EGERTON

Before Charleston's Church Shooting, a Long History of Attacks

(June 18, 2015)

In 1868, three men assassinated the Reverend Benjamin Randolph in broad daylight as he was boarding a train in Abbeville County, South Carolina. Randolph, a black man, had recently won a seat in the State Senate and was then campaigning for the Republican slate. Having served as an army chaplain with the Twenty-sixth Regiment United States Colored Troops, Randolph asked the Freedmen's Bureau to send him "where he can be most useful to his race." He settled in South Carolina in time to take part in the 1865 rededication of the Emanuel African Methodist Episcopal Church in Charleston. It was that church's long history of spiritual autonomy and political activism that caught the attention of the white vigilantes who gunned him down and rode away. Randolph's fate was repeated yesterday with the murder of nine people, including the pastor of the church, the Reverend Clementa Pinckney, who, like Randolph, also served as a state senator.

Reports of yesterday's tragedy have invariably noted that an earlier incarnation of the Emanuel Church was home to Denmark Vesey, a lay minister who was one of the church's founders, but the connections between Vesey, the congregation's long history of activism, and the events of June 17 run far deeper than that.

South Carolina was unique in early America for its black majority. No other southern colony or state had a white minority until 1855, when Mississippi also earned that particular status. In 1822, Charleston housed 24,780 people, only 10,653 of whom were white. Free people of color were a tiny percentage, at 623, and most of them were the mixed-race offspring of white fathers and black mothers. One of the few free blacks in the city was a former slave turned carpenter, Denmark Vesey.

Vesey's early life was so unusual that if it were the plot of a novel or film, most would regard the saga as an absurd fiction. (The fact that his story has not attracted modern filmmakers is in itself curious, and perhaps a commentary on Hollywood's disinclination to wrestle seriously with the American past.) Born around 1767 on what was then the Danish island of St. Thomas, he was purchased in 1781 by Capt. Joseph Vesey, who shipped slaves around the Caribbean. Vesey briefly kept the child as a cabin boy, but upon reaching the French sugar colony of St. Domingue—modern Haiti—he sold the child, whom he had rechristened Telemaque, to French planters. Even by the standards of slave societies, St. Domingue was hell on earth. Telemaque pretended to have epileptic fits, rendering him unfit for the fields. When the captain returned with another cargo of humans, he had to take the child back, at which time the fits stopped. Captain Vesey, who settled in Charleston after the British evacuation in 1783, kept Telemaque—whose name had evolved into Denmark—as a domestic servant and assistant.

Denmark's life took yet another turn in the fall of 1799, when he won $1,500 in the city lottery. The captain might simply have confiscated the earnings of his human property, but instead he agreed to sell Denmark his freedom for $600. The bargain was completed on New Year's Eve, and Denmark Vesey woke up in the new century as a free man. But his wife, and therefore his two sons, Robert and Sandy, remained enslaved by a man named James Evans. At length, with his wife in bondage, Vesey married another woman, named Susan, and Vesey was able to buy her freedom. Their children grew up free in their rented house on Bull Street.

A practicing Presbyterian, Vesey was outraged by the pro-slavery brand of Christianity preached from the city's pulpits. White ministers were advised to lecture their black congregants on "their duties and obligations" and avoid troublesome stories, like the exodus out of Egypt, or Christ's sermons on human brotherhood. When 4,376 black Methodists quit their white-controlled church in protest over the elders' decision to construct a hearse house—a garage—over a black cemetery, Vesey was an early convert. As a carpenter, he may even have assisted in constructing the first Emanuel Church, which stood not far from the present building.

The African Church, as black Charlestonians called it, promptly attracted the animosity of the authorities. As a lay minister, Vesey, in his off hours, taught congregants to read and write—a violation of the state's ban on black literacy. State and city ordinances allowed for blacks to worship only in daylight hours and only with a majority of white congregants. City authorities raided the church in 1818, arresting and whipping 140 "free Negroes and Slaves," one of them presumably Vesey. In 1819 they again shuttered the church, and in 1820 the city council warned the Reverend Morris Brown not to allow his church to become "a school for slaves."

Had the city not declared war on Emanuel, Vesey might not have participated in the plot that got him killed in 1822. Enslaved Carolinians were never content with their lot, of course, but every slave in the state knew the odds of a successful rebellion. To protect the region's white minority, the city militia was ever active, and Secretary of War John C. Calhoun always stood ready to ship soldiers to his native state. But the assaults on the church, which the Old Testament taught was a capital offense, reminded blacks that authorities would never allow them even the smallest spiritual freedom.

President Jean-Pierre Boyer of Haiti had recently placed advertisements in American newspapers, urging free blacks to bring their tools and skills and start life anew in his black republic. So, meeting in Vesey's Bull Street home and within the walls of the Emanuel, Vesey and his lieutenants called for domestic slaves to kill their masters in their beds and fight their way to the docks, where they would seize ships and sail south. Originally, the plan was set for July 14, 1822—Bastille Day—but the plot began to unravel, and Vesey moved the plans forward to the night of June 16. The uprising would begin when the city's churches tolled midnight, meaning that the actual black exodus out of Charleston would take place on June 17. Either the shooter in Charleston yesterday knew the importance of this date, or the selection of June 17 was a ghastly coincidence.

As was too often the case, a handful of nervous bondmen informed their masters of what was afoot. In the aftermath of the failed plot, Vesey and dozens of his lieutenants were executed, and city authorities razed the church. Robert Vesey, Denmark's son, rebuilt Emanuel at its current location in 1865. After the pine structure was destabilized by an earthquake in the 1880s, congregants rebuilt the church that exists today. Even as white Americans forgot the story of Denmark Vesey, his struggle, and that of his church, lived on in the black memory. Frederick Douglass invoked his name during the Civil War, and in later years, the church honored his commitment to civil rights by hosting activists, including the Reverend Martin Luther King Jr. In 1963, the church sponsored a peaceful protest march for civil rights, which city authorities dubbed a "negro riot" and called in state troops to put down.

More recently, the church, and particularly Pinckney himself, worked tirelessly to memorialize Vesey. Charleston is crammed with countless monuments and markers dedicated to white Carolinians, most of them slaveholders, but until last year, there was nothing to adequately mark the black struggle for freedom and equality. Pinckney was instrumental in funding the statue of Vesey that was finally erected in February 2014. Many white Charlestonians opposed the monument. Letter writers filled the pages of Charleston's newspaper, The Post and Courier, with complaints.

In the coming days, the world will find out more about Dylann Storm Roof and his state of mind. But to dismiss him as simply a troubled young man is to disregard history. For 198 years, angry whites have attacked Emanuel AME and its congregation, and when its leaders have fused faith with political activism, white vigilantes have used terror to silence its ministers and mute its message of progress and hope. Denmark Vesey's story should never be forgotten—nor should the tragedy of June 17.

MAURIE MCINNIS

The First Attack on Charleston's AME Church

(June 19, 2015)

In the dark of night, a white man entered the AME church in Charleston, South Carolina, and opened fire. Nine people were killed.

In the dark of night, a white man entered the AME church in Charleston and started a fire. The structure was completely consumed and the church destroyed.

One is a headline from 2015, the other from 1822. The shooting this week has evoked horror and outrage across the nation; the event two hundred years ago provoked only satisfaction among the city's white inhabitants. Charleston, the wealthiest city in pre–Civil War America, was also the city with the largest percentage of residents of African descent, greater than 50 percent in every census until 1860. It has a long history of racialized violence and of violence inflicted against the black church. The shooting this week at the African Methodist Episcopal Church is another bloody chapter in that long history.

The fire in 1822 destroyed a small wooden church located a few blocks away from the present structure affectionately called "Mother Emanuel." The church had been founded in 1818 by Morris Brown, a member of Charleston's small free black population (nearly 1,500 in 1820). Charleston was then a city of 25,000 (more than 12,000 of whom were enslaved), and it is estimated that several thousand African Americans joined the church in the early years. On the corner of Reid and Hanover streets, this earlier church was in an area called Charleston Neck, just north of the city boundary then on Calhoun Street, where today's AME church stands. The early congregants had chosen this location in part because it was not in the city limits, and thus stood outside the close scrutiny of the city's authorities.

Being away from the watchful eye of the authorities was important because that watchful eye was often a harassing one. The most systematic and visible form of racial control in Charleston was the City Guard. Founded in 1783 as one of the first acts of the newly created City Council after American independence, the city's police force was created to control what was the largest enslaved population in an American city. It was given authority over a wide range of behaviors, both black and white. From the beginning, however, black and white residents were treated differently: the police could "inflict corporal punishment, by whipping, on persons of color."

The authority to whip and physically punish people of African descent, with little or no due process, was an important element of the slave regime. We know well that many slave owners used physical punishment and the threat thereof to control the people they owned, but such violence also had state sanction, regulations that were only to increase as the decades passed. As one visitor noted, they "know and they dread the slaveholder's power." With the church being in Charleston Neck, however, it meant that the City Guard did not regularly patrol there, which gave its members some degree of freedom in their worship.

The primary concern of the police was to guard against servile insurrection. And as a white population living among an enslaved majority, they had reason to fear. In addition to the police force, they established a curfew for African Americans. Every night curfew was announced by the tolling of the bells of St. Michael's and the beating of drums for a quarter-hour. After "drum beat," the City Guard patrolled the streets, arresting black Charlestonians out after curfew. Visitors often noted that the city felt as if it were under constant threat. When landscape architect and journalist Frederick Law Olmsted visited Charleston, he noted that when curfew rang, the city felt like a "military garrison," under a "general siege."

Charleston's City Guard arrested people of color for many reasons, most of them mere excuses to harass and intimidate: being on the streets without a pass after the ringing of the bells; not wearing a slave badge (if required); participating in merriment; smoking a cigar; hollering; selling goods in the market without a pass; or gathering in groups of greater than seven. These are just a few of the supposed offences specified in the city's ordinances.

The city's pervasive fear of servile unrest was confirmed one day in May 1822 when an enslaved man named Peter Desverneys told his owner what he had heard about plans for a slave uprising. The city authorities jumped into action (or overreaction), arresting men and confining them in the city's Work House, the notorious institution for the punishment and incarceration of people of color. The City Guard was on high alert for weeks, patrolling its streets in greater numbers and with enhanced vigilance.

The city, under the leadership of Mayor James Hamilton Jr., convened a court and initiated proceedings. The testimony that emerged, most of it coerced through violence and threats of hangings, only heightened the city's fears. A white resident told a friend elsewhere that during those weeks, "no one, not even children ventured to retire" and that the "the passing of every patrol and every slight noise excited attention."

A free black man named Denmark Vesey was fingered as the leading organizer. Born into slavery in the Caribbean, Vesey had purchased his freedom in 1799 with the proceeds from a lottery. Though named by several of the accused, Vesey himself never spoke to the court. He was not allowed to face his accusers. He did not admit guilt. Nevertheless, he was condemned to execution by hanging. On July 2, Vesey and five other men were carried in wagons from the Work House to a site in Charleston Neck called "the Lines." There they swung from trees, "their bodies . . . delivered to the surgeon for dissection, if requested," according to the newspaper announcement. It was a site carefully crafted to send fear throughout the African American community. More hangings followed later in the month.

Eventually more than 131 men were arrested, 35 were hung, and 43 were ordered to leave the state or the country. In August of that year, the court proceedings were published. This document, voraciously read and consumed by all in the city, told a story that deviated somewhat from the surviving court transcripts. It seemed calculated to frighten the city's slaveholding elite, emphasizing certain parts of the testimony more than others. One of the principal points emphasized was that many of the men involved in the plot were the "indulged and trusted" domestic servants who were intimately connected with their slave-owning families. Now every Charlestonian was looking at the people they owned and wondering, *What if?*

The other chilling fact for many Charlestonians was the supposed role of religion, especially the "African Church," as they called it then. According to the printed testimony, Vesey was "considered the Champion in the African church business. . . . [I]t is generally received opinion that this church commenced this awful business." Of those arrested, nineteen were members of the AME church. Rolla Bennett, one of the men eventually hanged who belonged to the then-governor of South Carolina, Thomas Bennett, supposedly told the court that Vesey "was the first to rise up and speak, and he read to us from the Bible, how the Children of Israel were delivered out of Egypt from bondage." Preaching a liberation theology, Vesey supposedly met with enslaved men in the city, convincing them to work with him in plotting the takeover of the city's armories, and commencing a massacre of all the whites, "not permitting a white soul to escape."

Today historians disagree on the extent of the planning for the insurrection. Did Vesey and his men have a plan for as many as nine thousand men ready to attack the city from the countryside? Or was there merely talk of freedom and liberty that was then exaggerated by the city's leaders in order to spread fear? Or is the answer somewhere in between?

Though we may never know for certain if the plot was real, the fear aroused was very real. The outcome of that fear was an increase in violence and intimidation aimed at the city's enslaved residents. These actions took many forms. For example, in 1822, Charleston passed the Negro Seaman Act and incarcerated *all* free black sailors who entered Charleston until the time of embarkation, on account of their race alone. In 1825, Charleston started construction on a massive building called the Arsenal (later home to the Citadel), to fortify the city with weapons in preparation against insurrection. That same year, the city added a new form of punishment to the Work House: the treadmill. The enslaved were forced to walk for eight hours a day, three minutes on and three minutes off. Perhaps most shocking of the Work House's provisions was that a master could send the people he owned to the Work House, where, for a fee, they would be "corrected by whipping," confined to a cell, or forced to walk on the treadmill. No proof of wrongdoing was required. A master could do this on a whim. No questions were asked.

The city's white leadership also saw to it that the African Church was burned. Not long afterward, the city outlawed all black churches. The enslaved were not allowed to meet for worship without a white person in attendance.

The church has always been a symbol of black community and of resilience in the face of racism, violence, and hatred. It has also been a frequent target of racial hatred. Throughout American history, burning and bombing churches has been used as a way to intimidate. After the Vesey insurrection scare, one Charlestonian wrote that "some plan must be adopted to subdue them." That sounds chillingly like what Dylann Storm Roof, the alleged shooter in this week's attack, supposedly said: "I have to do it. You rape our women and you're taking over our country, and you have to go."

It appears that Roof may have driven from near Columbia, South Carolina, to Charleston. It therefore seems likely that he chose this church for its historic and symbolic importance. Located in the heart of the city, just off Marion Square, only a few hundred yards from the Arsenal built to protect the city against servile insurrection, it stands there defiant: a historic AME congregation in a beautiful, soaring building of an architectural style and grandeur reminiscent of many of the city's white churches. The church is proud of its history. Just under the steps leading to the church's front door is a sculptural monument to Denmark Vesey. It shows the faces of young children, supposedly listening to his preaching. Erected after the passage of the Civil Rights Act, their eager young faces speak to the promise of liberty that Vesey supposedly fought for and that the post–Civil Rights era supposedly promised. Now the faces of those young children, and the entire nation, are streaked with tears as we realize how deeply rooted racial violence and hatred remain in the heart of at least one young man who walked into the AME church in Charleston and opened fire.

There was no justice for Denmark Vesey and the others who were executed and banished in 1822. There was no justice for the members of the AME church when their building was burned. There was no justice for the millions of African Americans who were wrongly held in bondage. Justice in this case will not merely be a guilty verdict for the accused shooter. Justice demands that we acknowledge and address our nation's continuing racial prejudice and disparities. Justice demands that we address police brutality, mass incarceration, and the lack of equal access to opportunity for millions of black Americans. The shooting is not simply the action of one deranged and evil individual, but instead springs from our nation's long history of racial prejudice and violence against black Americans.

LESLIE SCHWALM

From "'Sweet Dreams of Freedom': Freedwomen's Reconstruction of Life and Labor in Lowcountry South Carolina"

(1997)

The women who had been held in slavery in mainland lowcountry South Carolina were situated in a region marked by a specific geography, a unique African American culture, and a particular plantation setting organized around a single crop cultivated under a distinctive system of slave labor. African American women enslaved elsewhere in the South were faced with a very different set of circumstances before, during, and after the Civil War. The rice-planting region of lowcountry South Carolina contained some of the South's largest plantations and wealthiest planters, and before the war, some of its largest, most stable, and culturally autonomous slave communities. On the eve of the war, rice agriculture rested squarely on the shoulders of slave women whose lives were spent in the fields and ditches that marked the distinctive lowcountry terrain. As in other advanced plantation regimes, slave women on rice plantations were a significant proportion of "prime" field hands. However, to paraphrase from the introduction to an anthology on slave labor in the Americas, it was the particulars of slaves' labor which "determined, in large measure, the course of their lives." Slave labor in the rice fields was organized under the task system, so that the work of preparing fields, and cultivating and processing the rice crop, was assigned to women by the task—a portion of an acre for hoeing, a certain number of linear feet for ditch digging, a certain number of rice sheaves cut and tied. This distinguished slave women's task labor from women's dawn-to-dusk gang labor in almost every other plantation economy. The pace of task labor was set by slaves, who—with considerable effort—could often complete their tasks by mid-afternoon. For slave women, this translated into more daylight hours for the labor of raising and caring for families and for a variety of activities related to independent production.

Slave women's work in the rice fields and the elaborate residences of rice planters not only shaped their experience of slavery but also influenced their wartime struggle to escape or destroy slavery. The naval blockade of southern ports and the subsequent disruption of trade, the withdrawal of white men from agriculture to military service, and demands by the Confederate military and state authorities for slave labor and slave-produced goods all disrupted the long-established patterns of plantation life and labor in the lowcountry. The forced removal of lowcountry slaves to the state's more protected interior further undermined the traditional cycle of rice agriculture as well as the local ties which for many generations had anchored lowcountry plantation production and slavery. With the occupation of Port Royal by Union forces early in the war, the threat posed by the proximity of the enemy exacerbated the war's domestic interruptions in South Carolina.

For lowcountry slave men and women, these wartime conditions translated into incremental disruptions of the traditions, customary rights, social relations, and domestic networks that they had forged over several generations of struggle against slavery. Yet even as wartime shortages forced a deterioration in the standard of living in the slave quarters, slave women accelerated the wartime collapse of slavery by slowing plantation production, resisting the new forms of exploitation introduced during the war, and escaping lowcountry plantations in unprecedented numbers and making their way to the fleet of federal ships blockading the coast. When slave women seized the opportunities presented by the war to further weaken the institution of slavery or to secure their own freedom, it was not only slavery which they hoped to leave behind but also the worsening conditions of life on lowcountry plantations. Long before emancipation became a part of Union policy, slave women were struggling to alter the conditions of life and labor on South Carolina plantations.

It bears stressing that war affected not only the material conditions of lowcountry slave life but also the relationships of power that were integral to slavery. As planters became increasingly unable to purchase or afford the most basic necessities; as they became subject to impressment of their plantation products and slaves; as they, their overseers, and their sons became vulnerable to conscription; and, as increasing numbers of plantation mistresses assumed unprecedented and unanticipated responsibility for plantation operations in light of the absence of husbands and sons, slaves watched the weakening of their masters' ability to dominate. Slave women not only observed, but tested and acted upon, the wartime crisis of plantation mastery. Overseers and planter families alike complained during the war of slave women disrupting the peaceful operation of their plantations, threatening to run away, and slowing the pace of work. One rice plantation mistress complained early in the war of the "license" increasingly taken by slaves; they "all think this a crisis in their lives that must be taken advantage of. . . . [T]imes and slaves, have changed" since secession. The weaknesses in the bedrock of slavery exposed by the war were seized upon and widened by slave women who were determined to make the war's trajectory towards emancipation irreversible.

Thousands of slave women fled lowcountry plantations during the war and made their way to the Union-occupied Sea Islands, beginning their transition from slavery to freedom under the dominion of northern missionaries, civilians, and military authorities. Unlike native Sea Islanders who staked out their own portion of plantation lands and continued to live in their slave quarters, slave women from the mainland rice plantations constituted a refugee population. They found living quarters in refugee camps, abandoned buildings, or temporary barracks, and pieced together a living from the employment they found in the Quartermaster's Department, as regimental laundresses or cooks, from the pay of their enlisted kin or husbands, or by marketing provisions to Union soldiers stationed on the islands. Yet their appreciation for the protection, schooling, and charity offered by northern military and civilian authorities did not slow women's response when the freedom offered under northern tutelage was less than what they expected. Whether this meant shaming the northern missionary women who pointedly ignored the pressing needs of young "unmarried" slave mothers, challenging military authorities who tried to prevent their entry into soldiers' camps to sell provisions or to "see and be seen," or leading groups of women to protest unacceptably low wages, these refugees from mainland slavery were hardly content to await passively the redefinition of black life and labor by others. Before the war had ended, these contraband women were already engaged in the process of defining and defending their freedom.

Women's pursuit of freedom gained momentum and breadth in the immediate aftermath of the war. The final dissolution of lowcountry slavery in early 1865, coinciding with the chaotic closing weeks of war in the wake of Sherman's advance through the state, inspired newly freed slave women to attack former overseers, raid planter residences and storehouses, and confiscate or destroy planter property. From the smallest luxuries to the most expensive furnishings, freedwomen clothed themselves and their children in confiscated and previously forbidden finery "in pride of their freedom." In the aftermath of the war, former slave women's defining acts of freedom were also found in their efforts to reunite their families, separated before or during the war; in the strategies they adopted to endure calamitous material conditions and to evade violent attacks by white reactionaries and northern soldiers; and in the ways they reorganized and reallocated their agricultural, domestic, and household labor. . . .

. . . In the fall and early winter of 1865, lowcountry planters complained with growing frequency that freedpeople left the plantations without permission, refused work orders, and made threats against planters. Planters complained that freedpeople "not only will not work now, but tell you so openly & plainly. . . ." They accused former slaves of being saucy, insolent, intractable, disobedient, and dangerous. Even in this general climate of conflict and resistance, men and women of the lowcountry planter class, white overseers, soldiers, and agents of the Freedmen's Bureau all complained pointedly about the insubordinate behavior of former slave women. Freedwoman Jane, who rejected work orders and slapped her white mistress, was denounced by her employers as "an audacious creature." Mary Ann "boldly [and] unblushingly" confronted her former owner in the field, refused his assignment of work unrelated to the present crop, and "frequently contradicted me and spoke to me as roughly and as defiantly as if I had been the meanest old negro in the country." He was as alarmed by Mary Ann's defiant bearing towards him as by her insistence on determining for herself which work she would and would not perform. Another planter characterized freedwomen as idle and insolent, vagrant, playing sick and doing no work; the driver's wife thought she was "too fine a lady to think of doing any work," and even Eve, while admittedly "an old woman," he described as "very impertinent." It was the behavior of women like these that prompted the agent on one lowcountry plantation to complain that "[t]he more kindness offered to them the more ingratitude & abuse we receive," an unwitting admission that freedwomen were challenging the facade of reciprocal relations that had masked the abusive and exploitative nature of antebellum paternalism.

Beyond their insistence on bringing radical change to their relationships with lowcountry elites, lowcountry freedwomen's reputation for insubordination was in part a consequence of the specific kinds of demands they made in postwar labor arrangements. Freedpeople needed to innovate new family economies to cope with conditions of starvation and want; they sought a balance between their ties to specific communities and plantation lands and their need for cash, or food and basic goods. After the harvest, freedmen (husbands and fathers) left the plantations in pursuit of day labor, sold firewood or fruit to passing steamers or in nearby towns, or found other temporary avenues into the cash economy. Freedwomen—often wives and mothers—remained on the plantations and assumed a frontline role in ongoing plantation battles over the shape of postemancipation labor while caring for family and tending independent crops. Some families on mainland plantations managed to plant "private crops of their own," and the men "hire out now & then . . . to neighbors" while freedwomen and children remained on the plantation. This strategy not only exacerbated planters' concern about securing essential postharvest labor from freedpeople, it also placed freedwomen in direct conflict with planters.

Freedwomen fueled the escalating labor conflict by their refusal to perform postharvest domestic chores for planters. Planters had customarily assigned female slaves a range of postharvest labor that included spinning and weaving, the manufacture of clothing, butchering and preserving meat, and other kinds of domestic production critical to the maintenance and support of plantation operations. That labor had eaten into the hours slavewomen might otherwise have spent with, and working for, their own families. In the fall of 1865, freedwomen who had contracted to work as field hands were no longer willing to perform "double duty" in domestic production for their employers. This included freedwoman Mary Ann, who "shewed the virago from the start"; according to her former owner, "she has refused to rake[,] fence[,] or do any work," leading him to fear that her behavior "will poison all the rest of the people of the place." Freedwomen on one of the Allsten plantations brought an end to the extra burden of postharvest wool production, first by killing off the plantation sheep, and then eating them. One planter's wife reported that in order to get former slaves to work even half tasks in the field, chores related to domestic production, such as spinning, had to be totally abandoned. Another planter's wife found herself reported to a local bureau agent for trying to compel female field hands to do her spinning and weaving. Even young women like sixteen-year-old Margaret Brown rejected "weaving after night" for her employer, who took her refusal as provocation enough to beat her with his bare hands and with a stick.

Freedwomen's contributions to lowcountry labor conflicts did not go unnoticed or unanswered. According to bureau and military records, many freedwomen paid a dear price for the audacity of insisting on their right to define free labor on their own terms. Their experience of violence at the hands of an outraged employer was not unusual. Hagar Barnwell had been ordered by her former owner to go into the kitchen and work, but "she refused . . . as she had contracted to work in the field." When Barnwell vowed she would leave the plantation rather than work in his kitchen, the man threatened her with his pistol, stated he would kill her if not for the need to get his crop in, and then he took her to a shed and tied her up by her thumbs so that her feet barely touched the ground. Barnwell eventually escaped but appealed to three different army officers as well as a local magistrate before she found someone willing to investigate her mistreatment. In another instance, "a Woman named Sarah . . . was tied up by the thumbs" by a planter and two accomplices, as punishment for violating plantation rules; "Sarah was pregnant and . . . she was kept suspended for nearly two hours," reported the agent, and "in consequence of this brutality the birth of the child was forced." The infant "was dead when delivered" and Sarah "has not been expected to live." Their refusal to withdraw from disputes over the meaning of black freedom meant that freedwomen became targets for physical attack. . . .

. . . With the arrival of Union troops, former slave women began to abandon the mask of subservience they had been forced to wear as domestic slaves, and, in the immediate aftermath of war, female domestic servants, like field hands, first resorted to a work stoppage. Some servants preferred to leave their former owners and find new employers rather than fight with former owners over what they would and would not continue to do now that they were free. . . .

. . . Far from passive or retreating figures withdrawing to the shadows of southern life, freedwomen played a visible and instrumental role in the reconstruction of life and labor in the postbellum South. They fought for greater freedom of movement between their household and family economies and the plantation economy, for greater insularity from the supervision of overseers and other hated figures from their recent past, and for the freedom to make their own decisions about how best to allocate their time and their labor.

WALTER JOHNSON

From *Soul by Soul: Life inside the Antebellum Slave Market*

(1999)

When Richard Winfield went to the slave market to buy Elvira and Samuel Brown, he took James Calvitt along to help him see. As a witness remembered it, Calvitt had more experience in the slave market than did Winfield, and the sale went something like this: "The Negroes were called in and the girl was examined by Mr. Calvitt in the presence of Winfield. Winfield looked at the slaves. Calvitt asked the slaves some questions." Calvitt remembered the sale similarly. Winfield "looked" at Elvira and then Calvitt "put his hand where her breast ought to be and found nothing but rags." If he had been purchasing on his own behalf, Calvitt added "he would have made her pull her dress off." Soon after Winfield bought her, it became apparent that Elvira was mortally ill—the rags filled out a chest ravaged by consumption—and she died within a few weeks of the sale. Another witness to the sale drew a slaveholder's moral from the story: "Thinks Winfield a poor judge of slaves or he would not have purchased said girl. She is the first girl Winfield ever owned." The observers described the nonslaveholder's inexperience as a matter of insight: Winfield was a poor judge of slaves. Indeed, comparisons of the depth of the slaveholder's insight with that of the nonslaveholder run through all of the descriptions of the sale: Calvitt "examined" while Winfield "looked"; Calvitt touched while Winfield stood by. Calvitt, by all accounts, could see things that Winfield could not.

Being able to see that way was a talent, and inexperienced buyers often took someone along with them when they went to the slave market. Friends, physicians, even slave dealers went to the slave market "at the request" of uncertain buyers. These more experienced men examined the lots of slaves for sale in the market, reading their bodies aloud and helping buyers select the "likely" and the healthy from among them. The presence of these slave-pen guides hints at a masculine social world in which being a "good judge of slaves" was a noteworthy public identity, a world of manly one-upsmanship in which knowledge of slaves' bodies was bandied back and forth as white men cemented social ties and articulated a hierarchy among themselves through shared participation in the inspection and evaluation of black slaves. And as these white men watched one another examine and choose slaves, and as the slave-pen mentors helped inexpert buyers choose slaves, they daily reproduced and passed on the racial "knowledge" by which southern slavery was justified and defended.

A savvy slave buyer knew enough to try to look past the fancy clothes, bright faces, and promising futures lined up against the walls of the slave pens. Mississippi planter John Knight was presumably passing on the opinion of the "old planters" upon whom he regularly relied for advice when he sent his slave-market wisdom to his father-in-law. "The fact is," Knight wrote, "as to the character and disposition of all of the slaves sold by the traders, we know nothing whatever, the traders themselves being generally such liars. Buyers therefore can only judge the *looks* of the Negroes." The effects of the traders' practice—the invisibility of slaves' origins and the obscurity of their histories—and their reputation for dishonesty limited buyers' options as they tried to see through to slaves' pasts and prospects. In the absence of reliable information the buyers began with the physical coordinates of the people who stood before them in the pens.

The axes of physical comparison used by the buyers were prefigured in the traders' practice. Slaves in the market were advertised by their sex, racial designation, age, and skill, and they were lined out for sale according to height. They were arrayed as physical specimens even as their origins, attitudes, and infirmities were covered over by the traders' arts. Buyers preferred darker to lighter people for work in their fields and lighter to darker people for skilled and domestic labor; they generally preferred slaves of "prime age" (between fifteen and twenty-five for laborers), although skilled slaves reached their prime at a later age (around thirty-five). Buyers favored men for work outdoors and women for domestic service; and they apparently paid higher prices for taller slaves. As telling as they are, however, these broad correlations tell us very little about what buyers saw when they looked at slaves, about what was behind the "singular look" that so impressed Joseph Ingraham. What did skin color or sex or size mean to slaveholders?

Asked to explain what they looked for in a slave, most slave buyers would have responded with the word "likely." Today the word means probable, but as slave buyers used it [it] was as much a description as it was a prediction. As they singled out the "likely" from among the many they saw in the pens, slave buyers made detailed inspections of people's bodies which went well beyond the traders' advertisements and the age, sex, and racial designation that were commonly recorded on an Act of Sale. The standard slave inspection, as one buyer described it, went like this: "my inspection was made in the usual manner: their coats being taken off and the breast, arms, teeth, and general form and appearance looked at." The whole process, according to another buyer, might take, anywhere from fifteen minutes to half an hour, and bargaining might be stretched over three or four days. The inspections, at least at the outset, were public. The white male buyers in the yard mingled as they walked the rows of slaves; they observed the inspections made by one another and shared their own reckonings of part..icular slaves; they talked about and joked about the slaves standing before them. All the while they invoked ever more elaborate notions of physiological meaning to make ever finer distinctions among the people they evaluated.

As the slaves were paraded before them, slave buyers began by reading the slaves' skin color, groping their way from visible sign to invisible essence. No doubt buyers were seeing skin color when they described a slave as "a Negro or griff boy," "a griff colored boy," "dark Griff color," or "not black nor Mulatto, but what I believe is usually called a griff color, that is a Brownish Black, or a bright Mulatto." But in describing the blurred spectrum they saw before them, buyers used descriptive language that was infused with the reassuring certitudes of race. The words they used attempted to stabilize the restless hybridity, the infinite variety of mixture that was visible all over the South, into measurable degrees of black and white. They suggested that slaves' skin color could be read as a sign of a deeper set of racial qualities. . . .

The spectrum of slaves ran in two directions along the walls of the slave pen: men on one side, women on the other. The bodies of those bought to work in the fields were comparable but not entirely fungible. W. H. Yos, comparing the men and women he found in the market, found the men "more likely" and put off buying women for another year—in the short run he could compare men to women, but in the long run he would have to have both. A similar perspective shows through John Knights plantation plans, which stipulated that his slaves be "half men and half women . . . young say from 16 to 25, stout limbs, large deep chests, wide shoulders and hips, etc." Knight's list of body parts ran male and female attributes together, describing a body that was to be, like his slave force, half and half: men and women bought to work in the fields were comparable in any instance but they had to be sexed and balanced in the aggregate. Having, like Knight, broken people down into parts, slaveholders could rebalance their attributes in the quest for slaves like those trader Samuel Browning called the "right sort" for the lower South. "Likely young fellows, stout girls the same and Black," was how Browning described the slaves who would sell best in Mississippi. Virginia trader Hector Davis similarly headed his slavemarket tables with "Best young men" and "Best black girls." Likely young women were not the same as likely young men, but likely young black women might be. If she was destined to be a field hand, being "black" was better; it made an enslaved woman look more like the men alongside whom she would work in the fields. In evaluating female slaves, the traders were imagining composite slaves, matching the vitality they attributed to blackness with the vulnerability they expected from female-ness to make a better slave.

As well as comparing women to men, buyers compared women to one an-other. They palpated breasts and abdomens, searching for hernias and prolapsed organs and trying to massage bodies into revealing their reproductive history and capacity. Women passed through their "prime" interest to the slave traders at an earlier age than men. Males predominated in the slave trade among slaves over the age of nineteen; below that age, females did. Behind the aggregates lie the assumptions that slaveholders inscribed upon the bodies they bought. . . .

. . . These sex-specific age categories reflected different evaluations of which capacities of the human body made a slave useful: production in the case of males and reproduction in the case of females. Putting it scientifically, one might say that slaveholders emphasized full physical growth for males and menarche for females. . . .

The rituals of the slave pens taught the inexperienced how to read black bod-ies for their suitability for slavery, how to imagine blackness into meaning, how to see solutions to their own problems in the bodies of the slaves they saw in the market. Gazing, touching, stripping, and analyzing aloud, the buyers read slaves' bodies as if they were coded versions of their own imagined needs—age was longevity, dark skin immunity, a stout trunk stamina, firm muscles produc-tion, long fingers rapid motion, firm breasts fecundity, clear skin good character. The purposes that slaveholders projected for slaves' bodies were thus translated into natural properties of those bodies—a dark complexion became a sign of an innate capacity for cutting cane, for example. Daily in the slave market, buyers "discovered" associations they had themselves projected, treating the effects of their own examinations as if they were the essences of the bodies they exam-ined. Passed on from the experienced to the inexperienced, from the examiners to the onlookers, the ritual practice of the slave pens animated the physical co-ordinates of black bodies with the purposes of slavery.

Slave-pen blackness held another meaning for slaveholders: it brought the outlines of slaveholding whiteness into sharper relief. The gross physical ca-pacity of the slave was a rough background for the graceful motion of the slaveholder; all the talk about black "breeders" set off the elaborate rituals of white courtship; and the violation of black bodies emphasized the inviolability of white ones. Through shared communion in the rites of the slave market—the looking, stripping, touching, bantering, and evaluating—white men con-firmed their commonality with the other men with whom they inspected the slaves. . . .

In addition to outward delicacy and inward gentility, the racial gaze of the slaveholder projected sexual meaning onto the bodies of lightskinned women.

Phillip Thomas simply described a woman he had seen in Richmond as "13 years old, Bright Color, nearly a fancy for $1135." An age, a sex, a color, a price, and a fantasy. A longer description of Mildred Ann Jackson ran along the same lines: "She was about thirty years old. Her color was that of a quadroon; very good figure, she was rather tall and slim. Her general appearance was very good. She wore false teeth and had a mole on her upper lip. Her hair was straight." Jackson's body was admired for its form, for its delicacy and detail. Slave dealer James Blakeny made the density of the traffic between phenotype and fantasy explicit when he described Mary Ellen Brooks: "A very pretty girl, a bright mulatto with long curly hair and fine features . . . Ellen Brooks was a fancy girl: witness means by that a young handsome yellow girl of fourteen or fifteen with long curly hair." For slave buyers, the bodies of light-skinned women and little girls embodied sexual desire and the luxury of being able to pay for its fulfill-ment—they were projections of slaveholders' own imagined identities as white men and slave masters.

And so, at a very high price, whiteness was doubly sold in the slave market. In the first instance the hybrid whiteness of the slaves was being packaged and measured by the traders and imagined into meaning by the buyers: into deli-cacy and modesty, interiority and intelligence, beauty, bearing, and vulnerabil-ity. These descriptions of light-skinned slaves were projections of slaveholders' own dreamy interpretations of the meaningfulness of their skin color. Indeed, in the second instance, it was the buyers' own whiteness that was being bought. In buying these imagined slaves, they were buying for themselves ever more detailed fantasies about mastery and race. The qualities they projected onto their slaves' bodies served them as public reflections of their own discernment: they were the arbiters of bearing and beauty; their slaves were the show pieces of their pretensions; their own whiteness was made apparent in the proximate whiteness of the people they bought.

Ironically, these expensive flirtations with racial proximity, these commodi-fications of projected and imagined whiteness, were underwritten by the slave-holders' ideology of absolute racial difference. The saving abstraction "black blood" later codified inlaw as the "one drop rule" held the power to distin guish nearly white people from really white people. . . .

. . . The range of difference between these descriptions suggest that the racial-ized bodies these buyers thought they had discovered in the slave market were, in fact, being produced by their examinations—not in the sense that there was no physical body standing there until a buyer described it but in the sense that the racialized meaning of that body, the color assigned to it and the weight given to its various physical features in describing it, depended upon the examiner rather than the examined. . . .

. . . Employment, health, countenance, clothes, conversation, desire, any number of things might have guided slaveholders' imaginations as they looked at slaves' bodies. Which is to say that slaves' bodies were shaped and shaded by what the traders were selling and what potential buyers were seeking.

So powerful, indeed, was the acquisitive gaze of the slaveholder that slave-market "blackness" or "whiteness" could occasionally be produced in opposition to the phenotype of the body to which they were applied. . . . The "blackness" or "whiteness" associated with particular types of slavery could be mapped onto slaves' bodies according to coordinates other than color—gender, size, shape, visage, and conversation, for instance. . . . As they compared the people in the market to one another, slaveholders broke physical bodies into pieces and traded them back and forth. The vitality associated with blackness might cancel out the vulnerability associated with femininity in the search for a field hand, while a "bright disposition" might lighten a dark-skinned woman in the search for a domestic servant; a "rough" face might darken a light-skinned man, while "effeminacy" might lighten a dark-skinned one; an outwardly dull demeanor and the presence of wife and child might make a light-skinned man seem less likely to run away; and so on. In the slave market, buyers produced "whiteness" and "blackness" by disaggregating human bodies and recomposing them as racialized slaves.

The racism of the slave pens, however, was less an intended effect than a tool of the trade. To paraphrase the historian Barbara Jeanne Fields, the business of the slave pens was the buying and selling of slaves, not the production of wide-ranging ideas about racial proximity and inferiority. The buyer's most immediate interest in detailing an account of a slave's racial characteristics was getting a lower price. And the more accomplished he was at using the verities of antebellum racism to detail "faults and failings" of the slaves in the market, the less he could expect to pay for the slave he wanted to take home. . . .

If necromancy was the slave market's magic, race was its technology. Just as the magic of alchemy based its claims on the scientific techniques of chemistry and mineralogy, the necromancy of the slave pens was founded on the technology of biological racism. Without any reliable knowledge about the histories or identities of the people they met in the market, buyers turned to physical examination as the best method of comparison. In the slave market, the physical coordinates of human bodies—size, skin color, scars, physical carriage, and so on—were made meaningful through the application of slave buyers' medical, managerial, aesthetic, and sexual concerns. In the slave market, the racial ideologies by which slaveholders organized their society were put to work doing the hard work of differentiating commodities and negotiating prices.

As the experienced guided the eyes of the inexperienced, slaves' bodies were made racially legible. The buyers' inspections, the parts they fingered, the details they fetishized, and the homosocial connections they made with one another gave material substance to antebellum notions of "blackness" and "whiteness" and outlined for observers the lineaments of a racial gaze. Out of the daily practice of slavery, they reproduced the notions of race that underwrote the system as a whole.

Many of the observers in the pens, however, were not white, and the conclusions they drew from watching the buyers' inspections were quite different from those drawn by a man like Joseph Ingraham. For the slaves in the market, the examinations were revealing accounts of the buyers themselves, accounts that allowed them to guess what a buyer was looking for and, sometimes, to shape a sale to suit themselves.

STEPHANIE E. SMALLWOOD

From *Saltwater Slavery:*
A Middle Passage from Africa
to American Diaspora

(2007)

For their part, ship captains and European agents in African and American ports well understood that the cargoes they assembled exhibited varying degrees of social and ethnic complexity. Indeed, traders were acutely aware that their well-being depended, at the very least, on awareness of the political dimensions of ethnicity among the persons placed in their possession. Aboard the *America*, for instance, unusually acute ethnic division appears to have been implicated in both an attempted shipboard uprising and its ultimate defeat. Sent to obtain a cargo of slaves from the Gambia River, the ship's captain, John Brome, sailed from the region in April 1693 en route to Jamaica with 461 captives on board: 421 of these came from trading networks developed by English factories along the Gambia River; the remaining 40 had been captured during an English assault on French trading posts at Gorée Island, situated some two hundred miles to the north, and Saint Louis, another two hundred miles beyond it, in the mouth of the Senegal River. As the vessel was preparing to leave the English fort at Gambia, the factor there reported "an insurrection amongst Bromes Negroes," in which "the Jellofes [Jolofs] rose" and "the Bambaras sided with the Master."

The term "Bambara," which entered the slaving lexicon of the region in the late seventeenth century, designated "interior people" (probably Malinke-speaking) who reached the coast via the Soninke trading state Gajaaga and are likely to have been the constituents of the *America*'s cargo assembled at the Gambia River. The Wolof-speaking peoples of the Jolof kingdom, a coastal state situated in the well-watered lands just south of the Senegal River, were important partners in Afro-European commercial networks throughout the slave-trading era, and as such they never figured prominently in slave exports after that region's contribution to the Atlantic traffic in people peaked in the sixteenth century. It is quite possible, in fact, that the rebels identified as "Jellofes" aboard the *America* had been domestic slaves employed at Gorée and Saint Louis, rather than captives held there to await export.

At the other end of the spectrum was the *Ferrers*, whose captain, a first-time commander of a slaving vessel, put in at Cape Coast Castle in 1722 boasting of the "good fortune" he met with in obtaining a cargo, having "purchased near 300 Negroes in a few Days, at a place called Cetre-Crue," on the Windward Coast. When the *Ferrers* arrived, the coastal people of the town had just completed a successful military assault on an enemy inland polity.

His seemingly fortuitous timing gave the captain "the opportunity of purchasing a great many of the Captives at an easy rate. For the Conquerors were glad to get something for them, at that instant, since, if a Ship had not been in the Road, they would have been obliged to have killed most of the Men-Captives, for their own Security." On hearing the captain's story, veteran slaving captain William Snelgrave cautioned the novice. "Understanding from him, that he had never been on the Coast of Guinea, before, I took the liberty to observe to him, 'That as he had on board so many Negroes of one Town and Language, it required the utmost Care and Management to keep them from mutinying.'" Worse yet, though the captives' staple diet consisted of rice, the captain had not purchased any of that commodity while on the Windward Coast, and he was now unable to come by anything like a sufficient quantity on the Gold Coast. Months later, when he reached Jamaica, Snelgrave received word that the slaves aboard the *Ferrers* had indeed staged a revolt, one that had taken the ship captain's life as well as the lives of eighty captives ten days following their departure from the African coast. Undeterred by their losses, the captives went on to attempt a rebellion on two separate occasions between the vessel's arrival in Jamaica and the cargo's sale to local planters.

Between these two extremes—the *America* representing a sharply drawn ethnic fault line aboard ship, the *Ferrers* representing ethnic affinity within the narrow compass of a single town—could be found most cargoes assembled in Atlantic Africa's eight major slave-exporting regions, including the Gold Coast. All the regions that exported people in the Atlantic market—Senegambia, Sierra Leone, the Windward Coast, the Gold Coast, the Bight of Benin, the Bight of Biafra, West-Central Africa, and southeast Africa—encompassed a plurality of ethnicities and speech communities. Some were more ethnically or linguistically heterogeneous than others, and in most the presence of powerful states figured heavily in their capacity to supply slaves in the first place. But in none of these regions did states yet correspond to national bodies in the eighteenth century. And although it is true that most ships obtained their entire cargo from only one or two ports, an equally important point is precisely that these were ports: collection sites, central places to which goods—in this case, people—flowed from afar and were collected for shipment.

Cargoes traveled from African to American ports bearing labels derived from the regional place names on the European map of Africa. Ships departing

[handwritten margin note:] Who and why did they export people into the Atlantic Market?

from the Gambia River carried "Gambian" slaves, while those from what modern historians now call West-Central Africa were described by the generic rubric "Angolans." Akin to a clothing tag that reads "made in the Gold Coast," this deliberately vague bit of information was all prospective buyers needed to know. But as they reflected a European rather than an African geography, the labels that attached to slave ships as they maneuvered into the transatlantic shipping lanes obscured the diversity actually represented in the cargoes they carried.

With regard to the Gold Coast, the regional system of supply enabled slave traders to "complete" cargoes by drawing from a stretch of territory along the coast that followed the east-west geography of port towns and their corresponding hinterlands, from Cape Three Points (the western border of the "Gold Coast" proper) as far as the Volta River, two hundred miles to the east. This, coupled with the fact that in the seventeenth century many cargoes whose production began on the Gold Coast were completed at ports in the Bight of Benin, meant that during this period, "Gold Coast" cargoes regularly comprised multiple ethnicities and often many linguistic and cultural threads as well.

Cargoes assembled at Gold Coast ports exhibited a diversity that can be measured by reference to the distinct languages represented among the slaves. Given that the slavers drew men and women from the length of the Gold Coast littoral, and in many cases from the Bight of Benin, the presence of three and sometimes four different major languages can be assumed. Two dialects of Akan were spoken along a hundred-mile stretch from Axim to Kormantin (the Anyi-Baule dialect from Axim as far as Shama, the Twi dialect from there to Kormantin). Guan—the language of the region's pre-Akan settlers—remained dominant around Winneba and Beraku, as well as among communities such as Latebi, in the Akwapim hills behind Accra. Ga was the language of the coastal Accra region, and closely related Adangbe was spoken by coastal communities just to the east at Ningo and Allampo. Captives from communities located on either side of the Volta River added Ewe-speakers to the mix; and those coming through the major Slave Coast ports at Whydah, Offra, and Jakin contributed Aja, Fon, and other variants of Gbe to the languages heard aboard ships like the *Edgar*.

Many of the captives that Akan-speaking traders from Akwamu sold into the Atlantic market were a by-product of the state's depredations against such small hill polities as Latebi, so Guan was probably the language spoken by those whom the factor at Accra purchased in 1693, for example. Describing social complexities that were plain to those responsible for the day-to-day work of slave trafficking, the factor stationed there explained: "The slaves we buy here are not all Quamboers [Akwamus] but I know they are natives not far from thence altho they speak another lingua. However," he continued, getting to the fundamental point, "they do not cost the Company £4 sterling per head which the Captains are allowed for Whydah negroes."

It was thus that the cargo put aboard the *Coast* frigate elicited the following complaint upon the arrival of the ship in Barbados in February 1686. "Those . . . by you stild [styled] good Gold Coast negroes we here found not to be so," the company agent wrote, "but of several nations and languages as Alampo the worst of Negroes, Papas & some of unknown parts & few right Gold Coast negroes amongst them." By the latter term the agents referred to those known to American buyers as "Coromantis" and as Akan-speakers distinguished from others by language. If the *Coast* stood out among astute American buyers for its near-absence of "right Gold Coast negroes" evidence indicates that, on the whole, the group aboard this ship was more typical than not.

When the Asante state entered into the orbit of the Atlantic market in the eighteenth century, and what had been a modest tributary became a fast-moving torrent of people that could be culled to make up slave cargoes at the coastal ports, Asante's reach into its northern hinterland reconfigured the slave ship's ethnic profile. In the absence of the kind of documentary material for the earlier period, it is not possible to map those historically shifting contours in detail, but some sense of the ethnic politics of captivity can be discerned in European observations. A group of Asante merchants came to the Royal African Company's fort at Komenda in August 1715, for instance, with the news that the "great many more" traders who were yet on their way "have abundance of both gold & teeth but no slaves, what they have caught in their last battel with Gingebea, a countrey beyond Ashantee, being so very maugre & lean that are not as yet able to undergo the fatigue of so farr a journey to be vendable when come here." As the "Gold Coast" from which captives departed in 1715 was a place different from that of a few decades earlier, so too were the social contours of the cargoes they constituted. The trajectory of historical change in the region thus contributed additional layers of complexity to the diaspora of captives from the region.

Identifying the ethnic composition of the Gold Coast peoples raises still further questions. What meaning did ethnic labels actually have in people's daily lives? At what level(s) of social and political organization did "identity" reside? Here again, contemporary European representations of the region's geography offer a useful point of departure. Europeans defined their "Gold Coast" by mapping it, marking the details deemed relevant to the European agenda of commercial expropriation: which people had gold and which did not; which were known to steal gold from merchants seeking to trade with Europeans at the coast and which were reliable partners in economic exchange; and so on. Cartographic representations of what Europeans needed to know about the region's politico-economic landscape provide a useful framework for exploring questions about the socioethnic landscape of the Gold Coast.

One of the earliest extant European maps of the region is a 1629 Dutch rendering of "the Regions of the G[old] C[oast] in Guinea." Its layout defined spatially by forty-three *landschapen* (territorial units), the map told its viewers that the territory called Aquemboe stood adjacent to the territory called Akim or Great Acanij; that the inhabitants of the former were "Thievish people" but those of the latter were "Very delicate people and rich in slaves"; and that abutting "Akim or Great Acanij" was the territory called simply Acanij. "Here," the map's notation explained, "live the most principal merchants who trade gold with us."

Gold Coast historian Ray Kea has interpreted the Dutch term *landschapen* as "a Dutch rendering of two Akan terms: *oman* (in the plural, *aman*), which refers to political units, and *afamu*, which refers to geographical ones." The Gold Coast on this map, then, comprised polities or states (*aman*) whose limits were neatly defined by corresponding territorial boundaries. Comparing this map with two others, one drawn in 1602 and another prepared around 1720 (but dated 1746), Kea has observed that all but two of the territorial units depicted on the later map are found also on the 1629 map, and many also appear on the earliest of the three. Through this correspondence, "the spatial and historical continuity of political and geographical units over a period of 170 years (1550–1720) is clearly affirmed," writes Kea. Indeed, he continues, the three maps "indicate a historical and spatial continuity of towns, and, by extension, of settlement systems, both on the coast and in the interior."

But if indeed the boundaries of political authority corresponded neatly to geographic boundaries, did these correspond in turn to the other varied elements of ethnic belonging that define group identity? In other words, to what extent did states (such as Wassa, or Acquemboe, or Acanij) correspond to ethnic groups, and if so, to which people did such neatly correlated social-political-geographic identities extend? Who among the inhabitants of the place called Bonnoe identified themselves exclusively or primarily as "the Bonnoe" people? To put it somewhat more abstractly, what complex factors shaped the relationship between place and people—correspondence to a speech community, a ruling group, a community of original settlers, a recent migration, displacement and assimilation by way of enslavement?

The nation-state, with its posited correspondence of social, political, and territorial boundaries, was emerging at this time as Europe's approach to the problematic interplay of identity, place, and assent to political authority; but as the literature on early modern Europe continues to make ever clearer, there the nation-state turned on correspondences as much imagined as real, produced as much by coercion from above as by processes from below. It is no surprise that viewed through another lens, a different geography for the peoples of the Gold Coast can be discerned from the one mapped by narrow European interest in the region's "subterraneous treasures."

Invisible to Europeans until the unfortunates appeared at the littoral to be sold, the anonymous thousands who came together aboard slave ships had inhabited a social landscape whose contours we must attempt to map, even if only in rudimentary fashion. Of greatest concern here is not which places possessed gold and which did not, but rather who occupied this landscape from which captive people were expelled to fill the holds of European ships, and how did those inhabitants define themselves? Stories of origin provide a means for prying open another window onto the region's social landscape.

LESLIE M. HARRIS

From *In the Shadow of Slavery: African Americans in New York City, 1626–1863*

(2003)

In the decades between 1741 and the Revolutionary War, some white Americans slowly and haltingly began to question the role of slavery in society. Partially in response to the Great Awakening, Quakers and Methodists began to reexamine the religious basis for the enslavement of Africans. By the early 1770s, New York's Methodists and Quakers had begun to fight against slavery within their own congregations by excluding slaveholders from their midst. Anglicans, although less overtly antislavery, continued to educate and baptize blacks, implying at least blacks' religious equality with whites. Such actions encouraged enslaved blacks to agitate for their freedom. But the attempts by religious denominations and by blacks to call attention to the wrongs of slavery had little material impact in New York before the Revolutionary War.

The political ideology of the Revolution, with its emphasis on the American colonies' enslavement to Britain, provided a secular language with which to critique the holding of blacks as slaves, one that an emerging coalition of antislavery New Yorkers could embrace across differing religious affiliations. Additionally, the practical effects of the war gave large numbers of enslaved people an opportunity to seize their freedom; both the British and American armies made limited offers of freedom to those who would fight for them, and the disorder of the war gave slaves greater opportunities to flee their masters.

Ultimately, however, the Revolution did not lead to the end of slavery in New York. There were strong economic reasons for retaining slaves in New York City and the Hudson Valley immediately after the war. Slaves continued to be an important labor source for urban and rural New York until European immigration increased in the 1790s. There were also ideological and political reasons for retaining slavery. The ideology of republicanism that emerged from the Revolutionary War depicted a society whose success depended on a virtuous, self-sufficient, independent citizenry that was not beholden to any social group or individual. Slaves, as the property of masters, were symbolically and literally the inverse of the ideal republican citizen. Although the new nation celebrated colonists who resisted "enslavement" to England as revolutionary patriots, African Americans who sought their freedom by siding with the occupying British during the war were considered traitors. Whites viewed even those slaves and free blacks who assisted the colonists during the Revolutionary War as unable to throw off the degradation of their enslavement. New Yorkers only reluctantly granted freedom to those slaves who fought on behalf of the new nation.

After the Revolutionary War failed to provide freedom for all blacks, New York's blacks and a growing group of whites continued to struggle to end slavery and, in the meantime, to ameliorate the harshest aspects of the system. Many blacks maintained cultural independence and built community against the isolation of New York slavery through participation in Pinkster celebrations. Some slaves negotiated with masters to purchase family members or spouses. Those able to hire out their labor for wages could buy their freedom. Other slaves chose the path of outright rebellion. During this period, the numbers of slave runaways again increased, and some slaves resorted to arson conspiracies to free themselves and others. . . .

. . . The failure of Americans to address the problem of slavery gave the British powerful rhetorical and military weapons against them during the war. Samuel Johnson chided, "How is it that we hear the loudest *yelps* for liberty among the drivers of negroes?" More dangerous to the American cause were the British offers of freedom to slaves. In 1775, Lord Dunmore, the royal governor of Virginia, promised freedom after the war to any slaves who fought for the British. Based on military service, Dunmore's proclamation only applied to male slaves. By 1780, however, Sir Henry Clinton, the British commander in chief based in New York, had expanded the offer of freedom "to every Negro who shall desert the Rebel standard," thus opening British lines to black men, women, and children. In response, tens of thousands of slaves joined the British during the course of the war. . . .

Blacks served both the British and American forces in a variety of ways. Black soldiers served the British in all-black companies such as the Black Guides and Pioneers, the Ethiopian Regiment, and the Black Brigade. The British commissioned the first Black Pioneer company in New York in 1776. Two white officers led the company, but blacks filled the positions below the rank of lieutenant and ensign. In contrast, the Americans interspersed blacks among white troops. Both the British and the Americans used blacks as combatants in their navies. The British in particular relied on blacks who had knowledge of the American waterways as sailors and guides. Privateers, private boats commissioned by their respective governments but not subject to their enlistment rules, also employed blacks on their crews. . . .

When the British occupied New York in 1776, the city became a center for blacks from all colonies seeking freedom. The swelling numbers of blacks alarmed the British, but ultimately their need for labor led them to accept the aid of the growing population. The British housed black refugees in "Negro Barracks" in the city; blacks socialized at "Ethiopian balls" with British officers and soldiers. The British army also called upon blacks to labor for them. After the Americans retreated from the area in 1776, blacks assisted the British army in raiding patriot property in New York City and the surrounding rural areas. They seized supplies, particularly food, and generally helped terrorize the patriots into submission. Blacks also served in more mundane tasks. Black men helped to build fortifications and served as cartmen, woodcutters, cooks, and military servants. Black women labored as cooks, washerwomen, and prostitutes. Because the British were desperate for workers, they paid black laborers wages equal to those of whites.

Whether laboring for the British or for the Americans, blacks expected freedom and equality in return for their services. At war's end, many who had served the British and were willing to relocate achieved liberty by traveling to British territories. Between three and four thousand blacks left through New York's port for England, Nova Scotia, and Sierra Leone; about one thousand were natives of New York State. Their resettlement was not easy; they faced racism in England and Nova Scotia and difficult pioneer conditions in Africa. But they believed, at least initially, that their chances for freedom and equality were greater outside the newly forming United States.

The rhetoric of revolutionary Americans and the reality of blacks' service to the patriot cause led most northern states to emancipate their slaves during and immediately after the Revolutionary War. Vermont, with its tiny population of slaves, provided for immediate emancipation in its 1777 constitution. In 1780, the Pennsylvania state legislature enacted gradual emancipation. Three years later, a Massachusetts Supreme Court decision declared slavery unconstitutional in the state. In 1784, Connecticut and Rhode Island enacted gradual emancipation laws. But New York's continued reliance on slave labor in the city and in the rural Hudson Valley through the 1780s led whites to resist including general abolition in their state constitution or in legislative actions. Only those slaves who had served in place of their masters in the war were granted freedom. These men then negotiated with slave masters to free their wives, children, and other relatives, usually in return for labor or cash.

By 1790, the free black population in New York City had grown to an unprecedented 1,036 out of a total black population of 3,092. But slavery remained firmly entrenched in the city. The tenuousness of black freedom in New York City was revealed in 1784 when slave traders attempted to seize a group of free blacks and sell them south illegally. . . .

. . . From the end of the Revolutionary War to the early 1800s, New York City blacks were part of the greatest round of slave resistance and rebellion the Americas had yet seen. Some were inspired by the Revolutionary War in the United States. Disappointed by the retreat of Americans on the issue of slavery in the new nation's constitution, some slaves plotted individual or group freedom. The number of runaways increased, particularly from southern plantations to those northern states where emancipation laws had been enacted. The era's greatest success was Haitian revolutionaries' defeat of the French government and liberation of the slaves of Saint Domingue by 1800. In the 1790s, the example of the Haitian revolution also inspired some slaves in the United States. Slaves throughout the United States overheard their masters discussing the massive rebellion. Along the coast from Louisiana to New York, white refugees arrived with their slaves from Saint Domingue; both slaves and masters brought stories of the rebellion. In at least one instance, in Louisiana in 1811, a slave brought from Saint Domingue, Charles Deslondes, led American slaves to rebellion. . . .

Slaves in New York City and the surrounding rural areas who were unable to escape bondage attempted to mitigate the isolation and hardships of slavery through participation in Pinkster celebrations in the late 1780s and 1790s. Pinkster had not played a large role among slaves in New York City prior to this time; rather, it was a tradition of rural slaves and centered more in Albany. Its appearance in New York City at the end of the eighteenth century indicates a growing sense of community between New York City slaves and their rural counterparts. Slaves incorporated the Dutch festival into their strategies for building community to combat the isolated nature of rural slavery. . . . Although whites were not participating in Pinkster by the late eighteenth century, they observed and approved of the festival's continuation as a slave celebration. Slaves combined African and Dutch traditions in their version of the festival. In the spring, they elected a king to a three-day reign. As in the Dutch tradition, this king collected tributes from blacks and whites throughout the city, and for the three days of the festival he settled all disputes. Additionally, blacks performed a variety of dances during the celebration, dances that white observers considered distinctively African or "negro" in nature. These dances continued African traditions that emphasized the centrality of dance to community and religious celebrations.

In New York City, blacks celebrated Pinkster in the markets. Black slaves from New Jersey who sold their wares at Bear Market joined slaves from Long

Island and New York City at Catharine Market after completing their day's peddling. Together, these slaves perfected the dances for which they were known throughout New York State, with the best dancers picking up prizes of money or dried fish or eels before returning to their masters. Through such approved autonomous activities, slaves and free blacks in the 1790s and 1800s could reunite briefly with family members; they could also pass along information, from gossip about friends to methods of escape from slave masters.

PART 2

Religious Life, Spirituality, and Racial Identity

KEISHA N. BLAIN

Since the beginning of the transatlantic slave trade, which resulted in the forced migration of an estimated twelve million Africans from the sixteenth to the nineteenth centuries, people of African descent have drawn on multiple religious faiths and traditions. Black religious life, with its focus on personhood and liberation, has served as a vital counterweight to the violent and dehumanizing aspects of life for blacks in the United States and other parts of the African diaspora. As Eddie Glaude's essay in this section argues, black religious practice in the United States and other parts of the African diaspora was, and continues to be, richly diverse. From the colonial period to the present, people of African descent have drawn on a myriad of religious traditions including Christianity, Islam, Judaism, conjure, and Yoruba.

The experiences forged by slavery in the United States and in the Atlantic World have had a profound impact on black religious practices. On the one hand, white masters generally attempted to destroy any traces of African religious practice and belief among their slaves through horror and violence. In the context of the United States, many of the enslaved were forced to outwardly practice Christianity but secretly maintained their own traditional beliefs. By arranging secret meetings and clandestine worship practices and services and establishing their own form of religious hierarchies, slaves covertly challenged white masters and thereby asserted their political agency.

While the institution of slavery threatened the survival of African religious heritage, enslaved men and women employed various strategies to retain African religious traditions. As Jermaine Archer's essay in this section demonstrates, African influences thrived in slave societies in the United States and other parts of the globe. Many enslaved men and women practiced religious syncretism, blending aspects of Christianity with various West African religious practices such as conjuration, divination, and folk medicine. In places such as Brazil, Jamaica, and Trinidad, African cultures remained salient in the religious lives of people of African descent. Among the practitioners of various global black religions, including voodou, rastafari, and candomblé, traces of African cultural practices can still be found—in worship styles, music, and rituals. Through these varied religious practices, people of African descent have found hope and healing in response to slavery and racial segregation and their legacies of mass incarceration and police violence.

Historically, people of African descent have always used religion and religious institutions as avenues for resisting white supremacy. On slave plantations, black men and women who embraced Christianity sang redemption songs such as "Amazing Grace," expressing hope in a glorious afterlife—far removed from the pain and despair of life under slavery. These men and women also created Negro spirituals that reflected their newfound faith. According to religious scholar Horace Clarence Boyer, Negro spirituals "not only spoke to the slaves' relationship to God but also gave special attention to their position on earth and the difficult fate that had befallen them."[1] These songs served multiple functions on the slave plantations, often as a coping mechanism and certainly as an act of resistance. According to Christa K. Dixon, Negro spirituals, such as popular songs like "Steal Away," "offer[ed] a physiological 'out' where no physical 'out' [was] possible."[2] In this sense, these spiritual songs functioned as a means of survival, offering hope for a better future in light of present painful realities.

Significantly, Negro spirituals also functioned as code messages for organizing acts of resistance. As part of the abolitionist movement, for example, slaves often used the song "Steal Away" to signal that guides to the Underground Railroad had arrived on a plantation. At other times, the song was used to initiate secret meetings to plot escapes.[3] Such examples highlight the myriad functions of Negro spirituals and other songs of faith on the slave plantation. Indeed, as theologian James Cone has argued in *The Spirituals and the Blues*, these songs contained a power of their own; they served as a spiritual medium through which the antebellum slave community transcended plantation life entirely.[4] By their very existence on the plantation, spirituals connected slaves to God and strengthened their faith in God's ability to free them—both physically and spiritually.[5]

Enslaved men and women who wholeheartedly embraced Christianity were not oblivious to the contradictions inherent in their white masters' violent and inhumane practices. Writing in his 1845 narrative, abolitionist and former slave Frederick Douglass pointed out the contradictions: "Between the Christianity of this land, and the Christianity of Christ, I recognize the widest possible difference—so wide, that to receive the one as good, pure, and holy, is of necessity to reject the other as bad, corrupt, and wicked."[6] Many other black men and women agreed with these sentiments and attempted to reshape Christian theological practices in response to their social conditions. Jarena Lee, whose narrative is included in this section, challenged social conventions concerning women's roles in black churches and set out to spread the gospel in hopes of transforming both hearts and minds concerning the "national sin" of slavery.

Enslaved men and women found inspiration in biblical stories and verses to justify their unwavering acts of resistance and efforts to overturn the slave system. These men and women were unwilling to accept the slave masters' version of Christianity, which encouraged slaves to be docile and obedient. In his 1820 speech Richard Allen—founder of the African Methodist Episcopal (AME) Church—drew on biblical teaching to openly condemn the institution of slavery and call for its immediate end.[7] Efforts to end chattel slavery and white supremacy were not confined to the United States. On the African continent, for example, black religious leaders not only condemned chattel slavery but also were at the forefront of social movements to end colonialism, racial injustice, and inequality. James Campbell's chapter, included in this section, highlights the influence of AME leaders in South Africa. As Campbell argues, the AME church in South Africa, as in other parts of the continent, became one of the crucial sites for black men and women to engage in social and political activism. In these religious spaces, churchgoers not only debated Africa's place in the black cultural identity but also attempted to forge transnational political and religious ties in their struggles for freedom and equality.

Women of African descent have played vital roles in this struggle, including as leaders of and participants in various religious movements from the colonial era to the present. Jarena Lee's religious activities during the nineteenth century, for example, laid the groundwork for the kinds of activities in which women would be engaged in black churches and in religious groups in general. The reading by Charles Marsh sheds light on the integral role black women have played in religious organizations and movements for centuries.

In addition to addressing the emotional and spiritual needs of the communities in which they reside, black places of worship have provided sanctuaries for education and political organizing and mobilizing. Because of the significant role black religious institutions have played in sustaining black political action, these spaces have always been subjected to white supremacist violence and terror. Manisha Sinha's op-ed emphasizes this point, highlighting some of the most infamous acts of violence in black churches in the decades leading up to the Charleston shooting. Perhaps one of the most well-known church bombings took place in Birmingham, Alabama, in 1963, when four little girls were killed at the hands of white vigilantes. This act of terror, combined with countless other acts of violence in black churches and communities, compelled Rev. Jeremiah Wright, former pastor of then-senator Barack Obama, to openly condemn the United States for its treatment of people of color.

While Rev. Wright's speech generated much controversy, especially because of the pastor's ties to Obama during his presidential campaign, the speech captured some of the frustrations felt by black religious leaders concerning the continued struggles against racial violence and discrimination, which have, as Claudia Rankine argues, created a permanent state of black mourning. Rev. Wright's speech called attention to the failures of American society. Yet, in a reflection of the religious spirit of many black leaders before him, Rev. Wright appealed to his parishioners not to lose sight of their faith despite the challenges ahead: "When God says it, it's done. God never fails. When God wills it, you better get out the way. 'Cause God never fails."[8]

NOTES

1. Horace Clarence Boyer, *How Sweet the Sound: The Golden Age of Gospel* (Urbana: University of Chicago Press, 2000), 9.

2. Christa K. Dixon, *Negro Spirituals: From Bible to Folksong* (Philadelphia: Fortress Press, 1976), 81.

3. Ibid.

4. James Cone, *The Spirituals and the Blues: An Interpretation* (New York: Maryknoll, 1982), 32.

5. Ibid., 29, 43.

6. Frederick Douglass, *Narrative of the Life of Frederick Douglass, an American Slave, Written by Himself* (Boston: Anti-Slavery Office, 1845).

7. Richard Allen, "An Address to Those Who Keep Slaves and Approve the Practice," in *Preaching with Sacred Fire: An Anthology of African American Sermons, 1750–Present*, ed. Martha Simmons and Frank Thomas. Ca. 1820; New York: W. W. Norton, 2010.

8. Jeremiah Wright, "Confusing God and Government," *BlackPast.org: An Online Reference Guide to African American History*, http://www.blackpast.org/2008-rev-jeremiah-wright-confusing-god-and-government.

JARENA LEE

From *Religious Experience and Journal of Mrs. Jarena Lee, Giving an Account of Her Call to Preach the Gospel*

(1849)

And it shall come to pass . . . that I will pour out my Spirit upon all flesh, and your sons and your *daughters* shall prophesy.

JOEL 2.28

I was born February 11th, 1783, at Cape May, State of New Jersey. At the age of seven years I was parted from my parents, and went to live as a servant maid, with a Mr. Sharp, at the distance of about sixty miles from the place of my birth.

My parents being wholly ignorant of the knowledge of God, had not therefore instructed me in any degree in this great matter. Not long after the commencement of my attendance on this lady, she had bid me do something respecting my work, which in a little while after she asked me if I had done, when I replied, Yes—but this was not true.

At this awful point, in my early history, the Spirit of God moved in power through my conscience, and told me I was a wretched sinner. On this account so great was the impression, and so strong were the feelings of guilt, that I promised in my heart that I would not tell another lie.

But notwithstanding this promise my heart grew harder, after a while, yet the Spirit of the Lord never entirely forsook me, but continued mercifully striving with me, until his gracious power converted my soul.

The manner of this great accomplishment was as follows: In the year 1804, it so happened that I went with others to hear a missionary of the Presbyterian order preach. It was an afternoon meeting, but few were there, the place was a school room; but the preacher was solemn, and in his countenance the earnestness of his master's business appeared equally strong, as though he were about to speak to a multitude. . . .

Soon after this I again went to the city of Philadelphia, and commenced going to the English Church, the pastor of which was an Englishman, by the name of Pilmore, one of the number who at first preached Methodism in America, in the city of New York.

But while sitting under the ministration of this man, which was about three months, and at the last time, it appeared that there was a wall between me and a communion with that people, which was higher than I could possibly see over, and seemed to make this impression upon my mind, *this is not the people for you.*

But on returning home at noon I inquired of the head cook of the house respecting the rules of the Methodists, as I knew she belonged to that society, who told me what they were; on which account I replied, that I should not be able to abide by such strict rules not even one year—however, I told her that I would go with her and hear what they had to say.

The man who was to speak in the afternoon of that day, was the Rev. Richard Allen, since bishop of the African Episcopal Methodists in America. During the labors of this man that afternoon, I had come to the conclusion, that this is the people to which my heart unites, and it so happened, that as soon as the service closed he invited such as felt a desire to flee the wrath to come, to unite on trial with them—I embraced the opportunity. Three weeks from that day, my soul was gloriously converted to God, under preaching, at the very outset of the sermon. The text was barely pronounced, which was "I perceive thy heart is not right in the sight of God," when there appeared to *my* view, in the centre of the heart, *one* sin; and this was *malice* against one particular individual, who had strove deeply to injure me, which I resented. At this discovery I said, *Lord I forgive every* creature. That instant, it appeared to me as if a garment, which had entirely enveloped my whole person, even to my fingers' ends, split at the crown of my head, and was stripped away from me, passing like a shadow from my sight—when the glory of God seemed to cover me in its stead.

That moment, though hundreds were present, I did leap to my feet and declare that God, for Christ's sake, had pardoned the sins of my soul. Great was the [ecstasy] of my mind, for I felt that not only the sin of *malice* was pardoned, but all other sins were swept away together. That day was the first when my heart had believed, and my tongue had made confession unto salvation—the first words uttered, a part of that song, which shall fill eternity with its sound, was *glory to God.* For a few moments I had power to exhort sinners, and to tell of the wonders and of the goodness of Him who had clothed me with *His* salvation. During this the minister was silent, until my soul felt its duty had been performed, when he declared another witness of the power of Christ, to forgive sins on earth, was manifest in my conversion. . . .

Between four and five years after my sanctification, on a certain time, an impressive silence fell upon me, and I stood as if some one was about to speak to me, yet I had no such thought in my heart.—But to my utter surprise there seemed to sound a voice which I thought I distinctly heard, and most certainly understand, which said to me, "Go preach the Gospel!" I immediately replied aloud, "No one will believe me." Again I listened, and again the same voice seemed to say—"Preach the Gospel; I will put words in your mouth, and you will turn your enemies to become your friends."

In consequence of this, my mind became so exercised, that during the night following, I took a text and preached in my sleep. I thought there stood before me a great multitude, while I expounded to them the things of religion. So violent were my exertions and so loud were my exclamations, that I awoke from the sound of my own voice, which also awoke the family of the house where I resided. Two days after I went to see the preacher in charge of the African Society, who was the Rev. Richard Allen, the same before named in these pages, to tell him that I felt it my duty to preach the gospel. But as I drew near the street in which his house was, which was in the city of Philadelphia, my courage began to fail me; so terrible did the cross appear, it seemed that I should not be able to bear it. Previous to my acting out to go to see him, so agitated was my mind, that my appetite for my daily food failed me entirely. Several times on my way there, I turned back again; but as often I felt my strength again renewed, and I soon found that the nearer I approached to the house of the minister, the less was my fear. Accordingly, as soon as I came to the door, my fears subsided, the cross was removed, al things appeared pleasant—I was tranquil.

I [now] told him, that the Lord had revealed it to me, that I must preach the gospel. He replied, by asking, in what sphere I wished to move in? I said, among the Methodists. He then replied, that a Mrs. Cook, a Methodist lady, had also some time before requested the same privilege; who, it was believed, had done much good in the way of exhortation, and holding prayer meetings; and who had been permitted to do so by the verbal license of the preacher in charge at the time. But as to women preaching, he said that our Discipline knew nothing at all about it—that it did not call for women preachers. This I was glad to hear, because it removed the fear of the cross—but no sooner did this feeling cross my mind, than I found that a love of souls had in a measure departed from me; that holy energy which burned within me, as a fire, began to be smothered. This I soon perceived.

O how careful ought we to be, lest through our by-laws of church government and discipline, we bring into disrepute even the word of life. For as unseemly as it may appear now-a-days for a woman to preach, it should be remembered that nothing is impossible with God. And why should it be thought impossible, heterodox, or improper for a woman to preach? seeing the Saviour died for the woman as well as for the man.

If the man may preach, because the Saviour died for him, why not the woman? seeing he died for her also. Is he not a whole Saviour, instead of a half one? as those who hold it wrong for a woman to preach, would seem to make it appear.

Did not Mary *first* preach the risen Saviour, and is not the doctrine of the resurrection the very climax of Christianity—hangs not all our hope on this, as argued by St. Paul? Then did not Mary, a woman, preach the gospel? for she preached the resurrection of the crucified son of God.

But some will say that Mary did not expound the Scripture, therefore, she did not preach, in the proper sense of the term. To this I reply, it may be that the term *preach* in those primitive times, did not mean exactly what it is now *made* to mean; perhaps it was a great deal more simple then, than it is now—if it were not, the unlearned fishermen could not have preached the gospel at all, as they had no learning.

To this it may be replied, by those who are determined not to believe that it is right for a woman to preach, that the disciples, though they were fishermen and ignorant of letters too, were inspired so to do. To which I would reply, that though they were inspired, yet that inspiration did not save them from showing their ignorance of letters and of man's wisdom; this the multitude soon found out, by listening to the remarks of the envious Jewish priests. If then, to preach the gospel, by the gift of heaven, comes by inspiration solely, is God straitened: must he take the man exclusively? May he not, did he not, and can he not inspire a female to preach the simple story of the birth, life, death, and resurrection of our Lord, and accompany it too with power to the sinner's heart. As for me, I am fully persuaded that the Lord called me to labor according to what I have received, in his vineyard. If he has not, how could he consistently bear testimony in favor of my poor labors, in awakening and converting sinners?

. . . I firmly believe that I have sown seed, in the name of the Lord, which shall appear with its increase at the great day of accounts, when Christ shall come to make up his jewels.

JOHN NEWTON

Amazing Grace

(1779)

Amazing grace! How sweet the sound
That saved a wretch like me!
I once was lost, but now am found;
Was blind, but now I see.

'Twas grace that taught my heart to fear,
And grace my fears relieved;
How precious did that grace appear
The hour I first believed.

Through many dangers, toils and snares,
I have already come;
'Tis grace hath brought me safe thus far,
And grace will lead me home.

The Lord has promised good to me,
His Word my hope secures;
He will my Shield and Portion be,
As long as life endures.

Yea, when this flesh and heart shall fail,
And mortal life shall cease,
I shall possess, within the veil,
A life of joy and peace.

The earth shall soon dissolve like snow,
The sun forbear to shine;
But God, who called me here below,
Will be forever mine.

When we've been there ten thousand years,
Bright shining as the sun,
We've no less days to sing God's praise
Than when we'd first begun.

Love and Terror in the Black Church

(June 20, 2015)

At the sprawling Friendship-West Baptist Church in Dallas one day last spring, I was met by five men with earpieces who escorted me to the pastor's office. As I prepared to preach that morning, a rolling phalanx of bodyguards shadowed my every move—when I greeted parishioners in the church's spacious narthex and even as I made a stop at the men's room. We walked from the church study into the 4,200-seat sanctuary, the security team whispering into their wrists.

I was entering a sanctuary, a sacred space to speak the word of the Lord and to lift the spirits of God's people. But I was also entering a black church, a site of particular power in this country, and a site of unspeakable terror.

That is what the Emanuel African Methodist Episcopal Church in Charleston, South Carolina, became on Wednesday, when a young white male wielding a .45-caliber handgun unloaded his rage on nine souls, and that is why for the foreseeable future we will enter our houses of worship wary of violence.

Sites and spaces of black life have come under attack from racist forces before, but the black church is a unique target. It is not just where black people gather.

In too many other places, black self-worth is bludgeoned by bigotry or hijacked by self-hatred: that our culture is too dumb, our lives too worthless, to warrant the effort to combat our enemies. The black sanctuary breathes in black humanity while the pulpit exhales unapologetic black love.

For decades, these sites of love have been magnets for hate.

In June 1958, a dynamite bomb rocked the Bethel Baptist Church in Birmingham, Alabama, led by the Reverend Fred L. Shuttlesworth, a civil rights luminary. It would take more than two decades to bring the white supremacist perpetrator to justice. In 1963, four girls were killed when the Sixteenth Street Baptist Church in the same city was bombed. As the drive to register black voters heated up during Freedom Summer in 1964, nearly three dozen black churches in Mississippi were bombed or burned.

The hatred of black sacred space didn't end in the 1960s. In July 1993, the FBI uncovered a plot to bomb the First AME Church in Los Angeles, wipe out its congregation with machine guns, and then assassinate Rodney G. King in hopes of provoking a race war. In 1995, several men took sledgehammers to the pews and kitchens of black churches in Sumter County, Alabama. A year later, the Inner City Church in Knoxville, Tennessee, was bombarded with as many as eighteen Molotov cocktails as its back door was splashed with racist epithets.

President Clinton appointed a task force in 1996 to investigate church fires, which by 1998 had singed the holy legacies of 225 black churches. In November 2008, three white men set the Macedonia Church of God in Christ in Springfield, Massachusetts, ablaze hours after Barack Obama was elected the nation's first black president.

And this wasn't the first time Emanuel AME Church, founded in 1816, faced racist violence. After Denmark Vesey, one of the church's founding members, plotted a slave rebellion but was foiled in the effort by a slave who betrayed his plans, Emanuel was burned to the ground by an angry white mob.

Despite this history, black churches are open and affirming of whoever seeks to join their ranks—unlike white churches, which have often rigidly divided along racial lines. The AME church was born when the founder, Richard Allen, spurned segregation in the white Methodist church and sought to worship God free of crippling prejudice. Early church leaders took seriously the scripture in Acts 17:26, which claims of God: "From one man he made all the nations, that they should inhabit the whole earth," even as they embraced the admonition in Hebrews 13:2: "Do not forget to show hospitality to strangers, for by so doing some people have shown hospitality to angels without knowing it."

That is how it is possible that the doors of Emanuel were open to a young white participant who, after an hour of prayer, raised a weapon and took nine lives. Sylvia Johnson, a cousin of the murdered pastor, the Reverend Clementa C. Pinckney, said one of the survivors told her that the gunman argued: "I have to do it. You rape our women and you're taking over our country, and you have to go." The vortex of racist mythology spun into a plan of racial carnage.

The black church is a breeding ground for leaders and movements to quell the siege of white racist terror. From the start, black churches sought to amplify black grievance against racial injustice and to forge bonds with believers to resist oppression from the broader society. The church's spiritual and political mission were always intertwined: to win the freedom of its people so that they could prove their devotion to God.

Some critics see black church leaders as curators of moral quiet in the face of withering assault. Religious people are accused of being passive in the wake of social injustice—of seeking heavenly reward rather than earthly action. In truth, the church at its best has nurtured theological and political resistance to white supremacy and the forces of black hatred. The church has supplied leaders and blueprints for emancipation—whether in the preaching of Frederick

Douglass or Prathia Hall or in the heroic activism of the Reverend Dr. Martin Luther King Jr.

But the church is also the place where black people are most vulnerable. Oddly, stereotypes of the sort the killer nursed are unmasked in such a setting. It is not murderous venom that courses in black veins but loving tolerance for the stranger, which is the central moral imperative of the Gospel.

I recall an instance of such generosity when I led a dialogue for a black men's group at another Dallas church a few years ago. A white man entered the church and joined our group. We introduced ourselves, and welcomed him. He sought to counter my message of affirmation for gay men and lesbians. After he had his say, I asked him if the tables were turned could such a thing occur: Could I, as a black man, show up at his white church and be received with open arms and permitted to publicly denounce the teachings of the white male lecturer? He at least had the honesty to admit it could never happen. Yet no black man asked him to leave our ranks.

Adherence to the moral imperative to treat strangers kindly may have led to the black parishioners' death in Charleston. The shooter exploited the very kindness and humanity he found before him. The black folk gathered in that church were the proof that he was wrong; they were the living, breathing antithesis of bigoted creeds cooked up in the racist fog he lived in. It is not their barbarity, but the moral beauty of black people, that let an angel of death hide in their religious womb.

Its openness and magnanimity are what make the black church vital in the quest for black self-regard. When I stand in the house of God to deliver the word I embrace the redemption of black belief—a belief in self and community.

In a country where black death is normal, even fiendishly familiar, black love is an unavoidably political gesture. And that is what happens in our churches: the act of black love, which seems to make our houses of worship a target of hate. It is a political act in this culture that must remind the nation, once again, as hate and terror level our community, that black lives matter.

MANISHA SINHA

The Long and Proud History of Charleston's AME Church

(June 19, 2015)

When twenty-one-year-old Dylann Roof opened fire at the historic Emanuel African Methodist Episcopal (AME) Church in Charleston, South Carolina, on Wednesday night killing nine worshippers, including its pastor, the Reverend Clementa Pinckney, he struck at the very heart of black America. Established by the Reverend Richard Allen, a former slave and Methodist preacher, the AME is the oldest black denomination in the country. Its roots lie in one of the first black religious and mutual help societies, the Free African Society founded by Philadelphia blacks in 1787. Like other independent churches and societies founded by newly free African Americans, it has a proud history of black protest and community activism.

In 1792, Allen and the Reverend Absalom Jones, led a walkout at St. George's Methodist Church in Philadelphia. They had dared to pray in the front pews reserved for whites rather than in the segregated gallery constructed for blacks. Zealous church authorities had interrupted their prayers and forced them to rise to their feet. As the story goes, this unseemly incident was the impetus for the founding of independent black churches. In 1794, with black contributions and donations from the British abolitionist Granville Sharp, President George Washington, and the Pennsylvania Abolition Society, Jones's African Episcopal Church of St. Thomas opened its doors, boasting over four hundred members. Founded the same year, Allen's Mother Bethel Methodist Church was incorporated in 1796. Later Allen composed an "African Supplement" to proclaim his church's autonomy. In 1816, he issued a call to all black Methodists in the surrounding area. Delegates from Pennsylvania, New Jersey, Delaware, and Maryland, including Moses Brown from Charleston, South Carolina, met and founded the African Methodist Episcopal Church in 1816, and Allen became its first bishop.

AME churches soon spread north, west, and even to the south acquiring a large congregation in Charleston, South Carolina, in the midst of one of the largest slave societies in the United States. In 1818, the Reverend Brown, replicating Allen's and Jones's actions, led a walkout of black members from the

Methodist church protesting the treatment of black burial grounds by whites and established the AME church in Charleston with four thousand members.

Right from the start, the AME, like other independent black churches, gave birth to antislavery protest. Allen and Jones were authors of early abolitionist pamphlets and petitions. Their "An Address to Those Who Keep Slaves and Uphold the Practice" reminded whites that slavery is "hateful . . . in the sight of God" and that "God himself was the first pleader of the cause of the slaves." The most potent challenge to slavery came from the AME church in Charleston. One of its founders and class leaders, Denmark Vesey, a literate black carpenter who had bought his freedom after winning a lottery, was implicated in a slave conspiracy scare in 1822. State authorities had harassed church members and used the conspiracy as an excuse to destroy the church. Its ministers, Brown and the Reverend Henry Drayton, were forced to leave South Carolina. Brown became the second bishop of the AME on Allen's death. Black Charlestonians rebuilt their church until the city outlawed independent black churches in 1834. In a fitting coda, Robert Vesey, Denmark Vesey's son, helped rebuild the Charleston church in 1865, after the Civil War and emancipation. It was renamed Emanuel AME church, a name that it carries until today.

During the civil rights movement, the Emanuel AME Church of Charleston continued to be the site of black protest. In 1969, the South Carolina National Guard arrested the church's pastor and nine hundred others at a demonstration for hospital workers led by Coretta Scott King. The black church lay at the organizational base of the mass movement for black rights and equality in the South. With good reason, white supremacists and segregationist have targeted it, most infamously in the 1963 Birmingham church bombing that killed four young black girls. A resurgence of black church burnings in the South in the 1990s led the Justice Department to launch a civil rights investigation and civil rights activists volunteered to rebuild them. This latest attack on a black church is all too reminiscent of this tragic history.

Just a year ago, the city of Charleston finally honored Denmark Vesey with a statue after years of controversy when some conservative commentators labeled him a "terrorist." One might well paraphrase the great black abolitionist Frederick Douglass, who asked, "Pray, tell me who is the barbarian here?" during the height of lynching in the post–Civil War South. On the 150th anniversary of Juneteenth or June 19, the day many of the enslaved celebrated as the day of emancipation, one might ask, Pray, who is the terrorist here?

CLAUDIA RANKINE

The Condition of Black Life
Is One of Mourning

(June 22, 2015)

A friend recently told me that when she gave birth to her son, before naming him, before even nursing him, her first thought was, I have to get him out of this country. We both laughed. Perhaps our black humor had to do with understanding that getting out was neither an option nor the real desire. This is it, our life. Here we work, hold citizenship, pensions, health insurance, family, friends, and on and on. She couldn't, she didn't leave. Years after his birth, whenever her son steps out of their home, her status as the mother of a living human being remains as precarious as ever. Added to the natural fears of every parent facing the randomness of life is this other knowledge of the ways in which institutional racism works in our country. Ours was the laughter of vulnerability, fear, recognition, and an absurd stuckness.

I asked another friend what it's like being the mother of a black son. "The condition of black life is one of mourning," she said bluntly. For her, mourning lived in real time inside her and her son's reality: At any moment she might lose her reason for living. Though the white liberal imagination likes to feel temporarily bad about black suffering, there really is no mode of empathy that can replicate the daily strain of knowing that as a black person you can be killed for simply being black: no hands in your pockets, no playing music, no sudden movements, no driving your car, no walking at night, no walking in the day, no turning onto this street, no entering this building, no standing your ground, no standing here, no standing there, no talking back, no playing with toy guns, no living while black.

Eleven days after I was born, on September 15, 1963, four black girls were killed in the bombing of the Sixteenth Street Baptist Church in Birmingham, Alabama. Now, fifty-two years later, six black women and three black men have been shot to death while at a Bible-study meeting at the historic Emanuel African Methodist Episcopal Church in Charleston, South Carolina. They were killed by a homegrown terrorist, self-identifed as a white supremacist, who might also be a "disturbed young man" (as various news outlets have described him). It has been reported that a black woman and her five-year-old grand-

daughter survived the shooting by playing dead. They are two of the three survivors of the attack. The white family of the suspect says that for them this is a
difficult time. This is indisputable. But for African American families, this living
in a state of mourning and fear remains commonplace.

The spectacle of the shooting suggests an event out of time, as if the killing
of black people with white-supremacist justification interrupts anything other
than regular television programming. But Dylann Storm Roof did not create
himself from nothing. He has grown up with the rhetoric and orientation of racism. He has seen white men like Benjamin F. Haskell, Thomas Gleason, and Michael Jacques plead guilty to, or be convicted of, burning Macedonia Church of
God in Christ in Springfield, Massachusetts, just hours after President Obama
was elected. Every racist statement he has made he could have heard all his life.
He, along with the rest of us, has been living with slain black bodies.

We live in a country where Americans assimilate corpses in their daily com-
ings and goings. Dead blacks are a part of normal life here. Dying in ship hulls,
tossed into the Atlantic, hanging from trees, beaten, shot in churches, gunned
down by the police, or warehoused in prisons: historically, there is no quotidian
without the enslaved, chained, or dead black body to gaze upon or to hear about
or to position a self against. When blacks become overwhelmed by our culture's
disorder and protest (ultimately to our own detriment, because protest gives
the police justification to militarize, as they did in Ferguson), the wrongheaded
question that is asked is, What kind of savages are we? Rather than, What kind
of country do we live in?

In 1955, when Emmett Till's mutilated and bloated body was recovered
from the Tallahatchie River and placed for burial in a nailed-shut pine box, his
mother, Mamie Till Mobley, demanded his body be transported from Mississippi, where Till had been visiting relatives, to his home in Chicago. Once the
Chicago funeral home received the body, she made a decision that would create
a new pathway for how to think about a lynched body. She requested an open
coffin and allowed photographs to be taken and published of her dead son's disfigured body.

Mobley's refusal to keep private grief private allowed a body that meant nothing to the criminal-justice system to stand as evidence. By placing both herself
and her son's corpse in positions of refusal relative to the etiquette of grief, she
"disidentified" with the tradition of the lynched figure left out in public view as
a warning to the black community, thereby using the lynching tradition against
itself. The spectacle of the black body, in her hands, publicized the injustice
mapped onto her son's corpse. "Let the people see what I see," she said, adding,
"I believe that the whole United States is mourning with me."

It's very unlikely that her belief in a national mourning was fully realized, but her desire to make mourning enter our day-to-day world was a new kind of logic. In refusing to look away from the flesh of our domestic murders, by insisting we look with her upon the dead, she reframed mourning as a method of acknowledgment that helped energize the civil rights movement in the 1950s and 1960s.

The decision not to release photos of the crime scene in Charleston, perhaps out of deference to the families of the dead, doesn't forestall our mourning. But in doing so, the bodies that demonstrate all too tragically that "black skin is not a weapon" (as one protest poster read last year) are turned into an abstraction. It's one thing to imagine nine black bodies bleeding out on a church floor, and another thing to see it. The lack of visual evidence remains in contrast to what we saw in Ferguson, where the police, in their refusal to move Michael Brown's body, perhaps unknowingly continued where Till's mother left off.

After Brown was shot six times, twice in the head, his body was left face-down in the street by the police officers. Whatever their reasoning, by not moving Brown's corpse for four hours after his shooting, the police made mourning his death part of what it meant to take in the details of his story. No one could consider the facts of Michael Brown's interaction with the Ferguson police officer Darren Wilson without also thinking of the bullet-riddled body bleeding on the asphalt. It would be a mistake to presume that everyone who saw the image mourned Brown, but once exposed to it, a person had to decide whether his dead black body mattered enough to be mourned. (Another option, of course, is that it becomes a spectacle for white pornography: the dead body as an object that satisfies an illicit desire. Perhaps this is where Dylann Storm Roof stepped in.)

Black Lives Matter, the movement founded by the activists Alicia Garza, Patrisse Cullors, and Opal Tometi, began with the premise that the incommensurable experiences of systemic racism creates an unequal playing field. The American imagination has never been able to fully recover from its white-supremacist beginnings. Consequently, our laws and attitudes have been straining against the devaluation of the black body. Despite good intentions, the associations of blackness with inarticulate, bestial criminality persist beneath the appearance of white civility. This assumption both frames and determines our individual interactions and experiences as citizens.

The American tendency to normalize situations by centralizing whiteness was consciously or unconsciously demonstrated again when certain whites, like the president of Smith College, sought to alter the language of "Black Lives Matter" to "All Lives Matter." What on its surface was intended to be interpreted as a humanist move—"aren't we all just people here?"—didn't take into account a system inured to black corpses in our public spaces. When the judge in the

Charleston bond hearing for Dylann Storm Roof called for support of Roof's family, it was also a subtle shift away from valuing the black body in our time of deep despair.

Anti-black racism is in the culture. It's in our laws, in our advertisements, in our friendships, in our segregated cities, in our schools, in our Congress, in our scientific experiments, in our language, on the Internet, in our bodies no matter our race, in our communities, and, perhaps most devastatingly, in our justice system. The unarmed, slain black bodies in public spaces turn grief into our everyday feeling that something is wrong everywhere and all the time, even if locally things appear normal. Having coffee, walking the dog, reading the paper, taking the elevator to the office, dropping the kids off at school: all of this good life is surrounded by the ambient feeling that at any given moment, a black person is being killed in the street or in his home by the armed hatred of a fellow American.

The Black Lives Matter movement can be read as an attempt to keep mourning an open dynamic in our culture because black lives exist in a state of precariousness. Mourning then bears both the vulnerability inherent in black lives and the instability regarding a future for those lives. Unlike earlier black-power movements that tried to fight or segregate for self-preservation, Black Lives Matter aligns with the dead, continues the mourning, and refuses the forgetting in front of all of us. If the Reverend Martin Luther King Jr.'s civil rights movement made demands that altered the course of American lives and backed up those demands with the willingness to give up your life in service of your civil rights, with Black Lives Matter, a more internalized change is being asked for: recognition.

The truth, as I see it, is that if black men and women, black boys and girls, mattered, if we were seen as living, we would not be dying simply because whites don't like us. Our deaths inside a system of racism existed before we were born. The legacy of black bodies as property and subsequently three-fifths human continues to pollute the white imagination. To inhabit our citizenry fully, we have to not only understand this, but also grasp it. In the words of playwright Lorraine Hansberry, "The problem is we have to find some way with these dialogues to show and to encourage the white liberal to stop being a liberal and become an American radical." And, as my friend the critic and poet Fred Moten has written: "I believe in the world and want to be in it. I want to be in it all the way to the end of it because I believe in another world and I want to be in that." This other world, that world, would presumably be one where black living matters. But we can't get there without fully recognizing what is here.

Dylann Storm Roof's unmediated hatred of black people; Black Lives Matter; citizens' videotaping the killings of blacks; the Ferguson Police Department leaving Brown's body in the street—all these actions support Mamie Till Mobley's belief that we need to see or hear the truth. We need the truth of how the bodies died to interrupt the course of normal life. But if keeping the dead at the forefront of our consciousness is crucial for our body politic, what of the families of the dead? How must it feel to a family member for the deceased to be more important as evidence than as an individual to be buried and laid to rest?

Michael Brown's mother, Lesley McSpadden, was kept away from her son's body because it was evidence. She was denied the rights of a mother, a sad fact reminiscent of pre–Civil War times, when as a slave she would have had no legal claim to her offspring. McSpadden learned of her new identity as a mother of a dead son from bystanders: "There were some girls down there had recorded the whole thing," she told reporters. One girl, she said, "showed me a picture on her phone. She said, 'Isn't that your son?' I just bawled even harder. Just to see that, my son lying there lifeless, for no apparent reason." Circling the perimeter around her son's body, McSpadden tried to disperse the crowd: "All I want them to do is pick up my baby."

McSpadden, unlike Mamie Till Mobley, seemed to have little desire to expose her son's corpse to the media. Her son was not an orphan body for everyone to look upon. She wanted him covered and removed from sight. He belonged to her, her baby. After Brown's corpse was finally taken away, two weeks passed before his family was able to see him. This loss of control and authority might explain why after Brown's death, McSpadden was supposedly in the precarious position of accosting vendors selling T-shirts that demanded justice for Michael Brown that used her son's name. Not only were the procedures around her son's corpse out of her hands; his name had been commoditized and assimilated into our modes of capitalism.

Some of McSpadden's neighbors in Ferguson also wanted to create distance between themselves and the public life of Brown's death. They did not need a constant reminder of the ways black bodies don't matter to law-enforcement officers in their neighborhood. By the request of the community, the original makeshift memorial—with flowers, pictures, notes, and teddy bears—was finally removed by Brown's father on what would have been his birthday and replaced by an official plaque installed on the sidewalk next to where Brown died. The permanent reminder can be engaged or stepped over, depending on the pedestrian's desires.

In order to be away from the site of the murder of her son, Tamir Rice, Samaria moved out of her Cleveland home and into a homeless shelter. (Her family eventually relocated her.) "The whole world has seen the same video like I've seen," she said about Tamir's being shot by a police officer. The video, which was played and replayed in the media, documented the two seconds it took the police to arrive and shoot; the two seconds that marked the end of her son's life and that became a document to be examined by everyone. It's possible this shared scrutiny explains why the police held his twelve-year-old body for six months after his death. Everyone could see what the police would have to explain away. The justice system wasn't able to do it, and a judge found probable cause to charge the officer who shot Rice with murder. Meanwhile, for Samaria Rice, her unburied son's memory made her neighborhood unbearable.

Regardless of the wishes of these mothers—mothers of men like Brown, John Crawford III, or Eric Garner, and also mothers of women and girls like Rekia Boyd and Aiyana Stanley-Jones, each of whom was killed by the police—their children's deaths will remain within the public discourse. For those who believe the same behavior that got them killed if exhibited by a white man or boy would not have ended his life, the subsequent failure to indict or convict the police officers involved in these various cases requires that public mourning continue and remain present indefinitely. "I want to see a cop shoot a white unarmed teenager in the back," Toni Morrison said in April. She went on to say: "I want to see a white man convicted for raping a black woman. Then when you ask me, 'Is it over?' I will say yes." Morrison is right to suggest that this action would signal change, but the real change needs to be a rerouting of interior belief. It's an individual challenge that needs to happen before any action by a political justice system would signify true societal change.

The Charleston murders alerted us to the reality that a system so steeped in anti-black racism means that on any given day it can be open season on any black person—old or young, man, woman, or child. There exists no equivalent reality for white Americans. The Confederate battle flag continues to fly at South Carolina's statehouse as a reminder of a history marked by lynched black bodies. We can distance ourselves from this fact until the next horrific killing, but we won't be able to outrun it. History's authority over us is not broken by maintaining a silence about its continued effects.

A sustained state of national mourning for black lives is called for in order to point to the undeniability of their devaluation. The hope is that recognition will break a momentum that laws haven't altered. Susie Jackson; Sharonda Coleman-Singleton; DePayne Middleton-Doctor; Ethel Lee Lance; the Reverend Daniel Lee Simmons Sr.; the Reverend Clementa C. Pinckney; Cynthia Hurd; Tywanza Sanders and Myra Thompson were murdered because they were black. It's extraordinary how ordinary our grief sits inside this fact. One friend said, "I am so afraid, every day." Her son's childhood feels impossible, because he will have to be—has to be—so much more careful. Our mourning, this mourning, is in time with our lives. There is no life outside of our reality here. Is this something that can be seen and known by parents of white children? This is the question that nags me. National mourning, as advocated by Black Lives Matter, is a mode of intervention and interruption that might itself be assimilated into the category of public annoyance. This is altogether possible; but also possible is the recognition that it's a lack of feeling for another that is our problem. Grief, then, for these deceased others might align some of us, for the first time, with the living.

EDDIE S. GLAUDE

From *African American Religion:*
A Very Short Introduction

(2014)

. . . [W. E. B.] Du Bois described in *The Souls of Black Folk* (1903) . . . three things that characterized the religion of the slave: the preacher, the music, and the frenzy. For him, each one of these accounts for the distinctiveness of black religious life and sets the stage for the importance of "the Negro church" as a civic institution in African American life more generally. The preacher is the paradigmatic figure for black leaders; the music offers a glimpse into the blues-soaked soul of a people—it is their plaintive cry under the storm and stress of American life. The frenzy (the shouting), for Du Bois, captures that delicate balance between joy and terror that shadows black life in the United States. It is the eruption of the spirit in ordinary time that assures the presence of God amid the absurdity of white supremacy.

All three features are powerfully expressed in what Du Bois called "the Negro church." This institution stood at the epicenter of black life. Voluntary associations that addressed the social and economic needs of the community formed within its walls. Church buildings provided the physical space for the education of children. They also offered space for political debate and organizing. Here one acquired a sense of the religious worldview of a captured people, for "the Negro church," under the brutal weight of slavery and Jim Crow, gave its members and its community languages to imagine themselves apart from the dehumanizing practices of white supremacy. . . .

But to think of the preacher, the music, and the frenzy or, more generally, "the Negro or black church," as definitive of *all* of African American religious life denies the religious differences and complexity within black communities. Not all African Americans are Christian nor are they specifically Protestant. American soil has always been and remains fertile ground for a plurality of religious views and practices. Black religious life is no different. Black Christians, Muslims, Jews, practitioners of conjure, voodoo, Yoruba, or other traditional African religions all flourish in black communities throughout the United States. . . .

What is African American religion? An informative body of literature has been written about the difficulties in the study of religion generally. Many of the concerns evidenced in these conversations (debates about whether religion is reducible to some other more fundamental notion) are interestingly complicated when we think about religion in tandem with race. Or, more specifically, the issue becomes even messier when the modifier "black" or "African American" describes religion. These adjectives bear the unusual burden of a difficult history that colors the way religion is practiced and understood in the United States. They register the horror of slavery and the terror of Jim Crow as well as the richly textured experiences of a captured people, for whom sorrow stands alongside joy. It is in this context, one characterized by the ever-present need to account for one's presence in the world in the face of white supremacy, that African American religion takes on such significance.

African American religious life is not reducible to those wounds. That life contains within it avenues for solace and comfort in God, answers to questions about who we take ourselves to be and about our relation to the mysteries of the universe; moreover, meaning is found, for some, in submission to God, in obedience to creed and dogma, and in ritual practice. Here evil is accounted for. And hope, at least for some, is assured. In short, African American religious life is as rich and as complicated as the religious life of other groups in the United States, but African American religion emerges in the encounter between faith, in all of its complexity, and white supremacy. . . .

African Americans drew on the cultural knowledge, however fleeting, of their African past. They selected what they found compelling and rejected what they found unacceptable in the traditions of white slaveholders. In some cases, they reached for traditions outside of the United States altogether. They took the bits and pieces of their complicated lives, the received knowledge and the newly experienced insight, and created distinctive expressions of the general order of existence that anchored their efforts to live amid the pressing nastiness of life. . . .

. . . I have chosen three representative examples of African American religion. Each demonstrates how African American religion can be seen as a practice of freedom, a sign of difference, and as an open-ended mode of living religiously. Conjure, for example, draws our attention to the continuity and discontinuity with African religious practices as well as particular instances of religious imagination, which differentiates itself from those who enslaved and discriminated against others. . . .

Conjure expressed a religious worldview that enabled African American slaves to see themselves apart from white slaveholders. It is an African-derived spirituality that empowered its practitioners, through special knowledge, to garner some semblance of control over their environment. This special knowledge did not require rejecting Christianity or other religions of the book—Islam or

Judaism. In most cases, practices of conjure stood alongside or within religious expressions readily recognized as Christian. Some charms or spells even used the Bible explicitly.

The use of magic is not unique to African-descended people. Magic, the ability to possess a special knowledge to affect the outcomes of daily living, has been an important feature of the social landscape of all human beings. One can readily see its presence in all facets of American life. For African Americans, conjure presupposes a vast knowledge about the natural and supernatural world, knowledge rooted in an African past disrupted by the transatlantic slave trade and transformed by the institution of slavery in the New World. Here, "Africa" speaks through accumulated wisdom about an enchanted world that held black folk as slaves. That wisdom became a resource for maintaining a sense of humanity under captive conditions.

. . . [C]onjure played a critical role in the religious imagination of slaves. Whether or not they believed in it, the presence of the conjurer affected how they grabbed hold of the world around them. Conjure offered resources for the daunting task of sense-making, of dealing with the mysteries and disappointments of life with a little more than luck. It provided a little elbow room to imagine freedom and power apart from white slaveholders. But conjure cannot be located solely as a feature of the slave's religious imagination; it is not a relic of a long, forgotten past.

Conjuring practices continued to thrive after slavery and became an integral part . . . of the religious landscape of black America. . . .

. . . For the most part, African American conversion to Christianity took place against the backdrop of the economic imperative of slavery. As such, American Christianity has been indelibly shaped by what the historian David Wills describes as "the encounter between black and white," the domination of the slave by free, and that encounter has involved, among other things, a vacillation between an embrace of the abolition of slavery on Christian grounds and a justification for slavery on the same grounds. Here the typical American religious story of Puritans in New England or the narrative about religious pluralism and toleration in the middle colonies takes a backseat to the brutal and ironic reality of slavery and Christianity in a place committed, ostensibly at least, to democratic principles.

The encounter between black and white was marked by a radical difference: the gap or distance between Southern whites and African-descended slaves. Not only was this distance cultural—that the slave looked different, talked differently, and acted differently, what Alexis de Tocqueville described in his classic

1835 book, *Democracy in America*, as "this stranger brought into our midst—is hardly recognized as sharing the common features of humanity. His face appears to us hideous, his intelligence limited, and his tastes low; we almost take him for being intermediate between beast and man." The reality of power and the profound prejudice that attended the exercise of that power characterized the gap between black and white.

The system of slavery sought to reduce the slave to mere chattel. It attempted to deprive her of personality and agency, and generated a host of meanings about who the slave was and what were her capacities that affected her relationship and her children's children's relationship with whites. African American Christianity takes its initial shape in this moment: in the distance between professed belief in the Gospel and in the practice of slavery and the ideology of white supremacy.

Not until after 1760 and up to the 1830s was there widespread conversion of slaves to Christianity. Prior to this period, the ambivalence about religious instruction and the accommodation of Christianity with slavery blocked the way to successful missions among slaves. Missionaries often told slave owners that Christian slaves made better slaves. They cited biblical verses such as Ephesians 6:5, where St. Paul says, "Slaves be obedient to them that are your masters according to the flesh, with fear and trembling, in singleness of your heart, as unto Christ" (KJV). Many slave owners came to believe that religion worked as a means of control. But this same religious impulse also served as a basis for what would later become the abolitionist movement as many white Christians viewed slavery as an affront to God. . . .

. . . African Americans converted to Christianity in relatively large numbers during the Great Awakenings of the eighteenth and early nineteenth centuries. The revivals emphasized individual experience and ecstatic worship. The preachers held that all were equal before God. The revivals became important vehicles for reshaping Christianity in the image of the common folk. Religious leaders had to be unpretentious; the experience of God's grace was available to anyone without mediation; religious instruction was clear and direct; and churches were in the hands of those who attended them. One of the distinctive features of this period was the democratization of the emerging nation's religious life, the result of which was a fascinating fragmentation of the religious landscape as different and independent interpretations of the Gospel resulted in a proliferation of religious groups.

In these revivals, African Americans sat alongside white Christians, and together they experienced the power of God's word and the transforming quality of his presence. White and black alike groaned and cried out as they felt the power of God's presence. This emphasis on immediate experience—that the emotional worship services resembled African forms of religious expression, that many of the revival preachers licensed black preachers, and that early on Baptists and Methodists condemned slavery—resulted in the conversion of large numbers of African Americans. . . .

The early phase of African American Christianity is defined by two distinctive tendencies: the significance of the "invisible institution" in the slaveholding South, and the emergence of independent black denominations in the North. In the Southern interior, African American Christianity took the form of an invisible institution. On the Southern seaboard, black religious expression was more visible but constantly policed by a white, and fearful, gaze. In the North, the maturation of black communities began, with independent black denominations like the African Methodist Episcopal Church and the African Methodist Episcopal Zion Church. . . .

Most black churches conducted their ministries under the watchful eyes of white slave owners. . . . Many whites believed that independent gatherings fomented slave insurrections and were deeply suspicious of their presence within their communities. As independent gatherings were frowned upon, slaves were permitted to attend the churches of their white masters or churches pastored by white clergy. There the accommodation of Christianity with the peculiar institution would be on full display as white ministers urged the slaves in attendance to "serve your masters. . . . Do whatsoever your master tell you to do."

Vigilant surveillance characterized the economic system of slavery. Slaves were required to carry passes to move from plantation to plantation. They could not display any sense of individual agency or autonomy that would threaten the foundations of the institution. To do so was to risk severe punishment, such as "the lash" or being sold away from loved ones. . . .

Given the surveillance and its potential consequences, many slaves were forced to worship in secret—to steal away to worship God apart from the gaze of white slave owners. And it is here, in the brush arbors and cabins of slaves, that black Christians forged a singular style of worship and a distinctive theological outlook to speak to their unique experiences. That distinctive theology offered those who "took up the cross" an empowering language to see beyond their present condition and to imagine a future defined by freedom, not by slavery or white supremacy. This open-endedness became a signature feature of African American Christian practice, which indelibly shaped African American cultural and political life.

Most black preachers offered a different reading of the Gospel, one that did not accommodate the system of slavery, and preached that slaves, despite their wretched condition, were in fact the chosen people of God. In the story of Exodus, black preachers found an analogy to their captive condition. African Americans emerged in their powerful sermons as the Israelites and America as Egypt, a house of bondage. . . .

The troubles of today dimmed in the face of the promise of tomorrow. In short, Christian slaves imagined a new world by drawing on the language of the Gospel and in doing so transcended their captive experience. As one slave noted, "my body may belong to the master but my soul belongs to Jesus." Such imaginings put in place the conditions for Christian slaves to see themselves beyond the relationship of slave and master. They also enabled the slave to reach backward into the world of the early Christians (as well as that of the children of Israel) and blur the lines between the experience recounted in scripture and their own.

Here we see the political significance of African American Christianity. Apart from questions of whether the practice of Christianity among slaves was otherworldly (an escapist fantasy that left the power relation of slavery intact) or this-worldly (a revolutionary ideology that upended the peculiar institution), the religion provided tools to create a sense of personhood—a means to step outside of a relation of domination that sought to reduce human beings to mere chattel—and offered a theology of history in which freedom was possible because of God's very activity in the lives of his chosen people. In prayer meetings and in fellowship with other like-minded Christians, slaves forged a sense of identity, created meaning in the context of an absurd existence, grabbed hold of an idea of freedom rooted in the power of God's love and, in the process, left an indelible mark on the expression of Christianity in the United States. . . .

The modern phase of black Christianity is marked by three distinctive moments. First, the "invisible institution" emerges out of the shadows of slavery, and northern black denominations extend their mission work to the South as well as abroad. Both result in the nationalization of black Christendom. Second, large numbers of African Americans leave the South (what is known as the Great Migration) and relocate to cities in the North and in the West. Their movement occasioned the appearance of what would be called the "institutional church," a church that has social activism and social services at the heart of its theological mission. And, finally, the black freedom struggle of the twentieth century transformed the substance of African American life and the form and content of black Christendom by ending legal segregation.

. . . To tell the story of Islam in America by beginning with slavery does not reveal much, beyond the important historical fact that Islam was indeed practiced among slaves. But to assert some connection between that fact and subsequent iterations of Islam in America is all too often to engage in a broader political project to think about African-descended people in the United States apart from the racist practices of white people.

None of the elements of African Islam actually shows up in the various expressions of African American Islam. Islam is embraced here under particular circumstances and in specific ways. Understanding African American Islam then is not a matter of uncovering a continuous practice of the religion. Beyond the actual presence of Muslims in the slave population, there is little to no inheritance to trace from that moment to now. Instead, we do better to think about Islam among African Americans as a feature of the rapid modernization and radicalization of black America—that period when African Americans entered cities, fought wars, experienced new forms of labor discipline, and organized formally and informally to resist white supremacy in the South and in the North. To put the point more baldly, Islam heralds "the modern" in black life. . . .

The story of African American Islam, then, is not one that starts with slavery. It begins with the religious imagination of black urban dwellers in the twentieth century who deployed Islam in their efforts to forge a distinctive identity as free black men and women, and whose children would later struggle to join more fully a global Muslim community that often viewed them and the history of their unique expression of Islam with skepticism. The story of African American Islam charts that journey from the proto-Islamist movements of Noble Drew Ali and the early Nation of Islam to the efforts of the late Warith Deen Muhammad. It entails an account of the impact of what has been called immigrant Islam on the form and content of African American Islam and questions whether this expression of the Islam should be thought of as an example of African American religion.

. . . Among African Americans, Islam served as a sign of difference: a way of differentiating a religious path supposedly unsullied by the nastiness of white supremacy and a geopolitical identity that enabled African Americans to see themselves as part of an imagined community beyond the borders of the United States. Just as Marcus Garvey took up the symbolic dressings of empire to give voice to an idea of black identity that embraced notions of self-determination, dynamic black personalities at the dawning of the twentieth century who embraced Islam gave voice to a religious and political identity, which radically defined black folk over and against the patriarchal bonds of the U.S. context. In other words, Islam-as-sign in the hands of African Americans such Noble Drew Ali and Elijah Muhammad became a path to a kind of global blackness, which, in turn, recast its meanings within the United States. But this reimagining was not solely limited to the idea of blackness. These figures took hold of Islam as their own. They not only reconstructed the idea of blackness, they reimagined the meaning of Islam by bending and shaping it to respond to the conditions of black people in the United States.

. . . African American religious life remains a powerful site for creative imaginings in a world still organized by race. Churches, mosques, communions of all kinds offer African Americans who participate in them languages and identities that speak back to their conditions of living. What is required is a thick description of what is going on in the religious life of this diverse and complicated community. And if African American religion helps us in doing that work, then it remains useful. If it does not, if the phrase blocks the way to a fuller understanding of religion and race in the United States because it is an outmoded description, then it is time we got rid of it.

JERMAINE O. ARCHER

From "Bitter Herbs and a Lock of Hair: Recollections of Africa in Slave Narratives of the Garrisonian Era"

(2002)

. . . James Albert Ukawsaw, Olaudah Equiano, and Venture Smith were all African-born slaves and each of their narratives includes references to the religious and spiritual world from which they came. Expressions of cultural memory found in the narratives from both men and women of the [Garrisonian era of the 1830s] suggest that despite the increase in an American-born population and an emerging African-American identity, African culture did not necessarily dissipate with each passing decade of the nineteenth century. In fact, some of the more popular book-length narratives of the antebellum period demonstrate the persistence of memory within the slave quarters. . . .

. . . Root doctoring, divination, and ceremonial dance along with the symbolism of dreams, prophesies, ancestral reverence, and flight are themes that reappear throughout the texts published during the Garrisonian period. The authors, a number of whom were key figures in the abolitionist movement, offer insightful observations and thoughts on these particular expressions of African culture that animated the lives of large numbers of slaves. . . .

While conjure doctors and diviners played a significant role in the slave community, the good fortune of one's life also had much to do with his or her relationship to the ancestors. It was a widespread belief that the improper burial of a family member would engender ill fortune. *A Narrative of the Life and Adventures of Charles Ball, a Black Man* was the first full-length book narrative published during the Gar[r]isonian period. Ball provides an account of a burial ceremony that took place in South Carolina in which the father of the deceased, who had been a priest in West Africa, placed a specific talisman around the corpse, which he claimed would help his son travel back to his countrymen. Ball believed that this notion of returning to Africa after death was a belief held by a number of Africans. "They are universally of opinion," he says, "and this opinion is founded in their religion, that after death they shall return to their own country, and rejoin their former companions and friends, in some happy region, in which they will be provided with plenty of food, and beautiful women, from the lovely daughters of their own land."

Harriet Jacobs also maintained a spiritual connection to her parents after they died. In fact, it was at their burial grounds that she vowed to free herself. She believed that "there the wicked cease from troubling, and there the weary be at rest. There the prisoners rest together; they hear not the voice of the oppressor; the servant is free from his master." As Jacobs walked through the graveyard she recalled the blessing her mother had given her before she died and thought about the many times that she heard her voice either chiding her or "whispering loving words." As she prayed for guidance and protection while walking past the old dwelling where the slaves use to worship before the Turner insurrection, she also heard her father's voice emanating from it—encouraging her to push forward until freedom was hers. The burial grounds never seemed so sacred to her as they were on this occasion. "My trust in God," Jacobs says, "had been strengthened by that prayer among the graves."

Slaves honored and invoked the power of their ancestors through the African-influenced counterclockwise dance known as the ring shout. [Historian] Sterling Stuckey has convincingly demonstrated that the ceremony was largely responsible for strengthening bonds among slaves across ethnic lines. Perhaps Frederick Douglass was referring to the ring shout when he wrote about the songs that he heard while he was a slave in Maryland:

> I did not, when a slave, understand the deep meaning of those rude and apparently incoherent songs. I was myself within the *circle*; so that I neither saw nor heard as those without might see and hear. They told a tale of woe which was then altogether beyond my feeble comprehension; they were tones loud, long, and deep; they breathed the prayer and complaint of souls boiling over with the bitterest anguish.

Given the accounts of the ceremony in the urban areas of Maryland by Bishop Daniel Alexander Payne of the African Methodist Episcopal Church during the second half of the nineteenth century, it should not surprise us that Douglass while still a slave would have observed and even participated in the ritual in rural Maryland. The Lloyd plantation was very much an African enclave and Douglass quickly learned that an important spiritual exercise of its inhabitants was the ring shout. It was not uncommon for one to "hear a wild, hoarse *laugh* arise from a circle, and often a song" when the slaves were allowed a brief amount of leisure time following their evening meals. . . .

William Wells Brown also discussed his observations of the ring shout. Consider his rather detailed account of one such gathering in St. Louis:

The noise was hushed, and the assembled group assumed an attitude of respect. They made way for their queen, and a short, black, old negress came upon the scene, followed by two assistants, one of whom bore a cauldron, and the other, a box. The cauldron was placed over the dying embers, the queen drew forth, from the folds of her gown, a magic wand, and the crowd formed a ring around her. Her first act was to throw some substance on the fire, the flames shot up with a lurid glare—now it writhed in serpent coils, now it darted upward in forked tongues, and then it gradually transformed itself into a veil of dusky vapors. At this stage, after a certain amount of gibberish and wild gesticulation from the queen, the box was opened, and frogs, lizards, snakes, dog liver, and beef hearts drawn forth and thrown into the cauldron. Then followed more gibberish and gesticulation, when the congregation joined hands, and began the wildest dance imaginable, keeping it up until the men and women sank to the ground from mere exhaustion.

Brown knew that these practices were not uncommon "throughout the Southern states," where one could easily find "remnants of the old time Africans, who were stolen from their native land and sold in the Savannah, Mobile, and New Orleans markets, in defiance of all law." According to Brown, New Orleans was the center of such explicit activity:

Congo Square takes its name, as is well known, from the Congo Negroes who used to perform their dance on its sward every Sunday. They were a curious people, and brought over with them this remnant of their African jungles. In Louisiana there were six different tribes of negroes, named after the section of the country from which they came, and their representatives could be seen on the square, their teeth filed, and their cheeks still bearing tattoo marks.

As many as three thousand onlookers would show up on any given Sunday to observe the "dusky dancers." The dancing was accompanied by banjoes, drums, and shakers and when the participants became aroused by the rhythmic synchronization of the instruments nothing could "faithfully portray the wild and frenzied motions" that caused many to *faint*. After exhaustion overcame one group another would enter the circle. The Igbo, Fulani, Congolese, Mandingos, and Kormantins were some of the groups involved in the ceremonies. "These dances," Brown declared, "were kept up until within the memory of men still living, and many who believe in them and who would gladly revive them, may be found in every state in the Union."

Harriet Tubman became quite fond of the dances she observed at midnight funeral ceremonies in the South Carolina Sea Islands. She recalled that after a preacher delivered his sermon at one particular funeral ceremony the entire congregation while shaking one another's hand and calling each by name engaged in a circular solemn dance known as the "spiritual shuffle" at which time they sang:

> My sis'r Mary's boun' to go;
> My sis'r Nanny's boun' to go;
> My brudder Tony's boun't to go;
> My brudder July's boun' to go.

Harriet, a stranger among the faithful, was a participant in this ring shout ceremony and when it came time for her name to be called during the song they sang:

> Eberybody's boun' to go!

Harriet Tubman and Henry Bibb seem to have incorporated in their narratives the African notion that certain persons possessed the supernatural power to fly. The Bight of Biafra contributed significant imports into North America and Igbo from the region were largely responsible for spreading the belief. Folktales of "flying Africans" and their frequent place of departure "Ebo Landing," located off the coast of the Georgia and South Carolina Sea Islands, are found in the Works Progress Administration slave narrative collection of the 1930s. It has been suggested that the comparatively high rate of suicide among Igbo slaves can be attributed in large part to the idea that through this process they were actually returning to Africa via flight. While we do not have precise numbers of how many Igbo made their way into Bibb's home state of Kentucky, he does provide us with evidence that this notion of "flying Africans" did exist there. After being carted to Louisville after he was captured by four slavehunters for an attempted escape, Bibb was briefly left in the care of slaveholder Daniel Lane. The man was notorious for his "slave selling, kidnapping, and negro hunting." As soon as he turned his back on his prisoner, Bibb with no hesitation seized the opportunity and took off. Yet few believed Lane's account of Bibb's escape: "Dan imputed my escape to my godliness! He said that I must have gone up in a chariot of fire, for I went off by flying; and that he should never again have anything to do with a praying negro." That Lane connected flight with the spirituality of slaves can likely be attributed to his familiarity with the customs of Igbo and others who subscribed to their notion of "flying Africans."

Prior to Harriet Tubman's escape, she often dreamt of flying "like a bird" over a variegated landscape which came to signify her flight to the North. In her dream she would approach a barrier either in the form of a huge fence or a river above which she would attempt to soar. "But it' peared like I wouldn't hab de strength," she says, "and jes as I was sinkin' down, dere would be ladies all drest in white ober dere, and de would put out dere arms and pull me 'cross." When she eventually reached the North she came face to face with the places and people she observed in her dreams. It is quite possible that Tubman's reference to flight might have been more than just an allegory for her escape. The motif of the flying African may actually be at work here. Igbo and Akan comprised considerable numbers in Maryland. There is evidence to suggest that the notion of flying Africans would not have been lost on the Akan. Commenting on this phenomenon among the Akan, Anthony Ephirim-Donkor explains that "the Akan people also believe that the soul can be put to flight (*ne kra eguan*)." This would happen when one is incarcerated. While Tubman's encounter with flight occurred only in her dream, that it was a reoccurring dream which eventually came true seems to demonstrate the prevalence of such a belief among Maryland slaves. . . .

. . . [N]ineteenth-century slave narratives published after 1836 can be used as a cultural lens for spiritual memory and identity formation in the slave South. . . . [E]x-slave narratives served as a collective memory of Africans on this side of the Atlantic by pointing to corresponding cultural examples. These narratives not only reflect the individual lives of those few persons fortunate enough to tell their stories but also serve as critical sources for the slave community, as the authors tell of their experiences with slaves across plantations and states, thus making this project more than an intellectual analysis of a select few who had the opportunity to use such mediums. These memoirs are much more than tales of bondage and freedom. Indeed, they are vital tools for all students of African American folklore and should now be considered as texts for uncovering African cultural continuities. When one wonders how slaves endured their condition, an important part of the answer may be found in African spiritual and artistic practices found in the genre of the slave narratives.

EDWARD E. CURTIS IV

From *Islam in Black America:*
Identity, Liberation, and Difference in
African American Islamic Thought

(2002)

Born on August 3, 1832, in the Dutch West Indies, Edward Wilmot Blyden became one of the more remarkable intellectual and political figures of the black English-speaking world during the nineteenth century. An immigrant to Liberia, Blyden was a largely self-taught Presbyterian missionary who went on to become a professor and President of Liberia College, two-time Ambassador to Great Britain, Liberian Secretary of State, Minister of the Interior, Director of Muslim Education in Sierra Leone, a Liberian presidential candidate, and one of the most noted black authors of his time. As a critic of missionary Christianity and an ardent Liberian nationalist, Blyden was also the first English-speaking black author to tout Islam as a more "natural" tradition for blacks than Christianity.

 . . . Blyden argued that Islam was a far better vehicle of black self-determination than Christianity. For in contrast to the Christian faith, he said, Islam encouraged African nationalism, the development of black civilization, and racial equality. But many of Blyden's arguments on Islam were inconsistent or at least ambiguous and prone to change, depending on what audience he was addressing and what his political motives were in so doing. When Blyden was seeking support from European or American Christian missionaries, for example, he might present Islam as a menacing adversary to Christianity, trying to spur his missionary audience to fund his education projects or other concerns of the young Liberian state, which he hailed as a Christian outpost in the infidel wilderness. When in Sierra Leone, however, he might actually call for better cooperation between Muslim "natives" and Christian immigrants. Later in life, his quest for international support of African nationalism led him to challenge the parochialism that he viewed as endemic among Christians, Jews, and Muslims everywhere. . . . Blyden constantly shifted his rhetorical strategies in his life-long mission to build black nation-states in West Africa, which was the only truly consistent theme in his intellectual life. . . .

By the time Blyden had arrived in West Africa, the region had undergone a re-markable period of religious and political change. While Islam had been present in the western Sudan from at least the eleventh century, it was mainly the re-ligion of ruling elites, merchants, and missionaries. From the seventeenth un-til the nineteenth century, however, a number of reformers emerged who were committed to sponsoring *jihads* that would make their Islamic vision the guid-ing force in people's lives. Most famous among these leaders was Uthman dan Fodio, whose Sokoto jihad of 1804 created the largest Islamic empire of its time in the central Sudan. The power of Uthman's political and social reforms, which were based on certain Islamic traditions of law, mysticism, and saint worship, reverberated throughout the entire region. By the late nineteenth century, at the dawn of Europe's imperialist scramble for the region, "Islam had come to be the almost universal language of political ambition and moral reform" in West Africa. . . .

In criticizing Christianity and simultaneously promoting Islam, Blyden hoped to convince his white audience that all Africans, both immigrant and indigenous, should be allowed to develop their own authentic civilization. For instance, in "Mohammedanism and the Negro race," published in November 1875, Blyden praised R. Bosworth Smith's claims that Islam provided a sense of dignity to its adherents that Christian converts did not possess. Blyden magni-fied Smith's comments, asserting that "whenever the Negro is found in Christian lands, his leading trait is not docility, as has been often alleged, but servility." Devoid of self-reliance and true independence, countries like Haiti existed only by the whims of white power, according to Blyden. "On the other hand," Blyden continued, "there are numerous Negro Mohammedan communities and states in Africa which are self-reliant, productive, independent and dominant," in-cluding Sierra Leone, for example. Whereas missionary Christianity's arrival in Africa was associated with colonialism and slavery, Islam had spread, Blyden ar-gued, by "choice" and "conviction," finding Africa in the midst of its "manhood." Christianity, on the other hand, "subdued," "soothed," and inspired sympathy even for the enslavers—so much so, in fact, that black "ideas and aspirations could be expressed only in conformity with the views and tastes of those who held rule over them." Conversely, Islam managed to inspire spiritual feelings "to which they [African pagans] had before been utter strangers," while simulta-neously strengthening and hastening "certain tendencies to independence and self-reliance which were already at work."

Blyden amplified this view in "Christianity and the Negro Race," an article published in 1876 in which he turned the common European notion of black inferiority on its head, implying that it was European culture rather than the African "jungle" that had transformed blacks into apes. "From the lessons he ev-

eryday receives," Blyden protested, "the Negro unconsciously imbibes the conviction that to be a great man he must be like the white man." Blacks, according
to Blyden, were not taught to be the companions, equals, or comrades of whites,
but the "imitator, his ape, his parasite. . . . To be like the white man as much as
possible—to copy his outward appearance, his peculiarities, his manners, the
arrangement of his toilet." Worse yet, Blyden argued in "Christian Missions in
West Africa," European and American missionaries often measured their success by how much the "natives" had become imitators of white culture. They
mistook the "thin varnish of European civilization" left with the native as a genuine "metamorphosis." The result was that the convert's "Christianity, instead of
being pure is superstitious, instead of being genuine is only nominal, instead of
being deep is utterly superficial."

In full view of his white audience, Blyden had begun to question more fundamentally the entire missionary enterprise and Christianity itself. In "Islam
and Race Distinctions," published in 1876, Blyden focused not only on the ill
effects of European Christianity on blacks, but also on its complicity in the advancement of a secular Western culture. Why, Blyden demanded, has "the grand
Semitic idea of the conversion to Divine truth of all the races of mankind, and
their incorporation into one spiritual family" made such slow progress under
the direction of Europeans? The answer, he offered, was that Christianity had
been subsumed under the more general Western tendency to divide and con-
quer the world as a material possession. The West, he remarked, was anthro-
pocentric, power-hungry, and materialistic. Even "religion is . . . cherished as
a means of subserving temporal and material purposes." In the Middle Ages,
Blyden argued, Roman Catholicism advanced this obsession with material
things through its emphasis on the "visible" rather than the "unseen and spiritual," while Protestantism, through the actions of the Puritans, Presbyterians,
and Episcopalians, focused on "material aggrandisement at any cost," including
the enslavement of Africans and the wholesale murder of Indians. But if the absence of a true spirituality in Christian Europe made slavery and genocide possible there, Islamic spirituality had the opposite effect in Islamdom. Because the
Muslim has a deeper trust in God and reliance in God's revelation in the Qur'an,
Blyden said, Islam "extinguishes all distinctions founded upon race, colour, or
nationality. . . . [T]hroughout the history of Islam, in all countries, race or 'previous condition' has been no barrier to elevation." A true faith, Blyden implied in
this article, led to true brotherhood. . . .

Blyden's legacy with regard to Islam was anything but conservative, for his
innovative thinking about Islam foreshadowed most of the central themes of
African-American Islamic thought in the twentieth century. Like many of his
African-American heirs, Blyden indicted white Christianity on the grounds that

it stunted the development of black self-determination. Instead, he promoted Islam as a tradition more in tune with the political, social, and cultural aspirations of blacks. Specifically, he believed that Islam had contributed to black nation-building, the development of the black racial "essence," and historic black achievements, especially in the area of black civilization. . . . Ultimately, Blyden left it to others to make the hard theoretical choices about how black Muslims should perceive themselves in relation to other blacks, other Muslims, and the rest of humanity. Left unresolved, then, was also a more complete explanation of what the central message of Islam would be within the story of black liberation.

CHARLES MARSH

From *God's Long Summer:*
Stories of Faith and Civil Rights

(1997)

On a night in August of 1962, Fannie Lou Hamer attended a mass meeting at the Williams Chapel Church in Ruleville, Mississippi. A handful of civil rights workers from the Southern Christian Leadership Conference (SCLC) and the Student Nonviolent Coordinating Committee (SNCC) were in Sunflower County spreading news of voter registration. Sunflower County, in the heart of that "most southern place on earth," the Mississippi Delta, was perhaps the most solid core of the iceberg of southern segregation. Appropriately, SNCC had recently selected the Delta as one of the strategic points of its voter registration initiative. If the movement could crack the Delta, the reasoning went, it would send unsettling reverberations through the state's recalcitrant white majority.

There was great excitement in the chapel as James Bevel, one of Martin Luther Kings, Jr.'s, young colleagues in the SCLC, stood to address the people. His short sermon was taken from the sixteenth chapter of the Gospel of Matthew. He asked the congregation—mainly black men and women who worked on the nearby cotton plantations—to consider the words of the Lord when he rebuked the Pharisees and Sadducees. He read the Scripture: "Jesus answered and said unto them, When it is evening, ye say, It will be fair weather, for the sky is red and lowering. O ye hypocrites, ye can discern the face of the sky; but can ye not discern the signs of the times?" How can we discern the signs of the times, Bevel asked. How can we not recognize that the hour has arrived for black men and women to claim what is rightfully their own—indeed the right to vote? To be sure, most folk are not trained to discern the weather nor to forecast the future. But that is not our demand, Bevel told the people. Our demand is that we not ignore the clear signs before our eyes. God's time is upon us; let us not back down from the challenge.

Bevel's words stirred Mrs. Hamer's tired spirit. She had endured the burdens of white racism for forty-four years, living the hard life of a field hand on the Marlowe cotton plantation near Ruleville, a small town in the Delta. The youngest child born to Ella and Jim Townsend, by the age of seven Fannie Lou Hamer was in the fields picking cotton with her fourteen brothers and five sisters, the family working long days together and still not making "enough money to live on." "My parents moved to Sunflower County when I was two years old," Mrs. Hamer recalled. "I will never forget, one day [when I] was six years old and I was playing beside the road and this plantation owner drove up to me and stopped and asked me, 'could I pick cotton.' I told him I didn't know and he said, 'Yes, you can. I will give you things that you want from the commissary store,' and he named things like crackerjacks and sardines—and it was a huge list that he called off. So I picked the 30 pounds of cotton that week, but I found out what actually happened was he was trapping me into beginning the work I was to keep doing and I never did get out of his debt again. My parents tried so hard to do what they could to keep us in school, but school didn't last four months out of the year and most of the time we didn't have clothes to wear." . . .

Fannie Lou Hamer knew something was wrong with the world she inherited, yet on that night in August 1962, she had not even heard about her civil rights. "We hadn't heard anything about registering to vote because when you see this flat land in here, when the people would get out of the fields, if they had a radio, they'd be too tired to play it. So we didn't know what was going on in the rest of the state even; much less in other places." But Bevel's sermon, followed by SNCC member James Forman's talk on the constitutional right to vote, spoke deeply to Mrs. Hamer's longing for justice. Her imagination was charged by new moral and spiritual energies; she felt empowered to discern the signs of the time. And with more certainty than a red sky presages a fair tomorrow or a red sunrise stormy weather, Mrs. Hamer understood that her life would be very different from this point on. "When they asked for those to raise their hands who'd go down to the courthouse the next day, I raised mine. Had it up as high as I could get it. I guess if I'd had any sense I'd a-been a little scared, but what was the point of being scared. The only thing [the whites] could do was kill me and it seemed like they'd been trying to do that a little bit at a time since I could remember." She heard the call of Jesus—and James Bevel—a call demanding sacrifice, but a call also promising freedom and empowerment. She was excited by the speakers' description of the power of the vote. "It made so much sense to me," she said. These very women and men gathered at Williams Chapel Church—dirt-poor sharecroppers, field hands, and domestics—could force out of office the hateful politicians and sheriffs who had controlled the social oppressive order for as long as anyone could remember.

The call also made sense because the faith of the black church had prepared Mrs. Hamer for this moment. The church had sustained her wearied spirit when all other institutions had served contrary purposes. While Jim Crow society was designed to convince blacks they were nobodies, the black churches—even those that remained quiet on civil rights—preached a gospel that embraced the longings and desires of a disenfranchised people. A new social space took shape, offering an alternative to the social world of the segregated South—a "nation within a nation," as E. Franklin Frazier once wrote—a world displaying the very reversal of the racist patterns embedded in the segregated South. After enduring the indignities of demeaning jobs and discriminatory practices six days a week, black people could experience on Sunday mornings a rare though passionate affirmation of their humanity. The last could become first; a field hand or a janitor could become a deacon, the maid of the cook a leader in the women's union. Moreover, as a "nation within a nation," the black church not only awakened spiritual energies but also inspired the exercise of political ownership through such practices as electing officers and organizing church programs. Thus, by the time James Bevel delivered his testimony in Ruleville, Mississippi, in August of 1962, Mrs. Hamer had been made ready by her involvement in church life to "step out on God's word of promise"—to put her faith into action. She was ready to move, and did the next week when she joined a busload of people heading to the county courthouse to register to vote. . . .

Rough times would not end with the coming of the warm weather. In the summer of 1963, Mrs. Hamer was invited by Annelle Ponder, the SCLC field secretary in the Delta town of Greenwood, to attend the organization's citizenship school in South Carolina. Seven black Mississippians were chosen for the long bus ride to Charleston, where they were led by well-known civil rights activist Septima Clark in training sessions on voter registration. A week later, on June 9, near the end of the all-night ride home from South Carolina, the Continental Trailways bus stopped in Winona, Mississippi. When members of the group sat down at the lunch counter and asked to be served, several Winona policemen and highway patrolmen entered the station and forced them to leave. (As in much of the South, town officials had not accepted the ruling of the Interstate Commerce Commission outlawing segregated transportation facilities.) Once outside, Annelle Ponder made a point of writing down the license number of one of the patrol cars, so infuriating a police officer that he began arresting everyone in sight. Mrs. Hamer had returned to the bus because her left leg, disfigured from polio as a child, was sore from the strenuous week. But when she saw the officers herding her companions into police cars, she came out and asked Ponder what the folks left on the bus should do. Should they drive on to Greenwood or wait at the station? Before her friend could answer, an officer in one of the police cars noticed Mrs. Hamer and shouted to a colleague, "Get that one there, bring her on down in the other car!" Mrs. Hamer was then shoved into the back seat, kicked in the thigh, and cursed repeatedly on the drive to the jail. "They carried us on to the county jail. It wasn't the city jail, [but] the county jail, so we could be far enough out. [They] didn't care how loud we hollered, wasn't nobody gon' hear us. . . . When we got to the jail they started beatin' the man—his name was James West—and they put us in cells, two to a cell, and I could hear all this hollerin' and goin' on. Then they took Miss Ponder. I could hear these awful sounds and licks and screams, hear her body hit the concrete, and this man was yellin', 'Cain't you say yes sir, you nigger bitch?'"

Each time that Annelle Ponder refused to say "yes sir" to the police officers, the swing of the blackjack was harder. Mrs. Hamer heard the sounds from her cell down the hall. "She kept screamin', and they kept beatin' on her, and finally she started prayin' for 'em, and she asked God to have mercy on 'em, because they didn't know what they was doin'. . . . I don't know how long it lasted before I saw Annelle Ponder passing the cell with both her hands up. Her eyes looked like blood, and her mouth was swollen. Her clothes were torn. It was horrifying."

June Johnson, a fifteen-year-old black teenager who had attended the voter registration workshop, was the next person led by Mrs. Hamer's cell in this grim parade of tortured bodies. "The blood was runnin' down in her face, and they put her in another cell." In the booking room, whence Johnson was coming, the sheriff had pulled the young girl aside for his own personal whipping. He asked her whether she was a member of the NAACP. She told him yes. Then he hit her on the cheek and chin, and when she raised her arms to protect herself, he hit her on the stomach. He continued to ask her questions about the NAACP—"who runs that thing?" "do you know Martin Luther King?" Soon the four men in the room—the sheriff, the chief of police, the highway patrolman, and another white man—threw Johnson onto the floor, beat her, and stomped on her body in concert. The men ripped Johnson's dress and tore her slip off; blood soaked her tattered clothes.

The men came next for Mrs. Hamer. "Get up from there, fatso," one of the policemen barked. When the officers confirmed that this was Fannie Lou Hamer from Ruleville—the same woman stirring up trouble in the Delta—they began to revile her with insulting words. "I have never heard that many names called a human in my life," she said later. "You, bitch, we gon' make you wish you was dead," an officer said, as he brought two black inmates into the bullpen to carry out his ghastly design for torture. Mrs. Hamer asked them, "You mean you would do this to your own race?" But an officer quickly warned the men, "If you don't beat her, you know what we'll do to you." Mrs. Hammer recalled, "So they had me lay down on my face, and they beat with a thick leather thing that was wide. And it had sumpin' in it *heavy*. I don't know what that was, rocks or lead. But everytime they hit me, I got just as hard, and I put my hands behind my back, and they beat me in my hands 'til my hands . . . was as navy blue as anything you ever seen." She tried to put her hands over the leg that was damaged from polio, but this only made her hands vulnerable to the beating. When the first inmate grew exhausted, the blackjack was passed to the second inmate. "That's when I started screaming and working my feet 'cause I couldn't help it." One of the white officers became so enraged when he heard Mrs. Hamer's cries that "he just run there and started hittin' me on the back of my head." The torture became more brutal. "I remember I tried to smooth my dress which was working up from all the beating. One of the white officers pushed my dress up. I was screaming and going on—and the young officer with the crew cut began to beat me about [the] head and told me to stop my screaming. I then began to bury my head in the mattress and hugged it to kill out the sound of my screams." By the end, the flesh of her beaten body was hard, one of her kidneys was permanently damaged, and a blood clot that formed over her left eye threatened her vision. "They finally told me to get up, and I just couldn't hardly get up, and they kept on tellin' me to get up. I finally could get up, but when I got back to my cell bed, I couldn't set down. I would *scream*. It hurted me to set down." Back in her dark cell, Mrs Hamer was left alone to bear the physical and spiritual efforts of torture. . . .

Mrs. Hamer "really suffered in that jail from that beating," June Johnson said. The physical and psychological effects of Winona stayed with her for a long time—she almost never talked about her life without talking about Winona. Even so, her songs of freedom gave voice to her suffering and the suffering she shared with her friends. Their singing did not remove their suffering or the particularities of their humiliation; rather, it embraced the suffering, named it, and emplotted it in a cosmic story of hope and deliverance. At first tentatively, and then with growing confidence, their song floated freely throughout the jail, exploding the death grip of the cell. "Jail doors open and they walked out, let my people go." Despair turned into a steady resoluteness to keep on going. A miracle happened. And at least for Mrs. Hamer, a peaceable composure, incomprehensible apart from a deep river of faith, transformed not only her diminished self-perception but the perception of her torturers. She said astonishingly, "It wouldn't solve any problem for me to hate whites just because they hate me. Oh, there's so much hate, only God has kept the Negro sane."

During the days in jail that followed Mrs. Hamer's beating, she pondered once again the familiar paradox of white Christians who hate and mistreat black people. She even struck up a conversation with the jailer's wife about the life of faith. When the white woman showed some kindness to the prisoners by offering them cold water, Mrs. Hamer thanked her and remarked that she "must be Christian people." The jailer's wife picked up on Mrs. Hamer's remark, telling her that she really tried her best to live right and to please God. She tried to follow Jesus, she said; she certainly believed in him, and had been baptized as a child. Mrs. Hamer assumed the role of counselor and spiritual gadfly in her response. She told the jailer's wife to get out her Bible and read the verses in Proverbs 26:26 and Acts 17:26.

Mrs. Hamer's counsel, spoken in the spirit of gentleness and edification, offered at the same time an effective one-two punch of divine judgment and costly forgiveness. There is nothing sanguine about reconciliation in these passages. The jailer's wife could not have missed the barbed irony of Mrs. Hamer's devotional suggestions. The first verse speaks of those "whose hatred is covered by deceit," avowing that they will be brought down by divine wrath and "shall be shewed before the whole congregation." The entire twenty-sixth chapter of Proverbs is a litany of warnings for fools, transgressors, sluggards, and hateful men. "Whoso diggeth a pit shall fall therein: and he that rolleth a stone, it will return upon him," verse 27 adds. The New Testament passage came from St. Paul's address to the Athenians at Mars Hill. Before a people who took great pride in its collective piety—in this respect, a people much like the Mississippi's faithful white churchgoers—the apostle Paul had said, "I perceive that in all things ye are too superstitious" (Acts 17:22). He intended to make clear to the congregation at Athens, as Mrs. Hamer did to the jailer's wife, that the gods they "ignorantly worship" were idols. They must confess their sin of idolatry and worship instead the one true God, the one whom it may be said, "made the world and all things therein, seeing that he is Lord of heaven and earth, dwelleth not in temples made with hands; neither is worshipped with men's hands, as though he needed any thing, seeing he giveth to all life, and breath, and all things" (Acts 17:24–25). In other words, if you are going to be religious, then you need to understand the rich diversity of God's creation. Of course, this particular point may have been lost on the white woman in Winona—as it seems to have been lost on the Athenians. What would have hit hard was precisely the verse Mrs. Hamer singled out: "[God] hath made of one blood all nations of men for to dwell on all the face of the earth." Indeed, all races are as one in God's sight. Mrs. Hamer said of the white woman's response, "She's taken that down, but she never come back after then. I don't know what happened."

Later, when Mrs. Hamer was escorted by the jailer himself to her trial, she put the question to the very man who had helped carry out her beating just a few days earlier, "Do you people ever think or wonder how you'll feel when the time comes you'll have to meet God?" His response was full of embarrassment and vigorous denial. "Who you taking about?" he mumbled. In fact, Mrs. Hamer knew all too well what had happened. "I hit them with the truth, and it hurts them," she said.

JAMES CAMPBELL

From *Songs of Zion: The African Methodist Episcopal Church in the United States and South Africa*

(1995)

Over the course of the nineteenth century, the small seed of religious independence sown by Richard Allen and his comrades in Philadelphia blossomed into
a great institution. By the time of Allen's death in 1831, the AME Church boasted
congregations in every northern state and several southern ones, with a total
membership of more than ten thousand. By the beginning of the Civil War,
membership exceeded fifty thousand. In 1896, when the South African AME
Church was established, African Methodists numbered nearly half a million,
thanks to a vast infusion of southern freedpeople after the Civil War. As the
twentieth century dawned, few disputed the assessment of the young W. E. B.
Du Bois, whose epochal *The Souls of Black Folk* characterized the AME Church
as "the greatest Negro organization in the world." . . .

From the outset, African Methodism was an expansive creed. Fired by proph-
ecy, the leaders of the new church dispatched emissaries across the northern
states, inviting other African American Christians to join them in their Bethel.
Thousands heeded the call. In its first five years, the church absorbed congregations in New York State, New Jersey, eastern and central Pennsylvania, and
all along the Maryland shore. Although adherents came from a variety of denominational traditions, the lion's share appear to have been defectors from the
Methodist Episcopal Church, whose congregations hung, in the words of one
AME founder, "like ripe fruit, only waiting to be plucked." In 1823 Allen sent an
elder across the Alleghenies to begin organizing African American settlers in
the Ohio Valley. By the early 1830s, when the Pittsburgh, or Western, Annual
Conference was inaugurated, African Methodist elders plied a dozen circuits
across western Pennsylvania and Ohio. The church also boasted a handful of
congregations in Canada's growing black expatriate community.

 Just as the church plucked Methodist congregations, so did it rely on Methodist techniques. Itinerant ministers such as William Paul Quinn, David Smith,

Jordan Early, and the felicitously named Moses Freeman traveled the country-side, preaching at camp meetings and revivals, organizing congregations and circuits, and moving on. Surely the most extraordinary of these early itinerants was Paul Quinn, the AME Church's celebrated "missionary to the West" and later its fourth bishop. Although there are several versions of Quinn's origins, he seems to have been an Indian (of the South Asian rather than Native American variety). The son of a Calcutta mahogany merchant, Quinn first encountered Christianity in the late eighteenth century, probably through some British Quaker merchants or sailors. Disowned by his Hindu parents, he embarked for Britain in the early nineteenth century, carrying letters of introduction to several prominent Quakers. With their help, he proceeded on to America, eventually ending up in Bucks County, Pennsylvania, working at a sawmill. In the arbitrary racial taxonomy of his new home, this upper-caste Indian was now a Negro.

Soon after his arrival in the United States, Quinn converted to Methodism. He had already begun to preach when the AME Church was founded in 1816, and he quickly rallied to its banner. He attended the first AME-sponsored camp meeting in 1818, preaching alongside Richard Allen. A year later, he was ordained an AME deacon. Over the next quarter century, Quinn established himself as the church's most effective evangelist, organizing scores of congregations across Pennsylvania, Ohio, Indiana, and Illinois. In 1844 he was elevated to the bishopric.

Evangelist David Smith, less renowned in church annals, was scarcely less remarkable. An illiterate former slave, Smith began preaching in his native Maryland at the age of twelve. He was one of the first men to join the AME connection and attended the inaugural General Conference in 1816. He remained a minister for the next sixty years. In contrast to Quinn, who prided himself on being the AME Church's first minister on horseback, Smith traveled on foot, sowing congregations from Connecticut in the north to New Orleans in the south. Like Quinn, he enjoyed his greatest success in Ohio—in cities like Cincinnati, as well as in smaller towns like Chillicothe, Yellow Springs, and Xenia, where communities of African Americans huddled in the shadow of the state's notorious Black Codes. Excluded from schools, poor houses, and even cemeteries, black Ohioans found in African Methodism a vital spiritual resource, as well as a firm foundation for collective organizing. Smith, the self-proclaimed "father of Benevolent Societies in the West," established not only churches but schools, burial societies, masonic temples, and all manner of mutual aid schemes. Long after he had gone to his reward, the state of Ohio remained an AME stronghold.

Evangelization was not without its ambiguities, or its hazards. The "low class of whites," Smith later recalled, "were very much opposed to the prosperity of the colored people" and resented an independent, self-respecting institution like the AME Church. Paul Quinn survived a stab wound sustained when an Ohio camp meeting he had organized was attacked by a white mob. Opponents disrupted churches and schools, and AME itinerants endured harassment and arrest. To circumvent such hostility, many ministers became adept at cultivating the "better class" of whites. When entering a new town, Quinn presented authorities with letters from prominent Quakers in Britain and America, attesting to his good sense and moderation. Smith, who also traveled with a satchel full of testimonials from whites, capitalized on his status as a freemason, preaching in masonic halls when debarred from local churches. The masonic connection was even more critical to J. W. Early, another pioneering AME preacher. Arrested in Illinois and charged as a runaway, Early escaped almost certain reenslavement by flashing a masonic signal to the magistrate, who promptly ordered his release.

The hazards of evangelization were even greater in the South, where a series of uprisings led by Christian slaves had left southern whites deeply suspicious of black independent churches. A few AME itinerants did cross the Mason-Dixon line, but for the most part the church's growth was confined to border regions like the Maryland shore and the western counties of Virginia, where the plantation system was not well developed and restrictions on black movement were unevenly enforced. The church also established a foothold in several southern and border cities, where there was relative social fluidity and considerable overlap between slave and free populations. . . .

The contradictions of southern expansion were graphically illustrated by the church's meteoric rise and fall in Charleston, South Carolina. The roots of the Charleston church reached back to 1817, when several hundred black men and women, slave and free, withdrew from the local Methodist congregation. Having somehow heard of the AME Church, the seceders sent a request for affiliation to Bishop Allen. A year later, their leader, Morris Brown, traveled to Philadelphia to meet with Allen. In 1820 the AME General Conference formally welcomed the Charlestonians into connection. Despite constant white harassment and the periodic arrest of Brown and other leaders, the church grew. At the moment of connection, it counted fifteen hundred members, establishing South Carolina as the AME Church's second largest conference; over the next two years, membership reportedly doubled to nearly three thousand.

At that very moment, however, Charleston was convulsed by the Denmark Vesey conspiracy. Whether the uprising conceived by Vesey was as massive as panicky whites believed, and whether the AME Church played as pivotal a role in the plot as critics charged, are matters of considerable debate. What is clear is that the church bore the brunt of white reaction. Whites alleged that Vesey, who undoubtedly was a member of the church, had preached sedition from the pulpit and used weekly class meetings to plan his bloody insurrection. Morris Brown was cast as his counselor. The official commission that looked into the conspiracy, while somewhat more temperate, accepted the analysis: "On investigation, it appeared that all concerned in that transaction, except one, had seceded from the regular Methodist Church in 1817, and formed a separate establishment in connection with the African Methodist Society in Philadelphia. . . ." In the days that followed, the church was banned and dozens of alleged conspirators were hanged. Morris Brown, secreted out of the state by a sympathetic white politician, survived to become the AME Church's second bishop, but it was another forty years before African Methodism returned to Charleston.

. . . In a nation ruled by the descendants of Europe, Africa is and has always been the touchstone of black distinctiveness, the literal and figurative point of departure for the construction of African American identity, whatever one conceives it to be. And nowhere was the question of African Americans' relationship with Africa more explicitly confronted than in the AME Church. From the moment of its inception, the church was consumed by African issues—by debates on the merits of emigration and colonization, the value of African missions, the meaning of slavery itself. Long before the establishment of the South African AME Church in 1896, black Christians had gazed through the looking glass, searching for identity and explanation in the dim reflections of a distant continent. . . .

African American interest in Africa received an enormous spur with the founding of the Sierra Leone colony in 1787. Initially established as a dumping ground for "the Black Poor of London," Sierra Leone became a homeland for thousands of former slaves, mostly from Britain, Canada, and the West Indies, as well as for an untold number of Africans "recaptured" by the Royal Navy in its campaign against the slave trade. Word of the West African colony raced through the black community in the United States. In Boston, Prince Hall, founder of the first black Masonic lodge and a correspondent of Richard Allen's, led a group of petitioners in requesting transportation to the colony. In Newport, emigration was endorsed by the Free African Society, which presented its decision in a memorial to its parent body in Philadelphia. The Philadelphia chapter's carefully couched reply revealed how involved the African issue was already becoming. "If any apprehend a divine injunction is laid upon them to undertake such a long and perilous journey in order to promote piety and virtue," the Philadelphians wished them godspeed. At the same time, they committed themselves to remaining in America and working toward the full abolition of slavery. Significantly, even the qualified support they gave emigration was cast in terms not of racial affinity but of Christian universalism: "[E]very pious man is a citizen of the world."

The most influential of the early emigration advocates was a black ship's captain named Paul Cuffe. Cuffe was a man of many parts—of mixed African and Native American descent, he was a devout Quaker, a skilled sailor, and an ambitious entrepreneur who rose from poverty to become one of the wealthiest black men in the United States. Converted to the emigrationist banner in the first decade of the nineteenth century, he embarked in 1811 on a joint civilizing and commercial venture to the Windward Coast of Africa, an area he had often plied on whaling voyages. He visited Sierra Leone, returning via London, where he obtained a preferential trading agreement from the colony's sponsors in exchange for recruiting and transporting skilled colonists. In a circular published in 1812, Cuffe argued that emigration would remove the "yoke of oppression" from African Americans, enabling them to "rise to be a people." At the same time, emigration promised to "regenerate" Africa through the balm of Christianity, civilization, and, not coincidentally, commerce.

Cuffe's voluntary emigration plan appealed to at least a segment of America's free black population. In Baltimore, a pro-emigration group was formed under the leadership of future AME Church founder Daniel Coker. In Philadelphia, Cuffe met with several community leaders, including wealthy sailmaker James Forten, a confidante of Richard Allen's and a distinguished abolitionist in his own right. Cuffe easily recruited passengers for a voyage, but his plans were upset by the outbreak of war between Britain and the United States in 1812. The U.S. Congress refused to grant him a waiver to trade with an enemy colony, while the subsequent peace treaty explicitly excluded American merchants from British-controlled ports. Cuffe did succeed in transporting one company of thirty-eight settlers to Freetown in 1816, but the group received a frosty reception from local authorities. After some debate the settlers were allowed to land, but Cuffe was refused permission to offload the goods he had brought to trade. In the end, he lost about eight thousand dollars on the venture, the first of many commercial setbacks in the history of the African emigration movement. Cuffe died before he was able to muster the resources for a second voyage, allegedly leaving behind a waiting list of more than two thousand would-be emigrants. . . .

. . . [Th]e 1830s, a critical period in the development of black nationalist ideology, were marked by a recession of interest in and discussion about Africa. . . . Blacks were virtually united in their opposition to colonization, and most were [wary] of anything to do with Africa. Within the AME Church, a residuum of romance about Africa survived, expressed in occasional resolutions about redeeming souls "enshrouded in midnight darkness," but nothing came of them. The 1844 AME General Conference did establish a Home and Foreign Mission Society, but "foreign" at the time essentially meant Canadian. Richard Allen's episcopal successors—Morris Brown, Paul Quinn, and, later, Daniel Payne—all stressed the priority of "home missions" and showed little inclination to revive the West African work begun by Daniel Coker.

In the late 1840s, however, the cords tying African Americans to their ancestral home tautened once again. In 1847 Liberia became an independent republic. While primarily a product of the A.C.S.'s mounting debt, independence prompted many black Americans to reassess their position. Between 1847 and 1848 migration to Liberia grew tenfold. It continued to swell in the years that followed, as a series of devastating political defeats cast doubt on blacks' future in America. . . .

. . . The late-nineteenth-century back-to-Africa movement differed from its antebellum predecessor in several important respects. While a wizened American Colonization Society [ACS] continued to promote African American removal, control of the idea had long since passed out of its hands and into the hands of black ministers and politicians, most of whom had directly experienced the realities of the redeemed South. While some emigrationists maintained formal linkages with the ACS—Henry Turner, a man whose name would become synonymous with the postwar back-to-Africa movement, was a vice president of the Society—they insisted that emigration remain strictly voluntary and vigorously rejected any imputation of black incapacity for citizenship. Equally important, the geographical basis of emigrationism had shifted decisively. Debates over colonization and emigration in the prewar years had been centered, almost inevitably, in the North: the question, after all, was what to do with free people of color, the majority of whom lived in the free states. Postwar emigrationism, in contrast, was a distinctly southern affair. In South Carolina and in parts of Arkansas and Oklahoma, entire communities sold their belongings and embarked for the coast to meet ships—sometimes real, often imaginary—bound for the "promised land" of Liberia.

In other respects, however, the antebellum and postbellum back-to-Africa movements converged. Both traced the same skein of questions about identity and history, and posed the same cruel dilemmas. Both generated far more enthusiasm and opposition than actual emigration. Finally, debates over emigration in both periods were played out largely within the black church, nowhere more vociferously than within the AME Church. As in the antebellum period, the AME Church became an arena for debating the meaning of Africa, for organizing emigrationist schemes, and, simultaneously, for rallying emigrationist opposition.

PART 3

The Civil War and Reconstruction in History and Memory

KIDADA E. WILLIAMS

Preserving chattel slavery was the primary reason for secession and the establishment of the Confederate States of America. Americans had been fighting over slavery since the nation's founding. Whether they were enslaved or free, African-descended Americans overwhelmingly abhorred the institution and fought to destroy it from inside and out. As Matthew Clavin's piece in this section demonstrates, these men and women often drew on the memory of the Haitian Revolution to challenge slavery and global white supremacy. European-descended Americans were divided between those who were devoted to slavery, those who accepted the institution as long as it remained geographically bound to the South, and those who wanted to see it destroyed. From 1787 through 1860, these groups fought over these conflicting visions.

By the 1850s, both antislavery and proslavery forces had organized into political blocs. Reflecting conservative values, Democrats insisted on adherence to their strict interpretation of the Declaration of Independence and the Constitution and the values they believed informed the creation of the founding documents. They embraced localism and limited government. Slaveholding members of the party tended to support slavery and its expansion. Republicans, who emerged middecade from the Whig and Free Soil Parties, largely opposed slavery's expansion. These progressives, whose power lay in the northern states and territories, favored civil and political liberties and believed government intervention served the public good.

By the time the 1860 presidential election rolled around, the number of enslaved people had seen significant growth, rising from about one million in 1805 to just under four million in 1860. With decades of debate over the institution's expansion and continued existence, it was no surprise when slavery became the signature issue of the election.

Abraham Lincoln, running to stop slavery's expansion, won the Republican nomination. Democrats split their ticket, with southerners supporting John C. Breckenridge and northerners supporting Stephen A. Douglas. A third-party candidate, John Bell, further divided white southerners. Lincoln won the election, but his name was not even on the ballot in most slaveholding states.

The northern-based Republican victory not only in the White House but also in the Congress sent a shockwave across the slaveholding South. A Lincoln presidency meant the end of the enslaving class's domination of national politics. Slavery in the United States would be contained. For Americans invested in slavery this was untenable.

South Carolina took the lead, stating its justifications for secession in terms of slavery and race. Palmetto State resident Arthur P. Hayne summed up slavery's importance in a letter to outgoing President James Buchanan: "Slavery with us is no abstraction—but a great and vital fact. . . . Nothing short of separation from the Union can save us."[1] As the state's "Declaration of the Causes of Secession" makes clear, concerns about slavery's vulnerability to a Republican administration were the driving force behind the separation.

Lincoln tried to soothe slaveholders' fears. "Do the people of the South really believe that a Republican administration would interfere with their slaves?" the president-elect wrote to Alexander Stephens. "If they do, I wish to assure you . . . that there is no cause for such fears. . . . You think slavery is right, and ought to be extended; while we think it is wrong and out to be restricted. That I suppose is the rub. It is certainly the only substantial difference between us."[2]

As the Confederate States of America roared to life, Alexander Stephens's speech reveals clearly the centrality of slavery and white supremacy to secessionists' way of life. Excerpts from the Confederate Constitution relating to slavery, annotated by Stephanie McCurry, further reveal secessionists' intentions to create a white man's slaveholding republic.

When the war began, neither side knew that it would end with a U.S. victory and the abolition of slavery. Black Americans, who had watched the debates over slavery's expansion, knew their fate was tied to the outcome of the war. Enslaved people in particular, who had always been looking for weak spots in the institution of slavery and for opportunities to fight it, saw the clashing armies and navies as their opportunity to strike. As Stephanie McCurry's piece from *Confederate Reckoning* shows, just as enslaved people had used the cover of war to run during previous conflicts, southern slaves ran.

As popular as the Emancipation Proclamation has become in American memory, it did not vanquish slavery. Rebels ignored the order and stepped up their campaign to win the wars against the United States and their slaves. Officials in the White House and Congress knew that the only way to end slavery was to win the war and end the Constitution's tolerance of the practice.

When the armies stopped fighting, Americans still had a lot to resolve. How could they reunite the country after four bloody years of war? Would slavery be abolished? What place would African Americans have in the nation? No event reveals these divisions more than John Wilkes Booth's assassination of Abraham Lincoln after he raised the prospect of some equal rights for black veterans.

Slavery apologists have dismissed the institution as a harmless economic system. The spiritual "No More Auction Block For Me" illuminates African Americans' more comprehensive understandings of the institution. For enslaved people, slavery was never simply about money or stolen labor; it was about the physical, social, and psychological violence used to achieve it.

Freeing African Americans from chattel slavery was one thing, but giving them unobstructed access to American style liberty was another. Although most white Unionists supported emancipation as a war measure, they did not think blacks should have equal rights. Nothing underscored the irrepressible nature of Confederates' mentality after defeat more than southern legislators' enactment of Black Codes, laws designed for whites to retain control over black people's labor, freedom of movement, and way of life. Tera W. Hunter's work from *To 'Joy My Freedom* shows the efforts of African Americans to resist white supremacy by controlling their leisure time and expressing their joys and struggles as they saw fit.

The radical wing of the Republican Party believed equal civil and political rights should follow emancipation. They pushed for civil rights and a new citizenship in response to the Black Codes. The results were the Fourteenth and Fifteenth Amendments, which as Thomas C. Holt's work in *Black over White* shows, African Americans embraced.

As the excerpt from Hannah Rosen's *Terror in the Heart of Freedom* shows, however, carrying over old practices, postwar southern whites used violence to make African Americans accept something less than freedom. This violence included maintaining practices such as whipping for labor infractions. It also included attacks by white terror organizations, such as the Ku Klux Klan, sparked by black people's insistence on determining their own fate. Violence escalated during elections as white terrorists fought for and won political control of the South.

African Americans formed militias, defended their homes, and appealed to state and federal officials for relief. Thousands left the Deep South's rural areas and headed toward the region's cities. Others relocated to the Midwest, West, and Mid-Atlantic, and Northeast.

At the war's end, Confederates tried to make sense of their defeat and the incomprehensible loss of life. Robert E. Lee drafted the script apologists still use today: the men fought valiantly for states' rights, not slavery, but they were outnumbered and outgunned. Fellow ex-Confederates and their sympathizers repeated the refrain, and the Lost Cause narrative of the war was born. Such thinking absolved Confederates of responsibility for the war and the inhuman system of bondage they hoped to extend across the continent.

Frederick Douglass and other African American leaders attempted to push back against this narrative as they saw Confederate apologists stripping away the civil and political rights blacks gained during Reconstruction, reducing blacks to second-class status. In his 1874 speech, Congressman Robert Browne Elliott makes a passionate and constitutionally grounded case for a civil rights bill that would ensure African Americans had equal access to and treatment in places of public accommodation. The bill passed, but the Supreme Court overturned it less than a decade later.

African Americans ended Reconstruction legally free, but their ability to enjoy the full benefits of American citizenship had been restricted. In the last quarter of the nineteenth century, as Jim Crow took shape, they would face even more restrictions and violence.

NOTES

1. Quoted in Walter B. Edgar, *South Carolina: A History* (Columbia: University of South Carolina Press, 1998), 352.

2. Abraham Lincoln letter to Alexander Stephens, December 22, 1860, Teaching American History website, http://teachingamericanhistory.org/library/document/letter-to-alexander-h-stephens/.

Declaration of the Immediate Causes Which Induce and Justify the Secession of South Carolina from the Federal Union

(1860)

The people of the State of South Carolina, in Convention assembled, on the 26th day of April, A.D., 1852, declared that the frequent violations of the Constitution of the United States, by the Federal Government, and its encroachments upon the reserved rights of the States, fully justified this State in then withdrawing from the Federal Union; but in deference to the opinions and wishes of the other slaveholding States, she forbore at that time to exercise this right. Since that time, these encroachments have continued to increase, and further forbearance ceases to be a virtue.

And now the State of South Carolina having resumed her separate and equal place among nations, deems it due to herself, to the remaining United States of America, and to the nations of the world, that she should declare the immediate causes which have led to this act.

In the year 1765, that portion of the British Empire embracing Great Britain, undertook to make laws for the government of that portion composed of the thirteen American Colonies. A struggle for the right of self-government ensued, which resulted, on the 4th of July, 1776, in a Declaration, by the Colonies, "that they are, and of right ought to be, FREE AND INDEPENDENT STATES; and that, as free and independent States, they have full power to levy war, conclude peace, contract alliances, establish commerce, and to do all other acts and things which independent States may of right do."

They further solemnly declared that whenever any "form of government becomes destructive of the ends for which it was established, it is the right of the people to alter or abolish it, and to institute a new government." . . .

Thus were established the two great principles asserted by the Colonies, namely: the right of a State to govern itself; and the right of a people to abolish a Government when it becomes destructive of the ends for which it was instituted. And concurrent with the establishment of these principles, was the fact, that each Colony became and was recognized by the mother Country a FREE, SOVEREIGN AND INDEPENDENT STATE. . . .

Thus was established, by compact between the States, a Government with definite objects and powers, limited to the express words of the grant. This limitation left the whole remaining mass of power subject to the clause reserving it to the States or to the people, and rendered unnecessary any specification of reserved rights. . . .

The General Government . . . passed laws to carry into effect these stipulations of the States. For many years these laws were executed. But an increasing hostility on the part of the non-slaveholding States to the institution of slavery, has led to a disregard of their obligations, and the laws of the General Government have ceased to effect the objects of the Constitution. The States of Maine, New Hampshire, Vermont, Massachusetts, Connecticut, Rhode Island, New York, Pennsylvania, Illinois, Indiana, Michigan, Wisconsin, and Iowa, have enacted laws which either nullify the Acts of Congress or render useless any attempt to execute them. In many of these States the fugitive is discharged from service or labor claimed, and in none of them has the State Government complied with the stipulation made in the Constitution. . . . Thus the constituted compact has been deliberately broken and disregarded by the non-slaveholding States, and the consequence follows that South Carolina is released from her obligation. . . .

. . . The right of property in slaves was recognized by giving to free persons distinct political rights, by giving them the right to represent, and burthening them with direct taxes for three-fifths of their slaves; by authorizing the importation of slaves for twenty years; and by stipulating for the rendition of fugitives from labor.

We affirm that these ends for which this Government was instituted have been defeated, and the Government itself has been made destructive of them by the action of the non-slaveholding States. Those States have assume the right of deciding upon the propriety of our domestic institutions; and have denied the rights of property established in fifteen of the States and recognized by the Constitution; they have denounced as sinful the institution of slavery; they have permitted open establishment among them of societies, whose avowed object is to disturb the peace and to eloign the property of the citizens of other States. They have encouraged and assisted thousands of our slaves to leave their homes; and those who remain, have been incited by emissaries, books and pictures to servile insurrection.

For twenty-five years this agitation has been steadily increasing, until it has now secured to its aid the power of the common Government. Observing the *forms* of the Constitution, a sectional party has found within that Article establishing the Executive Department, the means of subverting the Constitution itself. A geographical line has been drawn across the Union, and all the States north of that line have united in the election of a man to the high office of President of the United States, whose opinions and purposes are hostile to slavery. He is to be entrusted with the administration of the common Government, because he has declared that that "Government cannot endure permanently half slave, half free," and that the public mind must rest in the belief that slavery is in the course of ultimate extinction.

This sectional combination for the submersion of the Constitution, has been aided in some of the States by elevating to citizenship, persons who, by the supreme law of the land, are incapable of becoming citizens; and their votes have been used to inaugurate a new policy, hostile to the South, and destructive of its beliefs and safety.

On the 4th day of March next, this party will take possession of the Government. It has announced that the South shall be excluded from the common territory, that the judicial tribunals shall be made sectional, and that a war must be waged against slavery until it shall cease throughout the United States.

The guaranties of the Constitution will then no longer exist; the equal rights of the States will be lost. The slaveholding States will no longer have the power of self-government, or self-protection, and the Federal Government will have become their enemy. . . .

We, therefore, the People of South Carolina, by our delegates in Convention assembled, appealing to the Supreme Judge of the world for the rectitude of our intentions, have solemnly declared that the Union heretofore existing between this State and the other States of North America, is dissolved, and that the State of South Carolina has resumed her position among the nations of the world, as a separate and independent State; with full power to levy war, conclude peace, contract alliances, establish commerce, and to do all other acts and things which independent States may of right do.

Adopted December 24, 1860

From "The Constitution of the Confederate States"

with Annotations by Stephanie McCurry

(March 11, 1861)

Article I

SECTION 2.3

> Representatives and direct taxes shall be apportioned among the several States, which may be included within this Confederacy, according to their respective numbers, which shall be determined by adding to the whole number of free persons, including those bound to service for a term of years, and excluding Indians not taxed, three-fifths of all slaves. The actual enumeration shall be made within three years after the first meeting of the Congress of the Confederate States, and within every subsequent term of ten years, in such manner as they shall by law direct. The number of Representatives shall not exceed one for every fifty thousand, but each State shall have at least one Representative; and until such enumeration shall be made, the State of South Carolina shall be entitled to choose six; the State of Georgia ten; the State of Alabama nine; the State of Florida two; the State of Mississippi seven; the State of Louisiana six; and the State of Texas six.

The Confederates copied the American Constitution's ration by which congressional representation is calculated. But in this section they also began to purge the document of the euphemisms adopted in the original. Most notably, whereas the word "slave" does not appear in the American Constitution, it is used repeatedly in the Confederate one. Unlike the original clause, which referred to a formula counting the whole number of free persons, excluding Indians, and "three fifths of all other Persons"—an ambivalent formulation clearly intended to allow for the possibility of an antislavery future—Confederates refer unapologetically to "three fifths of all slaves."

SEC. 9.1

> The importation of negroes of the African race from any foreign country other than the slaveholding States or Territories of the United States of America, is hereby forbidden; and Congress is required to pass such laws as shall effectually prevent the same.

The Confederate Constitution prohibited the reopening of the African slave trade. The movement to reopen the trade had been advanced by a cohort of southern rights activists and secessionists since at least 1850, and this clause was a clear defeat for radicals like Robert Barnwell Rhett of South Carolina. But this was no moral stance. It was a pragmatic inclusion, meant to recognize the interests of Virginia—a net-exporting slave state still in the Union—whose decision to join the Confederate States was viewed as critical to the new Deep South nation. . . .

SECTION 9.4

> No bill of attainder, ex post facto law, or law denying or impairing the right of property in negro slaves shall be passed.

This entirely new clause, the centerpiece of the Confederate Constitution, makes slavery a legal and permanent feature of the new society. It places human property on a positive constitutional foundation, and it puts owning slaves forever beyond the power of the Confederate Congress to restrict. It is this clause that makes the Confederate Constitution an explicitly proslavery document—something the original famously was not. It also establishes beyond any doubt the proslavery and antidemocratic purposes of secession and the founding of the Confederate nation.

Article IV

SECTION 2.3

> A person charged in any State with treason, felony, or other crime against the laws of such State, who shall flee from justice, and be found in another State, shall, on demand of the executive authority of the State from which he fled, be delivered up, to be removed to the State having jurisdiction of the crime.

Delegates added to the privileges and immunities clause to specify that it extended to property rights in slaves; citizens could travel through or visit any state or territory "with their slaves and other property." Taken together with other, later clauses, this article explicitly nationalized the property rights of slaveholders, thereby resolving old and agitating issues about the rights of slaveholders to carry their [human] property into free states and federal territories. . . .

SECTION 3.3

> The Confederate States may acquire new territory; and Congress shall have power to legislate and provide governments for the inhabitants of all territory belonging to the Confederate States, lying without the limits of the several Sates; and may permit them, at such times, and in such manner as it may by law provide, to form States to be admitted into the Confederacy. In all such territory the institution of negro slavery, as it now exists in the Confederate States, shall be recognized and protected by Congress and by the Territorial government; and the inhabitants of the several Confederate States and Territories shall have the right to take to such Territory any slaves lawfully held by them in any of the States or Territories of the Confederate States.

This is a wholly new clause. It rendered explicit both the Confederate government's imperial ambitions—it clearly planned to add new territories—and it secured the federal protection of slave property in the (hoped for) new territories. Constitutional protections for slavery in the territories had been a central issue in the split of the Democratic Party at its national convention in Charleston in May 1860 and the demands of secessionists after the election that fall. Confederates actually made some advances into New Mexico and Arizona in 1861 and 1862, but they were defeated as much by Indian warfare as by the Union army.

ALEXANDER H. STEPHENS

Corner Stone Speech

(March 21, 1861)
Savannah, Georgia

. . . [W]e are passing through one of the greatest revolutions in the annals of the
world. Seven States have within the last three months thrown off an old government and formed a new. This revolution has been signally marked, up to this
time, by the fact of its having been accomplished without the loss of a single
drop of blood. . . .

. . . The new constitution has put at rest, forever, all the agitating questions
relating to our peculiar institution African slavery as it exists amongst us the
proper status of the negro in our form of civilization. This was the immediate
cause of the late rupture and present revolution. Jefferson in his forecast, had
anticipated this, as the "rock upon which the old Union would split." He was
right. What was conjecture with him, is now a realized fact. But whether he
fully comprehended the great truth upon which that rock stood and stands, may
be doubted. The prevailing ideas entertained by him and most of the leading
statesmen at the time of the formation of the old constitution, were that the enslavement of the African was in violation of the laws of nature; that it was wrong
in principle, socially, morally, and politically. It was an evil they knew not well
how to deal with, but the general opinion of the men of that day was that, somehow or other in the order of Providence, the institution would be evanescent
and pass away. This idea, though not incorporated in the constitution, was the
prevailing idea at that time. The constitution, it is true, secured every essential
guarantee to the institution while it should last, and hence no argument can
be justly urged against the constitutional guarantees thus secured, because of
the common sentiment of the day. Those ideas, however, were fundamentally
wrong. They rested upon the assumption of the equality of races. This was an
error. It was a sandy foundation, and the government built upon it fell when the
"storm came and the wind blew."

Our new government is founded upon exactly the opposite idea; its foundations are laid, its corner-stone rests, upon the great truth that the negro is
not equal to the white man; that slavery subordination to the superior race is
his natural and normal condition. This, our new government, is the first, in the

history of the world, based upon this great physical, philosophical, and moral truth. This truth has been slow in the process of its development, like all other truths in the various departments of science. It has been so even amongst us. Many who hear me, perhaps, can recollect well, that this truth was not generally admitted, even within their day. The errors of the past generation still clung to many as late as twenty years ago. Those at the North, who still cling to these errors, with a zeal above knowledge, we justly denominate fanatics. All fanaticism springs from an aberration of the mind from a defect in reasoning. It is a species of insanity. One of the most striking characteristics of insanity, in many instances, is forming correct conclusions from fancied or erroneous premises; so with the anti-slavery fanatics. Their conclusions are right if their premises were. They assume that the negro is equal, and hence conclude that he is entitled to equal privileges and rights with the white man. If their premises were correct, their conclusions would be logical and just but their premise being wrong, their whole argument fails. I recollect once of having heard a gentleman from one of the northern States, of great power and ability, announce in the House of Representatives, with imposing effect, that we of the South would be compelled, ultimately, to yield upon this subject of slavery, that it was as impossible to war successfully against a principle in politics, as it was in physics or mechanics. That the principle would ultimately prevail. That we, in maintaining slavery as it exists with us, were warring against a principle, a principle founded in nature, the principle of the equality of men. The reply I made to him was, that upon his own grounds, we should, ultimately, succeed, and that he and his associates, in this crusade against our institutions, would ultimately fail. The truth announced, that it was as impossible to war successfully against a principle in politics as it was in physics and mechanics, I admitted; but told him that it was he, and those acting with him, who were warring against a principle. They were attempting to make things equal which the Creator had made unequal. . . .

. . . Many governments have been founded upon the principle of the subordination and serfdom of certain classes of the same race; such were and are in violation of the laws of nature. Our system commits no such violation of nature's laws. With us, all of the white race, however high or low, rich or poor, are equal in the eye of the law. Not so with the negro. Subordination is his place. He, by nature, or by the curse against Canaan, is fitted for that condition which he occupies in our system. The architect, in the construction of buildings, lays the foundation with the proper material—the granite; then comes the brick or the marble. The substratum of our society is made of the material fitted by nature for it, and by experience we know that it is best, not only for the superior, but for the inferior race, that it should be so. It is, indeed, in conformity with the ordinance of the Creator. It is not for us to inquire into the wisdom of His ordinances, or to question them. For His own purposes, He has made one race to differ from another, as He has made "one star to differ from another star in glory." The great objects of humanity are best attained when there is conformity to His laws and decrees, in the formation of governments as well as in all things else. Our confederacy is founded upon principles in strict conformity with these laws. This stone which was rejected by the first builders "is become the chief of the corner" the real "corner-stone" in our new edifice. I have been asked, what of the future? It has been apprehended by some that we would have arrayed against us the civilized world. I care not who or how many they may be against us, when we stand upon the eternal principles of truth, if we are true to ourselves and the principles for which we contend, we are obliged to, and must triumph.

GUSTAVUS D. PIKE

No More Auction Block For Me

(1873)

No more auction block for me
No more, no more
No more auction block for me
Many thousand gone

No more peck of corn for me
No more, no more
No more peck of corn for me
Many thousand gone

No more driver's lash for me
No more, no more
No more drivers' lash for me
Many thousand gone

No more pint of salt for me
No more, no more
No more pint of salt for me
Many thousand gone

No more hundred lash for me
No more, no more
No more hundred lash for me
Many thousand gone

No more mistress call for me
No more, no more
No more mistress call for me
Many thousand gone

No more children stole from me
No more, no more
No more children stole from me
Many thousand gone

No more slavery chains for me
No more, no more
No more slavery chains for me
Many thousand gone

ROBERT BROWN ELLIOTT

"The Civil Rights Bill"

Extracts from a Speech Delivered in the House of Representatives

(January 6, 1874)

While I am sincerely grateful for this high mark of courtesy that has been accorded to me by this House, it is a matter of regret to me that it is necessary at this day that I should rise in the presence of an American Congress to advocate a bill which simply asserts equal rights and equal privileges for all classes of American citizens. I regret, sir, that the dark hue of my skin may lend a color to the imputation that I am controlled by motives personal to myself in my advocacy of this great measure of national justice. Sir, the motive that impels me is restricted by no such narrow boundary, but is as broad as your Constitution. I advocate it, sir, because it is right. The bill, however, not only appeals to your justice, but it demands a response from your gratitude. . . .

But, sir, we are told by the distinguished gentleman from Georgia [Mr. Stephens] that Congress has no power under the Constitution to pass such a law, and that the passage of such an act is in direct contravention of the rights of the States. I cannot assent to any such proposition. The Constitution of a free government ought always to be construed in favor of human rights. Indeed, the thirteenth, fourteenth, and fifteenth amendments, in positive words, invest Congress with the power to protect the citizen in his civil and political rights. . . .

. . . Is it pretended, I ask the honorable gentleman from Kentucky or the honorable gentleman from Georgia—is it pretended anywhere that the evils of which we complain, our exclusion from the public inn, from the saloon and table of the steamboat, from the sleeping-coach on the railway, from the right of sepulture in the public burial-ground, are an exercise of the police power of the state? Is such oppression and injustice nothing but the exercise by the State of the right to make regulations for the health, comfort, and security of all her citizens? Is it merely enacting that one man shall so use his own as not to injure another[']s? Is the colored race to be assimilated to an unwholesome trade or to combustible materials, to be interdicted, to be shut up within prescribed limits? . . .

The distinction between the two kinds of citizenship is clear, and the Supreme Court has clearly pointed out this distinction, but is has nowhere written a word or line which denies to Congress the power to prevent a denial of equality of rights whether those rights exist by virtue of citizenship of the United States or of a State. Let honorable members mark well this distinction. . . . There are rights conferred on us by the state of which we are individually the citizens. The fourteenth amendment does not forbid a state to deny to all its citizens any of those rights which the state itself has conferred with certain exceptions which are pointed out in the decision which we are examining. What it does forbid is inequality, is discrimination or, to use the words of the amendment itself, is the denial "to any person within its jurisdiction, the equal protection of the laws." If a State denies to me rights which are common to all her other citizens, she violates this amendment, unless she can show, as was shown in the Slaughter-house cases, that she does it in the legitimate exercise of her police power. If she abridges the rights of all her citizens equally, unless those rights are specifically guarded by the Constitution of the United States, she does not violate this amendment. This is not to put the rights which I hold by virtue of my citizenship of South Carolina under the protection of the national Government; it is not to blot out or overlook in the slightest particular the distinction between rights held under the United States and rights held under the States; but it seeks to secure equality to prevent discrimination, to confer as complete and ample protection on the humblest as on this highest. . . .

. . . Now, sir, recurring to the venerable and distinguished gentleman from Georgia [Mr. Stephens] who has added his remonstrance against the passage of this bill, permit me to say that I share in the feeling of high personal regard for that gentleman which pervades this House. His years, his ability, and his long experience in public affairs entitle him to the measure of consideration which has been accorded to him on this floor. But in this discussion I cannot and will not forget that the welfare and rights of my whole race in this country are involved. When, therefore, the honorable gentleman from Georgia lends his voice and influence to defeat this measure, I do not shrink from saying that it is not from him that the American House of Representatives should take lessons in matters touching human rights or the joint relations of the State and national governments. While the honorable gentleman contented himself with harmless speculations in his study, or in the columns of a newspaper, we might well smile at the impotence of his efforts to turn back the advancing tide of opinion and progress; but, when he comes again upon this national arena, and throws himself with all his power and influence across the path which leads to the full enfranchisement of my race, I meet him only as an adversary; nor shall age or any other consideration restrain me from saying that he now offers this Government which he has done his utmost to destroy, a very poor return for its magnanimous treatment, to come here and seek to continue, by the assertion of doctrines obnoxious to the true principles of our Government, the burdens and oppressions which rest upon five millions of his countrymen who never failed to lift their earnest prayers for the success of this Government when the gentleman was seeking to break up the union of these States and to blot the American Republic from the galaxy of nations.

Sir, it is scarcely twelve years since that gentleman shocked the civilized world by announcing the birth of a government which rested on human slavery as its cornerstone. The progress of events has swept away that pseudo-government which rested on greed, pride, and tyranny; and the race whom he then ruthlessly spurned and trampled on is here to meet him in debate, and to demand that the rights which are enjoyed by its former oppressors—who vainly sought to overthrow a Government which they could no prostitute to the base uses of slavery—shall be accorded to those who even in the darkness of slavery kept their allegiance true to freedom and the Union. Sir, the gentleman from Georgia has learned much since 1861; but he is still a laggard. Let him put away entirely the false and fatal theories which have so greatly marred an otherwise enviable record. Let him accept, in its fullness and beneficence, the great doctrine that American citizenship carries with it every civil and political right which manhood can confer. Let him lend his influence with all his masterly ability, to complete the proud structure of legislation which makes this nation worthy of the great declaration which heralded its birth and he will have done that which will most nearly redeem his reputation in the eyes of the world, and best vindicate the wisdom of that policy which has permitted him to regain his seat upon this floor. . . .

Sir, I have replied to the extent of my ability to the arguments which have been presented by the opponents of this measure. I have replied also to some of the legal propositions advanced by gentlemen on the other side; and now that I am about to conclude, I am deeply sensible of the imperfect manner in which I have performed the task. Technically, this bill is to decide upon the civil status of the colored American citizen; a point disputed at the very foundation of our present form of government, when by a short-sighted policy, a policy repugnant to true republican government, one Negro counted as three-fifth of a man. The logical result of this mistake of the framers of the Constitution strengthened the cancer of slavery, which finally spread its poisonous tentacles over the southern portion of the body politic. To arrest its growth and save the nation we have passed through the harrowing operation of intestine war, dreaded at all times, resorted to at the last extremity, like the surgeon's knife, but absolutely necessary to extirpate the disease which threatened with the life of the nation the overthrow of civil and political liberty on this continent. In that dire extremity the members of the race which I have the honor in part to represent—the race which pleads for justice at your hands to-day,—forgetful of their inhuman and brutalizing servitude at the South, their degradation and ostracism at the North, flew willingly and gallantly to the support of the national Government. . . .

The results of the war, as seen in reconstruction, have settled forever the political status of my race. The passage of this bill will determine the civil status, not only of the Negro, but of any other class of citizens who may feel themselves discriminated against. It will form the cap-stone of that temple of liberty, begun on this continent under discouraging circumstances, carried on in spite of sneers of monarchists and the cavails of pretended friends of freedom, until at last it stands, in all its beautiful symmetry and proportions, a building the grandest which the world has ever seen, realizing the most sanguine expectations and the highest hopes of those who, in the name of equal, impartial, and universal liberty, laid the foundation-stone.

MATTHEW CLAVIN

From "A Second Haitian Revolution: John Brown, Toussaint Louverture, and the Making of the American Civil War"

(June 2008)

"One of the most extraordinary men of a time when so many extraordinary men appeared." The French historian Alphonse Beauchamp, who wrote these words in the *Universal Biography* at the opening of the nineteenth century as a series of democratic revolutions in Europe and throughout the Americas came to an end, did not intend them for George Washington, the Virginia planter who led Britain's thirteen North American colonies to independence. Nor did he intend them for Napoleon Bonaparte, the Corsican soldier who brought order out of the chaos of the French Revolution and conquered Europe, or Simon Bolivar, the Venezuelan aristocrat who ended Spanish rule throughout much of Latin America. They referred instead to François Dominique Toussaint Louverture, the black general and former bondman who led an army of rebel slaves to victory over their former masters as well as the armies of France, England, and Spain at the end of the eighteenth century in the Saint-Domingue or Haitian Revolution. It may come as a revelation that Beauchamp was not alone in his assessment. While today it is difficult to find people who revere the black slaves who centuries ago killed whites to be free, in the aftermath of the Haitian Revolution, men and women throughout the Atlantic world celebrated Louverture as a Great Man, a slave who compared favorably to other Great Men of the Age of Revolution. . . .

African Americans and their radical white allies put the memory of the Haitian Revolution to a different use. Throughout the first half of the nineteenth century, they joined the transatlantic commemoration of Louverture and in lectures, books, articles, pamphlets, and illustrations offered him to an American audience as a symbol of the virtue and potential of the black race. In addition to challenging the widespread belief in white supremacy, these abolitionists placed great emphasis on Louverture's *character* for another reason: to calm widespread fears of slave insurrection. By stressing his compassion and integrity at the expense of his militancy, abolitionists tried to soften the rock hard image of this indomitable black warrior. The strategy worked, for Louverture remained an anti-slavery icon among even the most conservative social reformers decades after his death. The convergence of European and American abolitionism around the memory of Haiti's preeminent founding father proved resilient. It was, however, only temporary.

An analysis of abolitionist oral, print, and visual culture reveals that in the decade before the Civil War, African Americans and their radical white allies transformed Louverture into a symbol of black masculinity and violence, which they deployed to bring about the destruction of the status quo. They insisted that if slavery did not end immediately, then they would follow Louverture's example and use violence to deliver freedom to their brothers and sisters in bondage. A look at radical abolitionism and in particular John Brown's raid on Harpers Ferry, Virginia, in October 1859 reveals the iconic stature of Louverture among American abolitionists; it moreover illuminates an important trajectory. The men who invaded Harpers Ferry not only carried on the memory of Louverture, but they joined their movement to a black revolutionary tradition deeply rooted in the eighteenth-century Atlantic world. . . .

At the beginning of the nineteenth century, public discourse on the Haitian Revolution was a transatlantic affair. With American print culture in its adolescence, American readers poured over foreign newspapers, periodicals, and books. In these texts, the memory of Louverture survived among African Americans and their radical white allies. In 1802, England's *Annual Register*, a widely read chronicle of the world's important events, devoted its pages to a biography of Louverture. The periodical detailed his great character and accomplishments. It compared him favorably to both Washington and Bonaparte, concluding, he was "undoubtedly the most interesting of all the public characters which appeared on the great stage of political events for the present year." At the same time that the *Annual Register* labeled Louverture its "man of the year," Marcus Rainsford, a British soldier and eyewitness to the Haitian Revolution published a history of the event. In the next two years, at a time when very few books enjoyed a second printing, London publishers reprinted the book twice more in revised and expanded editions. Popular periodicals reviewed these works and reprinted lengthy excerpts. Rainsford knew Louverture and venerated him. He referred to him as a "truly great man" who surpassed Napoleon in both personal character and political power. All three editions of Rainsford's book included detailed biographical accounts of Louverture's "character." . . .

African Americans embraced this memory of Louverture. The pages of Samuel Cornish's and John Russworm's *Freedom's Journal*, the first newspaper owned and operated by African Americans, included numerous accounts of the Haitian Revolution and the struggling independent black nation. A three-part biographical sketch on Louverture, which the editors copied directly from the *Quarterly Review* of London, illuminated Louverture's character as proof of the equality of the black race. The same English article influenced an oration on the Haitian Revolution delivered by the abolitionist medical doctor James Mc-Cune Smith in New York City in 1844. Like Rainsford's narratives and the article copied into *Freedom's Journal*, the oration included "a sketch of the character of Toussaint L'Ouverture." But this is where the similarities ended. Smith drew from the prominent works of American, British, and Haitian authors to offer a fresh perspective. Among his central ideas was that the French government did not emancipate the colony's enslaved people; it was rather something they seized "by force of arms." Led by a former bondman who "reached the prime of manhood, a slave," enslaved Haitians secured both individual liberty and national independence. Once free, "Like Leonidas at Thermopylae, or the Bruce at Bannockburn, Toussaint determined to defend from thralldom his sea-girt isle, made sacred to liberty by the baptism of blood. The oration was a commentary on the efficacy of violence that anticipated a significant transformation in the memory of Louverture, which would take place among American abolitionists on the eve of the Civil War. Considered alongside the articles in *Freedom's Journal* and the numerous other abolitionist accounts of the Haitian Revolution, it challenges those who find a reticence of African Americans to invoke the Haitian Revolution because of the images it evoked of race war and the failure of black government.

Given the high regard that prominent African Americans accorded foreign accounts of the revolution, biographies of Louverture written and published in Europe continued to figure prominently in American abolitionists' memory of the Haitian Revolution. Four widely read books published in England in the middle of the nineteenth century deserve attention, as they indicate an important modification of the symbol of Louverture. The authors of each of them, Henry Gardiner Adams, Wilson Armistead, John Relly Beard, and Harriet Martineau reinforced Louverture's construction as a Great Man. Beard ranked Louverture among history's greatest men in his lengthy biography: "If the world has reason to thank God for great men, with special gratitude should we acknowledge the divine goodness in raising up Toussiant L'Ouverture. Among the privileged races of the earth, the roll of patriots, legislators, and heroes, is long and well filled. As yet there is but one Toussaint L'Ouverture." Armisted perhaps had a copy of Martineau's *Penny Magazine* article at his side when he wrote in his biographical sketch of Louverture, he "was, emphatically, a Great Man; and what he was, others of his race may equally attain to." These writers continued to offer Louverture as proof of the equality of the races. . . .

Memory of Louverture fueled [John] Brown's faith in revolutionary black violence. While we do not know whether Brown attended any . . . lectures on Louverture, it is certain that he was aware of them. Brown followed the abolitionist newspapers that kept alive the memory of the Louverture—in his childhood his father subscribed to William Lloyd Garrison's *Liberator*. Brown drew inspiration from these articles, as well as the books and conversations on the Haitian Revolution. Richard J. Hinton, one of Brown's allies, recounted that one evening Brown stopped to rest while helping eleven slaves escape from Bloody Kansas. At the home of a frontier abolitionist, Brown recounted the history of American slave resistance. He impressed Hinton by also reciting the history of the Haitian Revolution. It was, Hinton remembered, a story Brown knew "by heart." Richard Realf, an English immigrant and abolitionist journalist who also befriended Brown in Kansas, testified before the U.S. Senate Investigating Committee after Brown's arrest. Asked about Brown's motivations, Realf responded that Brown "had posted himself in relation to the wars of Toussaint L'Ouverture; he had become thoroughly acquainted with the wars in Hayti and the islands round about; and from all these things he had drawn the conclusion, believing, as he stated there he did believe, and as we all (if I may judge from myself) believed, that upon the first intimation of a plan formed for the liberation of the slaves, they would immediately rise all over the Southern States." It was because of Brown's study of the Haitian Revolution and wars of liberation that his plan emerged "spontaneously" in his mind. Brown made these pronouncements before a room full of radical abolitionists in Chatham, Ontario, Canada, who gathered secretly to plot the end of slavery in the United States. One man suggested Brown reconsider his plan to provoke an American slave insurrection, due to his concern that enslaved Americans might not rally behind an invading abolitionist force. According to the abolitionist, Brown laughed off the idea that enslaved Americans were "different from those of the West India island of San Domingo." Enslaved Saint Domingans rose when the opportunity presented itself; Brown knew that enslaved Americans would too. . . .

Throughout the first half of the nineteenth century abolitionists on both sides of the Atlantic remembered Toussaint Louverture. In public speeches, published illustrations, and printed texts they celebrated him as a Great Man, a former slave who compared favorably to Napoleon Bonaparte, George Washington, and the other Great Men of the Age of Revolutions. It was a resonant image that survived throughout the early national and antebellum periods in spite of the spread of plantation slavery across the American southwest and the triumph of white supremacy. Public memory of Louverture influenced the American abolitionist movement throughout the nineteenth century. But it had its most powerful impact in the 1850s, because it was then that so many abolitionists abandoned their hopes of the natural and peaceful demise of the institution of slavery. Indeed, the U.S. Congress's passage of both the Fugitive Slave Law and the Kansas and Nebraska Act, in conjunction with the Supreme Court's decision in the Dred Scott case, ensured both the expansion and perpetuation of the "peculiar institution." It was for this reason that African Americans and their radical white allies remembered Louverture. Frustrated with the nonviolent tactics of their movement, they interpreted the Great Man of Haiti as a militant bondman who willingly died and eagerly killed for freedom. Louverture was for them a symbol of the efficacy of violence in both ending slavery and redeeming black manhood. On the eve of the Civil War, radical abolitionists threatened to emulate Louverture by taking up arms in hopes of toppling the institution of slavery. Some, like John Brown, actually did.

STEPHANIE MCCURRY

From *Confederate Reckoning: Power and Politics in the Civil War South*

(2010)

The problem of slaves' political allegiance arose with the birth of the republic. At the very dawn of the nation Thomas Jefferson admitted that slavery destroyed slaves' love of country: that it turned slaves into enemies and nurtured traitors at the American breast. It was a harrowing thought, never more so than in war. The problem it names runs through the history of not one but two slaveholding republics in North America. . . .

In their judgment of what war would involve, Confederate founders and ordinary citizens counted slaves out. They could not have been more wrong. Among the four million people enslaved in the American South in 1861, most of them in Confederate territory, were many who moved with great determination to make their political loyalty count, prove the truth of Jefferson's fear that slavery destroyed slaves' love of country, made them into traitors and enemies, and nurtured allegiance to any country that countenanced their emancipation. . . . Slave men and women would of necessity take very different paths through war to emancipation, but each group would prove formidable enemies of slaveholders and their new national government. There would be a reckoning. . . .

Secessionists had no sooner begun trumpeting the advantages of slavery to a society at war than slaves registered their challenge to that flatly instrumental view. The slaves' war opened simultaneously with—some would have said predated—the Confederate war for independence. "Your late and [our] all time enemies," a group of South Carolina freedmen pointedly said of Confederates when talking to Union soldiers in October 1865, succinctly conveying slaves' different chronology of, and political stakes in, the American Civil War. . . .

It was on plantations that slaves' politics registered first. Take Gowrie, the rice plantation in the Georgia low country where the wartime battle between masters and slaves reached epic proportions. "The people," as the owner Charles Manigault called his slaves, had been actively resisting his government for a long time before Confederate independence. But with secession Manigault immediately recognized the new stakes: the destruction of slavery itself. "They have very generally got the idea of being emancipated when 'Lincon' comes in," he said in January 1861. With its ninety-eight enslaved men, women, and children, and one powerful white slaveholding family, the struggle on Gowrie was old but the political terrain was new.

Charles Manigault, the patriarch, owned two plantations and a small farm: Gowrie, on Argyle Island, eight miles upriver from Savannah; Silk Hope, a rice plantation on the Cooper River, forty miles inland from Charleston; and Marshlands, a farm seven miles from Charleston. The slaves on Gowrie were managed by Louis, Charles's oldest son; most had been moved there in 1844. Another son, Gabriel, managed Silk Hope, where about 126 slaves lived when the war began. . . .

Late January 1861 thus found South Carolina grappling with the consequences of its secession from the Union. . . . The war between the masters and slaves had entered a new phase, and even the masters acknowledged it.

As the new phase opened, Louis Manigault managed a few wins on Gowrie. He brought in the five runaways still out in January. But the correspondence makes it clear that the Manigault men regarded their slaves as formidable adversaries. They worried most about slaves' communication networks. Gabriel alerted his brother Louis to the scale of the problem. In November he had gone with a parcel of overseers and professional Negro hunters to search the woods near Gordon's brickyard, a refuge for runaways in the vicinity of Silk Hope. But notwithstanding their knowledge of the location of the hideout, they "saw no one at all." The experience taught him a few things: that he had to go armed and be prepared to shoot any Negro who attempted to resist or escape after being caught. Even more important, he had to observe "the utmost secrecy and caution" in making plans, "as it is extremely difficult to prevent the runaways from being informed of a search after them." Gabriel attributed the failure of his mission to "their intention having been communicated by house negroes." "No overseer or Planters should speak on such subjects before a small house boy or girl." Because rice planters did practically nothing without the aid of their slaves, that was a tall order. It always proved difficult for planters to make preparations without revealing themselves to the enemy. The Manigault men clearly saw themselves arrayed against not just particular runaways but the collectivity of slaves now imbued with emancipationist hopes and potentially powerful allies.

What ensued on Gowrie after Confederate independence can only be described as a war. Few, if any, Manigault slaves made it to Union lines before Savannah fell, despite the plantation's proximity to the coast and the Union fleet. Confederates fortified the city early in 1862, and Savannah River plantations were thereafter more secure than those elsewhere in the low country. Jack Savage, Big Hector, and the other Gowrie slaves thus had to wage their war with their master behind Confederate lines, on Confederate terrain, using strategies and networks built up under slavery. Nonetheless, from January 1861 until Christmas 1864, when the low country fell to Sherman's troops, Gowrie was in a state of barely suppressed insurrection and marronage. Developments on plantations like Gowrie threw a significant wrench into Confederate officials' plans to use slaves to national advantage, if only because they made planters extremely cautious about anything that disrupted routine or diminished surveillance. From early on, planters like Charles Manigault were under no illusions about their slaves' intentions.

In November 1861, after the "day of the gun shoot at Bay Point" (as low-country slaves called it) when Union troops took Port Royal and all of Savannah was packed to run upcountry, a number of Gowrie slaves made their move. Louis Manigault had no sooner finished congratulating himself that "the Negroes give no trouble" than Big George, Jack Savage, and at least two other slaves tried to reach Union lines by canoe. When a search of the plantation quarters revealed that another slave, Jack Savage's younger brother Ishmael, had stockpiled a "quantity of plantation guns and powder," Ishmael openly confessed "his intention to go with the Yankees." From that point on, Louis Manigault was, and knew himself to be, in a state of open warfare with at least a portion of his slaves.

What ensued on Gowrie was a relentless campaign to suppress revolt by removing "bad negroes"—identifying the ringleaders and rebels, sending them to the workhouse, selling them away, but most commonly moving them inland to Silk Hope, "sufficiently remote," they hoped, "from all excitement." Admitting that the slaves' heads had been "turned by recent military events," the Manigaults responded with an intensification of the usual violence. After the November 1861 escape attempt, they removed ten Gowrie slaves, three by force; caught in the act of running away, the slaves went to Silk Hope in handcuffs and soon thereafter to the Charleston workhouse, where they spent three months. The overseer, William Capers, advised Louis to sell Big George and send him to Cuba: "Let him go or you will lose him," he wrote, "he should not be among a gang of negroes." The logic of infection and quarantine was quite explicit. Louis thought about returning the remaining seven to Gowrie over Christmas (he resented the loss of their labor) but decided against it, worried that "Christmas is always a very bad time for Negroes . . . any year but far more so this." But on Gowrie, the ever widening circle of Manigault's quarantine testifies only to the increasing intensity of the struggle. By February 1862 Charles Manigault was convinced that planters had learned a valuable lesson: that "the Government of our Negroes" was far too slack and that many of the slaves had "got their heads more or less turned by recent military events and intercourse with bad Negroes." At the end of the month, Louis removed more slaves from Gowrie to Silk Hope, where he intended to keep them until the declaration of peace.

The identity of the twenty-three he removed is telling and a bit surprising, given the prominence of women among those identified as rebels and leaders. The original ten prime hands removed included the usual suspects but also "Jenny." And among the eighteen more removed in February 1862 were "Bess and her Infant," "Betty and infant," "Catherine," "Betty," "Amey" (Jack Savage's wife), "Louisa," "Tilla," "Polly," "Katrina," and "Kate." Fully ten of the eighteen and almost half of the total twentythree finally removed to Silk Hope were women, two with infants. Indeed, like a lot of planters, Louis Manigault believed that women house servants were the chief conduits of political intelligence: they are "often the first to have their minds polluted with evil thoughts," he observed. His father, Charles, never got over the fact that when the Yankees took Charleston, "every one of our house and yard Negroes immediately left us." Indeed, his sense of betrayal by women slaves was so strong that in April 1865 he was "looking for a white woman to do the drudgery . . . resolved never to have a Negro in our house again." Like planters everywhere the Manigaults were accustomed to viewing women as laborers—and recalcitrant ones at that. Almost a third of the slaves who ran away from Gowrie before and during the war were women, and so were four of the twelve judged so incorrigible as runaways that they suffered the ultimate Manigault punishment: sale. Women were regularly found among the runaway slaves who tried to survive in swamp settlements or maroon colonies before and during the war. Dissidence was not the preserve of men alone.

Discussion of slaves' politics almost always focuses on slave men, because in war it was the men whom state officials saw as a threat. But that was not how it looked to planters. None of the Manigaults ever made the mistake of underestimating the Gowrie women. Nor did they show any reluctance to deal with them roughly. Those who proved hard to break were sent to the workhouse or jail, where they were subjected to courses of professional whipping, just like the men. In 1863 William Capers found himself in a brutal struggle with Rose, the slave nurse of Louis's child, who not only resisted a whipping, she fought him, he said, "until she had not a rag of clothes on." "Before she is turned loose," Capers wrote his boss, "she will know she is a negro." Like planters all over the South, the men who managed Gowrie developed a distinct view of slave women's capacity for resistance and struggled throughout the war with the evidence of their betrayal and leadership in revolt.

The plantation was a school of political instruction during the Civil War, although it was the masters who struggled to learn the lessons slaves were teaching. Jack Savage did his part. Only weeks out of a stint in the workhouse and under constant surveillance, he made a successful break in February 1862, the very night he was to be removed to Silk Hope with his wife, Amey. Savage managed to stay out for "upwards of a year . . . in the dense Carolina swamp near the McPherson plantation in company with 'Charles Lucas' [another Gowrie slave] and other runaway Negroes." In this, obviously, he had help. Jack Savage emerged from the swamp after a year, half starved, his owner said. But he stayed only a month before he threatened to run again, saying "he had not come home to be killed up with work." Manigault, whose family had owned Savage since 1839, finally sold him in the fall of 1863, allegedly to a man in Columbus, Georgia, for the hefty sum of $1,800. Rumors persisted that Savage had foiled the sale and was still in the area. On Gowrie, marronage was an antislavery strategy used especially by slaves—men and women alike. . . .

. . . There was nothing particularly unusual about the way emancipation unfolded in the Confederate States of America. . . . In the Civil War South slaves moved tactically and by stages, men and women both, equal and active participants in the whole array of insurrectionary activities calculated to destroy the institution of slavery, their masters' power, and the prospects of the CSA as a proslavery nation. Emancipation there was indeed regionally uneven, temporally protracted, and linked to the Union army's invasion and federal emancipation policy. But to planters and slaves alike, it was unmistakably, too, the consequence of a massive rebellion of the Confederacy's slaves.

THOMAS C. HOLT

From *Black over White: Negro Political Leadership in South Carolina during Reconstruction*

(1977)

Most Reconstruction legislators in South Carolina—white as well as black—were political novices when they first arrived in Columbia. Democrats who had held state office before and during the war shunned any association with the new regime and left the field largely to less experienced men. The northern white Republicans were former army officers, teachers, and missionaries. In one sense or another they were men on the make and, as such, not likely to have left successful political offices in the North for an uncertain competition in the war-torn South. And of course the Negroes had had little opportunity to gain experience in partisan politics, irrespective of status, color, or nativity. In most northern states they had not been able to vote, much less run for office. They more than either of the other two groups would have to be recruited and learn the art of politics, either on the job or under the auspices of non-political institutions.

The opportunity to learn on the job was terribly abbreviated for most Negro legislators, because their tenures were short even by Reconstruction standards. It was possible to serve four full terms in the House during Reconstruction, but 61 percent of the 212 Negroes were one-term members. Only ten men served three terms or more, and of these only two, William M. Thomas of Colleton and Joseph D. Boston of Newberry, served for the entire period. Since but fifteen of these House members moved up to higher positions at the federal or state level, many must simply have failed to gain renomination or reelection. Of course, some may have chosen to take more financially rewarding local appointments. But while the brevity of their service may not be a comment on their capacities, it certainly indicates that for most of the period the House was composed of large numbers of freshmen legislators, unfamiliar with its routines and uncertain of their jobs. . . .

Such preliminary experiences were not possible at all for Negroes elected to the 1868 Constitutional Convention and the 1868–70 General Assembly. For them the Freedmen's Bureau, the army, and the missionary societies and churches were important factors in their personal and political development. Out of the total group of Negro elected officials serving between 1868 and 1876, at least seventy-three individuals, more than one-fourth, were affiliated with one or more of these institutions. Eighteen of these men served as state senators, congressmen, or executive officers. Furthermore, these organizations had greater impact on the group which served during the early years of Reconstruction than on those serving later in the decade. Of the early convention delegates and legislators, forty-three individuals—more than 37 percent of all Negroes who served in those years—gained their formative experiences through one or more of these institutions.

The churches, missionary societies, army, and Freedmen's Bureau did not set out purposefully to recruit blacks into politics or to prepare them for political leadership. But most northern leaders, white or black, came to South Carolina because of their employment in one or the other of these organizations and gained their earliest experiences and contact with the freedmen through this employment. Although their experiences were diverse, a common factor appears to have been the opportunity such employment allowed for the growth of an ethic of public service and the development of a system of public contacts which could later form a basis for a political constituency. The role of these institutions in the recruitment and development of the Negro leadership was more accidental than deliberate and generally passive rather than active. Indeed, in some cases institutional policies and orientations prevented Negro operatives from fully utilizing the political potential of their clients. Finally, it was in these organizations that the whites and Negroes who would form and lead the Republican party had their first and perhaps their most intimate professional interaction. Significantly, this interaction often resulted in conflicts, mutual hostilities, and suspicions which resemble those that developed in subsequent years.

The Freedmen's Bureau provides one example of the limitations, as well as the potential, of such institutional affiliations. Only fifteen of the Negro legislators were connected with the Bureau, either as agents or as teachers, but several of these men held major offices during Reconstruction. Congressman Robert C. De Large and state senators Stephen A. Swails, Henry E. Hayne, Charles Hayne, Henry J. Maxwell, Samuel E. Gaillard, and Benjamin F. Randolph all gained their initial experience in public service with the Bureau. Employment there was not an unmixed blessing, however, because of the anti-black, pro-planter biases and policies of many Bureau operatives. Always inadequately financed and understaffed, it had to rely on the active and reserve military service for the bulk of its employees. To many of these men this was simply another patronage job to which they were attracted for strictly pecuniary reasons. Not only were many of them not moved by abolitionist sentiments, but some were described as being "more pro-slavery than the rebels themselves. Doing justice seems to mean, to them, seeing that the blacks don't break a contract and compelling them to submit cheerfully if the whites do," complained one northern teacher. And while one scholar has found that most Bureau agents in South Carolina were fair and conscientious, his and other evidence indicates that the Bureau's posture was in most instances clearly nonpolitical.

This nonpolitical posture of the agency did not, of course, deter individual employees from using their positions to curry favor with a potential electorate. Yet only one black agent, Major Martin R. Delany, appears to have had either long enough service or broad enough authority to make effective use of his position. Delany was transferred to the Bureau services from his post as the first black commissioned officer of field grade in the 104th U.S. Colored Troop; though classified as a surgeon, he had worked mainly at recruiting Negro regiments. He served with the South Carolina Freedmen's Bureau from its inception in 1865 to its virtual termination in the summer of 1868. His position as a black abolitionist leader of international reputation probably provided him the security with which to go beyond the mandate of the bureaucracy and to be pretty much self-directed in his duties and goals. Delany was openly political in his activities, speeches, and advice to the freedmen. He developed labor agreements between freedmen and the planters which were broader in scope than those recommended by the Bureau. For a time he succeeded in establishing an independent cotton press which allowed black tenants an alternative market to the one manipulated by the Charleston cotton factors. All of these activities brought a storm of protests from planters, military authorities, and other Bureau personnel, all of which Delany survived and to some extent overcame. Yet Delany, the most effective black Bureau agent, was one of the few who never held elective office. He ran for lieutenant governor in 1874 on a fusion ticket with a former Confederate but lost badly, and he held a few minor appointive offices in Charleston County. But though he was a ubiquitous figure at Republican rallies and always an effective speaker, he was never an elected delegate to any of these rallies or conventions.

It is very doubtful that any other black Bureau agent could have operated as independently or effectively as Delany. Most were young and inexperienced men with no effective political contacts on either the local or the national level. Their activities were probably restricted by directives like the one received by Benjamin F. Randolph at the beginning of his brief service with the Bureau. He was instructed to visit the plantations in the parishes of St. Thomas, Christ Church, and St. James Santee and "induce the Freed people on the Plantations to labor faithfully, exhort them to be prompt and diligent in the discharge of their duties." . . .

Randolph was cautioned that his role was "merely advisory." Thus he was given responsibility without authority; he could offer advice, but little else....

... [T]he army may have been a more important contributor to the leadership pool than the Bureau. Twenty-four of the Negro legislators had records of military service, and two-thirds of them were either officers (2) or noncommissioned officers (12). Some of the states top political leaders in future years—William James Whipper, Benjamin A. Bosemon, Stephen A. Swails— were northern-born Negroes brought to the state by the army. Recognizing that the hopes for the future of black people were more sanguine in the South than in the North, they generally settled in or returned to the state in which they had served shortly after being mustered out. The native ex-soldiers gained other advantages from their military experiences. Some received their first formal education while in the army; others received an education in human relationships that was less formal but perhaps just as important to their personal and political development.

The wartime service of some of these men had been action-filled and heroic. Robert Smalls's exploit in abducting the Confederate steamer *Planter* was clearly the most daring of all, and it became the central part of his repertoire on the stump in later years. His audiences never seemed to tire of hearing how he conspired with his fellow slaves to stow away their families and boldly bluff their way past the Confederate batteries in Charleston harbor and into Union lines in 1862. Nor did Smalls tire of telling it. One cannot determine exactly how much this image of daring and shrewdness contributed to his more than two decades of practically unchallenged political supremacy in Beaufort County, but it surely endeared him to many voters and almost deified him with others....

But for most legislators military experience had bestowed benefits other than the glory of battle and the red badge of courage. The army had given many of the ex-slaves their first opportunity to command other men, in addition to bestowing the respect and confidence that might accrue to such positions. Sergeant Richard H. Humbert sought to apply his expertise for direct political advantage during the postwar years. After his election to the lower house in the summer of 1868, Humbert wrote to the newly inaugurated Governor Robert K. Scott to inform him that he had organized two militia companies in Darlington County, and that he planned to form several others in preparation for the presidential elections that fall. He saw his previous military experience as essential to this enterprise and requested a commission from the governor. Humbert did not mince words when he stated that "the organization of the militia will be of great benefit to the Republican Party in this district."...

The activities of the army and later the Freedmen's Bureau were followed closely by the northern missionary societies and churches, all of which had a significant impact on black legislators. Early in the spring of 1865 the Reverend Mansfield French described the relationship aptly: "The sword has hewn a way for the cross." Parson French was pointing exultantly to the great field for missionary activities opened up by the advancing Union armies. Even as he wrote, every major denomination worth its evangelical salt had workers in the field, to use their favorite metaphor, "harvesting the crop." French's denomination, the Northern Methodists, had been especially favored in securing the special passes and transportation that admitted them into the war zones; they followed, literally, in the track of the Union Army. . . .

. . . Lawyers make up the bulk of most American deliberative assemblies, but in South Carolina ministers and teachers constituted a significant proportion of the 194 Negro legislators whose postwar occupations can be determined. Of the total black delegation, 42 were ministers and 29 were teachers, most of whom had missionary affiliation and support. Of the ministers, 12 were affiliated with the Methodist Church, North; at least nine, possibly 11, were with the African Methodist Episcopal Church; six with the Baptist; two with the Presbyterian; and one with the Congregational church . Yet their particular institutional affiliation appears to have been less important to the political development of these men than the nature of the experience itself. Missionary and church experience apparently encouraged Negro leaders to develop their leadership abilities, and opened a wide range of public contacts on which a future political constituency could be built. . . .

Other Negro legislators were members of a large group of ministers affiliated with or supported by various religious denominations; some of them had been sent from the North to work among the freedmen. While most of these missionaries were primarily interested in converting the freedmen to their particular version of Christian faith, their day-to-day labors were as much secular as spiritual. Some of the ministers, like [Francis] Cardozo and [Hezekiah] Hunter, were also teachers; other missionaries, like [Jonathan J.] Wright, were not ministers at all but were hired exclusively to teach. . . .

To most northern Negroes, missionary work was difficult but inspiring. Some felt that their talents and skills could be better utilized in the South, and that they were needed here more than in the North. Cardozo was convinced that the moral education of southern youth was more important than an exclusively ministerial career. "If I can influence and shape the future life of a great number, if I can cause them to love and serve Christ, I could not aspire to a nobler work," he explained to George Whipple. "There are so many of these boys and girls that are just at that age when their whole future may be determined." This was surely a new and unaccustomed role for these black men, to be movers and shapers of their people's future. Cardozo had come to New Haven from England in 1864 after spending seven years training for the ministry, but his primary ambition was to teach in a normal school. After pastoring a church in New Haven from 1864 to 1865, he offered his services to the AMA in June, 1865. From the outset, he told Whipple, the prospect of eventually founding such a school was his reason for coming South. "It is the object for which I left all the superior advantages and privileges of the North and came South, it is the object for which I am willing to remain here and make this place my home." . . .

There is little evidence that any of the Negro missionaries had chosen this career as a purely political instrumentality. Nevertheless, it is evident that their normal daily activities—widespread contacts with freedmen, counseling them, advocacy in their behalf, the attempt to uplift them materially as well as spiritually—bestowed some political advantages. Such activities were clearly adaptable to political canvassing and organizing later on. Indeed, the allegiance that the church commanded might itself prove to be politically powerful on occasion. . . .

. . . The political effectiveness of ministers was probably related more to their personal orientation and the nature of their personal activities than to any denominational allegiance, with its implication of a ready-made constituency. The church provided an arena for leadership development and was likely to attract people who aspired—like the politicians—to be leaders of the flock. The daily activities of a minister were sometimes demanding, but were particularly suited to the development of a personal constituency. . . .

As with the Bureau and the army, however, there were also limitations to the political usefulness of the church. Conflicts among the various churches and between the missionaries show how competition could restrict the influence of all. It is clear, too, that despite their good intentions the missionaries were sometimes limited in their understanding of the freedmen and grossly manipulative in their dealings with them. Such attitudes may have accounted for some of the hostility that native blacks sometimes displayed toward Northerners, white and black—hostility which might affect their acceptance of these men as political leaders. . . .

. . . Obviously, such divisions and conflicts decreased the possibility that a given church membership or denomination could provide a potent or reliable political constituency in itself. . . .

Therefore, like the other postwar institutions from which black leaders were recruited, the churches were not available for automatic and unrestricted political uses. Like these others, the church provided a flexible and sustaining employment, an opportunity for developing leadership qualities, and a pattern of public contacts with a potential political constituency. . . .

. . . The political usefulness of the church per se may have been limited, but, like the Bureau and the army, it served an important function in the identification and development of native as well as northern political leaders. Indeed, all of these institutions encouraged new social vistas and presented new opportunities which enabled blacks to assume significant leadership roles among their people. The postwar institutions also provided a setting in which blacks interacted with and grew to know the people who would be their white political allies in the coming decade. Perhaps the fact that misunderstandings between these allies had sometimes limited the potential of black leaders to develop and serve their constituents was a lesson that would grow more significant during the critical years ahead.

TERA W. HUNTER

From *To 'Joy My Freedom:*
Southern Black Women's Lives
and Labors after the Civil War

(1997)

Nighttime leisure on Atlanta's Decatur Street was incomplete without a stop in the popular dance halls. Domestic workers were conspicuous among the dedicated dancers in the city who sought pleasure in the "jook joints"—night clubs devoted to dance and music. They contributed to the moment in American history in the 1910s when urban America "danced like mad." But public dance halls were among the most controversial popular amusement sites; they were often associated with crime, drinking, and illicit sex. "When Lugenia Burns Hope and Henry Hugh Proctor constructed "wholesome" recreational programs to compete with Decatur Street entertainment, they singled out public dancing as the most egregious activity contributing to the moral decay of the black race. White reformers and city officials were also strong critics of public dancing and dance halls. The contests that ensued between the opponents of public dancing and the resilient devotees reveal broader tensions and anxieties about race, class, and sexuality.

A central issue at stake was control over black women's and men's bodies. Employers insisted it was their prerogative to limit the physical exertions of black women's bodies to domestic service. Black middle-class reformers tried to mollify white animosity and racial prejudice, especially in the post-riot era, by insisting that blacks conform to the standards of a chaste, disciplined, servile labor force—on and off the job. African-American wage-earners, however, asserted their own right to recuperate their bodies from exploitation. Their defiance exhibited more than creative release. The substance, style, and form of black vernacular dancing were profound expressions of a cultural aesthetic grounded in an emerging musical form, the blues.

The blues represented the music of post-slavery generations that bore the signs of a historical consciousness, as seen in its borrowings from plebeian art forms such as work songs, spirituals, and field hollers, and in its use of such traditional African-American devices as polyrhythm, falsetto, improvisation, and call and response. The blues also reflected the changing conditions of black life in its marked departure from the past. The centrality of the singer's individual persona, the highly personalized subject matter of songs, the thematic shifts toward the material world and the pursuit of pleasure were all characteristic of an emergent modern ethos. The philosophical underpinnings of the blues informed and reflected broader African-American working-class self-understandings in the modern world. This is revealed most poignantly in the ongoing battles over dancing.

The popularity and controversy of black dance have a long history. Slaves incorporated dance into their everyday lives to diminish the harsh realities of forced labor. They turned events like corn-shuckings into festive occasions, performing dances that mimicked their routine labor activities such as pitching hay, hoisting cotton bales, and hoeing corn. They also danced for pleasure on Saturdays and holidays and to express sadness in funeral rituals. Slaveholders tolerated dancing, and even enjoyed watching it, as long as it pacified bound labor, enhanced morale, and stayed within the boundaries of acceptable behavior. But dancing sometimes threatened the social order, as when slaves ridiculed masters through song lyrics and dance movement, when slaves defied orders by organizing clandestine dances, or when group solidarity was transformed into insurrections.

Following emancipation, dancing continued to be an important expression of black culture and a source of conflict with white authorities. In the 1870s, African Americans in Atlanta danced in public places near the railroad depot downtown, in halls, bars, and in the privacy of their homes, much to the chagrin of the police. By the 1890s, public officials called for "Negro dance halls" to be outlawed because they were "crime breeders and a disgrace to the city." The ties between drinking, dancing, and the sex trade led moral reformers throughout urban America to advocate regulations or prohibitions against public dance halls as eager working-class patrons flocked to them in droves. . . .

Domestic laborers and others escaped from their workaday worries through dance in "jook joints" and settings also referred to as "dives." These were among the most important (re)creative sites of black working-class amusements at the turn of the century, where old and new cultural forms, exhibiting both African and European influences, were syncretized. The music and the movements invented there became cultural wares that traveled back and forth via migrants and itinerant entertainers moving from country to town to city and from South to North, forming common ties with people of African descent all over the nation. . . .

As working-class women and men danced the night away in dark, dingy, public, and, sometimes, shady places, the black elite danced to a different beat in more immaculate surroundings, demonstrating the class privileges they openly embraced. Their gala, private, and formal affairs purposely rejected the African influences conspicuous in the "snake hips" and "buzzard lope" in favor of more European-inspired polkas, waltzes, quadrilles, and pinafore lancers. A white journalist in the conventional mocking tone used to deride the "pompous ethics" of the black bourgeoisie described these elite dances as events where "etiquette and decorum are painfully emphatic . . . [and] a grotesque exaggeration of politeness, and affectation [run] riot." In less burlesque fashion, Perry Bradford recalled well-to-do black Atlantans doing setdancing. As a youth, around 1905, he had attended dancing school on Wednesday afternoons. For ten cents he received lessons in EuroAmerican dance and a glass of lemonade). This is not to say, however, that the black elite blindly aped white culture. Despite their statements to the contrary, black elites often incorporated distinctive African-American elements in their dancing, giving novel twists to quadrilles and polkas with improvised breaks, solos, and varied tempos.

It was not dancing per se that the black elites rejected; rather, as their own balls indicated, they disdained dancing of a certain type: they criticized the physical surroundings and social atmosphere of public dance halls, and they condemned the character of working-class body language. . . .

For middle-class blacks throughout the South dedicated to racial uplift, dance halls presented some of their greatest challenges to instilling the virtues that would lead the masses out of the spiral of so-called degradation. . . . The self-described elites persistently framed their pejorative descriptions of dancing and dance halls in the language of class. They disparaged people who made scanty livings through wage work as they sought to construct their own identity above the common fray. How one moved one's body constituted one's rank in society. . . .

Black vernacular dance also generated controversy because of its distinctive physical characteristics, which challenged Euro-American conceptions of proper bodily etiquette. African-American dance emphasized the movement of body parts, often asymmetrically and independent of one another, whereas Euro-American dance demanded rigidity to mitigate its amorous implications. Black dance generally exploded outward from the hips; it was performed from a crouching position with the knees flexed and the body bent at the waist, which allowed a fluidity of movement in a propulsive rhythmic fashion. The facial gestures, clapping, shouting, and yelling of provocative phrases reinforced the sense of the dancer's glee. A woman might shout, for example, "C'mon Papa grab me!" as she danced. . . .

Vernacular dance assumed these characteristics in large part from the inspiration of the music, reflecting the fact that in black culture, music and dance were virtually inseparable. African-American music is an engaging so-cial practice where audience and performers are expected to respond to one another with oral and physical gestures. The complex rhythmic patterns of voice and instruments prompt the desire to mimic the emotions they evoke through bodily movement such as foot stomping, hand clapping, and leaping around. African-American music acknowledges the power of the body to be moved.

The music that couples enjoyed in the dance halls was varied and fluid, typ-ically characterized as ragtime or "lowdown" blues, performed live before the advent of records and the radio. The blues, which arose toward the end of the nineteenth century, grew to maturity in dance halls, rent parties, and vaudeville theaters and became more formalized in the 1910s and 1920s. In some clubs, the blues were generated by a pianist, a fiddler, or by one or more individuals "pat-ting juba"—a practice dating back to slavery that involved clapping hands, snap-ping fingers, and patting limbs and armpits rhythmically. In other instances, a piano was the sole instrument driving the rhythmic beat. The dancers them-selves would shout and yell as they moved.

The blues and popular dance reflected a new aesthetic that was beginning to emerge in black cultural life. Like its ancestors, the blues inspired active move-ment rather than passive reception, and dance provided the mechanism for the audience to engage the performer in a ritual communal ceremony. Despite the connotations of its name, the blues was "good-time" music that generated a positive rhythmic impulse to divert and drive away depression and resignation among workers whose everyday lives were filled with adversity. The blues served as the call and dance as the response in a symbiotic performance in which ec-static bodily movements mocked the lyrics and instrumentation that signified pain and lamentation. . . .

Black women domestic workers were singled out in these attacks against danc-ing in public halls. The black bourgeoisie lamented the shame and disgrace that befell the entire race when workers failed to live up to the highest expectations of dutiful service. White employers opposed the violation of what they consid-ered their rightful claim to restrict black women's exertions to manual work. Dance halls were a menace, declared Proctor, because "the servant class tried to work all day and dance all night." He warned employers that household laborers would not perform well if they used their leisure unproductively-dancing in-stead of resting in preparation for the next day of work. Not missing the lesson of subservience proposed in Proctor's counsel, the white newspaper seized the opportunity to offer a reform: "Let the dance halls and places of low resort for the negro give way to schools for the domestic training of the race—schools for cooking and housework." It continued, "instead of dancing and carousing the night away, he (and especially she) will learn to become proficient in the task [for which] he is employed." . . .

Ironically, the castigating remarks made by middle-class blacks and whites had something in common with the meaning conferred by the working class itself. Both sides understood that dancing interfered with wage work, though clearly from antithetical perspectives. The elite saw dancing as a hindrance to the creation of a chaste, disciplined, submissive, and hard-driving labor force—the hallmarks of the Protestant work ethic. Workers saw it as a respite from the deadening sensation of long hours of poorly compensated labor—critical to the task of claiming one's life as one's own.

Black dance itself embodied a resistance to the confinement of the body solely to wage work. The transformation of physical gestures in black dance from slavery to freedom demonstrates the rejection of wage work as the only outlet for physical exertion. . . . Consumption, entertainment, and personal gratification were also vital to working-class livelihoods and essential to an emergent modern ethos or blues aesthetic.

Though dancing was seen as interfering with wage labor, the connotation of "work" in black culture had multiple meanings. Work not only meant physical labor, it also meant dancing. In addition, it meant engaging in sex. Dancing enabled a momentary escape from wage work, even as dance itself was considered work—of a different order. The ethics of drive, achievement, and perseverance took on a different meaning when removed from the context of wage relations. Dancers put a high value on mastery of technique and style, and they also competed with one another in jest and formal contests in which "working hard" became the criterion of a good performance. The proof could be found in the zeal and agility of body movements or in the perspiration that seeped through one's clothes. James P. Johnson, a pianist, suggested another way: "I saw many actually wear right through a pair of shoes in one night. They danced hard." . . .

Further evidence of black women creating an alternative ethos can be seen in their dress. Domestic workers wore uniforms to work, or other plain outfits that signified poverty and low social status. But when they put away the wash tubs or left the kitchen stoves and sinks, they shed the sartorial symbols of servility for garments that reflected personal style and self-worth. This new mode of dressing emerged in the transition from slavery to freedom. In the antebellum era, African American clothing was designed to be suitable for physical labor or to be reverent for religious worship. But when blacks became free people, their changing status could be seen in their adornment for leisure activities, unhindered by the requirements for either the practicality of work or the appropriate exhibition of piety for church. . . .

No doubt, women were increasingly wearing clothing that was less modest and restrictive than former fashions. But a few rare photographs of black women and men in dance halls show them "dressed up" in clothing typically associated with the middle class. They used this opportunity to construct their own notions of masculinity and femininity. The men donned hats, vests, jackets, and trousers held up by suspenders. The women wore flat-top or wide-brimmed hats, fulllength skirts that hugged the hips and flared out at the bottom, blouses with pouter pigeon bodices and sleeves that were puffed out near the shoulders and fitted around the forearms. The women gave careful attention to their dress style from their hairdos down to their underwear—the disclosure of pretty petticoats made of fine linen and crocheted edges was incorporated into certain dances such as the Funky Butt. Moreover, the emphasis and glorification of body parts such as the buttocks subverted dominant standards of beauty. Black women were endlessly caricatured as grotesque and ugly in popular representations in the dominant culture. But in dance halls, black beauty could be highlighted and celebrated. The anthropologist Zora Neale Hurston summed up one alternative criterion of good looks in a colorphobic society: "Even if she were as black as the hinges of hell the question was 'Can she jook?'"

. . . The blues and dance were developed with a fierce sense of irreverence—the will to be unencumbered by any artistic, moral, or social obligations, demands, or interests external to the community which blues and dance were created to serve. While the blues and vernacular dance forms borrowed from traditions of both Euro-America and AfroAmerica, they ultimately paid homage only to their own interpretations. Despite protests by white authorities or black reformers, black workers persisted in their public dancing to "lowdown" music, continually reaffirming the value that they placed on upholding a collective culture. . . .

The blues and dance marked a new departure in the assertion of individualism, as well as a redefinition of the conventional Western meaning of that term. Slavery had largely denied this concept among African Americans, but as free people they reclaimed the importance of the self without diminishing the imperatives of the collective. In slavery, blacks were denied ownership of their bodies. In freedom, they reclaimed their right to use their bodies beyond their needs for subsistence alone. But their assertion of their individual rights did not preclude the expression of a collective sensibility. Blues was personal music; dance was a reclamation of one's individual body; yet both allowed and demanded an integral link between the person and the group. Some of the salient characteristics of the blues and of black music and dance in general, such as polyrhythm, improvisation, and antiphony, reinforced this notion of the simultaneity of the individual and the collective—of various elements going their own way, but still being held together by their relationship to each other. . . .

The blues aesthetic is the key to understanding why African-American vernacular dance was such a contested terrain in Atlanta and the urban South and how it generated conflict over the black body. As an object of discipline and liberation, the body is a site where a society's ideas about race, class, gender, and sexuality are constructed to give the appearance of being mandates of nature while actually conforming to cultural ideologies. The body is the vehicle through which labor produces wealth, although the powerful usually resist acknowledging and rewarding the centrality of labor in the production of wealth. The importance of laboring bodies in the political economy is revealed, however, in the obsession of employers to repress and contain the autonomy of workers in order to reap the maximum benefits of their exertions. The mere sight of African Americans, especially domestic workers, deriving pleasure and expressing symbolic liberation in dance halls by posing alternative meanings of bodily exertion seemed threatening to employers. . . .

Yet despite the tirades of incensed critics, dancing did have the effect of renewal and recovery, even if on the workers' own terms. It reinvigorated them for the next day of work and enabled them to persevere. It helped to maintain the social order by providing an outlet for workers to release their tensions, to purge their bodies of their travails on the dance floor. Dancing hard, like laboring hard, was consistent with the work ethic of capitalism. Black working-class dance, like the blues, looked back to vernacular roots and forward to the modern world. Black women had played a pivotal role in asserting this expressive practice, replicating dimensions of the social order around them.

HANNAH ROSEN

From *Terror in the Heart of Freedom:*
Citizenship, Sexual Violence,
and the Meaning of Race in the
Post-Emancipation South

(2009)

Late in May 1871, eleven disguised men rode up to a cabin on a plantation in Gwinnett County, Georgia. After tying up their horses about 100 yards away, they approached the house yelling, "Open the door." A former slave named Hampton Mitchell was inside with his wife, his son-in-law, and his wife's father. Before anyone inside the house was able to get to the door, the men outside had forced it open. Mitchell recognized three of the intruders, despite their masks, as white men from the area. After grabbing Mitchell's gun, these men ordered him to kneel beside the cabin's threshold. "Hampton, is this your house?" the intruders demanded. "Yes, sir," Mitchell replied. They repeated the question, "Is this your house?" and Mitchell repeated his reply. Then, with Mitchell remaining on his knees in the doorway, guarded and intermittently struck by two of the men, others forced members of his family to come out of the house one at a time. First, they called to his son-in-law and "gave him a severe whipping." Next, they beat Mitchell's wife with their guns. And last, they ordered his father-in-law to come outside, beat him, sent him back into the house, and then called him out and beat him again. Finally, they ordered Mitchell to go inside and close the door.

Former slaves living throughout the South in the years following emancipation would have recognized this scene. The years of Reconstruction saw extensive campaigns of vigilante terror, making this one of the most violent eras in U.S. history. Bands of white men roamed the rural areas of the South, attacking African Americans in their homes. From groups known as "bush whackers" or "jayhawkers" during the war, to local vigilante gangs of returned Confederate soldiers just after southern surrender, to men in costume claiming membership in the Ku Klux Klan during congressional Reconstruction, intrusions in the night by companies of hostile white men were experienced by many and feared by most former slaves. Although freedpeople made distinctions between these groups, they also labeled them all "night riders" and perceived in all of them conspiracies of terror with similar overall practices, objectives, and effects. Former slaves understood attacks by any of these vigilante gangs as violent efforts to crush their newly won rights and to limit the meaning of their freedom.

Freedpeople went to great lengths to report night riders' actions to officials and to seek redress, leaving extensive documentation of violence in the records of the Freedmen's Bureau, of state and federal prosecutions of Klan members, and of an 1871 congressional investigation into Klan activity that conducted hearings in Washington, D.C., North Carolina, South Carolina, Georgia, Alabama, Mississippi, and Florida. These records reveal consistent patterns of violence across the South as well as local and individual variations. Forcing Hampton Mitchell to identify the site where he and his family were attacked as his domain—and thereby mocking his power within it—may have been unique. However, testimony suggests that night rider violence during Reconstruction often operated through similar kinds of performance. These attacks were not brief encounters. Assailants might have produced similar states of terror simply by shooting at freedpeople from a distance. Instead, akin to the practices of assailants during the Memphis Riot, intrusions in the night lasted at times for hours and involved prolonged interaction and dialogue between assailants and victims. Through this interaction and dialogue, through their words and actions, assailants staged meanings for race that contested the rights and identities claimed by African Americans in freedom. These scenes drew on gendered imagery to represent blackness as subordination and vice and whiteness as authority and power. In this way, assailants invented and communicated a fantasy post–Civil War world wherein white men's power approximated that before the war, thereby erasing military defeat and reclaiming the political privileges of whiteness bestowed by the system of slavery even on nonslaveholding white men. And the stage for acting out these scenes charged with race and gender symbolism was most often the homes of former slaves. . . .

. . . White gangs directed violence at agents of the radical social transformations that followed emancipation, particularly those people who most visibly exercised, promoted, or enabled the citizenship of former slaves. Common targets were black Union soldiers, black teachers, and black preachers. Freedpeople involved in labor disputes or able to purchase land coveted by local whites could also anticipate being the victims of a nighttime attack. Assailants undermined the independence of freedpeople by seizing their land or stealing their means of support and self-defense, such as weapons, food, cash, clothing, and other valuables. They interfered with collective action by preventing nighttime travel and assembly of African Americans. And when black men gained the right to vote in

1868, organized night riding moved directly onto the terrain of electoral politics, targeting Republican leaders, Union League members, black men suspected of voting Republican, and the families of these men. Night rider violence was, in fact, so seemingly instrumental and so explicitly targeted for political ends that it is difficult to resist reducing its meaning entirely to its apparent function. Yet this violence also took striking forms seemingly unrelated to function that were consistent across a wide region and over several years. Most saliently, this politically targeted and instrumental violence was suffused with imagery of gender and sexuality beyond anything necessitated by the explicit political ends of its assailants. . . .

The symbolic dimensions of night riding are demonstrated in the accounts of violence recorded by freedpeople wherein assailants are represented as positioning themselves in and forcing victims to enact certain gendered roles and identities that disavowed the changes in social relations resulting from emancipation. Night rider violence can be read as a type of performance, a theatrical form of political expression that drew on gender to resignify race and to undermine African American citizenship. The symbolism enacted through violence conveyed assailants' visions for a hierarchical racial order for southern society despite emancipation and formal legal equality. From the perspective of their creators, these brutal scenes righted a world turned upside down. In scenes such as the attack on Hampton Mitchell's house, white men acted out the impossibility of black men demonstrating the same kinds of mastery over their households, their property, and the security of their family members that white men claimed for themselves, a mastery powerfully linked to popular constructions of white manhood and of citizenship. In other scenes, particularly those involving sexual insult, assault, and rape, white men also rejected black women's potential identities as honorable wives and daughters, caring for and protected within their families. Instead, assailants' words and actions positioned black women and men outside proper domestic relationships and inside realms of the illicit, transgressive, and criminal.

This schema necessitated highly ironic patterns of displacement, wherein white men insisted on the criminal nature of black men and women while representing their own violent and criminal behavior as "justice," acting out the role of legitimate arbiters of an (extralegal) law governing the conduct of former slaves. This was most obvious in scenes involving sexual violence or its threat. Although black men were often attacked by white men for alleged illicit or violent sexual conduct with white women, it was black women who faced the greatest threat of rape from these same white men. Part of what allowed such obvious contradiction was the representation of blackness upon which night riders' violence rested and which it helped to produce—representations of extreme otherness that positioned black homes as marginal spaces outside the community of respectable citizens. This allowed white men to behave within these spaces in ways they could not have in their own homes or under the gaze of their neighbors and families and still maintain the posture of honorable men. The theatrical nature of the night riding—wearing disguises and taking on identities different from those embodied during the day—further sustained white men's self-representation as honorable even as they participated in dishonorable acts.

Though they rarely, if ever, communicated directly, throughout the South local vigilantes enacted similar scenes. What they did share was an antebellum culture that linked political and domestic authority in the idealized figure of a white citizen and patriarch whose exclusive claim to political power rested on fulfillment of his role and responsibilities in his household, as a supposedly benevolent lord providing for and protecting virtuous wives and chaste daughters. In other words, they shared assumptions about representing worthiness for public power through private roles.

It was these shared assumptions that shaped the patterns evident in night rider violence. White men contested both the domestic and political identities achieved in freedom by former slaves by attacking freedpeople in their homes. Through violence in domestic spaces, assailants staged gendered forms of racial difference and inequality that had profound political implications.

Assailants throughout the South were also loosely connected through an informal public sphere built around the circulation of rumor. White southerners apologizing for night rider attacks spread rumors of black criminality and illicit sexual activity meant to explain the necessity and legitimacy of vigilante violence. Fabrications traveling from assailants to their neighbors to local officials to state judges and then to other assailants, often then invoked in the midst of violent attacks, depicted a world of rampant black vice and violence. These rumors invested broad political significance in white men's local conflicts with their black neighbors, now evidence of the supposed widespread danger unleashed on southern society by emancipation, and authorized white men's violent reactions as part of a larger campaign to preserve order. These rumors also appear to have given shape to nighttime attacks, providing an overall script replicated and adapted to local conditions throughout the South. The shared script of night rider violence, passed from neighborhood to neighborhood, town to town, and county to county, helped establish an imagined community of white men and drew them into a world of vigilantism that restored meaning to and bestowed privilege on their whiteness. . . .

Night riding was not a new practice during Reconstruction. In most southern states during the antebellum years, governments authorized and conscripted groups of white men to enforce slave codes by patrolling roads and slave quarters after dark. These slave patrols were designed to prevent slaves' clandestine nighttime meetings, running away, and theft by limiting their mobility. Patrols also often intruded into slave cabins and inflicted physical punishment on their inhabitants, sometimes for specific infractions such as visiting with other slaves or holding a religious meeting on another plantation without a pass from an owner, at other times for no reason at all. The bands of white men attacking freedpeople in numerous regions of the Reconstruction-era South drew upon these practices of antebellum slave discipline and control. . . .

The domestic setting of most night rider violence also echoed past practice. Although schools and churches were occasional targets for arson and political meetings were regularly broken up, the vast majority of violent encounters occurred in and around homes. Rather than waylay victims on roads as they returned from church, meetings, or markets or confront them at work in a field, assailants preferred to catch freedpeople at home and most often in bed. Attacks almost always occurred after sundown and usually after midnight, when victims were asleep. White men in disguise surrounded houses and called for a particular resident to come out or banged on doors and forced their way inside. Assailants dragged victims outside in their bedclothes, destroyed or stole their furnishings and clothing, and burned or tore down their houses. They whipped and beat freedpeople, sometimes in front of family members or at other times a distance away from their house and its other occupants. These practices imitated the conduct of slave patrols but also differed crucially as well. The houses in which attacks occurred were not slave cabins within the household of a white planter but, rather, the independent homes of free African Americans. . . .

Former slaves living in homes independent of white control and constituting domestic identities that had, from the perspective of white southerners, been signifiers of the distinction between freemen and slaves represented a powerful challenge to antebellum constructions of racial difference. The meanings assailants expressed through violence asserted not only white dominance and black subordination but also racial difference via asymmetric access to patriarchal rights and privileges. Night riders' intrusion into African American homes asserted that claims to a secure and autonomous domestic space, a man's authority over his home and his dependents, and a woman's protected status when in the company of her family were exclusively privileges of whiteness. When Klansmen asked Hampton Mitchell, "Is this your house?" they were, in fact, contesting his claim to it and asserting to him and his family that freedom did not mean that former slaves could now claim the right to privacy, autonomy, and authority within the boundaries of a home. Instead, the intruders enacted their own authority to rule over the members of the Mitchell household. Thus, rather than autonomous realms of black patriarchal power, freedpeople's homes were to continue to be penetrable at any and all moments by the power of white men. Neither were private black domains to constitute independence and the rights of citizenship. When white men attacked freedpeople's private identities as husbands and wives, they were also attacking their worthiness for public rights as citizens. The fact that white opposition to African American freedom and citizenship was expressed through attacks on gender identities embedded within domestic domains shaped the kind of violence that freedpeople suffered.

PART 4

Jim Crow, Racial Politics, and Global White Supremacy

KIDADA E. WILLIAMS

When southern African Americans took their stand in the political sun as voters and officeholders during Reconstruction they helped produce some of the country's most democratic governments. This was especially the case in places like South Carolina, Louisiana, and Georgia, where their large populations gave them great political sway.

Centuries of bondage and antiblack racism instilled in African Americans visions of freedom that were always more radically inclusive than those of white Americans. For freedpeople, abolition was nothing if it did not include freedom. During the Civil War era African Americans stretched the parameters of American freedom beyond the end of chattel slavery. Aided by the Fourteenth and Fifteenth Amendments and exercising their authority in governance and the filing of lawsuits, African Americans across the country turned what had been the social rights of attending schools and visiting parks, cemeteries, and theaters into civil rights, "universal standards that [every citizen] could claim" with the federal backing of Congress.[1]

Aside from progressive members of Congress, most whites still believed that emancipation only meant the end of slavery not racial equality. Many chafed at African Americans running for and holding political office or having not just the temerity to demand access to public spaces of higher education and leisure but the financial means and intellectual capacities to do so.

Many white southerners used violence to restrict black people's freedoms. White citizens had the consent of state officials who gleefully joined them in doing what they could to preserve white supremacy. Just as whites were constructing blackness, they were constructing notions of whiteness and determining who could enjoy the full benefits of American freedom.

Under Jim Crow, white conservatives continued using violence to harness black southerners' aspirations for equality. White terrorists, operating either as private vigilantes or as agents of the state, killed thousands of African Americans both inside and outside the law. These killings increased exponentially in the 1880s.

White terrorists operated differently across the nation. Mobs and gangs snatched African Americans charged with crimes against whites from jails and courthouses. On some occasions, they advertised the killings in advance, and hundreds and thousands of whites of all ages and sexes attended and participated, watching staged events where blacks were tortured and killed. These spectacle killers often hung the victims' bodies in public places—from bridges and lampposts, in town squares and parks—to serve as a reminder to African Americans of the penalties they faced for threatening white supremacy.

Lynchers and their allies offered countless excuses for refusing to let the law take its course, many of which played on existing stereotypes of African Americans. Drawing on postemancipation caricatures of black men lusting after helpless and vulnerable white women, lynchers defended their actions as a defense of white womanhood, claiming to avenge white women and girls raped by black males. Ida B. Wells-Barnett's *Red Record* deconstructs the lies lynchers and their apologists told and the cover-ups they made of their own sexual crimes. The rape myth was frequently refuted by white women's assertions, by the lynchings of black women, and by white men's conspicuous silence with regard to and denial of their rapes of black women and girls as a weapon of white supremacy, as the excerpt from Crystal N. Feimster's *Southern Horrors* shows.

African Americans fought back. They tried to repulse attacking whites by shooting back. The excerpt from Robin D. G. Kelley's "We Are Not What We Seem" highlights the diversity of black people's resistance to the antiblack racism they faced in everyday life.

Conservatives in the judiciary withdrew support for African Americans' expansive vision of civil rights. In a series of legal cases, the Supreme Court decided that southern states could handle issues relating to violence and discrimination against blacks. It even overturned the Civil Rights Act of 1875, which prohibited racial discrimination in parks and railroads. With the court's consent individuals, businesses, and governments at all levels expanded existing practices of denying African Americans service or access. African Americans fought the new wave of restrictions to their civil rights with little success. *Plessy v. Ferguson* (1896) allowed white supremacists at all levels of government to segregate in all areas of life—schools, parks, medicine, housing.

With the Supreme Court's consent, whites insisted on segregated elementary and secondary schools. Seeking to maintain white supremacy and to legitimize ideas that blacks neither wanted nor needed higher education, lawmakers and their constituents underfunded schools blacks attended, violating even the *Plessy* doctrine of "separate but equal."

Although rigid legal segregation was pervasive throughout the South, it was not solely a southern phenomenon. It was national, and it was global. White supremacists established similar racial caste systems in other parts of the country and abroad. The excerpt from W. E. B. Du Bois's *Darkwater* and the essay by Benjamin Foldy capture the global dimensions of white supremacy and black resistance.

Most of the effects of Jim Crow in the United States were decidedly negative. But culturally, the caste created sanctuaries where African Americans could escape the horrors of antiblackness in everyday life. Congregating in their own institutions and establishments, blacks could avoid racial violence and practice their culture outside the presence of whites. African Americans opened and supported schools to educate pupils of all ages and instill them with a respect for their culture and history and a commitment to racial advancement. Entrepreneurs living in cities opened businesses and financial institutions to provide desperately needed services denied under Jim Crow. These men and women hired people from the black community, and the community in turn patronized their establishments in a style of economic and cultural black nationalism promoted by Booker T. Washington and Marcus Garvey, whose "Declaration of the Rights of the Negro People of the World" is included here.

Prosperous blacks tried presenting themselves to the world as respectable and deserving of fair treatment. They also participated in "uplift," providing what they thought was insight and assistance to help the struggling masses advance. African Americans from the lower classes had their own values and sense of the good life and worked to preserve it.

Blacks seethed under Jim Crow not because they wanted to be in physical proximity to whites but because they had been promised equal treatment during Reconstruction and their dreams of equality had been dismissed and deferred by the blunt fists of segregation and disfranchisement. Horrified by the racial caste and the violence used to maintain it, African Americans across the nation intensified their efforts to organize their communities to topple Jim Crow.

Ida B. Wells-Barnett was part of a critical contingent of African American reformers who resisted Jim Crow. Through her investigative journalism, Wells wielded a mighty pen, exposing the lies lynchers and their apologists told. Joining her were countless black journalists, artists, and public figures, such as Booker T. Washington, Mary Church Terrell, and W. E .B. Du Bois, who would constitute the New Negro Movement. Claude McKay, whose protest poem "If We Must Die" is included in this section, reflects the fighting spirit as African Americans from all walks of life were mobilizing.

Blacks wouldn't wage this battle on their own. They had numerous allies among white liberals. Abel Meeropol responded to a macabre photograph of lynching by penning the poem "Strange Fruit," referencing the black bodies hanging from trees that dotted the southern landscape. Blues songstress Billie Holiday turned it into one of the growing movement's first protest songs.

At the front of the movement would be activists like Asa Philip Randolph, who in 1941 called upon black Americans to march on Washington to protest segregation in the armed forces and racial discrimination in federal hiring for the defense industries. As nearly one hundred thousand African Americans indicated their willingness to answer Randolph's call, President Franklin D. Roosevelt passed Executive Order 8802, banning discrimination in the defense industries. Activists in the civil rights and Black Power movements would come to appreciate the benefits of demanding reform.

NOTE

1. Laura F. Edwards, *A Legal History of the Civil War and Reconstruction: A Nation of Rights* (New York: Cambridge University Press, 2015), 131.

IDA B. WELLS-BARNETT

From *A Red Record*

(1895)

1. The Case Stated

The student of American sociology will find the year 1894 marked by a pronounced awakening of the public conscience to a system of anarchy and outlawry which had grown during a series of ten years to be so common, that scenes of unusual brutality failed to have any visible effect upon the humane sentiments of the people of our land.

Beginning with the emancipation of the Negro, the inevitable result of unbridled power exercised for two and a half centuries, by the white man over the Negro, began to show itself in acts of conscienceless outlawry. During the slave regime, the Southern white man owned the Negro body and soul. It was to his interest to dwarf the soul and preserve the body. Vested with unlimited power over his slave, to subject him to any and all kinds of physical punishment, the white man was still restrained from such punishment as tended to injure the slave by abating his physical powers and thereby reducing his financial worth. While slaves were scourged mercilessly, and in countless cases inhumanly treated in other respects, still the white owner rarely permitted his anger to go so far as to take a life, which would entail upon him a loss of several hundred dollars. The slave was rarely killed, he was too valuable; it was easier and quite as effective, for discipline or revenge, to sell him "Down South."

But Emancipation came and the vested interests of the white man in the Negro's body were lost. The white man had no right to scourge the emancipated Negro, still less has he a right to kill him. But the Southern white people had been educated so long in that school of practice, in which might makes right, that they disdained to draw strict lines of action in dealing with the Negro. In slave times the Negro was kept subservient and submissive by the frequency and severity of the scourging, but, with freedom, a new system of intimidation came into vogue; the Negro was not only whipped and scourged; he was killed.

Not all nor nearly all of the murders done by white men, during the past thirty years in the South, have come to light, but the statistics as gathered and preserved by white men, and which have not been questioned, show that during these years more than ten thousand Negroes have been killed in cold blood, without the formality of judicial trial and legal execution. And yet, as evidence of the absolute impunity with which the white man dares to kill a Negro, the same record shows that during all these years, and for all these murders only three white men have been tried, convicted, and executed. As no white man has been lynched for the murder of colored people, these three executions are the only instances of the death penalty being visited upon white men for murdering Negroes. . . .

The first excuse given to the civilized world for the murder of unoffending Negroes was the necessity of the white man to repress and stamp out alleged "race riots." For years immediately succeeding the war there was an appalling slaughter of colored people, and the wires usually conveyed to northern people and the world the intelligence, first, that an insurrection was being planned by Negroes, which, a few hours later, would prove to have been vigorously resisted by white men, and controlled with a resulting loss of several killed and wounded. It was always a remarkable feature in these insurrections and riots that only Negroes were killed during the rioting, and that all the white men escaped unharmed.

From 1865 to 1872, hundreds of colored men and women were mercilessly murdered and the almost invariable reason assigned was that they met their death by being alleged participants in an insurrection or riot. But this story at last wore itself out. No insurrection ever materialized; no Negro rioter was ever apprehended and proven guilty, and no dynamite ever recorded the black man's protest against oppression and wrong. It was too much to ask thoughtful people to believe this transparent story, and the southern white people at last made up their minds that some other excuse must be had.

Then came the second excuse, which had its birth during the turbulent times of reconstruction. By an amendment to the Constitution the Negro was given the right of franchise, and, theoretically at least, his ballot became his invaluable emblem of citizenship. In a government "of the people, for the people, and by the people," the Negro's vote became an important factor in all matters of state and national politics. But this did not last long. The southern white man would not consider that the Negro had any right which a white man was bound to respect, and the idea of a republican form of government in the southern states grew into general contempt. It was maintained that "This is a white man's government," and regardless of numbers the white man should rule. . . .

The white man's victory soon became complete by fraud, violence, intimidation and murder. The franchise vouchsafed to the Negro grew to be a "barren ideality," and regardless of numbers, the colored people found themselves voiceless in the councils of those whose duty it was to rule. With no longer the fear of "Negro Domination" before their eyes, the white man's second excuse became valueless. With the Southern governments all subverted and the Negro actually eliminated from all participation in state and national elections, there could be no longer an excuse for killing Negroes to prevent "Negro Domination."

Brutality still continued; Negroes were whipped, scourged, exiled, shot and hung whenever and wherever it pleased the white man so to treat them, and as the civilized world with increasing persistency held the white people of the South to account for its outlawry, the murderers invented the third excuse—that Negroes had to be killed to avenge their assaults upon women. There could be framed no possible excuse more harmful to the Negro and more unanswerable if true in its sufficiency for the white man.

Humanity abhors the assailant of womanhood, and this charge upon the Negro at once placed him beyond the pale of human sympathy. With such unanimity, earnestness and apparent candor was this charge made and reiterated that the world has accepted the story that the Negro is a monster which the Southern white man has painted him. And today, the Christian world feels, that while lynching is a crime, and lawlessness and anarchy the certain precursors of a nation's fall, it can not by word or deed, extend sympathy or help to a race of outlaws, who might mistake their plea for justice and deem it an excuse for their continued wrongs. . . .

If the Southern people in defense of their lawlessness, would tell the truth and admit that colored men and women are lynched for almost any offense, from murder to a misdemeanor, there would not now be the necessity for this defense. But when they intentionally, maliciously and constantly belie the record and bolster up these falsehoods by the words of legislators, preachers, governors and bishops, then the Negro must give to the world his side of the awful story.

A word as to the charge itself. In considering the third reason assigned by the Southern white people for the butchery of blacks, the question must be asked, what the white man means when he charges the black man with rape. Does he mean the crime which the statutes of the civilized states describe as such? Not by any means. With the Southern white man, any misalliance existing between a white woman and a colored man is a sufficient foundation for the charge of rape. The Southern white man says that it is impossible for a voluntary alliance to exist between a white woman and a colored man, and therefore, the fact of an alliance is a proof of force. In numerous instances where colored men have been lynched on the charge of rape, it was positively known at the time of lynching, and indisputably proven after the victim's death, that the relationship sustained between the man and woman was voluntary and clandestine, and that in no court of law could even the charge of assault have been successfully maintained.

It was for the assertion of this fact, in the defense of her own race, that the writer hereof became an exile; her property destroyed and her return to her home forbidden under penalty of death, for writing the following editorial which was printed in her paper, the *Free Speech*, in Memphis, Tenn., May 21,1892:

> Eight Negroes lynched since last issue of the *Free Speech* one at Little Rock, Ark., last Saturday morning where the citizens broke(?) into the penitentiary and got their man; three near Anniston, Ala., one near New Orleans; and three at Clarksville, Ga., the last three for killing a white man, and five on the same old racket—the new alarm about raping white women. The same programme of hanging, then shooting bullets into the lifeless bodies was carried out to the letter. Nobody in this section of the country believes the old threadbare lie that Negro men rape white women. If Southern white men are not careful, they will overreach themselves and public sentiment will have a reaction; a conclusion will then be reached which will be very damaging to the moral reputation of their women.

But threats cannot suppress the truth, and while the Negro suffers the soul deformity, resultant from two and a half centuries of slavery, he is no more guilty of this vilest of all vile charges than the white man who would blacken his name.

During all the years of slavery, no such charge was ever made, not even during the dark days of the rebellion, when the white man, following the fortunes of war went to do battle for the maintenance of slavery. While the master was away fighting to forge the fetters upon the slave, he left his wife and children with no protectors save the Negroes themselves. And yet during those years of trust and peril, no Negro proved recreant to his trust and no white man returned to a home that had been dispoiled.

. . . It must appear strange indeed, to every thoughtful and candid man, that more than a quarter of a century elapsed before the Negro began to show signs of such infamous degeneration.

. . . It is not the purpose of this defense to say one word against the white women of the South. Such need not be said, but it is their misfortune that the chivalrous white men of that section, in order to escape the deserved execration of the civilized world, should shield themselves by their cowardly and infamously false excuse, and call into question that very honor about which their distinguished priestly apologist claims they are most sensitive. To justify their own barbarism they assume a chivalry which they do not possess. True chivalry respects all womanhood, and no one who reads the record, as it is written in the faces of the million mulattoes in the South, will for a minute conceive that the southern white man had a very chivalrous regard for the honor due the women of his own race or respect for the womanhood which circumstances placed in his power. That chivalry which is "most sensitive concerning the honor of women" can hope for but little respect from the civilized world, when it confines itself entirely to the women who happen to be white. Virtue knows no color line, and the chivalry which depends upon complexion of skin and texture of hair can command no honest respect.

From *Plessy v. Ferguson*

(May 18, 1896)

The statute of Louisiana, acts of 1890, c. 111, requiring railway companies carrying passengers in their coaches in that State, to provide equal, but separate, accommodations for the white and colored races, by providing two or more passenger coaches for each passenger train, or by dividing the passenger coaches by a partition so as to secure separate accommodations; and providing that no person shall be permitted to occupy seats in coaches other than the ones assigned to them, on account of the race they belong to; and requiring the officer of the passenger train to assign each passenger to the coach or compartment assigned for the race to which he or she belong; and imposing fines or imprisonment upon passengers insisting on going into a coach or compartment other than the one set aside for the race to which he or she belongs; and conferring upon officers of the train power to refuse to carry on the train passengers refusing to occupy the coach or compartment assigned to them, and exempting the railway company from liability for such refusal, are not in conflict with the provisions either of the Thirteenth Amendment or of the Fourteenth Amendment to the Constitution of the United States.

This was a petition for writs of prohibition and certiorari, originally filed in the Supreme Court of the State by Plessy, the plaintiff in error, against the Hon. John H. Ferguson, judge of the criminal District Court for the parish of Orleans, and setting forth in substance the following facts:

That petitioner was a citizen of the United States and a resident of the State of Louisiana, of mixed descent, in the proportion of seven eighths Caucasian and one eighth African blood; that the mixture of colored blood was not discernible in him, and that he was entitled to every recognition, right, privilege and immunity secured to the citizens of the United States of the white race by its Constitution and laws; that, on June 7, 1892, he engaged and paid for a first class passage on the East Louisiana Railway from New Orleans to Covington, in the same State, and thereupon entered a passenger train, and took possession of a vacant seat in a coach where passengers of the white race were accommodated; that such railroad company was incorporated by the laws of Louisiana as a common carrier, and was not authorized to distinguish between citizens according to their race. But, notwithstanding this, petitioner was required by the conductor, under penalty of ejection from said train and imprisonment, to vacate said coach and occupy another seat in a coach assigned by said company for persons not of the white race, and for no other reason than that petitioner was of the colored race; that, upon petitioner's refusal to comply with such order, he was, with the aid of a police officer, forcibly ejected from said coach and hurried off to and imprisoned in the parish jail of New Orleans, and there held to answer a charge made by such officer to the effect that he was guilty of having criminally violated an act of the General Assembly of the State, approved July 10, 1890, in such case made and provided.

That petitioner was subsequently brought before the recorder of the city for preliminary examination and committed for trial to the criminal District Court for the parish of Orleans, where an information was filed against him in the matter above set forth, for a violation of the above act, which act the petitioner affirmed to be null and void, because in conflict with the Constitution of the United States. . . .

MR. JUSTICE BROWN, after stating the case, delivered the opinion of the court.

This case turns upon the constitutionality of an act of the General Assembly of the State of Louisiana, passed in 1890, providing for separate railway carriages for the white and colored races. . . .

The constitutionality of this act is attacked upon the ground that it conflicts both with the Thirteenth Amendment of the Constitution, abolishing slavery, and the Fourteenth Amendment, which prohibits certain restrictive legislation on the part of the States.

1. That it does not conflict with the Thirteenth Amendment, which abolished slavery and involuntary servitude, except as a punishment for crime, is too clear for argument. Slavery implies involuntary servitude — a state of bondage; the ownership of mankind as a chattel, or at least the control of the labor and services of one man for the benefit of another, and the absence of a legal right to the disposal of his own person, property and services. . . .

A statute which implies merely a legal distinction between the white and colored races—a distinction which is founded in the color of the two races and which must always exist so long as white men are distinguished from the other race by color—has no tendency to destroy the legal equality of the two races, or reestablish a state of involuntary servitude. . . .

2. By the Fourteenth Amendment, all persons born or naturalized in the United States and subject to the jurisdiction thereof are made citizens of the United States and of the State wherein they reside, and the States are forbidden from

making or enforcing any law which shall abridge the privileges or immunities of citizens of the United States, or shall deprive any person of life, liberty, or property without due process of law, or deny to any person within their jurisdiction the equal protection of the laws. . . .

The object of the amendment was undoubtedly to enforce the absolute equality of the two races before the law, but, in the nature of things, it could not have been intended to abolish distinctions based upon color, or to enforce social, as distinguished from political, equality, or a commingling of the two races upon terms unsatisfactory to either. Laws permitting, and even requiring, their separation in places where they are liable to be brought into contact do not necessarily imply the inferiority of either race to the other, and have been generally, if not universally, recognized as within the competency of the state legislatures in the exercise of their police power. The most common instance of this is connected with the establishment of separate schools for white and colored children, which has been held to be a valid exercise of the legislative power even by courts of States where the political rights of the colored race have been longest and most earnestly enforced. . . .

. . . [W]e think the enforced separation of the races, as applied to the internal commerce of the State, neither abridges the privileges or immunities of the colored man, deprives him of his property without due process of law, nor denies him the equal protection of the laws within the meaning of the Fourteenth Amendment. . . .

We consider the underlying fallacy of the plaintiff's argument to consist in the assumption that the enforced separation of the two races stamps the colored race with a badge of inferiority. If this be so, it is not by reason of anything found in the act, but solely because the colored race chooses to put that construction upon it. The argument necessarily assumes that if, as has been more than once the case and is not unlikely to be so again, the colored race should become the dominant power in the state legislature, and should enact a law in precisely similar terms, it would thereby relegate the white race to an inferior position. We imagine that the white race, at least, would not acquiesce in this assumption. The argument also assumes that social prejudices may be overcome by legislation, and that equal rights cannot be secured to the negro except by an enforced commingling of the two races. We cannot accept this proposition. If the two races are to meet upon terms of social equality, it must be the result of natural affinities, a mutual appreciation of each other's merits, and a voluntary consent of individuals. . . .

Legislation is powerless to eradicate racial instincts or to abolish distinctions based upon physical differences, and the attempt to do so can only result in accentuating the difficulties of the present situation. If the civil and political rights of both races be equal, one cannot be inferior to the other civilly or politically. If one race be inferior to the other socially, the Constitution of the United States cannot put them upon the same plane. . . .

The judgment of the court below is, therefore, Affirmed.

MR. JUSTICE HARLAN, dissenting.

. . . [W]e have before us a state enactment that compels, under penalties, the separation of the two races in railroad passenger coaches, and makes it a crime for a citizen of either race to enter a coach that has been assigned to citizens of the other race.

Thus, the State regulates the use of a public highway by citizens of the United States solely upon the basis of race.

However apparent the injustice of such legislation may be, we have only to consider whether it is consistent with the Constitution of the United States. . . .

In respect of civil rights common to all citizens, the Constitution of the United States does not, I think, permit any public authority to know the race of those entitled to be protected in the enjoyment of such rights. Every true man has pride of race, and, under appropriate circumstances, when the rights of others, his equals before the law, are not to be affected, it is his privilege to express such pride and to take such action based upon it as to him seems proper. But I deny that any legislative body or judicial tribunal may have regard to the race of citizens when the civil rights of those citizens are involved. Indeed, such legislation as that here in question is inconsistent not only with that equality of rights which pertains to citizenship, National and State, but with the personal liberty enjoyed by everyone within the United States. . . .

It was said in argument that the statute of Louisiana does not discriminate against either race, but prescribes a rule applicable alike to white and colored citizens. But this argument does not meet the difficulty. Everyone knows that the statute in question had its origin in the purpose not so much to exclude white persons from railroad cars occupied by blacks as to exclude colored people from coaches occupied by or assigned to white persons. Railroad corporations of Louisiana did not make discrimination among whites in the matter of accommodation for travelers. The thing to accomplish was, under the guise of giving equal accommodation for whites and blacks, to compel the latter to keep to themselves while traveling in railroad passenger coaches. No one would be so wanting in candor as to assert the contrary. The fundamental objection, therefore, to the statute is that it interferes with the personal freedom of citizens. . . .

It is one thing for railroad carriers to furnish, or to be required by law to furnish, equal accommodations for all whom they are under a legal duty to carry. It is quite another thing for government to forbid citizens of the white and black races from traveling in the same public conveyance, and to punish officers of railroad companies for permitting persons of the two races to occupy the same passenger coach. If a State can prescribe, as a rule of civil conduct, that whites and blacks shall not travel as passengers in the same railroad coach, why may it not so regulate the use of the streets of its cities and towns as to compel white citizens to keep on one side of a street and black citizens to keep on the other? Why may it not, upon like grounds, punish whites and blacks who ride together in streetcars or in open vehicles on a public road or street? Why may it not require sheriffs to assign whites to one side of a courtroom and blacks to the other? And why may it not also prohibit the commingling of the two races in the galleries of legislative halls or in public assemblages convened for the consideration of the political questions of the day? . . .

The white race deems itself to be the dominant race in this country. And so it is in prestige, in achievements, in education, in wealth and in power. So, I doubt not, it will continue to be for all time if it remains true to its great heritage and holds fast to the principles of constitutional liberty. But in view of the Constitution, in the eye of the law, there is in this country no superior, dominant, ruling class of citizens. There is no caste here. Our Constitution is color-blind, and neither knows nor tolerates classes among citizens. In respect of civil rights, all citizens are equal before the law. The humblest is the peer of the most powerful. The law regards man as man, and takes no account of his surroundings or of his color when his civil rights as guaranteed by the supreme law of the land are involved. It is therefore to be regretted that this high tribunal, the final expositor of the fundamental law of the land, has reached the conclusion that it is competent for a State to regulate the enjoyment by citizens of their civil rights solely upon the basis of race.

In my opinion, the judgment this day rendered will, in time, prove to be quite as pernicious as the decision made by this tribunal in the Dred Scott Case. . . .

. . . Sixty millions of whites are in no danger from the presence here of eight millions of blacks. The destinies of the two races in this country are indissolubly linked together, and the interests of both require that the common government of all shall not permit the seeds of race hate to be planted under the sanction of law. What can more certainly arouse race hate, what more certainly create and perpetuate a feeling of distrust between these races, than state enactments which, in fact, proceed on the ground that colored citizens are so inferior and degraded that they cannot be allowed to sit in public coaches occupied by white citizens. That, as all will admit, is the real meaning of such legislation as was enacted in Louisiana. . . .

The arbitrary separation of citizens on the basis of race while they are on a public highway is a badge of servitude wholly inconsistent with the civil freedom and the equality before the law established by the Constitution. It cannot be justified upon any legal grounds. . . .

I am of opinion that the statute of Louisiana is inconsistent with the personal liberty of citizens, white and black, in that State, and hostile to both the spirit and letter of the Constitution of the United States. If laws of like character should be enacted in the several States of the Union, the effect would be in the highest degree mischievous. Slavery, as an institution tolerated by law would, it is true, have disappeared from our country, but there would remain a power in the States, by sinister legislation, to interfere with the full enjoyment of the blessings of freedom to regulate civil rights, common to all citizens, upon the basis of race, and to place in a condition of legal inferiority a large body of American citizens now constituting a part of the political community called the People of the United States, for whom and by whom, through representatives, our government is administered. Such a system is inconsistent with the guarantee given by the Constitution to each State of a republican form of government, and may be stricken down by Congressional action, or by the courts in the discharge of their solemn duty to maintain the supreme law of the land, anything in the constitution or laws of any State to the contrary notwithstanding.

For the reasons stated, I am constrained to withhold my assent from the opinion and judgment of the majority.

CLAUDE MCKAY

If We Must Die

(1919)

If we must die, let it not be like hogs
Hunted and penned in an inglorious spot,
While round us bark the mad and hungry dogs,
Making their mock at our accursed lot.
If we must die, O let us nobly die,
So that our precious blood may not be shed
In vain; then even the monsters we defy
Shall be constrained to honor us though dead!
O kinsmen! we must meet the common foe!
Though far outnumbered let us show us brave,
And for their thousand blows deal one death-blow!
What though before us lies the open grave?
Like men we'll face the murderous, cowardly pack,
Pressed to the wall, dying, but fighting back!

From "Declaration of the Rights of the Negro Peoples of the World: The Principles of the Universal Negro Improvement Association"

(1920)

Preamble

Be It Resolved, That the Negro people of the world, through their chosen representatives in convention assembled in Liberty Hall, in the City of New York and United States of America, from August 1 to August 31, in the year of Our Lord one thousand nine hundred and twenty, protest against the wrongs and injustices they are suffering at the hands of their white brethren, and state what they deem their fair and just rights, as well as the treatment they propose to demand of all men in the future.

We complain:

1. That nowhere in the world, with few exceptions, are black men accorded equal treatment with white men, although in the same situation and circumstances, but, on the contrary, are discriminated against and denied the common rights due to human beings for no other reason than their race and color.

   We are not willingly accepted as guests in the public hotels and inns of the world for no other reason than our race and color.

2. In certain parts of the United States of America our race is denied the right of public trial accorded to other races when accused of crime, but are lynched and burned by mobs, and such brutal and inhuman treatment is even practiced upon our women.

3. That European nations have parcelled out among them and taken possession of nearly all of the continent of Africa, and the natives are compelled to surrender their lands to aliens and are treated in most instances like slaves.

4. In the southern portion of the United States of America, although citi-

zens under the Federal Constitution, and in some States almost equal to the whites in population and are qualified land owners and taxpayers, we are, nevertheless, denied all voice in the making and administration of the laws and are taxed without representation by the State governments, and at the same time compelled to do military service in defense of the country.

5. On the public conveyances and common carriers in the southern portion of the United States we are jim-crowed and compelled to accept separate and inferior accommodations and made to pay the same fare charged for first-class accommodations, and our families are often humiliated and insulted by drunken white men who habitually pass through the jim-crow cars going to the smoking car.

6. The physicians of our race are denied the right to attend their patients while in the public hospitals of the cities and States where they reside in certain parts of the United States.

   Our children are forced to attend inferior separate schools for shorter terms than white children, and the public school funds are unequally divided between the white and colored schools.

7. We are discriminated against and denied an equal chance to earn wages for the support of our families, and in many instances are refused admission into labor unions and nearly everywhere are paid smaller wages than white men.

8. In the Civil Service and departmental offices we are everywhere discriminated against and made to feel that to be a black man in Europe, America and the West Indies is equivalent to being an outcast and a leper among the races of men, no matter what the character attainments of the black men may be.

9. In the British and other West Indian islands and colonies Negroes are secretly and cunningly discriminated against and denied those fuller rights of government to which white citizens are appointed, nominated and elected.

10. That our people in those parts are forced to work for lower wages than the average standard of white men and are kept in conditions repugnant to good civilized tastes and customs.

11. That the many acts of injustices against members of our race before the courts of law in the respective islands and colonies are of such nature as to create disgust and disrespect for the white man's sense of justice.

12. Against all such inhuman, unchristian and uncivilized treatment we here and now emphatically protest, and invoke the condemnation of all mankind.

In order to encourage our race all over the world and to stimulate it to overcome the handicaps and difficulties surrounding it, and to push forward to a higher and grander destiny, we demand and insist on the following Declaration of Rights:

1. Be it known to all men that whereas all men are created equal and entitled to the rights of life, liberty and the pursuit of happiness, and because of this we, the duly elected representatives of the Negro peoples of the world, invoking the aid of the just and Almighty God, do declare all men, women and children of our blood throughout the world free denizens, and do claim them as free citizens of Africa, the Motherland of all Negroes.

2. That we believe in the supreme authority of our race in all things racial; that all things are created and given to man as a common possession; that there should be an equitable distribution and apportionment of all such things, and in consideration of the fact that as a race we are now deprived of those things that are morally and legally ours, we believed it right that all such things should be acquired and held by whatsoever means possible.

3. That we believe the Negro, like any other race, should be governed by the ethics of civilization, and therefore should not be deprived of any of those rights or privileges common to other human beings.

4. We declare that Negroes, wheresoever they form a community among themselves should be given the right to elect their own representatives to represent them in Legislatures, courts of law, or such institutions as may exercise control over that particular community.

5. We assert that the Negro is entitled to even-handed justice before all courts of law and equity in whatever country he may be found, and when this is denied him on account of his race or color such denial is an insult to the race as a whole and should be resented by the entire body of Negroes.

6. We declare it unfair and prejudicial to the rights of Negroes in communities where they exist in considerable numbers to be tried by a judge and jury composed entirely of an alien race, but in all such cases members of our race are entitled to representation on the jury.

7. We believe that any law or practice that tends to deprive any African of his land or the privileges of free citizenship within his country is unjust and immoral, and no native should respect any such law or practice.

8. We declare taxation without representation unjust and tyran[n]ous, and there should be no obligation on the part of the Negro to obey the levy of a tax by any law-making body from which he is excluded and denied representation on account of his race and color.

9. We believe that any law especially directed against the Negro to his det-

riment and singling him out because of his race or color is unfair and immoral, and should not be respected.

10. We believe all men entitled to common human respect and that our race should in no way tolerate any insults that may be interpreted to mean disrespect to our race or color.

11. We deprecate the use of the term "nigger" as applied to Negroes, and demand that the word "Negro" be written with a capital "N."

12. We believe that the Negro should adopt every means to protect himself against barbarous practices inflicted upon him because of color.

13. We believe in the freedom of Africa for the Negro people of the world, and by the principle of Europe for the Europeans and Asia for the Asiatics, we also demand Africa for the Africans at home and abroad.

14. We believe in the inherent right of the Negro to possess himself of Africa and that his possession of same shall not be regarded as an infringement of any claim or purchase made by any race or nation.

15. We strongly condemn the cupidity of those nations of the world who, by open aggression or secret schemes, have seized the territories and inexhaustible natural wealth of Africa, and we place on record our most solemn determination to reclaim the treasures and possession of the vast continent of our forefathers.

16. We believe all men should live in peace one with the other, but when races and nations provoke the ire of other races and nations by attempting to infringe upon their rights[,] war becomes inevitable, and the attempt in any way to free one's self or protect one's rights or heritage becomes justifiable.

17. Whereas the lynching, by burning, hanging or any other means, of human beings is a barbarous practice and a shame and disgrace to civilization, we therefore declare any country guilty of such atrocities outside the pale of civilization.

18. We protest against the atrocious crime of whipping, flogging and overworking of the native tribes of Africa and Negroes everywhere. These are methods that should be abolished and all means should be taken to prevent a continuance of such brutal practices.

19. We protest against the atrocious practice of shaving the heads of Africans, especially of African women or individuals of Negro blood, when placed in prison as a punishment for crime by an alien race.

20. We protest against segregated districts, separate public conveyances, industrial discrimination, lynchings and limitations of political privileges of any Negro citizen in any part of the world on account of race, color or creed, and will exert our full influence and power against all such.

W. E. B. DU BOIS

From "The Souls of White Folk"

(1920)

High in the tower, where I sit above the loud complaining of the human sea, I know many souls that toss and whirl and pass, but none there are that intrigue me more than the Souls of White Folk.

Of them I am singularly clairvoyant. I see in and through them. I view them from unusual points of vantage. Not as a foreigner do I come, for I am native, not foreign, bone of their thought and flesh of their language. Mine is not the knowledge of the traveler or the colonial composite of dear memories, words and wonder. Nor yet is my knowledge that which servants have of masters, or mass of class, or capitalist of artisan. Rather I see these souls undressed and from the back and side. I see the working of their entrails. I know their thoughts and they know that I know. This knowledge makes them now embarrassed, now furious. They deny my right to live and be and call me misbirth! My word is to them mere bitterness and my soul, pessimism. And yet as they preach and strut and shout and threaten, crouching as they clutch at rags of facts and fancies to hide their nakedness, they go twisting, flying by my tired eyes and I see them ever stripped,—ugly, human.

The discovery of personal whiteness among the world's peoples is a very modern thing,—a nineteenth and twentieth century matter, indeed. The ancient world would have laughed at such a distinction. The Middle Age regarded skin color with mild curiosity; and even up into the eighteenth century we were hammering our national manikins into one, great, Universal Man, with fine frenzy which ignored color and race even more than birth. Today we have changed all that, and the world in a sudden, emotional conversion has discovered that it is white and by that token, wonderful!

This assumption that of all the hues of God whiteness alone is inherently and obviously better than brownness or tan leads to curious acts; even the sweeter souls of the dominant world as they discourse with me on weather, weal, and woe are continually playing above their actual words an obligato of tune and tone, saying:

"My poor, un-white thing! Weep not nor rage. I know, too well, that the curse of God lies heavy on you. Why? That is not for me to say, but be brave! Do your work in your lowly sphere, praying the good Lord that into heaven above, where all is love, you may, one day, be born—white!"

I do not laugh. I am quite straight-faced as I ask soberly:

"But what on earth is whiteness that one should so desire it?" Then always, somehow, some way, silently but clearly, I am given to understand that whiteness is the ownership of the earth forever and ever, Amen!

Now what is the effect on a man or a nation when it comes passionately to believe such an extraordinary dictum as this? That nations are coming to believe it is manifest daily. Wave on wave, each with increasing virulence, is dashing this new religion of whiteness on the shores of our time. Its first effects are funny: the strut of the Southerner, the arrogance of the Englishman amuck, the whoop of the hoodlum who vicariously leads your mob. Next it appears dampening generous enthusiasm in what we once counted glorious; to free the slave is discovered to be tolerable only in so far as it freed his master! Do we sense somnolent writhings in black Africa or angry groans in India or triumphant banzais in Japan? "To your tents, O Israel!" These nations are not white!

After the more comic manifestations and the chilling of generous enthusiasm come subtler, darker deeds. Everything considered, the title to the universe claimed by White Folk is faulty. It ought, at least, to look plausible. How easy, then, by emphasis and omission to make children believe that every great soul the world ever saw was a white man's soul; that every great thought the world ever knew was a white man's thought; that every great deed the world ever did was a white man's deed; that every great dream the world ever sang was a white man's dream. In fine, that if from the world were dropped everything that could not fairly be attributed to White Folk, the world would, if anything, be even greater, truer, better than now. And if all this be a lie, is it not a lie in a great cause?

Here it is that the comedy verges to tragedy. The first minor note is struck, all unconsciously, by those worthy souls in whom consciousness of high descent brings burning desire to spread the gift abroad,—the obligation of nobility to the ignoble. Such sense of duty assumes two things: a real possession of the heritage and its frank appreciation by the humble-born. So long, then, as humble black folk, voluble with thanks, receive barrels of old clothes from lordly and generous whites, there is much mental peace and moral satisfaction. But when the black man begins to dispute the white man's title to certain alleged bequests of the Fathers in wage and position, authority and training; and when his attitude toward charity is sullen anger rather than humble jollity; when he insists on his human right to swagger and swear and waste,—then the spell is suddenly broken and the philanthropist is ready to believe that Negroes are impudent, that the South is right, and that Japan wants to fight America.

After this the descent to Hell is easy. On the pale, white faces which the great billows whirl upward to my tower I see again and again, often and still more often, a writing of human hatred, a deep and passionate hatred, vast by the very vagueness of its expressions. Down through the green waters, on the bottom of the world, where men move to and fro, I have seen a man—an educated gentleman—grow livid with anger because a little, silent, black woman was sitting by herself in a Pullman car. He was a white man. I have seen a great, grown man curse a little child, who had wandered into the wrong waiting-room, searching for its mother: "Here, you damned black—" He was white. In Central Park I have seen the upper lip of a quiet, peaceful man curl back in a tigerish snarl of rage because black folk rode by in a motor car. He was a white man. We have seen, you and I, city after city drunk and furious with ungovernable lust of blood; mad with murder, destroying, killing, and cursing; torturing human victims because somebody accused of crime happened to be of the same color as the mob's innocent victims and because that color was not white! We have seen,—Merciful God! in these wild days and in the name of Civilization, Justice, and Motherhood, what have we not seen, right here in America, of orgy, cruelty, barbarism, and murder done to men and women of Negro descent. . . .

Think of the wars through which we have lived in the last decade: in German Africa, in British Nigeria, in French and Spanish Morocco, in China, in Persia, in the Balkans, in Tripoli, in Mexico, and in a dozen lesser places—were not these horrible, too? . . .

Behold little Belgium and her pitiable plight, but has the world forgotten Congo? What Belgium now suffers is not half, not even a tenth, of what she has done to black Congo since Stanley's great dream of 1880. Down the dark forests of inmost Africa sailed this modern Sir Galahad, in the name of "the noble-minded men of several nations," to introduce commerce and civilization. What came of it? "Rubber and murder, slavery in its worst form," wrote Glave in 1895.

Harris declares that King Leopold's régime meant the death of twelve million natives, "but what we who were behind the scenes felt most keenly was the fact that the real catastrophe in the Congo was desolation and murder in the larger sense. The invasion of family life, the ruthless destruction of every social barrier, the shattering of every tribal law, the introduction of criminal practices which struck the chiefs of the people dumb with horror—in a word, a veritable avalanche of filth and immorality overwhelmed the Congo tribes."

Yet the fields of Belgium laughed, the cities were gay, art and science flourished; the groans that helped to nourish this civilization fell on deaf ears because the world round about was doing the same sort of thing elsewhere on its own account.

As we saw the dead dimly through rifts of battlesmoke and heard faintly the cursings and accusations of blood brothers, we darker men said: This is not Europe gone mad; this is not aberration nor insanity; this *is* Europe; this seeming Terrible is the real soul of white culture—back of all culture,—stripped and visible today. This is where the world has arrived,—these dark and awful depths and not the shining and ineffable heights of which it boasted. Here is whither the might and energy of modern humanity has really gone. . . .

. . . It is the duty of white Europe to divide up the darker world and administer it for Europe's good.

This Europe has largely done. The European world is using black and brown men for all the uses which men know. Slowly but surely white culture is evolving the theory that "darkies" are born beasts of burden for white folk. It were silly to think otherwise, cries the cultured world, with stronger and shriller accord. The supporting arguments grow and twist themselves in the mouths of merchant, scientist, soldier, traveler, writer, and missionary: Darker peoples are dark in mind as well as in body; of dark, uncertain, and imperfect descent; of frailer, cheaper stuff; they are cowards in the face of mausers and maxims; they have no feelings, aspirations, and loves; they are fools, illogical idiots,—"half-devil and half-child." . . .

Such degrading of men by men is as old as mankind and the invention of no one race or people. Ever have men striven to conceive of their victims as different from the victors, endlessly different, in soul and blood, strength and cunning, race and lineage. It has been left, however, to Europe and to modern days to discover the eternal world-wide mark of meanness,—color! . . .

The using of men for the benefit of masters is no new invention of modern Europe. It is quite as old as the world. But Europe proposed to apply it on a scale and with an elaborateness of detail of which no former world ever dreamed. The imperial width of the thing,—the heaven-defying audacity—makes its modern newness. . . .

This theory of human culture and its aims has worked itself through warp and woof of our daily thought with a thoroughness that few realize. Everything great, good, efficient, fair, and honorable is "white"; everything mean, bad, blundering, cheating, and dishonorable is "yellow"; a bad taste is "brown"; and the devil is "black." The changes of this theme are continually rung in picture and story, in newspaper heading and moving-picture, in sermon and school book, until, of course, the King can do no wrong,—a White Man is always right and a Black Man has no rights which a white man is bound to respect. . . .

Instead of standing as a great example of the success of democracy and the possibility of human brotherhood America has taken her place as an awful example of its pitfalls and failures, so far as black and brown and yellow peoples are concerned. And this, too, in spite of the fact that there has been no actual failure; the Indian is not dying out, the Japanese and Chinese have not menaced the land, and the experiment of Negro suffrage has resulted in the uplift of twelve million people at a rate probably unparalleled in history. But what of this? America, Land of Democracy, wanted to believe in the failure of democracy so far as darker peoples were concerned. Absolutely without excuse she established a caste system, rushed into preparation for war, and conquered tropical colonies. She stands today shoulder to shoulder with Europe in Europe's worst sin against civilization. She aspires to sit among the great nations who arbitrate the fate of "lesser breeds without the law" and she is at times heartily ashamed even of the large number of "new" white people whom her democracy has admitted to place and power. Against this surging forward of Irish and German, of Russian Jew, Slav and [Italian] her social bars have not availed, but against Negroes she can and does take her unflinching and immovable stand, backed by this new public policy of Europe. She trains her immigrants to this despising of "niggers" from the day of their landing, and they carry and send the news back to the submerged classes in the fatherlands.

All this I see and hear up in my tower, above the thunder of the seven seas. From my narrowed windows I stare into the night that looms beneath the cloud-swept stars. Eastward and westward storms are breaking,—great, ugly whirlwinds of hatred and blood and cruelty. I will not believe them inevitable. I will not believe that all that was must be, that all the shameful drama of the past must be done again today before the sunlight sweeps the silver seas.

If I cry amid this roar of elemental forces, must my cry be in vain, because it is but a cry,—a small and human cry amid Promethean gloom?

Back beyond the world and swept by these wild, white faces of the awful dead, why will this Soul of White Folk,—this modern Prometheus,—hang bound by his own binding, tethered by a fable of the past? I hear his mighty cry reverberating through the world, "I am white!" Well and good, O Prometheus, divine thief! Is not the world wide enough for two colors, for many little shinings of the sun? Why, then, devour your own vitals if I answer even as proudly, "I am black!"

Strange Fruit

(1937; 1939)

Southern trees bear a strange fruit,
Blood on the leaves and blood at the root,
Black body swinging in the Southern breeze,
Strange fruit hanging from the poplar trees.

Pastoral scene of the gallant South,
The bulging eyes and the twisted mouth,
Scent of magnolia sweet and fresh,
And the sudden smell of burning flesh!

Here is a fruit for the crows to pluck,
For the rain to gather, for the wind to suck,
For the sun to rot, for a tree to drop,
Here is a strange and bitter crop.

ASA PHILIP RANDOLPH

Call to the March

(1941)

We call upon you to fight for jobs in National Defense.

We call upon you to struggle for the integration of Negroes in the armed forces, such as the Air Corps, Navy, Army and Marine Corps of the Nation.

We call upon you to demonstrate for the abolition of Jim-Crowism in all Government departments and defense employment.

This is an hour of crisis. It is a crisis of democracy. It is a crisis of minority groups. It is a crisis of Negro Americans.

What is this crisis?

To American Negroes, it is the denial of jobs in Government defense projects. It is racial discrimination in Government departments. It is widespread Jim-Crowism in the armed forces of the Nation.

While billions of the taxpayers' money are being spent for war weapons, Negro workers are being turned away from the gates of factories, mines and mills—being flatly told, "NOTHING DOING." Some employers refuse to give Negroes jobs when they are without "union cards," and some unions refuse Negro workers union cards when they are "without jobs."

What shall we do?

What a dilemma!

What a runaround!

What a disgrace!

What a blow below the belt!

Though dark, doubtful and discouraging, all is not lost, all is not hopeless. Though battered and bruised, we are not beaten, broken or bewildered.

Verily, the Negroes' deepest disappointments and direst defeats, their tragic trials and outrageous oppressions in these dreadful days of destruction and disaster to democracy and freedom, and the rights of minority peoples, and the dignity and independence of the human spirit, is the Negroes' greatest opportunity to rise to the highest heights of struggle for freedom and justice in Government, in industry, in labor unions, education, social service, religion and culture.

With faith and confidence of the Negro people in their own power for self-liberation, Negroes can break down the barriers of discrimination against employment in National Defense. Negroes can kill the deadly serpent of race hatred in the Army, Navy, Air and Marine Corps, and smash through and blast the Government, business and labor-union red tape to win the right to equal opportunity in vocational training and re-training in defense employment.

Most important and vital to all, Negroes, by the mobilization and coordination of their mass power, can cause PRESIDENT ROOSEVELT TO ISSUE AN EXECUTIVE ORDER ABOLISHING DISCRIMINATIONS IN ALL GOVERNMENT DEPARTMENTS, ARMY, NAVY, AIR CORPS AND NATIONAL DEFENSE JOBS.

Of course, the task is not easy. In very truth, it is big, tremendous and difficult.

It will cost money.

It will require sacrifice.

It will tax the Negroes' courage, determination and will to struggle. But we can, must and will triumph.

The Negroes' stake in national defense is big. It consists of jobs, thousands of jobs. It may represent millions, yes, hundreds of millions of dollars in wages. It consists of new industrial opportunities and hope. This is worth fighting for.

But to win our stakes, it will require an "all-out," bold and total effort and demonstration of colossal proportions.

Negroes can build a mammoth machine of mass action with a terrific and tremendous driving and striking power that can shatter and crush the evil fortress of race prejudice and hate, if they will only resolve to do so and never stop, until victory comes.

Dear fellow Negro Americans, be not dismayed in these terrible times. You possess power, great power. Our problem is to harness and hitch it up for action on the broadest, daring and most gigantic scale.

In this period of power politics, nothing counts but pressure, more pressure, and still more pressure, through the tactic and strategy of broad, organized, aggressive mass action behind the vital and important issues of the Negro. To this end, we propose that ten thousand Negroes MARCH ON WASHINGTON FOR JOBS IN NATIONAL DEFENSE AND EQUAL INTEGRATION IN THE FIGHTING FORCES OF THE UNITED STATES.

An "all-out" thundering march on Washington, ending in a monster and huge demonstration at Lincoln's Monument will shake up white America.

It will shake up official Washington.

It will give encouragement to our white friends to fight all the harder by our side, with us, for our righteous cause.

It will gain respect for the Negro people.

It will create a new sense of self-respect among Negroes.

But what of national unity?

We believe in national unity which recognizes equal opportunity of black and white citizens to jobs in national defense and the armed forces, and in all other institutions and endeavors in America. We condemn all dictatorships, Fascist, Nazi and Communist. We are loyal, patriotic Americans, all.

But, if American democracy will not defend its defenders; if American democracy will not protect its protectors; if American democracy will not give jobs to its toilers because of race or color; if American democracy will not insure equality of opportunity, freedom and justice to its citizens, black and white, it is a hollow mockery and belies the principles for which it is supposed to stand.

To the hard, difficult and trying problem of securing equal participation in national defense, we summon all Negro Americans to march on Washington. We summon Negro Americans to form committees in various cities to recruit and register marchers and raise funds through the sale of buttons and other legitimate means for the expenses of marchers to Washington by buses, train, private automobiles, trucks, and on foot.

We summon Negro Americans to stage marches on their City Halls and Councils in their respective cities and urge them to memorialize the President to issue an executive order to abolish discrimination in the Government and national defense.

However, we sternly counsel against violence and ill-considered and intemperate action and the abuse of power. Mass power, like physical power, when misdirected is more harmful than helpful.

We summon you to mass action that is orderly and lawful, but aggressive and militant, for justice, equality and freedom.

Crispus Attucks marched and died as a martyr for American independence. Nat Turner, Denmark Vesey, Gabriel Prosser, Harriet Tubman and Frederick Douglass fought, bled and died for the emancipation of Negro slaves and the preservation of American democracy.

Abraham Lincoln, in times of the grave emergency of the Civil War, issued the Proclamation of Emancipation for the freedom of Negro slaves and the preservation of American democracy.

Today, we call upon President Roosevelt, a great humanitarian and idealist, to follow in the footsteps of his noble and illustrious predecessor and take the second decisive step in this world and national emergency and free American Negro citizens of the stigma, humiliation and insult of discrimination and Jim-Crowism in Government departments and national defense.

The Federal Government cannot with clear conscience call upon private industry and labor unions to abolish discrimination based upon race and color as long as it practices discrimination itself against Negro Americans.

BENJAMIN FOLDY

Rhodesian Flag, Confederate Flag:
Roof and the Legacies of Racial Hate

(June 20, 2015)

When the perpetrator in the horrific massacre at the Emanuel AME church in Charleston was first publicly identified as Dylann Storm Roof, a near-instantaneous Twitter trawl of his social media uncovered his Facebook profile picture.

In the picture, Roof sports two flag patches on his left breast: the apartheid-era flag of South Africa and the flag of white Rhodesia, the colonial predecessor to current day Zimbabwe.

Most have at least a cursory understanding of the racist violence of apartheid in South Africa. Fewer are familiar with the history of Rhodesia, the short-lived pariah state that fought a vicious and dirty war rather than acquiesce to the British desire for its colonies to transition to majority (read: black) rule in the mid-1960s.

But this flag and its history provides crucial context for Roof's actions, perhaps even more so than the Confederate flag. If you wanted to look for a historical example of the kind of apocalyptic "race war" that white supremacists like Roof always claim to be fixing for, you'd be hard-pressed to find something resembling it more than the conflict between Rhodesia's white settler government and black nationalist Zimbabweans.

Shortly after the British colony of Northern Rhodesia transitioned to majority rule, independence, and its new name of Zambia, the colony of Southern Rhodesia—in defiance of British and international pressure—dropped the "Southern" and declared its own independence under the leadership of Ian Smith and his Rhodesian Front party.

Smith's unilateralism came at an immense cost, alienating both the UK's Labour government under Harold Wilson and Lyndon Johnson's Democratic administration, which was pursuing its own civil rights agenda at the time (and its own postcolonial war in Vietnam). As postcolonial struggles were intimately bound in the dynamics of the Cold War, China and the Soviet Union's support for "third world" liberation and postcolonial movements across Africa and the world ensured Rhodesia's pariah status, and solid support for the armed opposition.

The Rhodesian government and its white settler constituency faced steady opposition from black nationalists, whose efforts became increasingly militarized throughout the sixties and seventies. Known by Rhodesians as the Bush War and Zimbabweans as the Chimurenga (liberation war), the conflict took the form of traditional postcolonial insurgency, with rival factions of rebels using guerrilla tactics against a numerically inferior but qualitatively superior colonial force that felt it would have nowhere to go in the case of defeat.

With almost no international recognition and significant sanctions from the UN Security Council, Rhodesia's support came instead from neighbors also holding out against the postcolonial tide, namely Portuguese patrons fighting insurgencies in the colonies of neighboring Mozambique and nearby Angola, and apartheid South Africa.

But the collapse of Portugal's military dictatorship in 1974 imperiled the Rhodesian government's position, in terms of both its diplomatic isolation and its strategic situation. Surrounded by hostile Zambia and now FRELIMO-controlled Mozambique, the tenor of fighting between African nationalists (split into rival ZANU-PF and ZAPU factions) and the Rhodesian government grew more and more brutal.

In 1976, a contingent of Rhodesia's infamous Selous Scouts special forces unit carried out Operation Eland, in which they disguised themselves as Mozambican forces before massacring over one thousand nationalist guerrillas encamped at Nyadzonya. Nationalist guerrillas meanwhile sought to pressure Rhodesia by using mines and IEDs to target vehicles in government-controlled areas, bombed businesses, and downed Air Rhodesia airliners with portable surface-to-air missiles.

In the most disturbing (and forgotten) episodes of the war, there is significant evidence that the Rhodesian government deployed chemical and biological weapons against its opposition. Tactics included lacing food and uniforms with fatal doses of toxic chemicals before distributing them in the rebel-controlled countryside; poisoning wells and intentionally spreading cholera; and an intentional anthrax outbreak that decimated tribal cattle stocks, infected 10,000 Zimbabweans, and led to the deaths of 138 black Zimbabweans from cutaneous anthrax.

But even despite such apocalyptic efforts, the war was unwinnable for white Rhodesians. A late settlement between Smith's government and more "moderate" nationalists led to a brief, binational country of Rhodesia-Zimbabwe, but power soon fell to Robert Mugabe's ZANU-PF, holding power ever since and ending Rhodesia once and for all.

There are, of course, plenty of commenters looking to downplay the influence of race in Roof's actions. Fox News has already run a particularly dumbfounding segment in which the attack is discussed as an attack on Christians, as if it were some kind of logical extension of their ballyhooed "War on Christmas." But Dylann Roof's proud identification with such a regime and its race war are telling. Few flags represent racialized violence quite as sharply as that of white Rhodesia, a flag whose historical implications belong alongside the swastika.

Knowing this, it is nearly impossible then to not hear the echoes of Rhodesia's racist apocalypse in Roof's alleged preshooting declaration to his victims that "You rape our women, and you're taking over our country, and you have to go" or the claims of his confidants, who mention his desire to start "a civil war." Perhaps the fact that he proudly sported such a flag alongside his Confederate States of America license plate will finally put an end to the empty blathering that the Confederate flag can somehow be separated from its history of racial violence. Its defenders must be called to account, forced to answer how this young man's inspiration from one white supremacist regime can be somehow distinguished from his support of another.

CRYSTAL N. FEIMSTER

From *Southern Horrors: Women and the Politics of Rape and Lynching*

(2009)

In hopes of changing history, lda B. Wells-Barnett . . . boarded a train bound for Washington, D.C., in 1922. Wells-Barnett, however, did not make the journey alone. She traveled with a delegation of black clubwomen who had recently attended the 13th Biennial Session of the National Association of Colored Women (NACW) in Richmond, Virginia. Dressed in their Sunday best, with extravagant hats on their heads and prim white gloves on their hands, the fifteen NACW delegates had an appointment with President Warren Harding to urge him to hasten final action on the Dyer Bill, the first antilynching law to reach the U.S. Senate. Thirty years had passed since Wells-Barnett had single-handedly initiated the anti-lynching movement and first called on the federal government for protection for African Americans against southern lynch mobs. For Wells-Barnett, the bill's passage would mean that her lifelong anti-lynching plea would at last be answered. What were the chances that both Wells-Barnett, who had made a career campaigning against lynching and championing black women's rights, and [Rebecca] Felton, who had worked tirelessly on behalf of southern white women and advocated lynching for their protection, would both have their life's work validated by the 67th Congress of the United States?

In 1922, as Wells-Barnett looked back over her life it must have been difficult for her to fully appreciate the slow but steady impact of her radical protest politics on the larger movement to protect black women from sexual violence and black men from lynching. The "New Negro" of the early twentieth century, like Wells-Barnett, refused to tolerate white supremacist politics that relegated blacks to second-class status. And the "New Negro Woman" now also embraced a more politically radical image of black womanhood that recognized the limits of racial uplift and acknowledged the power of political action in the form of direct protest. But although Wells-Barnett had led the way, few were willing or able to credit her for helping to redefine uplift as agitation. Nevertheless, unwilling to sit on the sidelines, and still determined to have something "to show for all those years of toil and labor," Wells-Barnett continued to challenge the racial and sexual politics that served to justify lynching while ignoring the rape of black women.

The New Negro Woman's Political Power

In 1902, Mary Church Terrell published "What Role Is the Educated Negro Woman to Play in the Uplifting of Her Race?" In an eloquent conclusion, Terrell summed up, "Seeking no favors because of their color nor charity because of their needs they knock at the door of Justice and ask for an equal chance." Black clubwomen, however, would have to redefine their politics of uplift into a discourse of militant protest, force their way through the "door of Justice," and demand protection against white violence if they wanted "an equal chance" in twentieth century America. Roughly two decades later, World War I and the ratification of the Nineteenth Amendment helped foster the emergence of the New Negro Woman, who was indeed more willing to embrace militant agitation.

In 1919, black clubwomen sparked a new phase of the anti-lynching campaign that called for direct action and demanded white women's active involvement. And as they continued to fight for social justice and reform, and embraced female suffrage as a crucial weapon in the battle against lynching and the sexual exploitation of black women, their politics became decidedly more radical. Increasingly now, black clubwomen participated in and helped to lead the NAACP's campaign for federal anti-lynching legislation. They raised thousands of dollars for the cause, gave public lectures about the evils of lynching and the realities of rape, initiated and joined protest marches, lobbied senators, and testified before Congress. Working with the NAACP, the NACW engaged in speaking and petitioning campaigns against lynching and investigated instances of mob violence that kept the issue constantly before the American public.

In all these ways, black clubwomen were following in the footsteps of Wells-Barnett, who had paved the way for the New Negro Woman in her most radical incarnation. . . . Linking disenfranchisement to rape and lynching of African Americans, she insisted that woman suffrage was vital to the goals of reshaping local and national politics and ensuring protection. Since Reconstruction, African Americans had understood the power of the ballot and embraced black male suffrage as a means of acquiring and maintaining their rights as citizens. But Wells-Barnett, like many black women, was not willing to accept the idea that the dirty world of male politics was no place for a woman. Dedicated to ensuring equal rights and justice through direct political action, she embraced woman suffrage as essential to the survival of black communities. She understood all too well that white anti-suffragists feared the power that the ballot would extend to both white and black women. Ultimately, however, Wells-Barnett defined suffrage not simply as a woman's issue but as part of the larger campaign for racial and human justice. In this regard she formed part of a tradition of black women stretching back to the 1880s, but the new generation who came on the scene after 1910 now pushed for the right to vote more pointedly. And Wells, ever in the vanguard, sought to further sharpen the edge. The 1908 race riot in Springfield, Illinois, and the 1909 lynching in Cairo, Illinois, of William James, a black man accused of raping and murdering a white woman, reinforced not only her belief that blacks needed federal protection, but also her commitment to the ballot as black people's most powerful weapon in the battle against racial and sexual violence.

The events leading up to the Springfield riot began on August 14, 1908, when Nellie Hallam, a twenty-one-year-old white woman, alleged that George Richardson, a black man, had raped her. Although Richardson pled his innocence, he was arrested and placed in a jail cell with Joe James, a black vagrant from Birmingham, Alabama, accused of the attempted rape of a white woman and the murder of a white man. When rumors spread that a mob was en route to the jailhouse, local authorities moved the two men to Bloomington for safekeeping. The mob was furious to learn that the men had been taken to safer quarters. Prodded by Kate Howard, a white rooming-house owner, who called on the mob to live up to their duty to protect white womanhood, the men destroyed the restaurant and car of the white man whose vehicle had been used to transfer the prisoners to Bloomington. Still not satisfied, the mob, which had swelled to twelve thousand, began attacking any black person they could find. They beat black porters at the railroad depot and pulled blacks off the streetcars. After setting fire to the black business district and residential area, the bloodthirsty mob then lynched two innocent black men, Scott Burton, a barber, and William Donegan, a shoe cobbler, in the public square. Hundreds of blacks were injured and four whites were dead by the time the Illinois State Militia finally arrived and restored order. . . .

One thing that the Springfield riot had made very clear, Wells-Barnett emphasized, was that lynching was no longer just a southern problem. Northern whites were not immune to mob violence and northern white women were not above falsely crying rape—as in the case of Hallam, who two weeks after the riot signed an official statement clearing Richardson of the rape charges. She confessed that it had, in fact, been a white man (whom she refused to name) who was responsible for the assault. Wells-Barnett had long argued that black men were being lynched on trumped-up rape charges, but what had been defined as a particularly southern issue as clearly now a national problem that required federal intervention. . . .

On July 2, 1917, four months after the United States entered World War I, a race riot erupted in East St. Louis after a shoot-out in a middle-class neighborhood between a group of white men intent on terrorizing the black community and blacks defending themselves. Events escalated when plainclothes officers drove into the neighborhood and were shot and killed by black citizens who believed they were whites returning to do more damage. The next day, in response to the murder of the two white detectives, a white mob marched through the city attacking blacks wherever they could be found. Black men, women, and children were again pulled off streetcars and beaten unmercifully. The white mob set fire to homes and shot those trying to escape. While there were no reported rapes, white violence against black women nevertheless carried sexual overtones, with mob members stripping black women of their clothing. After two days of rioting, two hundred homes had been burned down, five thousand blacks had fled the city, and at least forty black people were dead, with many more brutalized.

As news of the riot spread, Wells-Barnett began organizing. On July 3, she called a meeting of the [National Fellowship League], which agreed to send her to East St. Louis to investigate. In a pamphlet titled *The East St. Louis Massacre: The Greatest Outrage of the Century*, Wells-Barnett recounted what she had learned during her trip. Using the victims' own words, together with reports from the white press, she exposed the brutality of the mob and the negligence and complicity of the local police and state militia. Not surprisingly, she opened her pamphlet with the words and experiences of black women and highlighted white women's brutality. Wells-Barnett was pleased when Congress, responding to outrage and protest across the country, launched an investigation. In a letter to the *Broad Ax* she praised Congress for acting, but called on people to engage in further action. Prayers, protests, and passing resolutions were not enough. She explained, "We all know that unless these parades are followed up by hard work in the trenches, and all the firing of guns by every conceivable active physical movement possible, the war will not be won." She insisted that blacks raise money to attend the congressional hearings en masse to ensure justice on the part of black victims and to prevent such riots from occurring in the future.

In general, World War I served to intensify the racist climate and sparked another deadly new wave of mob violence in America. In 1919 there were twenty-five race riots across the country, including one in Wells-Barnett's hometown of Chicago. White lynch mobs nationwide killed thirty-six blacks in 1917, sixty in 1918, and seventy-six in 1919. Wells-Barnett's predictions were coming to pass. In the midst of this epidemic of atrocities, the lynching of Mary Turner elicited an especially strong response from the NAACP and black clubwomen who had hoped the wartime rhetoric of democracy and justice would bring an end to mob violence. Turner was one of a total of eleven African Americans lynched in Brooks and Lowndes Counties, Georgia, between May 17 and May 22, 1918, for the alleged murder of Hampton Smith, a white farmer. Her husband, Hayes Turner, was implicated in the murder and was one of the first to be lynched. But Mary, who was eight months pregnant, complained that the lynching was unjust and called for the punishment of those responsible. . . . [S]he and her unborn child were brutally murdered by a mob of over five hundred white men and women. . . .

The Dyer Anti-Lynching Bill

Republican congressman Leonidas Dyer of Missouri first introduced the Dyer Anti-Lynching Bill in 1918. It held that "if any State or county fails, neglects or refuses to secure and maintain protection to the life of any person within its jurisdiction against a mob or riotous assemblage, such State or county shall by reason of such failure, neglect, or refusal be deemed to have denied to such person equal protection of the laws." It also declared that "any State or municipal officer" who refused to make all "reasonable efforts" to prevent a lynching or to pursue a person who participated in mob violence "shall be guilty of a felony and upon conviction shall be punished by imprisonment not exceeding five years or by a fine not exceeding $5,000 or both." Further, the proposed law provided that any county in which a mob murdered a person would have to pay $10,000 to family members of the victim. . . .

The bill drew little support until 1919, when race riots broke out in twenty-six cities, including Washington, D.C., and Chicago, and white mobs lynched at least seventy-six African Americans (twelve of them U.S. soldiers). . . . In addition to the activities of black women's clubs and other groups all over the country, new publications of Well-Barnett's "The Race Conflict in Arkansas" and the NAACP's *Thirty Years of Lynching, 1889–1918* helped keep black public attention focused. And at the 1920 Republication National Convention in Chicago, pressure from African American voters helped ensure that the anti-lynching bill was officially adopted as part of the party platform. . . .

. . . [T]he Republican dominated House of Representatives passed the Dyer Bill by a vote of 230 to 119 in January 1922. . . . The real battle would now come in the Senate. . . .

. . . [I]n July 1922 . . . the Senate Judiciary Committee voted 8 to 6 in favor of the Dyer Bill. . . . [Southern Democrats in the Senate voted as a bloc, scuttling the bill through filibuster.]

. . . In 1930, Jessie Daniel Ames, a white southern suffragist, founded the Association of Southern Women for the Prevention of Lynching (ASWPL) in Felton's home state of Georgia. Worried by the rise in the number of lynchings in the early months of 1930, and convinced that lynching did not function to protect white women, Ames insisted it was southern white women's responsibility to combat mob violence. . . . The ASWPL adopted strategies originally defined by Ida B. Wells: publicly attacking the idea that lynching was punishment for rape; engaging in onsite investigations of lynching; and collecting and reporting lynching statistics. They also developed their own tactics, such as asking sheriffs to sign pledges stating their intent to assist in the eradication of lynching and publicly praising local officials who acted to prevent mob violence. They convinced over 40,000 southern white women to sign the ASWPL's antilynching pledge, which declared, "Public opinion has accepted too easily the claim of lynchers and mobsters that they were acting solely in defense of womanhood. In the light of facts, we dare no longer permit this claim to pass unchallenged . . . . We solemnly pledge ourselves to create a new public opinion in the South, which will not condone, for any reason whatever, acts of mobs or lynchers." In many ways, the ASWPL represented an answer to the earliest calls, made by the Grimké sisters, for southern white women to take up the cause of racial justice as a women's rights issue.

. . . No doubt Wells-Barnett, who died on March 25, 1931, soon after the founding of the ASWPL, was pleased to learn that southern white women had taken up her plea to organize against lynching. Not until June 2005, almost seventy-five years after her death, however, was Wells-Barnett's antilynching crusade finally recognized on the floor of the U.S. Senate. Led by Democratic senator Mary Landrieu of Louisiana, the 109th Congress passed a resolution apologizing for the Senate's failure to pass anti-lynching legislation. The resolution noted that nearly two hundred anti-lynching bills had been introduced in Congress during the first half of the twentieth century, and all had been defeated. Now, however, it resolved:

That the Senate—
(1) apologizes to the victims of lynching for the failure of the Senate to enact anti-lynching legislation;
(2) expresses the deepest sympathies and most solemn regrets of the Senate to the descendants of victims of lynching, the ancestors of whom were deprived of life, human dignity, and the constitutional protections accorded all citizens of the United States; and

(3) remembers the history of lynching, to ensure that these tragedies will be neither forgotten nor repeated.

In the chambers of the Senate, Senator Landrieu recounted the 1892 Memphis lynching that sparked Wells-Barnett's anti-lynching crusade, and stated, "Without the work of this extraordinarily brave journalist, this story could never really have been told in the way it's being told now, today, and talked about here on the Senate floor. To her, we owe a great deal of gratitude."

ROBIN D. G. KELLEY

From "'We Are Not What We Seem': Rethinking Black Working-Class Opposition in the Jim Crow South"

(June 1993)

On the factory floor in North Carolina tobacco factories, where women stemmers were generally not allowed to sit or to talk with one another, it was not uncommon for them to break out in song. Singing in unison not only reinforced a sense of collective identity in these black workers but the songs themselves—most often religious hymns—ranged from veiled protests against the daily indignities of the factory to utopian visions of a life free of difficult wage work.

Throughout the urban South in the early twentieth century, black women household workers were accustomed to staging so-called incipient strikes, quitting or threatening to quit just before important social affairs to be hosted by their employers. The strategy's success often depended on a collective refusal on the part of other household workers to fill in.

In August 1943, on the College Hills bus line in Birmingham, Alabama, black riders grew impatient with a particularly racist bus driver who within minutes twice drew his gun on black passengers, intentionally passed one black woman's stop, and ejected a black man who complained on the woman's behalf. According to a bus company report, "the negroes then started ringing bell for the entire block and no one would alight when he stopped."

These daily, unorganized, evasive, seemingly spontaneous actions form an important yet neglected part of African-American political history. By ignoring or belittling such everyday acts of resistance and privileging the public utterances of black elites, several historians of southern race relations concluded, as Lester C. Lamon did in his study of Tennessee, that black working people "remained silent, either taking the line of least resistance or implicitly adopting the American faith in hard work and individual effort." But as Richard Wright, Zora Neale Hurston, and countless cases like those recounted above suggest, the appearance of silence and accommodation was not only deceiving but frequently intended to deceive. Beneath the veil of consent lies a hidden history of unorganized, everyday conflict waged by African-American working people. Once we explore in greater detail those daily conflicts and the social and cultural spaces where ordinary people felt free to articulate their opposition, we can begin to ask the questions that will enable us to rewrite the political history of the Jim Crow South to incorporate such actions and actors.

Drawing examples from recent studies of African Americans in the urban South, mostly in the 1930s and 1940s, I would like to sketch out a research agenda that might allow us to render visible hidden forms of resistance; to examine how class, gender, and race shape working-class consciousness; and to bridge the gulf between the social and cultural world of the "everyday" and political struggles. . . . The submerged social and cultural worlds of oppressed people frequently surface in everyday forms of resistance—theft, footdragging, the destruction of property—or, more rarely, in open attacks on individuals, institutions, or symbols of domination. Together, the "hidden transcripts" that are created in aggrieved communities and expressed through culture and the daily acts of resistance and survival constitute what [James C.] Scott calls "infrapolitics." As he puts it, "the circumspect struggle waged daily by subordinate groups is, like infrared rays, beyond the visible end of the spectrum. That it should be invisible . . . is in large part by design—a tactical choice born of a prudent awareness of the balance of power."

Like Scott, I use the concept of infrapolitics to describe the daily confrontations, evasive actions, and stifled thoughts that often inform organized political movements. I am not suggesting that the realm of infrapolitics is any more or less important or effective than what we traditionally consider politics. Instead, I want to suggest that the political history of oppressed people cannot be understood *without* reference to infrapolitics, for these daily acts have a cumulative effect on power relations. While the meaning and effectiveness of acts differ according to circumstances, they make a difference, whether they were intended to or not. Thus, one measure of the power and historical importance of the informal infrapolitics of the oppressed is the response of those who dominate traditional politics. Daily acts of resistance and survival have had consequences for existing power relations, and the powerful have deployed immense resources in response. Knowing how the powerful interpret, redefine, and respond to the thoughts and actions of the oppressed is just as important as identifying and analyzing opposition. The policies, strategies, or symbolic representations of those in power—what Scott calls the "official" or "public" transcript—cannot be understood without examining the infrapolitics of oppressed groups. The approach I am proposing will help illuminate how power operates, how effective the southern power structure was in maintaining social order, and how seemingly innocuous, individualistic acts of survival and opposition shaped southern urban politics, workplace struggles, and the social order generally. . . .

An infrapolitical approach requires that we substantially redefine our understanding of politics. Too often politics is defined by *how* people participate rather than *why*; by traditional definition the question of what is political hinges on whether or not groups are involved in elections, political parties, grass-roots social movements. Yet, the how seems far less important than the why since many of the so-called real political institutions have not proved effective for, or even accessible to, oppressed people. By shifting our focus to what motivated disenfranchised black working people to struggle and what strategies they developed, we may discover that their participation in "mainstream" politics—including their battle for the franchise—grew out of the very circumstances, experiences, and memories that impelled many to steal from an employer, to join a mutual benefit association, or to spit in a bus driver's face. In other words, those actions all reflect, to varying degrees, larger political struggles. For southern blacks in the age of Jim Crow, politics was not separate from lived experience or the imagined world of what is possible. It was the many battles to roll back constraints, to exercise power over, or create space within, the institutions and social relationships that dominated their lives. . . .

. . . Missing from most [historical] accounts of southern labor struggles are the ways unorganized working people resisted the conditions of work, tried to control the pace and amount of work, and carved out a modicum of dignity at the workplace.

Not surprisingly, studies that seriously consider the sloppy, undetermined, everyday nature of workplace resistance have focused on workers who face considerable barriers to traditional trade union organization. Black domestic workers devised a whole array of creative strategies, including slowdowns, theft (or "pan-toting"), leaving work early, or quitting, in order to control the pace of work, increase wages, compensate for underpayment, reduce hours, and seize more personal autonomy. These individual acts often had a collective basis that remained hidden from their employers. Black women household workers in the urban South generally abided by a code of ethics or established a blacklist so they could collectively avoid employers who had proved unscrupulous, abusive, or unfair. In the factories, such strategies as feigning illness to get a day off, slowdowns, sometimes even sabotage often required the collective support of co-workers. . . .

. . . [T]he relative absence of resistance at the point of production does not mean that workers acquiesced or accommodated to the conditions of work. On the contrary, the most pervasive form of black protest was simply to leave. Central to black working-class infrapolitics was mobility, for it afforded workers relative freedom to escape oppressive living and working conditions and power to negotiate better working conditions. Of course, one could argue that in the competitive context of industrial capitalism—North and South—some companies clearly benefited from such migration since wages for blacks remained comparatively low no matter where black workers ended up. But the very magnitude of working-class mobility weakens any thesis that southern black working-class politics was characterized by accommodationist thinking. Besides, there is plenty of evidence to suggest that a significant portion of black migrants, especially black emigrants to Africa and the Caribbean, were motivated by a desire to vote, to provide a better education for their children, or to live in a setting in which Africans or African Americans exercised power. The ability to move represented a crucial step toward empowerment and self-determination; employers and landlords understood this, which explains why so much energy was expended limiting labor mobility and redefining migration as "shiftlessness," "indolence," or a childlike penchant to wander. . . .

Location plays a critical role in shaping workplace resistance, identity, and—broadly speaking—infrapolitics. By location I mean the racialized and gendered social spaces of work and community, as well as black workers' position in the hierarchy of power, the ensemble of social relations. Southern labor historians and race relations scholars have established the degree to which occupations and, in some cases, work spaces were segregated by race. But only recently has scholarship begun to move beyond staid discussions of such labor market segmentation and inequality to an analysis of how spatial and occupational distinctions helped create an oppositional consciousness and collective action. Feminist scholarship on the South and some community histories have begun to examine how the social spaces in which people work (in addition to the world beyond work, which was also divided by race and, at times, sex) shaped the character of everyday resistance, collective action, and domination. . . .

Although gender undoubtedly shaped the experiences, work spaces, and collective consciousness of all southern black workers, historians of women have been the most forthright and consistent in employing gender as an analytical category. Recent work on black female tobacco workers, in particular, has opened up important lines of inquiry. Not only were the dirty and difficult tasks of sorting and stemming tobacco relegated to black women, but those women had to do the tasks in spaces that were unbearably hot, dry, dark, and poorly ventilated. The coughing and wheezing, the tragically common cases of workers succumbing to tuberculosis, the endless speculation as to the cause of miscarriages among co-workers, were constant reminders that these black women spent more than a third of the day toiling in a health hazard. If some compared their work space to a prison or a dungeon, then they could not help but notice that all of the inmates were black women like themselves. Moreover, foremen referred to them only by their first names or changed their names to "girl" or something more profane and regarded their bodies as perpetual motion machines as well as sexual objects. Thus bonds of gender as well as race were reinforced by the common experience of sexual harassment. . . . Women, unlike their black male co-workers, had to devise a whole range of strategies to resist or mitigate the daily physical and verbal abuse of their bodies, ranging from putting forth an "asexual" persona to posturing as a "crazy" person to simply quitting. Although these acts seem individualized and isolated, the experience of, and opposition to, sexual exploitation probably reinforced bonds of solidarity. In the tobacco factories, these confrontations usually took place in a collective setting, the advances of lecherous foremen were discussed among the women, and strategies to deal with sexual assault were observed, learned from other workplaces, or passed down. (Former domestics, for example, had experience staving off the sexual advances of male employers.) Yet, to most male union leaders, such battles were private affairs that had no place among "important" collective bargaining issues. Unfortunately, most labor historians have accepted this view, unable to see resistance to sexual harassment as a primary struggle to transform everyday conditions at the workplace. Nevertheless, out of this common social space and experience of racism and sexual exploitation, black female tobacco workers constructed "networks of solidarity." They referred to each other as "sisters," shared the same neighborhoods and community institutions, attended the same churches, and displayed a deep sense of mutuality by collecting money for co-workers during sickness and death and celebrating each other's birthdays. In fact, those networks of solidarity were indispensable for organizing tobacco plants in Winston-Salem and elsewhere. . . .

African-American workers' struggle for dignity did not end at the workplace. For most white workers public space—after intense class struggle—eventually became a "democratic space," where people of different class backgrounds shared city theaters, public conveyances, streets, and parks. For black people, white-dominated public space was vigilantly undemocratic and potentially dangerous. Jim Crow signs, filthy and inoperable public toilets, white police officers, dark bodies standing in the aisles of half-empty buses, black pedestrians stepping off the sidewalk or walking with their eyes turned down or away, and other acts of interracial social "etiquette"—all reminded black people every day of their second-class citizenship. The sights, sounds, and experiences of African Americans in white-dominated public spaces challenge the notion that southern black working-class politics can be understood by merely examining labor organization, workplace resistance, culture, and the family.

CHERISSE JONES-BRANCH

From "'To Speak When and Where I Can': African American Women's Political Activism in South Carolina in the 1940s and 1950s"

(July 2006)

... [B]lack women in South Carolina were critical actors in African Americans' epic struggle—from emancipation through the civil rights movement—to obtain access to electoral politics in [South Carolina]. During Reconstruction, after black men gained the right to vote, black women assumed important roles in African American political participation. After the vast majority of African Americans in South Carolina were disfranchised by the Constitution of 1895, this was no less the case. Well into the twentieth century, black women in South Carolina worked as leaders and followers at the grassroots level to enact political change for African Americans. This [essay] examines the collective and individual parts they played in South Carolina in the 1940s and 1950s as they fought for greater access to the political arena for all African Americans through such gender-integrated and female organizations as the South Carolina Progressive Democratic party, the South Carolina Federation of Colored Women's Clubs, and the Columbia Women's Council.

In August 1940, in the upcountry courthouse town of Gaffney, Lottie Polk Gaffney, teacher and principal of Petty Town School, went with four other women and several ministers to register to vote in the Cherokee County general election. When their turn to register came, the registrar informed Gaffney and those with her that "darkies ain't never voted in South Carolina and especially Cherokee County. I will not register you." Gaffney and her party promptly went to see the county attorney, who told them that they should have no trouble voting. Despite the county attorney's reassurance to the registrar that African Americans were eligible to vote, Gaffney and her party were still not allowed to register. In fact, when they returned on this second occasion, a member of the registration board slammed and locked the door before they could enter. Gaffney then wrote to NAACP officials in New York, who forwarded her letter to U.S. Attorney General Robert H. Jackson, asking that black voting rights be protected during the registration period. On September 2, 1940, the group returned to the registration office for a third time, where they were asked why they wanted to vote. Gaffney recalled:

> One member said that some God damned son of a bitch Republican put us up to want to vote. If the board would register us it would be dangerous for us—that our houses would be burned; that our heads would be scalped, etc. That if they would register us their heads would be cut off before night. If we registered it would do no good. If we are seeking social equality and a right to vote we had better go North.

Gaffney and the women who had accompanied her, with the assistance of the NAACP, brought suit against the Cherokee County Registration Board in March 1942 in the case of *United States v. Ellis et al.* Their efforts were to no avail. The Spartanburg County federal jury acquitted the officials of the charge of refusing to register African Americans, citing insufficient evidence. It is also likely that Gaffney and her group did not receive justice because the U.S. district attorney who represented them during the trial, Oscar H. Doyle, wanted to run for the U.S. Senate from South Carolina and was disinclined to jeopardize his political career by arguing the case too vigorously.

This court decision had further repercussions for Gaffney. For a time, local post office officials refused to deliver her mail. Even worse, because she had appeared as a witness in the case, Gaffney lost her position as a teacher and, despite an excellent record, was unable to gain employment in any South Carolina school district. When local black leaders learned of Gaffney's predicament, they asked school officials for an explanation and were told that the children's parents, displeased with her performance, had demanded her removal. They refused to accept this explanation and returned the following day with a petition supporting Gaffney that had been signed by the parent of every child in the school. School officials then told black leaders that Gaffney had been fired because she had "faked" the number of credits necessary for her college degree and had been receiving five dollars per month more in pay than she should have. Gaffney and her friends immediately went to the Colored Normal, Industrial, Agricultural, and Mechanical College of South Carolina (now South Carolina State University) at Orangeburg to check her credits. She had 150 units, thirty more than were necessary for a college degree. It was only after black leaders produced this evidence that school authorities were finally forced to admit that Gaffney had lost her job because she had taken part in the "voting case." Lottie Gaffney may have lost her case and her job, but by the early 1940s, black efforts to gain access to South Carolina's political arena were beginning to build momentum. Indeed, black leaders in South Carolina were well aware of court decisions and black political activism around the country that were presently reversing the tide of longstanding black political impotency in the South.

By the time Lottie Gaffney was prevented from registering to vote in Cherokee County in 1940, African Americans had been effectively excluded from participation in South Carolina politics for over four decades. For a time following the Civil War, black Republicans had enjoyed some political successes in the state. South Carolina had a black majority in the state assembly from 1868 through 1873, and the legislature was 40 percent black from 1874 to 1878. Even after the end of Reconstruction, blacks continued to hold political power in locales where they predominated. Black Republicans controlled Beaufort County politics through the mid 1890s, and the county sent five African American delegates to the state constitutional convention in 1895. But at the constitutional convention, U.S. Senator-Elect Ben Tillman installed a new plan for voting requirements: resembling the Mississippi Constitution of 1890, it was specifically designed to disfranchise African Americans and restore white supremacy. . . .

Marginalization and exclusion from the state Republican and Democratic parties made it clear to African Americans that the right to vote would not be easily won in South Carolina. Hence, they responded with an organization of their own to counteract such adamant denial of their rights. The Progressive Democratic party (PDP) was founded in May 1944 in Columbia by activist Osceola E. McKaine and John H. McCray, editor of the *Lighthouse and Informer*, a black newspaper, to counteract black exclusion from the state Democratic party. The PDP, which was open to all regardless of race, provided a necessary forum for African Americans in South Carolina to cultivate their increasing political activism. Three months after its founding, the PDP claimed 45,000 members in forty-four of the state's forty-six counties. . . .

In the early stages of the PDP's development, John H. McCray sought out black women willing to work with the organization. When the PDP held its first state convention at the Masonic Temple in Columbia, Lottie Gaffney was not only asked to lead the group in singing "America," but she also was elected as one of the PDP's three vice presidents and to a position on its national delegation selection committee. As further evidence of the PDP's commitment to female membership and active participation, in March 1945, less than one year after its founding, McCray wrote to Mrs. M. A. Morgan, offering his "best wishes to Mr. Morgan" and cautioning her "to get ready for some P.D.P. work which will be offered you a little later." As far as the leadership of the PDP was concerned, women's participation was critical. According to a 1944 flyer entitled "How To Organize For Voting," all men and women twenty-one years of age and older were urged to become members of the PDP, but women were recognized as particularly important in canvassing members for the organization: "Women should be used perhaps even more freely than men. At least, they should have equal footing in the organization." In July 1944, when the PDP went to the Democratic National Convention in Chicago, three women, including Lottie Gaffney, were part of its delegation.

The establishment of a women's auxiliary in 1945 offered black women a new opportunity to serve the PDP. In the same year, Sarah Z. Daniels, president of the Manning chapter of the NAACP, was appointed as auxiliary chairman. She had been working at the Palmer Memorial Institute in Sedalia, North Carolina, a private school for African Americans founded by Dr. Charlotte Hawkins Brown in 1902. For Daniels, helping blacks become politically empowered was so important that she resigned her post at Palmer Memorial in order to "come back to South Carolina, my home state where my service is needed most."

Daniels, who had also been a home demonstration agent and president of the Clarendon County Teachers' Association, organized two women's PDP auxiliaries in addition to leading the NAACP's voter-registration attempts in Clarendon County. In fact, she and other members of the auxiliaries made voter registration their "number one objective." Daniels expressed enthusiasm about becoming the PDP auxiliary chairman, seeing it as a further impetus to encourage eligible blacks to become politically involved. "I consider my appointment to speak when and where I can for the Progressive Democratic Party a privilege," she asserted, "and I am glad to accept." . . .

The number of women elected to positions within the PDP generally, not just the women's auxiliaries, evinces the importance of their participation to the welfare of the party. Women were often elected as chairmen of city clubs. In Charleston, for example, women were elected as chairpersons of Ward 11 and the Jenkins Orphanage. Additionally, there were female chairpersons in Awendaw, Pageland, Round O, Georgetown, and Richland County. Several women from these clubs were national committeewomen as well. Black women clearly recognized that exercising the right to vote and leading a movement to do so, both as individuals and through their organizational memberships, was not the sole domain of black men. Through their PDP connections, black women were well positioned to enlighten their communities statewide about the benefits of political access.

But women were expected to serve the PDP in traditional and stereotypical roles as well. In almost every county in South Carolina, women were the secretaries of local PDP chapters. This trend was reflected in the state organization. At the second annual PDP convention in 1946, Annie Belle Weston, Mrs. F. M. Thomas, and Mrs. Richardson, were elected as secretary, assistant secretary, and recording secretary, respectively. These same women and others served on the "Committee on Young People," "Committee on Women Workers," and the district chairmen committee. . . .

Throughout the 1940s, black women and their organizations had been working to get African Americans to the polls. In fact, the SCFCWC prided itself on its political activism in South Carolina. For example, in 1945 Ethelyn Murray Parker, publicity chairman of the South Carolina and the Charleston Federation of Colored Women's Clubs, invited John H. McCray to speak to the organization about the importance of voter registration. McCray's female audience needed little convincing, however. In extending the invitation, Parker informed McCray that members of the SCFCWC had been given ten thousand bulletins about voter registration to distribute in their communities. Furthermore, she impressed upon him the depth of black women's and the SCFCWC's commitment to gaining first-class citizenship for African Americans. According to Parker, "The president of every club is being urged to keep before her members the importance of the ballot, and to have every member registered. Some clubs have already registered one hundred percent." When Judge J. Waties Waring handed down his decision easing formal barriers to black voting in 1947, black women's clubs celebrated, knowing that the part their political activism played in the victory was not small. They also insisted that they not rest on their laurels, instead using this long-overdue right to encourage other blacks to register.

Individual black women like Annie Belle Weston were members and leaders of female-led organizations like the SCFCWC, but they also used their membership and leadership positions in mixed-sex organizations to promote greater political access for African Americans by placing particular emphasis on the potential political strength of black women. In a 1947 speech entitled "Women Fail to Use Their Political Power," Weston focused on women's abilities to make changes in South Carolina, arguing that not only did they have the power to obtain the vote for African Americans, but also to erase the "corrupt the practices of the courts, the sadistic tendencies of the law enforcement officer, the inequalities of the educational systems and the unwholesome recreation conditions." . . .

Black women's political activism in the PDP, SCFCWC, and CWC persisted into the 1960s, when, with the enactment of federal civil rights legislation guaranteeing and protecting black voting rights, they harnessed additional power to ensure black political access and equality in South Carolina. Their organizations continued to advocate equitable access to voting polls by supporting programs like the Voter Education Project (VEP), which had been formed in 1962 to assist thousands of African Americans who felt acute frustration because they lacked the basic skills, such as elementary reading and writing, required for voter registration. In particular, individual black women like Modjeska Simkins remained in the forefront of efforts to further expand political rights for African Americans. In the 1960s, Simkins used the all-black Richland County Citizens' Committee (RCCC) to further promote change in South Carolina's political system. The RCCC had been formed under the auspices of the South Carolina Citizens' Committee, founded in 1944. The local group received its charter in 1956 and adopted as its motto "Leading the effort toward keen community awareness in Non-partisan Political Action in Richland County." Simkins was the public relations director and an official correspondent for the RCCC. As such, she produced written communications for the organization, including its charter.

A close examination of such organizations as the PDP, SCFCWC, and CWC not only reveals black women's political astuteness and desire for change in South Carolina politics, but also the ways in which they were able to navigate male-dominated political terrain. Certainly, black-male leaders recognized their skills as leaders and organizers. Black women like Lottie Gaffney, Annie Belle Weston, and Modjeska Simkins realized that, while they made good leaders in the traditional sense, they were also effective at exacting change as grassroots activists. Black women activists did not limit themselves to addressing the political impotency of blacks generally. They also encouraged women to recognize their strength as a force for political *and* racial equality, using their membership in all-female organizations to reach out to black women as wives and mothers, whom they felt were particularly responsible for helping blacks to obtain the right to vote. Without the traditional and nontraditional leadership provided by these women, male leaders would not have been able to secure the necessary support to obtain political access for South Carolina blacks. When it came to improving conditions for African Americans in South Carolina, black women proved themselves able, in the words of Sarah Z. Daniels, "to speak when and where I can."

GEORGE LIPSITZ

From *The Possessive Investment in Whiteness: How White People Profit from Identity Politics*

(1998)

Blacks are often confronted, in American life, with such devastating examples of the white descent from dignity; devastating not only because of the enormity of white pretensions, but because this swift and graceless descent would seem to indicate that white people have no principles whatever.
JAMES BALDWIN

Shortly after World War II, a French reporter asked expatriate Richard Wright for his views about the "Negro problem" in America. The author replied, "There isn't any Negro problem; there is only a white problem." By inverting the reporter's question, Wright called attention to its hidden assumptions—that racial polarization comes from the existence of blacks rather than from the behavior of whites, that black people are a "problem" for whites rather than fellow citizens entitled to justice, and that, unless otherwise specified, "Americans" means "whites." Wright's formulation also placed political mobilization by African Americans during the civil rights era in context, connecting black disadvantages to white advantages and finding the roots of black consciousness in the systemic practices of aversion, exploitation, denigration, and discrimination practiced by people who think of themselves as "white."

Whiteness is everywhere in U.S. culture, but it is very hard to see. As Richard Dyer suggests, "[W]hite power secures its dominance by seeming not to be anything in particular." As the unmarked category against which difference is constructed, whiteness never has to speak its name, never has to acknowledge its role as an organizing principle in social and cultural relations. To identify, analyze, and oppose the destructive consequences of whiteness, we need what Walter Benjamin called "presence of mind." Benjamin wrote that people visit fortune-tellers less out of a desire to know the future than out of a fear of not noticing some important aspect of the present. "Presence of mind," he suggested, "is an abstract of the future, and precise awareness of the present moment more decisive than foreknowledge of the most distant events." In U.S. society at this time, precise awareness of the present moment requires an understanding of the existence and the destructive consequences of the possessive investment in whiteness that surreptitiously shapes so much of our public and private lives.

Race is a cultural construct, but one with deadly social causes and consequences. Conscious and deliberate actions have institutionalized group identity in the United States, not just through the dissemination of cultural stories, but also through the creation of social structures that generate economic advantages for European Americans through the possessive investment in whiteness. Studies of racial culture too far removed from studies of social structure leave us with inadequate explanations for understanding and combating racism. . . .

The possessive investment in whiteness is not a simple matter of black and white; all racialized minority groups have suffered from it, albeit to different degrees and in different ways. The African slave trade began in earnest only after large-scale Native American slavery proved impractical in North America. Efforts to abolish African slavery led initially to the importation of low-wage labor from Asia. Legislation banning immigration from Asia set the stage for the recruitment of low-wage labor from Mexico. All of the new racial hierarchies that emerged in each of these eras revolved around applying racial labels to "nonwhite" groups in order to stigmatize and exploit them, while at the same time reserving extra value for whiteness.

Although reproduced in new form in every era, the possessive investment in whiteness has always been influenced by its origins in the racialized history of the United States—by the legacy of slavery and segregation, of "Indian" extermination and immigrant restriction, of conquest and colonialism. Although slavery has existed in many countries without any particular racial dimensions to it, the slave system that emerged in North America soon took on distinctly racial forms. Africans enslaved in North America faced a racialized system of power that reserved permanent, hereditary, chattel slavery for black people. White settlers institutionalized a possessive investment in whiteness by making blackness synonymous with slavery and whiteness synonymous with freedom, but also by pitting people of color against one another. Fearful of alliances between Native Americans and African Americans that might challenge the prerogatives of whiteness, white settlers prohibited slaves and free blacks from traveling in "Indian country." European Americans used diplomacy and force to compel Native Americans to return runaway slaves to their white masters. During the Stono Rebellion of 1739, colonial authorities offered Native Americans a bounty for every rebellious slave they captured or killed. At the same time, British settlers recruited black slaves to fight against Native Americans within colonial militias.

The power of whiteness depended not only on white hegemony over separate racialized groups, but also on manipulating racial outsiders to fight against one another, to compete with each other for white approval, and to seek the rewards and privileges of whiteness for themselves at the expense of other racialized populations.

Aggrieved communities of color have often curried favor with whites in order to make gains at each other's expense. In the nineteenth century some Native Americans held black slaves (in part because whites viewed slave ownership as a "civilized" European American practice that would improve Indians). Some of the first regular African American units in the U.S. army went to war against Comanches in Texas and served as security forces for wagon trains of white settlers on the trails to California. The defeat of the Comanches in the 1870s sparked a mass migration by Spanish-speaking residents of New Mexico into the areas of West Texas formerly occupied by the vanquished Native Americans. Immigrants from Asia sought the rewards of whiteness for themselves by asking the courts to recognize them as "white" and therefore eligible for naturalized citizenship according to the Immigration and Naturalization Act of 1790; Mexican Americans also insisted on being classified as white. In the early twentieth century, black soldiers accustomed to fighting Native Americans in the Southwest participated in the U.S. occupation of the Philippines and the punitive expedition against Pancho Villa in Mexico. Asian American managers cracked down on efforts by Mexican American farmworkers to form unions in the fields, while the Pullman Company tried to break the African American Brotherhood of Sleeping Car Porters by importing Filipinos to work as porters. Mexican Americans and blacks took possession of some of the property confiscated from Japanese Americans during the internment of the 1940s, and Asian Americans, blacks, and Mexican Americans all secured advantages for themselves by cooperating with the exploitation of Native Americans.

Yet while every racialized minority group has sometimes sought the rewards of whiteness, these groups have also been able to form interethnic antiracist alliances. Native American tribes often harbored runaway slaves and drew upon their expertise in combat against whites. In 1711, an African named Harry helped lead the Tuscaroras against the British. Native Americans secured the cooperation of black slaves in their attacks on the French settlement near Natchez in colonial Louisiana in 1729, and black Seminoles in Florida routinely recruited slaves from Georgia plantations to their side in battles against European Americans. African Americans resisting slavery and white supremacy in the United States during the nineteenth century sometimes looked to Mexico as a refuge (especially after that nation abolished slavery), and in the twentieth century the rise of Japan as a successful nonwhite world power served as one source of inspiration and emulation among African American nationalists. In 1903, Mexican American and Japanese American farm workers joined forces in Oxnard, California, to wage a successful strike in the beet fields, and subsequently members of the two groups organized an interracial union, the Japanese Mexican Labor Association. Yet whether characterized by conflict or cooperation, all relations among aggrieved racialized minorities stemmed from recognition of the rewards of whiteness and the concomitant penalties imposed upon "nonwhite" populations.

The possessive investment in whiteness today is not simply the residue of conquest and colonialism, of slavery and segregation, of immigrant exclusion and "Indian" extermination. Contemporary whiteness and its rewards have been created and recreated by policies adopted long after the emancipation of slaves in the 1860s and even after the outlawing of de jure segregation in the 1960s. There has always been racism in the United States, but it has not always been the same racism. Racism has changed over time, taking on different forms and serving different social purposes in each time period. Antiracist mobilizations during the Civil War and civil rights eras meaningfully curtailed the reach and scope of white supremacy, but in each case reactionary forces engineered a renewal of racism in new forms during succeeding decades.

Contemporary racism has been created anew in many ways over the past half century, most dramatically by the putatively race-neutral, liberal, social democratic reforms of the New Deal Era and by the more overtly race-conscious neoconservative reactions against liberalism since the Nixon years. It is a mistake to posit a gradual and inevitable trajectory of evolutionary progress in race relations; on the contrary, our history shows that battles won at one moment can later be lost. Despite hard-fought struggles for change that secured important concessions during the 1960s in the form of civil rights legislation, the racialized nature of social policy in the United States since the Great Depression has actually increased the possessive investment in whiteness among European Americans over the past five decades.

During the New Deal Era of the 1930s and 1940s, both the Wagner Act and the Social Security Act excluded farm workers and domestics from coverage, effectively denying those disproportionately minority sectors of the work force protections and benefits routinely afforded whites. The Federal Housing Act of 1934 brought home ownership within reach of millions of citizens by placing the credit of the federal government behind private lending to home buyers, but overtly racist categories in the Federal Housing Agency's (FHA) "confidential" city surveys and appraisers' manuals channeled almost all of the loan money toward whites and away from communities of color. In the post–World War II era, trade unions negotiated contract provisions giving private medical insurance, pensions, and job security largely to the white workers who formed the over-whelming majority of the unionized work force in mass production industries, rather than fighting for full employment, medical care, and old-age pensions for all, while avoiding the fight for an end to discriminatory hiring and promotion practices by employers in those industries.

Each of these policies widened the gap between the resources available to whites and those available to aggrieved racial communities. Federal housing policy offers an important illustration of the broader principles at work in the possessive investment in whiteness. By channeling loans away from older in-ner-city neighborhoods and toward white home buyers moving into segregated suburbs, the FHA and private lenders after World War II aided and abetted seg-regation in U.S. residential neighborhoods. . . .

During the 1950s and 1960s, local "pro-growth" coalitions led by liberal may-ors often justified urban renewal as a program designed to build more hous-ing for poor people. In reality, urban renewal destroyed more housing than it created. Ninety percent of the low-income units removed for urban renewal projects during the entire history of the program were never replaced. Com-mercial, industrial, and municipal projects occupied more than 80 percent of the land cleared for these projects, with less than 20 percent allocated for re-placement housing. In addition, the loss of taxable properties and the tax abate-ments granted to new enterprises in urban renewal zones often meant serious tax increases for poor, working-class, and middle-class homeowners and rent-ers. Although the percentage of black suburban dwellers also increased during this period, no significant desegregation of the suburbs took place. Four million whites moved out of central cities between 1960 and 1977, while the number of whites living in suburbs increased by 22 million; during the same years, the inner-city black population grew by 6 million, but the number of blacks living in suburbs increased by only 500,000. By 1993, 86 percent of suburban whites still lived in places with a black population below 1 percent. At the same time, cities with large numbers of minority residents found themselves cut off from loans by the FHA. Because of their growing black and Puerto Rican populations, not a single FHA-sponsored mortgage went to either Camden or Paterson, New Jersey, in 1966. . . .

Minority disadvantages craft advantages for others. Urban renewal failed to provide new housing for the poor, but it played an important role in trans-forming the U.S. urban economy from one that relied on factory production to one driven by producer services. Urban renewal projects subsidized the de-velopment of downtown office centers on previously residential land, and they frequently created buffer zones of empty blocks dividing poor neighborhoods from new shopping centers designed for affluent commuters. To help cities

compete for corporate investment by making them appealing to high-level ex-
ecutives, federal urban aid favored construction of luxury housing units and
cultural centers like symphony halls and art museums over affordable housing
for workers. Tax abatements granted to these producer services centers further
aggravated the fiscal crises that cities faced, leading to tax increases on existing
industries, businesses, and residences.

Workers from aggrieved racial minorities bore the brunt of this transformation. Because the 1964 Civil Rights Act came so late, minority workers who received jobs because of it found themselves more vulnerable to seniority-based
layoffs when businesses automated or transferred operations overseas. Although
the act initially made real progress in reducing employment discrimination,
lessening the gaps between rich and poor and between black and white workers
while helping to bring minority poverty to its lowest level in history in 1973,
that year's recession initiated a reversal of minority progress and a reassertion of
white privilege. In 1977, the U.S. Civil Rights Commission reported on the disproportionate impact of layoffs on minority workers. In cases where minority
workers made up only 10 to 12 percent of the work force in their area in 1974,
they accounted for 60 to 70 percent of those laid off. The principle of seniority,
a trade union triumph designed to protect workers from age discrimination, in
this case guaranteed that minority workers would suffer most from technolog-
ical changes, because the legacy of past discrimination by their employers left
them with less seniority than white workers. . . .

. . . Failure to acknowledge our society's possessive investment in whiteness
prevents us from facing the present openly and honestly. It hides from us the
devastating costs of disinvestment in America's infrastructure over the past two
decades and keeps us from facing our responsibility to reinvest in human resources by channeling resources toward education, health, and housing—and
away from subsidies for speculation and luxury. After two decades of disinvestment, the only further disinvestment we need is from the ruinous pathology
of whiteness. The possessive investment in whiteness undermines our best instincts and interests. In a society suffering so badly from an absence of mutuality, an absence of responsibility, and an absence of justice, presence of mind
might be just what we need.

"Blackness beyond Boundaries"

Navigating the Political Economies
of Global Inequality

(2008)

> The advance guard of the Negro people . . . must soon come to realize that if they
> are to take their just place in the van of Pan-Negroism, then their destiny is *not*
> absorption by the white Americans. That if in America it is to be proven for the first
> time in the modern world that not only Negroes are capable of evolving individual
> men like Toussaint, the Saviour, but are a nation stored with wonderful possibilities
> of culture, then their destiny is not a servile imitation of Anglo-Saxon culture, but a
> stalwart originality which shall unswervingly follow Negro ideals.
>
> W. E. B. DU BOIS, 1897

On March 5, 1897, the newly formed American Negro Academy met for its inaugural sessions in Washington, D.C., W. E. B. Du Bois, then a twenty-nine-year-old social scientist and recent PhD graduate of Harvard University, delivered the second paper to this gathering of black American intellectuals, "The Conservation of Races," that would foreshadow much of his future life's work. The paper centered in part on the question of what constituted "blackness," or the construction of black identity within the challenging contexts of white-dominated societies. Inside the United States, Du Bois argued, each African American must struggle to determine "what, after all, am I? Am I an American or am I a Negro? Can I be both?" Du Bois then sought to delineate the boundaries between Africanity, race, and citizenship that constantly confronted black Americans:

> We are Americans, not only by birth and by citizenship, but by our political ideals,
> our language, our religion. Farther than that, our Americanism does not go. At that
> point, we are Negroes, members of a vast historic race that from the very dawn of
> creation has slept, but half awakening the dark forests of its African fatherland. . . .
> We are that people whose subtle sense of song has given America its only American music, its only American fairy tales, its only touch of pathos and humor amid
> its mad money-getting plutocracy. As such, it is our duty to conserve our physical
> powers, our intellectual endowments, our spiritual ideals; as a race we must strive
> by race organization, by race solidarity.

For Du Bois at this time, the boundaries of blackness were defined largely by aesthetics, culture, and the highly charged construction of "race." But as the twentieth century unfolded, Du Bois expanded his understanding about the common grounds that people of African descent shared throughout the colonial and segregated world. This led him to embrace the politics of Pan-Africanism, and efforts by black activists in the Caribbean, the United States, and Africa itself to overthrow white minority regimes. Intellectually, it gave Du Bois a truly global concept of what today would be termed "Black Studies." Part of the mission of Black Studies as an intellectual project has been the remapping of collective identity and memory, in part by using Du Bois's criteria. But it should also combine theory with collective action, in the effort not simply to interpret but to transform the world, empowering black people in the process. . . .

It is impossible to relate the full narrative of the experiences of people of African descent in the United States, and throughout the Caribbean and the Americas, without close integration and reference to the remarkable history of the African continent, its many peoples, languages, and diverse cultures. The South Atlantic and especially the Caribbean were "highways" for constant cultural, intellectual, and political exchange between people of African descent, especially during the past three centuries. Pan-Africanist-inspired social protest movements like Marcus Garvey's Universal Negro Improvement Association and African Communities League (UNIA) started in Jamaica but accelerated into hundreds of chapters across the United States as a mass movement, and then grew hundreds of new chapters throughout Central America and Africa. Documenting the UNIA's complex story by focusing solely on the events of one nation, such as the United States, distorts the narrative and cripples our understanding of fundamental events. Similarly, South Africa's "Black Consciousness Movement" of the 1970s and the brilliant protest writings of Steven Biko cannot be interpreted properly without detailed references to the "Black Power Movement" in the United States during the 1960s, and to the influential speeches and political writings of Malcolm X of the United States and Frantz Fanon of Martinique.

"Blackness" acquires its full revolutionary potential as a social site for resistance only within transnational and Pan-African contexts. This insight motivated W. E. B. Du Bois to initiate the Pan-African Congress Movement at the end of World War I. George Padmore, Kwame Nkrumah, Du Bois, and others sponsored the Fifth Pan-African Congress, in Manchester, England, in October 1945, out of the recognition that the destruction of European colonial rule in Africa and the Caribbean, and the demise of the Jim Crow regime of racial segregation in the United States, were politically linked. Any advance toward democracy and civil rights in any part of the black world objectively assisted the goals and political aspirations of people of African descent elsewhere. An internationalist perspective, from a historian's point of view, also helped to explain the dynamics of the brutal transnational processes of capitalist political economy—the forced movement of involuntary labor across vast boundaries; the physical and human exploitation of slaves; the subsequent imposition of debt peonage, convict leasing, and sharecropping in postemancipation societies; and the construction of hypersegregated, racialized urban ghettoes, from Soweto to Rio de Janeiro's slums to Harlem. . . . [T]he twentieth century was full of examples of "blackness beyond boundaries as praxis"—intellectual-activists of African descent who sparked movements of innovative scholarship, as well as social protest movements, throughout Africa and the African Diaspora.

In 1900, Du Bois had predicted that the central "problem of the twentieth century" would be the "problem of the color line," the unequal relationship between the lighter versus darker races of humankind. Du Bois's color line included not just the racially segregated Jim Crow South and the racial oppression of South Africa but also the British, French, Belgian, and Portuguese colonial domination in Asia, the Middle East, Latin America, and the Caribbean among indigenous populations. Building on Du Bois's insights, we can therefore say that the problem of the twenty-first century is the problem of global apartheid: the racialized division and stratification of resources, wealth, and power that separates Europe, North America, and Japan from the billions of mostly black, brown, indigenous, undocumented immigrant, and poor people across the planet. The term "apartheid" comes from the former white minority regime of South Africa; an Afrikaans word, it means "apartness" or "separation." Apartheid was based on the concept of *herrenvolk*, a "master race" that was predestined to rule all non-Europeans. Under global apartheid today, the racist logic of *herrenvolk* is embedded ideologically in the patterns of unequal economic and global accumulation that penalizes African, South Asian, Caribbean, Latin American, and other impoverished nations by predatory policies.

Since 1979–80, with the elections of Ronald Reagan as U.S. president and Margaret Thatcher as prime minister of the United Kingdom, America and Great Britain embarked on domestic economic development strategies that are now widely known by the term "neoliberalism." Neoliberal politics called for the dismantling of the welfare state; the end of redistributive social programs designed to address the effects of poverty; the elimination of governmental regulations and regulatory agencies over capitalist markets; and "privatization," the transfer of public institutions and governmental agencies to corporations. Journalist Thomas B. Edsall has astutely characterized this reactionary process of neoliberal politics within the United States in these terms: "For a quarter-century, the Republican temper—its reckless drive to jettison the social safety net; its support of violence in law enforcement and national defense; its advocacy of regressive taxation, environmental hazard and probusiness dereg ulation; its 'remoralizing' of the pursuit of wealth—has been judged by many voters as essential to America's position in the world, producing more benefit than cost."

One of the consequences of this reactionary political and economic agenda, according to Edsall, was "the Reagan administration's arms race" during the 1980s, which "arguably drove the Soviet Union into bankruptcy." A second consequence, Edsall argues, was America's disastrous military invasion of Iraq. "While inflicting destruction on the Iraqis," Edsall observes, "[George H. W.] Bush multiplied America's enemies and endangered this nation's military, economic health and international stature. Courting risk without managing it, Bush repeatedly and remorselessly failed to accurately evaluate the consequences of his actions."

Edsall's insightful analysis significantly did not attempt to explain away the 2003 U.S. invasion of Iraq under President George W. Bush and subsequent military occupation as a political "mistake" or an "error of judgment." Rather, he located the rationale for the so-called "war on terrorism" within the context of U.S. domestic, neoliberal politics. "The embroilment in Iraq is not an aberration," Edsall observes. "It stems from core [Republican] party principles, equally evident on the domestic front." The larger question of political economy, left unexplored by Edsall and most U.S. mainstream analysts, is the connection between U.S. militarism abroad, neoliberalism, and macro-trends in the global economy. As economists, such as Paul Sweezy and Harry Magdoff, noted decades ago, the general economic tendency of mature, global capitalism is toward stagnation. For decades, in the United States and western Europe, there has been a steady decline in investment in the productive economy, leading to a decline in industrial capacity and lower future growth rates. Profit margins inside the U.S. have fallen over time, and corporations have been forced to invest capital abroad to generate higher rates of profitability. There is a direct economic link between the deindustrialized urban landscapes of Detroit, Youngstown, and Chicago with the expansion of industries in China, Vietnam, Brazil, and other developing nations. . . .

Although the majority of nations in the international community either openly opposed, or at least seriously questioned, the U.S. military occupation of Iraq, the neoliberal economic model of the United States has been now widely adopted by both developed and developing countries. Governments across the ideological spectrum—with the important exception of some Latin American countries in recent years—have eliminated social welfare, health, and education programs; reduced governmental regulations on business activity; and encouraged the growth income inequality and entrepreneurship. Even noncapitalist countries like Cuba have revived the sex-trade-oriented tourism business, which has contributed to new forms of gender and racial prejudice in that country. As

a result, economic inequality in wealth has rapidly accelerated, reinforcing traditional patterns of racial and ethnic domination.

A 2006 study by the World Institute for Development Economic Research of
the United Nations University established that, as of 2000, the upper 1 percent
of the globe's adult population, approximately 37 million people, averaged about
$515,000 in net worth per person, and collectively controlled roughly 40 percent
of the world's entire wealth. By contrast, the bottom one-half of the planet's adult
population, 1.85 billion people, most of whom are black and brown, owned only
1.1 percent of the world's total wealth. There is tremendous inequality of wealth
between nations, the UN report noted. The United States, for example, comprised
only 4.7 percent of the world's people, but it had nearly one-third, or 32.6 percent, of global wealth. By stark contrast, China, which had one-fifth of the world's
population, owned only 2.6 percent of the globe's wealth. India, which has 16.8
percent of the global population, controlled only 0.9 percent of the world's total
wealth. Within most of the world's countries, wealth was disproportionately concentrated in the top 10 percent of each nation's population. It comes as no surprise that in the United States, for example, that as of 2000 the upper 10 percent
of the adult population owned 69.8 percent of the nation's total wealth. However, Canada, a nation with much more liberal social welfare traditions than the
United States, nevertheless still exhibited significant inequality. More than one-
half (53 percent) of Canadian assets, were owned by only 10 percent of the population. European countries such as Norway, at 50.5 percent, and Spain, at 41.9
percent, had similar or slightly lower levels of wealth inequality.

The most revealing finding of the World Institute for Development Economics Research was that similar patterns of wealth inequality have come to be prev-
alent throughout the developing world. In Indonesia, for example, 65.4 percent
of the nation's total wealth belonged to the wealthiest 10 percent in 2000. In India, the upper 10 percent owned 52 percent of all Indian wealth. Even in China,
where the ruling Communist Party still maintains vestiges of what might be described as "authoritarian state socialism," the wealthiest 10 percent owned 41.4
percent of the national wealth.

But even these macroeconomic statistics, as useful as they are, obscure a
crucial dimension of wealth concentration under global apartheid's neoliberal
economics. In the past quarter century in the United States, where deregulation
and privatization have been carried to obscene extremes, we are presently witnessing a phenomenon that the media has described as "the very rich" who are
leaving "the merely rich behind." One study by New York University economist
Edward N. Wolff found that 1 out of every 825 households in the United States
in 2004 earned at least $2 million annually, representing nearly a 100 percent
increase in the wealth percentage recorded in 1989, adjusted for inflation. As of
2004, 1 out of every 325 U.S. households possessed a net wealth of $10 million or

more. When adjusted by inflation, this is more than four times as many wealthy households as in 1989. The exponential growth of America's "super-rich" is a direct product of the near elimination of capital gains taxes and the sharp decline in federal government income tax rates.

Inside the United States, the processes of global apartheid are best represented by the "New Racial Domain" (NRD). The NRD is different from other earlier systemic forms of racial domination inside the United States—such as slavery, Jim Crow segregation, and ghettoization or strict residential segregation—in several critical aspects. These earlier racial formations, or exploitative racial domains, were grounded or based primarily, if not exclusively, in the political economy of U.S. capitalism. Antiracist or oppositional movements that blacks, other ethnic minorities, and white antiracists built were largely predicated upon the confines or realities of domestic markets and the policies of the U.S. nation-state. Meaningful social reforms such as the Civil Rights Act of 1964 and the Voting Rights Act of 1965 were debated almost entirely within the context of America's expanding, domestic economy, and influenced by Keynesian, welfare-state public policies. The political economy of America's NRD, by contrast, is driven and largely determined by the forces of transnational capitalism, and the public policies of state neoliberalism. From the vantage point of the most oppressed U.S. populations, the NRD rests on an unholy trinity, or deadly triad, of structural barriers to a decent life. These oppressive structures are mass unemployment, mass incarceration, and mass disfranchisement. Each factor directly feeds and accelerates the others, creating an ever-widening circle of social disadvantage, poverty, and civil death, touching the lives of tens of millions of people in the United States.

[For centuries, various] individuals and organizations of African descent, primarily originating in the United States . . . challenged the legitimacy and power of the global color line and its oppressive political economies of inequality. Such examples varied widely in the tactics and strategies for social change they employed. What they held in common was a long memory of resistance to human exploitation, and the knowledge of African-descendant cultural heritages and rituals that connected the diverse peoples of the African Diaspora. For Du Bois over a century ago, there were certain "Negro ideals" worth fighting to preserve, which challenged the hegemonic materialism of Europe and America. Similarly, as the twenty-first century unfolds, and as the global color line's struggles for social justice intensify, the role of black activist-intellectuals and social protest movements will assume even greater significance transnationally.

PART 5

Civil Rights and Black Power

CHAD WILLIAMS

The Charleston massacre and the responses to it cannot be fully understood without clear recognition of how the civil rights and Black Power movements fundamentally transformed American society and the ways in which we think and talk about issues of race, violence, and national belonging. The struggle for African American civil rights did not begin in the 1950s. As a wealth of recent scholarship has demonstrated, struggles for black freedom and full citizenship began during the antebellum period and continued throughout the early to mid-twentieth century. Indeed, much of modern African American history is the story of how black men and women from across the country, employing all strategies and using every intellectual tool at their disposal, organized, argued, and protested for recognition of African Americans' full humanity and basic rights.

The civil rights and Black Power movements, commonly seen as encapsulating a time period from the mid-1950s to the late 1970s, represented the culmination of earlier struggles. At the same time, specific groups, individuals, and historical conditions converged to make this epoch in the black freedom struggle distinct.

In the aftermath of World War II, African Americans, especially those who served in the military, refused to return to a prewar racial status quo. A new generation of grassroots activists and leaders emerged that pushed African Americans, especially in the South, to bravely challenge white supremacy. These local people were complemented by the ascension of several inspiring and charismatic individuals, such as Malcolm X and Martin Luther King Jr., who commanded national attention and used their prophetic voice to galvanize African Americans across the country. Established civil rights organizations, such as the National Association for the Advancement of Colored People (NAACP) and the Urban League, were joined by new groups, such as the Southern Christian Leadership Conference (SCLC) and the Student Non-violent Coordinating Committee (SNCC), that together mobilized African Americans of varying backgrounds and beliefs around the shared goal of black freedom. Groups associated with the Black Power movement, such as the Black Panther Party for Self-Defense, the League of Revolutionary Black Workers, and the US Organization, inspired black people to see themselves and their potential for radical change in a fundamentally different light.

These developments took place in a larger international context of movements for black freedom throughout the African diaspora. World War II exposed the weaknesses of Western imperialism and created the space for colonized peoples to organize and fight for independence. Diasporic intellectuals and political leaders such as Franz Fanon, Kwame Nkrumah, and Julius Neyere offered inspiration to African Americans similarly seeking freedom in the United States. Taking advantage of the Cold War, African Americans challenged the U.S. government to live up to the democratic ideals it professed to the world. The advent of television and new media technologies allowed black civil and human rights activists to share their message with both domestic and international mass audiences and, through direct action protest and civil disobedience, showcase both the hypocrisy and brutality of American racism.

On the local level, Charleston, South Carolina, was a particularly important site of black activism. As the selection by Robert Korstad demonstrates, black people in Charleston built important movements for African American civil rights and economic justice, beginning immediately after World War II and continuing throughout the 1960s. The Emmanuel African Methodist Episcopal Church served as a key location for grassroots organizing, as well as a symbol of black communal strength in the heart of the former Confederacy. Indeed, Charleston was a central battleground in what many historians have characterized as a second Reconstruction, one defined by remarkable progress and courage in the face of white resistance.

White opposition to change regularly took the form of violence. Terrorist groups such as the Ku Klux Klan mobilized in the name of white supremacy—and often under the banner of the Confederate flag—to maintain the South's racial caste system. Transgressions of the region's codes of racial etiquette could result in loss of life, as fourteen-year-old Emmett Till brutally experienced. The assassinations of civil rights leaders like Medgar Evers and Martin Luther King Jr. sent the devastating message that no black person, regardless of his or her notoriety, was immune from killing. The violence of this period went beyond white vigilantism. Scenes of southern law enforcement viciously beating unarmed African American protesters in Birmingham, Selma, and other locations shocked the nation and compelled the federal government to act. The South was by no means unique. Black men and women in Oakland, Los Angeles, Detroit, Chicago, New York, and other major cities confronted police brutality on a daily basis, demonstrating the necessity for organizations such as the Nation of Islam and the Black Panther Party for Self-Defense.

As with the aftermath of the Charleston shooting in 2015, African Americans in the 1960s responded to racial violence in various ways. The Charleston shooting immediately drew comparisons with the September 15, 1963, bombing of the Sixteenth Street Baptist Church in Birmingham, Alabama, by a Ku Klux Klansman that killed four girls preparing for Sunday school service. Martin Luther King Jr., in his moving eulogy, found meaning for their deaths in his Christianity, tapping into a deep spiritual reservoir of African American perseverance and forgiveness through faith. In contrast, Nation of Islam minister Malcolm X, in his "Message to the Grassroots" speech delivered just two months later, saw the bombing and other atrocities as fundamentally American and expressed no desire to adhere to a philosophy of nonviolence while black people in the United States and beyond continued to die without any semblance of justice. As Akinyele Umoja demonstrates, debates about violence and self-defense were not merely theoretical but reflected the pressing everyday realities of confronting white racial terrorism in areas such as Mississippi and encouraged groups such as the Deacons of Defense to take it upon themselves to act.

We see from this history the roots of Black Power and how, as an ideology and movement, it emerged organically within the broader social, political, and cultural currents of the black freedom struggle of the 1950s, 1960s, and 1970s. Matthew Countryman reveals how Black Power migrated from the Deep South to Philadelphia, in the process adapting to the particular social, political, and economic conditions of African Americans in the North. Black Power took on many incarnations, including expressions of racial pride and political statements such as the 1972 Gary, Indiana, declaration. Black Power imparted a legacy that continues to inform contemporary black culture and politics, including the presence and symbolism of contemporary black elected officials like Clementa Pinckney and President Barack Obama.

Women and the politics of gender and sexuality stood at the center of the civil rights and Black Power movements. When Dylann Roof rationalized his actions by claiming that black men were "raping our women," he invoked a core element of southern white supremacist thought that, as Danielle McGuire demonstrates, associates both the potential and reality of interracial contact with sexual violence. However, the fact that the majority of Roof's victims were black women cannot be ignored. African American women, as they had been in the past, remained key participants and leaders in local grassroots organizing traditions, especially those based in the black church. As the movement evolved and expanded in the 1960s, the public presence and voice of individuals like Fannie Lou Hamer increased and highlighted how racism, sexism, and economic exploitation combined to uniquely oppress black women. Bringing awareness to these issues challenged the patriarchal structure of many organizations and exposed the shortcomings of many male leaders. By the 1970s, efforts to come to the defense of women like Joan Little, as Genna Rae McNeil recounts, reflected the evolution of not just the civil rights and Black Power movements but a growing black feminist movement as well.

Throughout this era, African Americans found multiple ways to sustain themselves in the midst of tragedy and in the face of seemingly insurmountable obstacles. Music proved especially important. Songs such as "We Shall Overcome," rooted in the black Christian church, expressed the hope of the movement, the power of faith, and the promise of victory. At the same time, other songs, like Nina Simone's "Mississippi Goddamn," articulated the pain, frustration, and rage African Americans grappled with as black progress clashed with the harsh reality of black death. No wonder that, in the aftermath of the Charleston shooting, many African Americans revisited Simone's song, substituting Mississippi with "South Carolina."

FANNIE LOU HAMER

Testimony before the Credentials Committee, Democratic National Convention, Atlantic City, New Jersey

(August 22, 1964)

Mr. Chairman, and to the Credentials Committee, my name is Mrs. Fannie Lou Hamer, and I live at 626 East Lafayette Street, Ruleville, Mississippi, Sunflower County, the home of Senator James O. Eastland, and Senator Stennis.

It was the 31st of August in 1962 that eighteen of us traveled twenty-six miles to the county courthouse in Indianola to try to register to become first-class citizens.

We was met in Indianola by policemen, Highway Patrolmen, and they only allowed two of us in to take the literacy test at the time. After we had taken this test and started back to Ruleville, we was held up by the City Police and the State Highway Patrolmen and carried back to Indianola where the bus driver was charged that day with driving a bus the wrong color.

After we paid the fine among us, we continued on to Ruleville, and Reverend Jeff Sunny carried me four miles in the rural area where I had worked as a timekeeper and sharecropper for eighteen years. I was met there by my children, who told me that the plantation owner was angry because I had gone down to try to register.

After they told me, my husband came, and said the plantation owner was raising Cain because I had tried to register. Before he quit talking the plantation owner came and said, "Fannie Lou, do you know—did Pap tell you what I said?"

And I said, "Yes, sir."

He said, "Well I mean that." He said, "If you don't go down and withdraw your registration, you will have to leave." Said, "Then if you go down and withdraw," said, "you still might have to go because we are not ready for that in Mississippi."

And I addressed him and told him and said, "I didn't try to register for you. I tried to register for myself."

I had to leave that same night.

On the 10th of September 1962, sixteen bullets was fired into the home of Mr. and Mrs. Robert Tucker for me. That same night two girls were shot in Ruleville, Mississippi. Also Mr. Joe McDonald's house was shot in.

And June the 9th, 1963, I had attended a voter registration workshop; was returning back to Mississippi. Ten of us was traveling by the Continental Trailway bus. When we got to Winona, Mississippi, which is Montgomery County, four of the people got off to use the washroom, and two of the people—to use the restaurant—two of the people wanted to use the washroom.

The four people that had gone in to use the restaurant was ordered out. During this time I was on the bus. But when I looked through the window and saw they had rushed out I got off of the bus to see what had happened. And one of the ladies said, "It was a State Highway Patrolman and a Chief of Police ordered us out."

I got back on the bus and one of the persons had used the washroom got back on the bus, too.

As soon as I was seated on the bus, I saw when they began to get the five people in a highway patrolman's car. I stepped off of the bus to see what was happening and somebody screamed from the car that the five workers was in and said, "Get that one there." When I went to get in the car, when the man told me I was under arrest, he kicked me.

I was carried to the county jail and put in the booking room. They left some of the people in the booking room and began to place us in cells. I was placed in a cell with a young woman called Miss Ivesta Simpson. After I was placed in the cell I began to hear sounds of licks and screams, I could hear the sounds of licks and horrible screams. And I could hear somebody say, "Can you say, 'yes, sir,' nigger? Can you say 'yes, sir'?"

And they would say other horrible names.

She would say, "Yes, I can say 'yes, sir.'"

"So, well, say it."

She said, "I don't know you well enough."

They beat her, I don't know how long. And after a while she began to pray, and asked God to have mercy on those people.

And it wasn't too long before three white men came to my cell. One of these men was a State Highway Patrolman and he asked me where I was from. I told him Ruleville and he said, "We are going to check this."

They left my cell and it wasn't too long before they came back. He said, "You are from Ruleville all right," and he used a curse word. And he said, "We are going to make you wish you was dead."

I was carried out of that cell into another cell where they had two Negro prisoners. The State Highway Patrolmen ordered the first Negro to take the blackjack.

The first Negro prisoner ordered me, by orders from the State Highway Patrolman, for me to lay down on a bunk bed on my face.

I laid on my face and the first Negro began to beat. I was beat by the first Negro until he was exhausted. I was holding my hands behind me at that time on my left side, because I suffered from polio when I was six years old.

After the first Negro had beat until he was exhausted, the State Highway Patrolman ordered the second Negro to take the blackjack.

The second Negro began to beat and I began to work my feet, and the State Highway Patrolman ordered the first Negro who had beat me to sit on my feet—to keep me from working my feet. I began to scream and one white man got up and began to beat me in my head and tell me to hush.

One white man—my dress had worked up high—he walked over and pulled my dress—I pulled my dress down and he pulled my dress back up.

I was in jail when Medgar Evers was murdered.

All of this is on account of we want to register, to become first-class citizens. And if the Freedom Democratic Party is not seated now, I question America. Is this America, the land of the free and the home of the brave, where we have to sleep with our telephones off the hooks because our lives be threatened daily, because we want to live as decent human beings, in America?

Thank you.

We Shall Overcome

We shall overcome, we shall overcome,
We shall overcome someday.
Oh, deep in my heart, I do believe,
We shall overcome someday.

The truth will make us free, the truth will make us free,
The truth will make us free someday,
Oh, deep in my heart, I do believe,
We shall overcome someday.

We'll walk hand in hand, we'll walk hand in hand,
We'll walk hand in hand someday.
Oh, deep in my heart, I do believe,
We shall overcome someday.

We are not afraid, we are not afraid,
We are not afraid today.
Oh, deep in my heart, I do believe,
We shall overcome someday.

The truth will make us free, the truth will make us free,
The truth will make us free someday,
Oh, deep in my heart, I do believe,
We shall overcome someday.

We shall overcome, we shall overcome,
We shall overcome someday.
Oh, deep in my heart, I do believe,
We shall overcome someday.

Mississippi Goddam

(1963)

The name of this tune is Mississippi Goddam
And I mean every word of it.

Alabama's gotten me so upset
Tennessee made me lose my rest
And everybody knows about Mississippi Goddam

Alabama's gotten me so upset
Tennessee made me lose my rest
And everybody knows about Mississippi Goddam

Can't you see it? Can't you feel it?
It's all in the air
I can't stand the pressure much longer
Somebody say a prayer

Alabama's gotten me so upset
Tennessee made me lose my rest
And everybody knows about Mississippi Goddam

This is a show tune
But the show hasn't been written for it, yet

Hound dogs on my trail
School children sitting in jail
Black cat cross my path
I think everyday's gonna be my last

Lord, have mercy on this land of mine
We all gonna get it in due time
I don't belong here, I don't belong there
I've even stopped believing in prayer

Don't tell me, I tell you
Me and my people just about due
I've been there so I know
They keep on saying, "Go slow!"

But that's just the trouble, do it slow
Washing the windows, do it slow
Picking the cotton, do it slow
You're just plain rotten, do it slow

You're too damn lazy, do it slow
The thinking's crazy, do it slow
Where am I going? What am I doing?
I don't know, I don't know

Just try to do your very best
Stand up be counted with all the rest
For everybody knows about Mississippi Goddam

I bet you thought I was kiddin', didn't you?

Picket lines, school boy cots
They try to say it's a communist plot
All I want is equality
For my sister, my brother, my people and me

Yes, you lied to me all these years
You told me to wash and clean my ears
And talk real fine just like a lady
And you'd stop calling me Sister Sadie

Oh, but this whole country is full of lies
You're all gonna die and die like flies
I don't trust you any more
You keep on saying, "Go slow! Go slow!"

But that's just the trouble, do it slow
Desegregation, do it slow
Mass participation, do it slow
Reunification, do it slow

Do things gradually, do it slow
But bring more tragedy, do it slow
Why don't you see it? Why don't you feel it?
I don't know, I don't know

You don't have to live next to me
Just give me my equality
Everybody knows about Mississippi
Everybody knows about Alabama
Everybody knows about Mississippi Goddam

That's it!

The Black Agenda

Gary Declaration: Black Politics at the Crossroads

(1972)

Introduction

The Black Agenda is addressed primarily to Black people in America. It rises naturally out of the bloody decades and centuries of our people's struggle on these shores. It flows from the most recent surgings of our own cultural and political consciousness. It is our attempt to define some of the essential changes which must take place in this land as we and our children move to self-determination and true independence.

The Black Agenda assumes that no truly basic change for our benefit takes place in Black or white America unless we Black people organize to initiate that change. It assumes that we must have some essential agreement on overall goals, even though we may differ on many specific strategies.

Therefore, this is an initial statement of goals and directions for our own generation, some first definitions of crucial issues around which Black people must organize and move in 1972 and beyond. Anyone who claims to be serious about the survival and liberation of Black people must be serious about the implementation of the Black Agenda.

What Time Is It?

We come to Gary in an hour of great crisis and tremendous promise for Black America. While the white nation hovers on the brink of chaos, while its politicians offer no hope of real change, we stand on the edge of history and are faced with an amazing and frightening choice: We may choose in 1972 to slip back into the decadent white politics of American life, or we may press forward, moving relentlessly from Gary to the creation of our own Black life. The choice is large, but the time is very short.

... From every rural community in Alabama to the high-rise compounds of Chicago, we bring to this Convention the agonies of the masses of our people. From the sprawling Black cities of Watts and Nairobi in the West to the decay of

Harlem and Roxbury in the East, the testimony we bear is the same. We are the witnesses to social disaster.

Our cities are crime-haunted dying grounds. Huge sectors of our youth—and countless others—face permanent unemployment. Those of us who work find our paychecks able to purchase less and less. Neither the courts nor the prisons contribute to anything resembling justice or reformation. The schools are unable—or unwilling—to educate our children for the real world of our struggles. Meanwhile, the officially approved epidemic of drugs threatens to wipe out the minds and strength of our best young warriors.

Economic, cultural, and spiritual depression stalk Black America, and the price for survival often appears to be more than we are able to pay. On every side, in every area of our lives, the American institutions in which we have placed our trust are unable to cope with the crises they have created by their single-minded dedication to profits for some and white supremacy above all.

Beyond These Shores

And beyond these shores there is more of the same. For while we are pressed down under all the dying weight of a bloated, inwardly decaying white civilization, many of our brothers in Africa and the rest of the Third World have fallen prey to the same powers of exploitation and deceit. . . .

White Realities, Black Choice

A Black political convention, indeed all truly Black politics must begin from this truth: The American system does not work for the masses of our people, and it cannot be made to work without radical fundamental change. (Indeed this system does not really work in favor of the humanity of anyone in America.)

In light of such realities, we . . . are confronted with a choice. Will we believe the truth that history presses into our face—or will we, too, try to hide? Will the small favors some of us have received blind us to the larger sufferings of our people, or open our eyes to the testimony of our history in America? . . .

Both Parties Have Betrayed Us

. . . [L]et us never forget that while the times and the names and the parties have continually changed, one truth has faced us insistently, never changing: Both parties have betrayed us whenever their interests conflicted with ours (which was most of the time), and whenever our forces were unorganized and dependent, quiescent and compliant. Nor should this be surprising, for by now we must know that the American political system, like all other white institutions in America, was designed to operate for the benefit of the white race: It was never meant to do anything else.

. . . If white "liberalism" could have solved our problems, then Lincoln and Roosevelt and Kennedy would have done so. But they did not solve ours nor the rest of the nation's. If America's problems could have been solved by forceful, politically skilled and aggressive individuals, then Lyndon Johnson would have retained the presidency. If the true "American Way" of unbridled monopoly capitalism, combined with a ruthless military imperialism could do it, then Nixon would not be running around the world, or making speeches comparing his nation's decadence to that of Greece and Rome.

. . . The profound crisis of Black people and the disaster of America are not simply caused by men nor will they be solved by men alone. These crises are the crises of basically flawed economics and politics, and or cultural degradation. None of the Democratic candidates and none of the Republican candidates—regardless of their vague promises to us or to their white constituencies—can solve our problems or the problems of this country without radically changing the systems by which it operates.

The Politics of Social Transformation

So we come . . . confronted with a choice. But it is not the old convention question of which candidate shall we support, the pointless question of who is to preside over a decaying and unsalvageable system. No, if we come . . . out of the realities of the Black communities of this land, then the only real choice for us is whether or not we will live by the truth we know, whether we will move to organize independently, move to struggle for fundamental transformation, for the creation of new directions, towards a concern for the life and the meaning of Man. Social transformation or social destruction, those are our only real choices.

If we have come . . . on behalf of our people in America, in the rest of this hemisphere, and in the Homeland—if we have come for our own best ambitions—then a new Black Politics must come to birth. If we are serious, the Black Politics of Gary must accept major responsibility for creating both the atmosphere and the program for fundamental, far-ranging change in America. Such responsibility is ours because it is our people who are most deeply hurt and ravaged by the present systems of society. That responsibility for leading the change is ours because we live in a society where few other men really believe in the responsibility of a truly human society for anyone anywhere.

We Are the Vanguard

The challenge is thrown to us here. . . . It is the challenge to consolidate and organize our own Black role as the vanguard in the struggle for a new society. To accept that challenge is to move independent Black politics. There can be no equivocation on that issue. History leaves us no other choice. White politics has not and cannot bring the changes we need.

We . . . are faced with a challenge. The challenge is to transform ourselves from favor-seeking vassals and loud-talking, "militant" pawns, and to take up the role that the organized masses of our people have attempted to play ever since we came to these shores. That of harbingers of true justice and humanity, leaders in the struggle for liberation. . . .

Towards a Black Agenda

So when we turn to a Black Agenda . . . , we move in the truth of history, in the reality of the moment. We move recognizing that no one else is going to represent our interests but ourselves. The society we seek cannot come unless Black people organize to advance its coming. We lift up a Black Agenda recognizing that white America moves towards the abyss created by its own racist arrogance, misplaced priorities, rampant materialism, and ethical bankruptcy. Therefore, we are certain that the Agenda we now press for . . . is not only for the future of Black humanity, but is probably the only way the rest of America can save itself from the harvest of its criminal past.

So, Brothers and Sisters of our developing Black nation, we now stand . . . as people whose time has come. From every corner of Black America, from all liberation movements of the Third World, from the graves of our fathers and the coming world of our children, we are faced with a challenge and a call:

Though the moment is perilous we must not despair. We must seize the time, for the time is ours.

. . . We begin with an independent Black political movement, an independent Black Political Agenda, and independent Black spirit. Nothing less will do. We must build for our people. We must build for our world. We stand on the edge of history. We cannot turn back.

ROBIN BLAKE

Is It Time to Reevaluate the Church's Role in the Civil Rights Movement?

(July 13, 2015)

Faith is a tenant of the black community, but [it] has been used against us in the past. Black people have become complacent and reliant upon a deity to solve real-world issues which require true effort and solidarity. Religion divides people just as easily as it brings them together, and its place in social progress needs to be evaluated.

I was raised in a devout Christian home, and that's why I personally feel infuriated when people insist that we need to pray and rely on a higher power in these situations. I was brought up to believe that faith without work is dead. Prayer is great; it has mental and spiritual benefits and brings people closer together. Where do we draw the line?

Not long ago, I attended one of many protests for Tamir Rice, a twelve-year-old boy shot by Cleveland police at a park in November of 2014. Local churches came out to show their support for the cause, which I initially thought was a lovely gesture. However, they came bearing white flags—the universal symbol of surrender—and that struck a chord with me. Did no one stop to think that maybe we were sending mixed signals to everyone? Does the appearance of submission really lend validity to the cause? Placing a flower in the barrel will not stop the bullet, regardless of the message sent. It doesn't particularly matter how righteous you are if, in the end, you're killed. I do believe Malcolm X said it best:

> The greatest miracle Christianity has achieved in America is that the black man in white Christian hands has not grown violent. It is a miracle that 22 million black people have not risen up against their oppressors—in which they would have been justified by all moral criteria, and even by the democratic tradition! It is a miracle that a nation of black people has so fervently continued to believe in a turn-the-other-cheek and heaven-for-you-after-you-die philosophy! It is a miracle that the American black people have remained a peaceful people, while catching all the centuries of hell that they have caught, here in white man's heaven!

This quote makes me think about the recent events in Charleston, South Carolina. A group of people welcomed a young, seemingly offbeat man into their congregation, only to be slaughtered by him, ending up nine members short after all was said and done. With enough of these circumstances, it won't take much effort for white supremacy to wipe us out in great numbers. While it won't work to sew in paranoia and live in constant distrust of anyone who isn't black, it's critical to note that open arms were met with a hail of gunpowder, fueled by hatred. We also cannot forget that initially, the image of Jesus was created in that of a white man so that slaves worshipping him would simultaneously conceive of whiteness as purity and salvation.

Oppressive institutions overlap and cannot be evaluated separately from one another. As a queer man of color, I find that I receive harsh judgment and stigmatization due to my membership in both of those groups. Sometimes, it even comes to be that I face aggression from black folks for identifying as queer, and vice versa. One major issue with the church being involved in the #BlackLives-Matter movement is that if the church is going to continue to impress a homo/transphobic dialogue into the ever-going conversation on race and white supremacy, then the movement is doomed to fail because it absolutely needs to be intersectional. Internalized homo/transphobia and destructive ideas divide us. Young black men especially are raised with a hypermasculine dogma that manifests a way of thinking that sabotages us from the inside. It's interesting to note that, on average, people from the church are the first ones arguing respectability politics and saying that we need to "stop black-on-black violence" without realizing that a great deal of these issues are created in their own personal circles and that most of this aforementioned black-on-black violence is often against members of the LGBT community, especially our trans brothers and sisters. #AllBlackLivesMatter needs to be weighed heavily against #BlackLivesMatter because there is a problem if we're allowing systems of privilege and inequality to perpetrate our own safe houses. One of the main beliefs of Christianity is that we are all created in the image of God and are perfect as we are; how can we use that justification when it suits our own personal political narrative and conveniently forget it when it doesn't? Let it be noted that white pastors used to use the Bible to justify slavery, beatings, and oppression. As interpretations of the Word change with the times, so should the viewpoints of our community. The first step is definitely to uplift each other and strengthen our own bonds, but this will never be achieved if we allow black people to suffer based on their divergence from hetero- and cisnormative standards, whether a personal choice or not.

Do I believe that religion is a valuable tool in revolution and an important part of humanity? I do. The black church has established itself as potentially the greatest source for religious enrichment and secular development. But it has its place. The church should be a place of reflection and reverence, where the faithful can come lay down their burdens and religious leaders can reinforce the community with faith, hope, and unconditional love. It should be a place where black people can speak out about their woes and struggles in a place of unconditional love and understanding. It does not need to act as a complete representation of the people, nor does it need to be an institution at the forefront of the wave, until this internal dissonance is worked out, or at least widely acknowledged.

No one is coming to save us from this.

DANIELLE MCGUIRE

More Than a Seat on the Bus

(December 1, 2015)

Today marks the sixtieth anniversary of the arrest of Mrs. Rosa Parks in Montgomery, Alabama. We all know the popular story of what happened on that cold December day in 1955. Indeed, it has become an American myth. A soft-spoken seamstress with tired feet refused to move to the back of the bus to make room for a white man. Her spontaneous action and subsequent arrest sparked a yearlong boycott of the city's buses that brought down Jim Crow in the cradle of the Confederacy. And the path to black equality was cleared.

But that story, of Rosa Parks tiptoeing into history, both oversimplifies the deep roots of the boycott and disregards the bold actions of the many black women who made the Montgomery movement about more than a seat on a bus. In truth, the Montgomery Bus Boycott was a protest against racial *and* sexual violence, and Rosa Parks's arrest on December 1, 1955, was but one act in a life devoted to the protection and defense of black people generally, and black women specifically. Indeed, the bus boycott was, in many ways, the precursor to the #SayHerName Twitter campaigns designed to remind us that the lives of black women matter.

In 1997, an interviewer asked Joe Azbell, former city editor of the *Montgomery Advertiser*, who was the most important person in the bus boycott. Surprisingly, he did not say Rosa Parks. "Gertrude Perkins," he said, "is not even mentioned in the history books, but she had as much to do with the bus boycott as anyone on earth." On March 27, 1949, Perkins was on her way home from a party when two white Montgomery police officers arrested her for "public drunkenness." They pushed her into the backseat of their patrol car, drove to a railroad embankment, dragged her behind a building, and raped her at gunpoint.

Left alone on the roadside, Perkins somehow mustered the courage to report the crime. She went directly to the Holt Street Baptist Church parsonage and woke the Reverend Solomon A. Seay Sr., an outspoken minister in Montgomery. "We didn't go to bed that morning," he recalled. "I kept her at my house, carefully wrote down what she said and later had it notarized." The next day, Seay escorted Perkins to the police station. City authorities called Perkins's claim "completely false" and refused to hold a lineup or issue any warrants since, according to the mayor, it would "violate the Constitutional rights" of the police. Besides, he said, "my policemen would not do a thing like that."

But African Americans knew better. What happened to Gertrude Perkins was no isolated incident. Montgomery's police force had a reputation for racist and sexist brutality that went back years, and black leaders in the city were tired of it. When the authorities made clear that they would not respond to Perkins's claims, local NAACP activists, labor leaders, and ministers formed an umbrella organization called the "Citizens Committee for Gertrude Perkins." Rosa Parks was one of the local activists who demanded an investigation and trial, and helped maintain public protests that lasted for two months.

By 1949 Rosa Parks was an experienced antirape activist. The campaign on behalf of Perkins, for example, was modeled on a protest Parks helped launch several years earlier for Recy Taylor, a young black mother kidnapped and brutally raped in 1944 in the town of Abbeville, Alabama, by a group of white men who threatened to kill her if she told anyone. Taylor reported the crime anyway and the Montgomery NAACP sent Parks to Abbeville to investigate. After gathering Taylor's testimony, Parks carried it back to Montgomery, where she and other activists launched "The Committee for Equal Justice for Mrs. Recy Taylor," a nationwide campaign that demanded protection for black womanhood and accountability for Taylor's assailants.

Two years after the protest on behalf of Gertrude Perkins, meanwhile, black activists rallied to defend yet another victim of white sexual violence in Montgomery. In February 1951, a white grocer named Sam Green raped a black teenager named Flossie Hardman whom he employed as a babysitter. After Hardman told her parents about the attack, they decided to press charges, and when an all-white jury returned a not-guilty verdict after five minutes of deliberation, the family reached out to community activists for help. Together, individuals such as Rufus Lewis, who organized voter registration campaigns, Rosa Parks, who was still serving as secretary of the Montgomery NAACP chapter, and members of the newly formed Women's Political Council, launched a boycott of Green's grocery store. After only a few weeks, African Americans delivered their own guilty verdict by driving Green's business into the red.

By the early 1950s, then, a history of sexual assaults on black women and of the use of the boycott as a powerful weapon for justice had laid the groundwork for what was to come. Given that history, it made sense that city buses served as the flashpoint for mass protest. Other than police officers, few were as guilty of committing acts of racist violence and sexual harassment of black women as Montgomery's bus operators, who bullied and brutalized black passengers daily. Worse, bus drivers had police power. They carried blackjacks and guns, and they assaulted and sometimes even killed African Americans who refused to abide by the racial order of Jim Crow.

In 1953 alone, African Americans filed over thirty formal complaints of abuse and mistreatment on the buses. Most came from working-class black women, mainly domestics, who made up nearly 70 percent of the bus ridership. They said drivers hurled nasty, sexualized insults at them, touched them inappropriately, and physically abused them. In May 1954, JoAnn Robinson, leader of the Women's Political Council, threatened a boycott of Montgomery's city buses, and only after months of futile efforts to get city officials to address the problem did the boycott finally come into being. Women walked rather than ride the buses, Rosa Parks said in 1956, not in support of her, but because she "was not the only person who had been mistreated and humiliated." Other women, she said, "had gone through similarly shameful experiences, most worse than mine."

These experiences propelled African American women into every conceivable aspect of the boycott. Women were the chief strategists and negotiators of the boycott and ran its day-to-day operation. Women helped staff the elaborate carpool system, raised most of the local money for the movement, and filled the majority of the pews at the mass meetings, where they testified publicly about physical and sexual abuse on the buses. And of course, by walking hundreds of miles to protest their humiliation, African American women reclaimed their bodies and demanded the right to be treated with dignity and respect.

Rooted in the struggle to protect and defend black womanhood from racial and sexual violence, the Montgomery Bus Boycott is impossible to understand and situate in its proper historical context without understanding the stories and *saying the names* of Gertrude Perkins, Flossie Hardman, Recy Taylor, and all the black women who were mistreated in Montgomery.

Today, as we celebrate the anniversary of Rosa Parks's arrest, witness the growth of the #BlackLivesMatter movement on city streets and campus quads across the country, and #SayHerName to demand an end to police violence against women of color, we should look to the past—and remember it correctly. Parks and the women who started the Montgomery bus boycott fought for more than a seat on the bus. They demanded the right to move through the world without being molested, fought against police brutality and racial and sexual violence, and insisted on the right to ownership and control of their own bodies.

GENNA RAE MCNEIL

From "'Joanne Is You and Joanne Is Me': A Consideration of African American Women and the 'Free Joan Little' Movement, 1974–75"

(2001)

Joanne Little, she's my sister
Joanne Little, she's our mama . . .
Joanne's the woman
Who's gonna carry your child . . .
Joanne is you and
Joanne is me
Our prison is
This whole society.
BERNICE JOHNSON REAGON

Joan Little, a twenty-year-old inmate in North Carolina's Beaufort County jail, stabbed Clarence Alligood. And in the early morning hours of August 27, 1974, she ran. About 5 feet 3 inches tall, weighing barely 120 pounds, Joan (pronounced Jo-Ann) Little was black, female, and poor. Clarence Alligood, who was closer to 5 feet 10 inches tall and weighed over 200 pounds, was Little's sixty-two-year-old white jailer. Little would later explain that the stabbing of Alligood was an act of resistance and self-defense. Moreover, she insisted that when she fled the jail she did not realize Alligood was dying. Little later testified that Alligood had come to the Beaufort County jail cell, where Little was being held awaiting disposition of a breaking and entering charge, and there her jailer, Alligood, forced her to perform oral sex. Alligood coerced her with an icepick, Little recounted. She made it a weapon of defense; then, she escaped. The memory of an injured Alligood yet vivid, Little hid in Washington, North Carolina, until she could decide what to do. Later coming to the jail, a colleague of Alligood discovered a bloody, partially nude Alligood dead with multiple stab wounds and a dried stream of semen on his thigh.

Declared a fugitive and suspected murderer, Little's life was particularly in jeopardy at the beginning of September 1974 because of an application from the authorities for the use of a Reconstruction era "Outlaw" statute. Contemplating a pending "shoot on sight" order and having read newspaper accounts of an intentional "brutal murder" of a night jailer who was acting "in the line of duty," Joan Little decided to seek assistance so that she might surrender somewhere outside of Beaufort County. On September 3, 1974, accompanied by supporters and attorneys, Jerry Paul and Karen Bethea Galloway, Little surrendered to the North Carolina State Bureau of Investigation (SBI). Following her surrender, rejecting Little's account of her act of resistance, the grand jury handed down an indictment of first-degree murder. Joan Little faced a penalty of death by execution.

In the next year, Joan Little and her case slowly became a *cause celebre*. Lawyers and nonlawyers collaborated as a defense team to save Joan Little from execution. Mounting the most effective defense included devising a unique defense strategy. The controversy over the indictment further polarized eastern North Carolina racially; this required a change of venue. The attorneys viewed several other tasks as necessary and urgent, including selecting more scientifically a jury committed to the verdict of innocence unless guilt was proven beyond a reasonable doubt, reducing the charge from first-degree murder, and obtaining a lesser penalty than death by execution. In the sociopolitical context of the early 1970s, the legal team also understood that unless the public's consciousness was raised about the multiple injustices inherent in this case, Joan Little was at even greater risk. Support from the public at large could not be guaranteed by legal maneuvers alone. Therefore, attorneys Jerry Paul and Karen Galloway encouraged the development of a statewide, regional, and ultimately national movement to promote a fair trial, to raise funds for Little's defense, and "to free Joan Little." After a five-week trial, on August 15, 1975, Joan Little was acquitted by a jury of six African Americans and six whites.

Unprecedented in North Carolina's history, *State vs. Joan Little* established a woman's right of self-defense against sexual assault and a defendant's right to have a change of venue beyond the boundaries of contiguous counties. It underscored, as well, the need for further scrutiny of the law that gave police the power to slay a suspected law-breaker. Within a few years, North Carolina's "Outlaw" statute would be struck down. For thousands of supporters and sympathizers, however, Joan Little's acquittal substantially represented the effective mobilization of progressive social organizations, networks of activists, and movements for justice. . . .

When Joan Little decided to stand trial in North Carolina for the stabbing death of Clarence Alligood rather than go into exile, it committed her to both the fight of her life and fight for her life. From the moment of the media's coverage of

Little's surrender and the inclusion of photographs of this twenty-year-old black girl-woman, the question became "who is this girl and what is she to you?"

Seeing her picture in North Carolina's newspapers, some could not help but recognize that Joan Little was the embodiment of a particular intersection of race, sex, and class—namely, her African descent, femaleness, and poverty—which constituted distinct disadvantages in the United States, despite the presumption of innocence. . . .

Hearing about Little on the radio or seeing her image in the print media, some wondered aloud if Joan Little was to be considered a political prisoner, like the recently acquitted Angela Davis, or activists like the "Wilmington Ten," and the local civil rights leader Golden Frinks, whose protests frequently landed him in jail. Neither at the height of the national Civil Rights–Black Power Movement, which had experienced serious decline by the early 1970s, nor during the numerous civil rights confrontations in North Carolina, where attempts to end de facto segregation continued to come under attack, was Joan Little involved in civil rights activism.

Outside of organized protest movements, however, Joan Little chose to assert her right to equal treatment and the sanctity of her person. Although she did not become a political activist, in one important sense she engaged in a "political" act, the consequences of which reached far beyond her intent or personal ideology. As [historian] Robin D. G. Kelley argues, "'[p]olitics' comprises the many battles to roll back constraints and exercise some power over, or create some space within, the institutions and social relationships that dominate our lives."

Joan Little mentally—and to some extent emotionally—had already created some space in her life for the exercise of a degree of freedom. Having made the decision to surrender on terms she and her lawyers established after her initial flight, Little was also taking steps to wrest some modicum of control from the oppressive white male authorities. Nevertheless, Little found herself physically confined again. This time, having been indicted for first-degree murder, she was held in Raleigh's correctional facility for women with bail set at $100,000. Joan Little would reflect upon her plight from behind bars throughout the fall of 1974 and into the winter of 1975. During that same time, several groups began to mobilize for her defense and to gain better treatment for Little while incarcerated. The groups included the Free Joan Little Committee, the JoAnn Little Defense Fund, the Commission for Racial Justice of the United Church of Christ (UCC), the Southern Christian Leadership Conference (SCLC), the Concerned Women for Fairness to JoAnn Little which later became the Concerned Women for Justice (CWJ), and the Southern Poverty Law Center (SPLC). . . .

Joan Little was born on May 8, 1954 in Washington, North Carolina to Jessie Ruth Little and Willis Williams. While still a teenager, Jessie Little fell in love with Willis Williams, a young black man who worked as a laborer. Before that relationship soured, Jessie Little and Willis Williams had four children. The two eventually separated, and soon afterward Jessie Little married Arthur Williams (no relation), a lumber man. They had four children. Unfortunately, Arthur Williams was an alcoholic who contributed little to the family income. As a result, Jessie Little Williams was forced to work long hours outside the home as a factory or domestic worker. As she became older, Joan Little was expected to take care of her seven siblings, and although she was close to her mother, Joan resented her strict parenting style, and also was disturbed by Arthur Williams's drinking. By November 1968, truancy and rebelliousness on Joan's part prompted her mother Jessie Little Williams to request that a Beaufort County court send Joan to Dobb's Farm, a minimum security training school for youth, located outside of Washington, North Carolina. When Joan ran away from Dobb's Farm, her mother decided to seek her release and allowed her to move to the North with relatives to attend school in Philadelphia, Pennsylvania and Newark, New Jersey. Unfortunately, when Joan returned to North Carolina in 1970, her northern school records were not available. Rather than be placed in a grade she believed was below her level of attainment, Little dropped out of school.

By the age of eighteen, Joan Little was on her own and working at low-paying jobs in eastern North Carolina. Falling in with the wrong crowd, she ran afoul of the law, and was arrested and charged with shoplifting and larceny, but was not convicted. Although she was employed at various jobs on and off, Little was arrested again, this time in 1974 in Greenville, North Carolina with her brother Jerome Little, on charges of breaking and entering. While out on bail she fled, but was later apprehended, and was being held in the Beaufort County jail, where she was attacked by her jailer Clarence Alligood.

By September 1974, Little had surrendered to the authorities in Raleigh, North Carolina. Having been charged with murder in Alligood's death, Joan Little concentrated on trying to make sense of where she was in light of whom she understood herself to be. . . .

Joan Little, insistent upon her right to defend herself and to have a voice in discussions about her life, became a catalyst for the continuing movement toward African American and women's liberation. Whether explored, contested, assumed, celebrated, or detested, talk of "sisterhood" could not be completely ignored in 1974 and 1975. For African Americans, sisterhood presented challenges and opportunities. The realities of disadvantage and oppression in a society that privileged white males were becoming more apparent and less tolerable for women, regardless of race, ethnicity, class, or sexual orientation. When Joan Little's ordeal came to national attention, it was in the wake of continued

FBI assaults upon civil rights and militant Black Power advocates and African American liberation groups, and only eight years after the founding of the National Organization for Women (NOW). In the same period, African Americans convened the National Black Political Convention. American citizens experienced other events relevant to women's issues and blacks' rights: the introduction of the Equal Rights Amendment (ERA), and a campaign for its ratification; the arrest, trial, and acquittal of Angela Davis; the Supreme Court decision in *Roe v. Wade* legalizing abortions; the founding of the National Black Feminist Organization; and a multiplicity of local struggles to eradicate racial oppression through desegregation, equal protection of the laws, equal opportunity in litigation, affirmative action, and nonviolent direct action protest.

In significant numbers, women, African Americans, and non–African Americans, conscious of systemic racism and patriarchal dominance, were becoming aware of the need to develop appropriate analyses, consider different ideologies, and make concerted efforts to raise their own and others' political consciousness. Some women had been active participants in the Civil Rights–Black Power Movement, while others in the late 1960s and early 1970s took up the struggle against sexism and joined the emerging women's liberation movement. Still other women came to view Joan Little's plight as an authentic opportunity to consider the possibilities of "sisterhood" across racial and class lines through the development of an integrated women's alliance. . . .

One of Joan Little's most vocal supporters was Bernice Johnson Reagon, former Student Nonviolent Coordinating Committee (SNCC) activist and founder of the musical group "Sweet Honey in the Rock." Reagon discovered that the various incidents that led to her involvement in the Civil Rights Movement provided her with startling insights into Joan Little's identity and a special sympathy for her plight. Joan Little's act of resistance as a woman revealed to Reagon the commonalities of all women in that their bodies have the potential to be both sites of conquest and effective instruments of resistance to violation. Reagon first met Joan Little in Washington, D.C., where Sweet Honey in the Rock had been invited to a rally to sing the song "Joanne Little." Bernice Reagon recalled that Little spoke about being hunted for the murder of the jailer, who was described as having acted "in the line of duty." "Little talked about being between the mattresses in a house when the sheriff came in, when they were looking for her. And I thought, 'Oh God, this is really something.'" Yet Reagon also remembered that "we sang the song and Joan Little came up. . . . She was this little woman and she . . . told us to 'help Jerry.' It was like she was saying help Jerry because Jerry is helping me. . . . And she was not quite yet standing on the ground her experience had placed her."

Bernice Reagon became involved in the political work to "Free Joan Little." Bernice Reagon wrote and performed the song, "Joanne Little," which became the anthem for the Free Joan Little Movement. Reagon recalled that people seemed to plug into the part of the song in that second verse, which is like the declaration of stance. "What did she do to deserve this name? Killed a man that thought she was fair game. When I heard the news I screamed inside. Lost my cool. My anger I could not hide. Joanne is you. Joanne is me. Our prison is this whole society." It was like something had been unleashed in the culture.

The particular genius of Bernice Reagon's song, "Joanne Little," was its capacity to galvanize all of Little's supporters, regardless of their degree of political consciousness or sophistication. This narrative and its refrain implicitly gave recognition to sisterhood in various manifestations, especially for persons of African descent and for women, regardless of race. It allowed the singer/activist to create for herself and others a space that could be occupied with Joan Little, the victim and resister. Reagon's lyrics contained progressive and critically conscious meanings that served to establish linkages and relationships among activists. The lyrics offered a way of understanding commonalities and sisterhood through personal identification. . . .

. . . Within the context of defining "sisterhood," public support and financial resources for Joan Little also came from members of the organized lesbian and feminist communities. Many women viewed oppression as the common concern; moreover, some lesbians, regardless of race, identified their oppression due to sexual orientation as an additional motive for political organization. Lesbian groups, such as the Alliance of Lesbian Feminists of Atlanta (ALFA) and North Carolina's Triangle Area Lesbian Feminists, found it politically beneficial to include themselves among the active supporters of Joan Little. In 1966, African American women, including politician Shirley Chisholm and attorney Pauli Murray, were among the founders of the leading feminist organization, the National Organization for Women (NOW); and in 1975, it was NOW's Rape Task Force leader, Mary Ann Largen, who enthusiastically supported Joan Little's cause. After making contact with attorney Karen Galloway, Largen organized NOW's special solicitations on Little's behalf.

A demonstrated sisterhood forged through a common commitment to civil and human rights did not alone bring women together in Little's defense. Angela Davis's article in *Ms.* magazine in June 1975 openly challenged men and women—regardless of race—to recognize their relationship to Joan Little. Writing at the invitation of the magazine's editor Gloria Steinem, Angela Davis's article "JoAnne Little: The Dialectics of Rape" generated new and important interest in the case, particularly among women's groups throughout the country. In the article Davis presented a nuanced, antiracist, and inclusive argument on Little's behalf, and ended with a call to action. . . .

. . . The wide range of organizations supporting and working to free Joan Little proved critical to the progress of the defense and her eventual acquittal. Among women it was significant that Little was supported by Concerned Women for

Justice (CWJ) as well as the National Organization for Women (NOW). At the same time, many African Americans became aware that Joan Little's defense movement encompassed a broad range of black organizations, including black church congregations, women's church groups, the Southern Christian Leadership Conference (SCLC), members of the black press, cultural nationalists and their organizations, such as Haki Madhubuti, Maulana (Ron) Karenga, Amiri Baraka, Bibi Amina Baraka, and the Black Women's United Front, as well as revolutionary nationalists in the Black Panther Party.

Organizations must transform individuals' feelings and ideologies into purposeful collective actions to bring about social and political change. The significance of *State vs. Joan Little*, Joan Little, and the Free Joan Little Movement for understanding the Civil Rights–Black Power Movement is inextricably linked to her symbolic representation of the right to resist oppression. The fluidity of the identification, unbound by a particular ideology, allowed a host of activists and organizations to coalesce around her cause and the movement for her freedom. For many African American women, Joan Little was the dramatic symbol, and the Free Joan Little Movement became the appropriate site, for raising feminist consciousness and strengthening the bonds of sisterhood.

ROBERT KORSTAD

From "Could History Repeat Itself? The Prospects for a Second Reconstruction in Post–World War II South Carolina"

(February 2005)

On the evening of November 26, 1945, several hundred white and black Charlestonians gathered at the Morris Street Baptist Church to hear Aubrey Williams, former director of the New Deal's National Youth Administration and, at the time, publisher of the *Southern Farmer*. Williams' presentation inaugurated the "New South Lecture Series," five talks by prominent southern progressives on the critical issues facing the region in the postwar world. In addition to Williams, the series featured Charles S. Johnson, the noted African American sociologist and soon to be President of Fisk University; Clifford Durr, an Alabama lawyer and a member of the Federal Communications Commission; Clark Foreman, chairman of the Southern Conference for Human Welfare; and Kelley Barnett, a minister from Chapel Hill who represented University of North Carolina president Frank Porter Graham.

The speakers were members of a well-positioned group of southern New Dealers (scholars, politicians, labor leaders, and civil rights activists) who, at the end of WWII, articulated a vision of a more democratic and prosperous New South. . . .

The New South Lecture Series grew out of an unlikely alliance between members of Local 15 of the Food, Tobacco, Agricultural, and Allied Workers, Congress of Industrial Organization (FTA-CIO) and a group of GIS stationed at Stark General Hospital. Workers at the American Tobacco Company, virtually all of who were women and a large majority of who were African Americans, had organized Local 15 in 1943. In the spring of 1945, my father, Karl Korstad, and a few of his army buddies began working with Local 15 as volunteers. They helped around the office, wrote leaflets and press releases, and taught literacy classes for union members. In the fall, they planned the lecture series.

On October 22, five weeks before the series was scheduled to begin, over one thousand black and white members of Local 15 walked off their jobs demanding wage increases, a union shop, paid sick leave, and better working conditions.

FTA members at American plants in Philadelphia had struck the week before, and a week later workers at Trenton, New Jersey would also walk out. The Charleston struggle is most remembered as the birthplace for the civil rights anthem, "We Shall Overcome." But the strike was also notable for the degree of interracial cooperation it engendered between black and white women.

Although caught up in a swirl of strike activities, union leaders decided to go ahead with the lecture series, hoping it could mobilize additional support for striking workers in both the black and white communities. Toward that end, they recruited three co-sponsors: the National Maritime Workers Union; the Citizens' Political Action Committee, the local chapter of the National Citizens' PAC, created in 1944 for middle-class supporters of the CIO's political program; and the Cosmopolitan Civic League, an organization of politically-minded African Americans.

After the first lecture, Karl was transferred to Alabama in preparation for his discharge from the army. My mother, Frances, a Charleston native, and an ad hoc committee of union leaders, black ministers, and black teachers took over the arrangements and publicity. Their big challenge was to get people to attend the lectures, and here the committee drew primarily on the organizational infrastructure of Charleston's African American community. They distributed blocs of tickets (one dollar for the series, fifty cents for a single lecture) to the ministers of local black churches, the teachers at the Avery Institute (a private high school for African Americans), and the leaders of the local chapter of the NAACP, who in turn, sold the tickets to their members and, in the process, discussed the goals of the lecture series. The sponsoring organizations did the same.

Although held at an African American church, the lecture series drew an interracial audience that numbered from a few hundred to over one thousand for Dr. Johnson, and without fanfare, organizers encouraged seating on a non-segregated basis. These gatherings were remarkable in part because of the cross-class composition of the audiences. Tobacco workers, merchant seamen, ministers, teachers, small shop owners, and a smattering of white-collar professionals sat side by side in the church pews.

Speakers took the occasion to carry their message to an even larger Charleston audience. All met with the Youth Interracial Fellowship at the Avery Institute. Clifford Durr spoke at a luncheon meeting of the Lions Club. Clark Foreman addressed the staff of the white YWCA. And several of the lectures were carried on local radio stations. . . .

By the 1940s, the South had emerged as the critical battleground in the effort to maintain the momentum of the New Deal. The region was home to the country's largest bloc of unorganized workers, and the long-term success of the CIO depended on its ability to bring southern workers into the house of labor.

Likewise, two out of three African Americans lived below the Mason-Dixon line, and the vast majority of these were working class. To survive and expand, New Dealers had to break the stranglehold of conservative southern Democrats, who owed their seniority and thus their domination of Congressional committees to the South's constricted electorate and one-party rule. To do so, they had to enfranchise millions of African Americans and mobilize the region's poor whites. . . .

Charleston may seem like an odd place to fire some of the first shots in the postwar battle to change the composition of the southern Congressional delegation and ultimately dislodge the planter/banker/industrial oligarchy that had ruled the South since the turn of the century. For no town better represented the Old South, and no state was more tethered to the myths of the past than South Carolina. Yet in the winter of 1945–46, no place better represented the remarkable changes of the past decade and the heightened expectations for the future. The New Deal and World War II had reshaped the social and economic geography of the city and the state. Thousands of new jobs had materialized. Military bases in Charleston and at Fort Jackson outside Columbia brought sailors and soldiers from around the country to the Palmetto State. Most important, workers and African Americans had begun to organize.

Perhaps the most notable of these democratic stirrings was the formation of the Progressive Democratic Party, a mostly middle-class African American challenge to the lily-white Democratic Party. NAACP membership had grown rapidly during the war, and by 1945 the state had a remarkable 40 chapters with over ten thousand members. Organized labor had a more tenuous toehold. The American Federation of Labor had scattered locals in printing, the building trades, and among longshoremen. The most dynamic unions were those affiliated with the CIO: FTA Local 15; the National Martime Union; a local of the Mine, Mill, and Smelter Workers in North Charleston; and a number of upstate outposts of the Textile Workers Union. Also critical were the individual efforts of white liberals in places like Charleston and Columbia. . . .

South Carolinians were not alone in these efforts to extend the reach of the New Deal. Similar mobilizations were occurring in other places and a network of capable leaders had sprung up in every southern state that crossed class lines and included blacks and whites, men and women. Regional organizations such as the Southern Regional Council, Highlander Folk School, and the Southern Conference for Human Welfare brought activists together to share experiences and strategies.

Each of the speakers at the New South Lecture series had played key roles in these regional organizations and each continued to play a part in national politics, trying to influence Truman's Fair Deal as they had FDR's New Deal. In all those capacities they spoke for what we might call the Southern Front, a loose coalition of labor unionists, civil rights activists, and southern New Dealers who saw a strong labor movement and the reenfranchisement of the southern poor as the key to reforming the South and a reformed South as central to the survival and expansion of the New Deal. . . .

The political, social, and economic policies advocated by southern progressives had five main objectives. The first was to extend citizenship rights to African Americans, as well as poor and working-class whites who had effectively been disfranchised for much of the century. The second was to end the racial discrimination that so constrained the talents and aspirations of ten million African Americans. A third goal was to institute a massive education program that would raise literacy rates as well as better prepare people for jobs in industry. A forth goal was to continue the organization of industrial workers that skyrocketed during the war and then to extend that organizational effort to small farmers and farm workers. The fifth goal was to spur growth in agriculture and industry. In all of these areas, progressives saw federal intervention as key.

Aubrey Williams devoted the first lecture to the crisis in southern agriculture, emphasizing especially the lack of effective organization among small farmers and the South's continued reliance on King Cotton. Small farmers, Williams insisted, needed organization as much as did industrial workers. "Fifty farmers, united, marketing their produce together can demand and receive much higher prices than can fifty farmers, divided," he said, echoing the rallying cry of the Populists. "And fifty farmers, united, buying their feed and gas and fertilizer . . . can demand and get a much lower price than can fifty farmers, divided." Williams warned small farmers not to view unions of industrial workers as enemies, which was the position of the Farm Bureau, an organization Williams claimed represented the interests of merchants, bankers, and large farmers, but not the small and medium farmers. Unions meant higher wages, and higher wages meant more purchasing power for workers, and that meant greater demand for farm products. . . .

Clifford Durr's December address focused on how to make the South "the nation's number one economic opportunity," instead of as FDR had called it, the nation's number one economic problem. The solution, according to Durr, lay in the better use of the region's human as well as natural resources. Arguing a variant of the colonial economy thesis, he said, "We have sought to hold our own in a competitive national economy by mining our farm lands as well as our mineral deposits, by mining our human resources through substandard wages rates and by exporting raw materials instead of finished products." Substandard wages and salaries made it impossible for many southerners to afford the goods they helped produce. Underconsumption was at the heart of poverty in the region, Durr claimed. . . .

Clark Foreman emphasized the role of electoral politics in fashioning a new South. Overthrowing the oligarchy that had ruled the region since the turn of the century required not only opening up the electorate to disfranchised African Americans, but also mobilizing the middle- and working-class voters who too often stayed away from the polls. Foreman also spoke about the importance of cross-class, interracial organizations such as the schw, a chapter of which had been organized in Charleston the day before.

Charles Johnson's lecture was the best attended, as African Americans in large numbers turned out to see the noted sociologist. Johnson stressed the need to address the South's social problems, particularly as they affected African Americans. For Johnson, improvements in housing, health care, and education had to be at the top of the progressive agenda.

When South Carolina's Progressive Democratic Party was formed in 1944, its vice-chairman Oceola McKaine evoked Reconstruction to describe what he believed was at stake in the years after World War II. "We are here," he said, "to help history repeat itself." But opponents of regional regeneration looked back to Reconstruction as well. They were determined not to let the past repeat itself, to forestall a "Second Reconstruction." William Watts Ball, editor of Charleston's *News and Courier*, was one of the most outspoken defenders of conservative rule. While his vitriolic polemics sometimes made him an embarrassment to his allies, his views on labor, African Americans, and the New Deal were in line with those of the major power brokers in the South: the plutocrats of North Carolina; the plantation owners and industrialists of Alabama; and the oilmen of Louisiana and Texas.

In the turbulent days at the end of the war, Ball's editorial page fired daily shots at each and every effort at change. And he closely followed the New South lecture series, honing in especially on what he—rightly—saw as the speakers' core message: the need to expand democratic citizenship in the South. "The ailment of South Carolina and of the whole United States is over dosage of democracy," Ball editorialized in December of 1945. "The infatuation for democracy is a disease. It is now epidemic." To state legislators who were at the time contemplating repeal of the poll tax, Ball recommended instead a "constitutional amendment that would reduce the potential negro vote by 90 percent and the potential white vote by a percentage that would shock the democrats." "It is possible," he continued, "that South Carolinians may some day have sense enough to return to the limited democracy that they had 86 years ago {before the Civil War} when government was good, decent, economical, and competent."

Ball was no less extreme in his denunciation of African Americans. "In our part of the country, the Southern United States, the white people have been more the victims of negro exploitation than the negroes have been of whites." In language that we have heard recently in the reparations debates, Ball continued,

"Negroes were brought to the South when slavery was common throughout the world, a great proportion of them brought out of slavery in Africa, and the negro population has been on the whole an economic burden on the Southern white people. Had never a negro landed in the South it would this day be not "the nation's economic problem number one" but one of the richest regions of the globe.

It was, however, the New Deal that took pride of place in Ball's pantheon of progressive horrors. Within weeks of Roosevelt's inauguration, Ball denounced the President and the federal government's intervention in the economy. Over the next decade, he never lost a chance to excoriate each New Deal program as a further step on the road to "state socialism." Convinced by the political realignments that brought Roosevelt to power that the national Democratic Party was not his true home, Ball supported the Dixiecrat revolt in 1948. This effort, led by South Carolina's own Governor Strom Thurmond, to unseat President Truman and reclaim southern control of the Democratic Party had limited success at the polls. But it laid the groundwork for massive resistance to desegregation in the 1950s and set the tenor for southern politics for years to come.

Faced with such opposition, what chance did progressives have of achieving a second reconstruction at the end of World War II? Could they mobilize the political support, both North and South, to defeat conservative congressmen, organize southern workers, and enfranchise African Americans? Could they persuade policy makers and elected officials to embrace an agenda of political and economic reform? . . .

Southerners such as Aubrey Williams, Charles Johnson, Clifford Durr, and Clark Foreman stood ready to assume the mantle of leadership for the South. They had years of experience in regional and national politics; they were members of influential organizations with a growing and diverse membership; and they had well-conceived plans for making the South the engine of postwar prosperity. They were, moreover, in touch with the grassroots, quite ready and willing, for instance, to show up in Charleston in response to the call of a few unknown GIs in league with tobacco workers on strike at a local plant.

In those heady days at the end of World War II, neither the speakers, nor the GIs, nor the tobacco workers could imagine what we know now: that Republicans and conservative southern Democrats would win control of the House and Senate in 1946 and forestall plans for Truman's Fair Deal; that the CIO's Operation Dixie would fizzle out in less than two years after it started; and that the whole nation would embrace a hysterical anticommunism reminiscent of the late-nineteenth century white supremacy campaigns.

The politics of polarization that was in place by the 1948 presidential campaign happened quickly, and it was both a response to and a result of the progressive push at the end of the war. The window of opportunity that was opened at the end of the war slammed shut. Karl's fears that without progressive leadership the nation would plunge into another depression proved unfounded, thanks in part to American expansion overseas. Nor did the region by any means succumb to fascism. Nevertheless, it would be safe to say that the history that was repeating itself was not Reconstruction but the mobilization of forces that cut short that grand experiment and made the dream of justice, equality, and prosperity once again a distant dream.

MATTHEW COUNTRYMAN

From *Up South: Civil Rights and Black Power in Philadelphia*

(2006)

At the same time that Cecil Moore and the Philadelphia NAACP were reinventing civil rights protest, a small group of community activists began meeting in a North Philadelphia storefront called the Freedom Library to discuss how to shift the focus of the movement to what they viewed as the fundamental causes of racial inequality and oppression in the city and nation. John Churchville, a twenty-three-year-old Philadelphia native who had worked as a Student Non-violent Coordinating Committee (SNCC) field secretary in Georgia and Mississippi, founded the Freedom Library in 1964 in order to bring the community organizing principles he had learned while working for SNCC to the issues facing the black poor in the urban North. Modeled on SNCC's Mississippi Freedom Schools, the library sponsored educational programs for neighborhood children that combined basic educational skills with black history during the day. And in the evenings, Churchville convened a series of lectures and discussions on black political and historical topics that were intended to attract activists who shared his frustration with the mainstream movement's integrationist agenda.

The Freedom Library's evening sessions drew a core group of community activists who were neither active in the student movement nor prominent in local civil rights activism. Rather they were longtime neighborhood activists . . . who shared an adamant opposition to what they saw as white and black middle-class domination of the mainstream civil rights movement. Inspired equally by Malcolm X's vision of a movement politics rooted in the black nationalist tradition and SNCC's commitment to developing movement leadership from within poor black communities, these activists set out to formulate and act on a movement politics that linked . . . black nationalist principles of race consciousness, intraracial unity, and black control over the social, political, and economic institutions operating within black communities to SNCC's radical democratic faith in indigenous political leadership.

A Black Nationalist in the Beloved Community

Even in its early years, SNCC's commitment to the discourse of the "beloved community" masked important similarities between its brand of movement activism and the black nationalist tradition. "By making southern blacks more confident of their capacity to overcome oppression," SNCC historian Clayborne Carson has written, "SNCC workers revived dormant feelings of racial consciousness." . . .

John Churchville was among the most vocal advocates of black nationalism on the SNCC staff. . . . Born and raised in North Philadelphia, Churchville attended Temple University before dropping out in 1961 to pursue a career as a jazz composer and pianist in New York. While in New York, he frequented the Harlem headquarters of the Nation of Islam where he met Malcolm X and became "enthralled by the Black Muslim movement." . . . "The black nationalist thing," Churchville remembers, "moved me emotionally at the very core of my being." . . .

. . . Despite [Churchville's] philosophical opposition to integration—"I was offended by the notion that the only way that blacks could develop was by being around white folks"—he was excited by SNCC's commitment to taking civil rights activism into the most isolated and dangerous areas of the South. . . . [H]e was able to distinguish between the racial separatism favored by the Nation of Islam and state-enforced jim crow segregation. "The problem with segregation," he remembers believing, "is that somebody else is in charge . . . somebody else controlled it." . . .

. . . In March 1963, Churchville [joined SNCC's] Greenwood, Mississippi [project] as part of an effort to overcome the violent repression of black voters and voter registration workers in the Mississippi Delta. Churchville calls his time in Greenwood his most important experience on the SNCC staff. In Greenwood, he shifted from canvassing to working in the Citizenship Schools, helping to train prospective voters to take the state's literacy test. In his literacy classes, Churchville found that he was doing "two things . . . you're trying to get people to pass this literacy test, but . . . you're giving a skill at the same time." As a result, he came to believe that the movement must be equally committed to grassroots organizing for short-term political goals and to effort to develop the basic skills of residents of poor communities. He recognized that in Mississippi, voter registration meant more than giving southern blacks the right to vote for one of the major parties; it meant that "if there were a lot black people registered to vote and . . . there was organization in that community about how one can vote, folks would begin to look at you better and treat you better because you could control whether they got in or out." It was not enough to win the right to vote, Churchville came to believe, blacks also needed to develop the skills and organizations that would enable them to use the political process to strengthen the communities in which they lived. He now viewed education as essential "to getting fundamental rights [and to] building an infrastructure for freedom."

Community Organizing with a Black Nationalist Agenda

. . . Churchville left . . . the SNCC staff in the summer of 1963. . . .

Back in Philadelphia, [he] started the Freedom Library Community Project in a Ridge Avenue storefront in North Philadelphia. Drawing on his work in the Mississippi Freedom Schools, he envisioned the Freedom Library as a community center that would simultaneously provide educational programming for neighborhood children and adults and serve as a staging point for community organization. . . .

For Churchville, however, the Freedon Library was to be more than a black nationalist-influenced educational program. Rather, he saw his efforts to promote black consciousness as the first step in a strategy to redirect the civil rights movement toward an agenda based on racial pride and black self-determination. "My perception of black power was never straight separatism," Churchville remembers. "It was come apart and be separate and get your act together . . . then you've got to get out there in the real world where other people are and you've got to argue with them." The next step was to create spaces in which black activists could come together free from the interference of well-meaning whites. To promote this vision of a black nationalist social movement, the Freedom Library sponsored an evening lecture and discussion series on issues ranging from black history to the current state of the civil rights movement. . . .

The success of the Freedom Library's evening discussions reflected the growing appeal within movement circles of Malcolm X's attempt to define a black nationalist political project in the months following his expulsion from the Nation of Islam. "The political philosophy of Black Nationalism," he had declared in a March 1964 press conference, "means we must control the politics and politicians of the our community. . . . We will organize, and sweep out of office all Negro politicians which are puppets for outside forces." . . .

. . . [The] Freedom Library might well have remained a largely self-contained neighborhood project had not Churchville had the good fortune to meet a thirty-eight-year-old hospital administrator and community activist named Mattie Humphrey. Excited by the Freedom Library's mix of youth programming and nationalist critique of mainstream black leadership, Humphrey recruited to the library's evening sessions many of the neighborhood activists who would work with Churchville to build the city's first Black Power organization, the Black People's Unity Movement (BPUM).

. . . Having admired the southern student movement from afar, she was immediately taken with what Churchville had established at the library. . . . [It] was the evening sessions, which she remembered attending a couple of times a week, that spoke to Humphrey's concerns about the impact of the civil rights movement on the collective well-being of the black community. Working as an administrator at black hospitals, . . . Humphrey had grown angry at what she shaw as the tendency of black doctors and other "professionals" to abandon the institutions that had taken responsibility for the collective strength of the black community as soon as they were given the opportunity to integrate "prestigious" white institutions. . . .

The Black People's Unity Movement

By the fall of 1965, the activists who had been convening at the Freedom Library were ready to present to a larger audience their vision of a new kind of movement politics, one committed to the black nationalist principles of racial unity, black consciousness, and community control over the key political and economic institutions operating within black communities. Drawing on Malcolm X's call for "all Afro-American people and organizations [to] henceforth unite so that the welfare and well-being of our people will be assured," the Freedom Library activists announced plans to start an all-black political organization—the Black People's Unity Movement (BPUM)—that would unite black Philadelphians across both class and ideological divisions free from the gaze of white allies and opponents alike. The discourse of racial unity had long been a powerful rhetorical weapon in the black nationalist critique of liberal interracialism. In a white supremacist society, black nationalists argued, the failure to establish intra-racial unity meant that the interracial coalitions favored by liberal integrationists were little more than tools for white control over the black agenda. . . .

. . . Churchville called on middle class blacks to join in a cross class coalition with the black poor and working classes . . . And in place of liberalism's emphasis on enabling individual blacks to escape the segregated ghetto, the founder of the Freedom Library declared that blacks must collectively "own, control and regulate the affairs of the so-called ghetto." . . .

. . . [BPUM's m]onthly mass meetings . . . brought together a diverse group of community activists and ideological nationalists while a number of subcommittees met regularly at the Freedom Library to work on issue areas such as education, economic development, and cultural consciousness. The group also sponsored a four-session training program, designed primarily for young activists, which combined the basics of community organizing with an introduction to black and precolonial African history. . . .

. . . Churchville was particularly proud that BPUM was able to attract people from across the class spectrum in the black community, bringing together 'teachers, doctors, at least one lawyer . . . professional and non-professional people . . . people on welfare." . . . Where BPUM did not differ from its predecessors in either the adult or student wings of the movement was in its assumption of male leadership. . . .

The peak of BPUM's influence came when the group hosted the Third National Conference on Black Power at the Church of the Advocate on the weekend of August 29, 1968. The conferences brought together many of Black Power's leading national figures, including Dr. Nathan Wright, an Episcopal priest who had hosted the previous summer's conference in Newark, New Jersey, the poet and playwright Amiri Baraka, Maulana Karenga of the Los Angeles–based U.S. Organization, Richard Henry of the Detroit-based Republic of New Africa, and the Revolutionary Action Movement's Max Stanford. According to Wright, the purpose of the conference was to forge a unified program for the Black Power movement. The conference delegates, Wright declared . . . , would consider the question of "reform or revolution as the only alternative for humanizing this society." The conference, he promised, would "deal with methods, techniques and strategies to forge a black nation in thought, experience, and commitment by unifying all black brothers and sisters." . . .

An estimated two thousand people attended the conference plenaries and workshop sessions on subjects like education, politics, economics, and culture. . . .

. . . The housing workshop, for example, emphasized strategies for accessing government funds for building and renovating low-income housing. . . . In the political workshop, activists began planning for a local Black Political Convention that would play a crucial role in the development of an independent black Democratic movement in the city. Finally, the work of the communications committee led Frankie Davenport (who would soon change her name to Falakha Fattah) to establish an underground black newspaper, *The Voice of Umoja*, to serve the city's black activist community.

SNCC Moves North

At the same time that the Black People's Unity Movement was establishing itself as the leading local advocate of the black nationalist politics of racial unity,

SNCC's national leadership decided to make Philadelphia the test site for its effort to bring its particular mix of community organizing and black empowerment to the urban North. Disillusioned by the unwillingness of the Democratic party's liberal wing to support fundamental political reform in the South, SNCC's community organizers had increasingly come to identify with Malcolm X's black nationalist political vision. . . .

. . . [SNCC National Chairman Stokley] Carmichael and his supporters saw the Harlem, North Philadelphia, and Watts riots as evidence that SNCC's brand of community organizing and independent electoral politics could win a significant following in the ghettoes of the urban North. . . . In 1965, Fred Meely, a longtime member of SNCC's Mississippi staff, arrived in Philadelphia to establish a full-fledged SNCC-sponsored community organizing project in the city. James Forman, who was SNCC's Executive Secretary from 1961 to 1966, would later write that the Philadelphia project was "the first attempt, in a major metropolitan area, to develop the concept of a national Freedom organization with the panther as its symbol."

. . . Meely recruited an all-black project staff made up of veterans of SNCC's southern projects, NSM members and local youth activists [to work on the Philadelphia project]. . . .

. . . Meely trained the staff in an organizing "model" in which . . . "the organizer . . . goes into the community, mobilizes the community, but does not make him or herself a permanent part of that structure, the idea being that you could walk out of it, and it would continue." [He] also taught that community people had to be allowed to make their own mistakes. . . .

Specifically, Meely and his staff envisioned the Philadelphia Freedom Organization (PFO) as a community-based organization led by and for residents of Philadelphia's black working class communities that could serve as an independent alternative to the city's mainstream political parties. The PFO's membership card listed eight "purposes and aims" including: "To Unify the People"; "To See that Black People Can Participate Freely in a True Democracy"; and "To Assure that the Negro Community Selects [its] Candidates." Canvassing the city's black working class neighborhoods, the staff sought . . . "to use the southern model to get people registered to vote and . . . involved in electoral politics. We'd give little booklets that . . . talked about . . . the Freedom organization." One booklet included sections on "What Is the Vote?," "What Is Politics?," and "Why Come Together?" . . .

From the start, the staff of Philadelphia SNCC made clear their commitment to promoting leadership from within the city's poor and working class black neighborhoods. . . . The PFO booklet asked "Do you know someone who lives on your street who would make a good city councilman, a good state senator, a good congressman, a good mayor or a good judge?" . . . Philadelphia SNCC saw poor black communities as the site of an authentic black identity. "If we could elect people who are not ashamed of us or of being black or Negro," the booklet continued, "they would work for us." . . . As part of their effort to demonstrate the relevance of electoral politics to the daily lives of black Philadelphians, SNCC canvassers focused on the issue of police brutality and, in particular, on "how damaging and dangerous" Deputy Police Commissioner Frank Rizzo was to the black community. They believed Rizzo's reputation for brutality, the threat that police violence posed to black lives in the city, and the fact that he had been appointed by a mayor who owed his election to black voters could provide the same object lesson of the importance of voting that the small-town sheriff had for SNCC's voter registration projects in the South.

Philadelphia SNCC, of course, faced a vastly different political terrain than the group had found in the Mississippi Delta and other areas of the rural South. While southern blacks had been excluded from the political process for generations, Philadelphia's black voters had played an active and increasingly important role in the patronage-based machine politics throughout the twentieth century. To promote its vision of an independent black political organization, Philadelphia SNCC had to convince the residents of the city's poor black communities not only of the relevance of electoral process but also to stop giving their votes to the Democratic machine. Much of SNCC's canvassing therefore focused on "how you put together a political party, how you get on the ballot, how you get enough votes, how you go through the paperwork." . . .

The effort to build the PFO reflected SNCC's continued belief that political action within the American electoral system was the key to ending racial oppression in the country. . . . SNCC's embrace of Black Power and community control represented not an abandonment of the electoral process but a shift from the coalition model of interracial liberalism to the ethnic mobilization model of urban political machine. "Black power," SNCC Chairman Stokely Carmichael wrote in 1966, "means the creation of power bases from which black people can work to change statewide or nationwide patterns of oppression. . . . Politically, black power means what it has always meant to SNCC: the coming-together of black people to elect representatives and *to force those representatives to speak to their needs*" (emphasis Carmichael's). Just as urban political machines had historically harnessed the resources of local government to support the economic advancement of European immigrants, SNCC believed that the mass organizations that it was building could use black votes to win control of the public resources necessary to fuel the economic development of poor black communities.

. . . Over the course of the late 1960s and early 1970s, a new generation of activists . . . would emerge in Philadelphia to challenge the liberal orthodoxy that had animated reform efforts in postwar Philadelphia. In their efforts to more justly distribute power and wealth in the city, this new generation of activists turned to the principles of community-based leadership, participatory democracy, and racial self-determination to replace liberalism's faith in antidiscrimination laws, technocratic government, and the Democratic Party's New Deal coalition.

Perhaps the most important legacy of the Black Power movement in Philadelphia, however, was its impact on the nature of black political leadership in the city. During the first half of the 1960s, Selective Patronage and Cecil Moore's reign as president of the Philadelphia NAACP [civil rights protest] had helped to shift the locus of black leadership in the city from the Center City offices of the city's liberal reform organizations to the city's black working class neighborhoods. But it was the Black Power movement's commitment to community-based leadership that truly democratized black leadership in the city. While charismatic national Black Power leaders conducted an endless search for more and more media attention, black student organizing and other forms of community-based activism in Philadelphia served to decenter the structure of black leadership in the city. No longer could . . . movement leadership be restricted to middle-class professionals. . . . [T]he leadership of all future black movement organizations and campaigns in Philadelphia would include significant and substantive representation of working-class activists from the city's poor black neighborhoods.

AKINYELE OMOWALE UMOJA

From *We Will Shoot Back:*
Armed Resistance in the
Mississippi Freedom Movement

(2013)

The March against Fear: Self-Defense and the Rise of Black Power

The [1966] March against Fear was considered "the last great march of the civil rights years." Designed to inspire and organize Black Mississippians to register and vote, the March against Fear had varying degrees of success in organizing Black communities and mobilizing the vote. The march would register new Black voters in the state and would have a lasting impact on the political participation of Blacks in the communities along the route of the march.

In Greenwood, SNCC field organizer Willie Ricks was put on the advance team. Ricks, a charismatic exhorter, went to Greenwood Black communities and implemented an agitation/propaganda campaign promoting the slogan of "Black Power." Conflict occurred when the march arrived in Greenwood on June 16th. Local police arrested Carmichael, SNCC worker Robert Smith, and CORE organizer Bruce Baines. The charge was violating a city order that prevented marchers from setting up tents for a campsite at a Black public high school. After being bailed out, Carmichael spoke at an evening rally in Greenwood. He had been encouraged by Ricks to include and emphasize the "Black Power" slogan in his presentation. Carmichael, a gifted and skillful orator, was fervent and inspiring, speaking to a crowd of six hundred at the Leflore County Courthouse. The SNCC chairman passionately asked them, "What do you want?" Ricks, an extremely effective "hype man," responded, "Black Power!" Carmichael asked the question again and again, and each time more people in the audience of mostly local people responded enthusiastically.

The inclusion of the "Black Power" slogan represented a more nationalist shift in the ranks of SNCC, CORE, and particularly in the younger generation of the Movement. The "Black Power" slogan was rejected by integrationists, including King, SCLC leaders, Charles Evers, and National Baptist Convention leader John H. Jackson. The development of incipient Black nationalism, along with the growing rejection of nonviolence by Movement activists and the presence of the Deacons, became a concern of integrationist and nonviolent forces in the Black Freedom Struggle and a major focus of national media covering the March against Fear. SNCC and SCLC leaders offered competing chants during the march. SNCC members led the march with, "What do you want . . . Black power." In response, SCLC chanted, "What do you want . . . Freedom."

The march inspired several Mississippi Black communities into political activity. Much of the media coverage and many of the scholarly accounts have emphasized the ideological difference among march participants, the emergence of the "Black Power" slogan, and the presence of the Deacons. The impact of the march on the political consciousness and participation of Mississippi Black communities and on individual Blacks in the state must not be lost. The charismatic appeal of Martin Luther King Jr. was a motivation for thousands of Black Delta residents to leave school, work, or their residences in order to march or rally at the respective county courthouses. The presence of King was a tremendous asset for the success of the march.

In some communities, the March against Fear was a significant moment that inspired individuals toward political action. The march entered the Delta town of Belzoni on June 19th, and as twelve hundred marchers arrived in the city, a Black citizen proclaimed, "There has never been anything like this in Belzoni." Hundreds of plantation workers and farmers in Humphreys County joined the march, increasing the number from the 150-person core of primarily SNCC, CORE, and SCLC field workers. Black Humphreys County residents responded to the call of the marchers and demonstrated support for the Movement, in spite of the threat of economic reprisal and violence. One Humphreys County resident remembered, "We was a little afraid, but we still stepped up." In Humphreys County, marchers witnessed conditions of life on plantations reminiscent of chattel slavery. During the march activities, 150 Blacks were registered at the Humphreys County courthouse in spite of intimidation tactics by plantation owners and local White supremacists. . . .

The March against Fear entered Yazoo County on June 22nd. The march and rally in the county seat, Yazoo City, would mark a turning point for many local residents. Prior to the march, Yazoo County had not been a significant Movement center in the state. The march initiated the beginning of dynamic Movement activity in the county. Nancella Hudson was a domestic and a mother of five. She went to the march with her youngest child, Rodney (an eight-month-old baby), in a stroller to shake the hand of King. She allowed her three older children, ages six, seven, and eight, to march with chaperones from the county courthouse to the Oak Grove African Methodist Episcopal Church. The church was located in the nearby Benton community (nearly seven miles away). Hudson decided to register to vote at the rally in front of the Yazoo County courthouse. Hudson remembered, "And then you know when I got home, I got scared, I said oh my goodness! You know, but at that time, you know there come a time when you just don't have no fear. I didn't have no fear." Hudson's overcoming her fear to register on that day is precisely the act [civil rights leader James] Meredith had wanted to encourage when he had initiated the march weeks earlier.

Arthur Clayborn was a postal worker in Yazoo County who had previously registered to vote. Clayborn did not fear losing his job for participating in the march since he was a federal employee. He was determined to see King at the march, so he carried his six children to the rally at the county courthouse for the opportunity to see the civil rights leader. Clayborn's oldest child wanted to march away from the rally to Canton. Two years later, he would actively participate in the boycott in Yazoo County.

Herman Leach was a teacher at the Saint Francis School in Yazoo City. His brother Wardell was teaching at a public school in Yazoo. Hundreds of Yazoo youth prepared to march downtown. Yazoo City mayor Jeffrey Barber mobilized local police and firemen with a fire truck to prevent the young people from marching through downtown. Wardell Leach warned Barber that for city law enforcement to attack young people would have political consequences. The Leach brothers escorted the students on the march. Herman Leach would become more politically active after the march, participating in organizing boycotts in Yazoo and serving as an elected official. Wardell Leach would become Yazoo City's first African American mayor.

The March, the Deacons, and the Growing Debate on Armed Resistance

U.S. Attorney General Nicholas Katzenbach agreed to grant the state of Mississippi the responsibility of securing the marchers. Mississippi governor Paul Johnson assumed responsibility for providing protection for the marchers, despite publicly exhibiting disdain for its participants. Johnson stated that state law enforcement's protection of the march was dependent on whether "they [the marchers] behave themselves, commit no acts of violence nor take any position of provocative defiance." Johnson also discouraged White Mississippians from disrupting the march, which he characterized as consisting of "agitators and radical politicians."

Governor Johnson originally provided twenty state patrol cars for this assignment. After early voter registration successes on the route, Johnson sliced the number of patrol cars to four, declaring that the march had "turned into a voter registration campaign." Johnson stated in a news conference, "We aren't going to wet-nurse a bunch of showmen." Carmichael believed that the Deacons' presence openly and legally carrying guns motivated the decision to scale the state police escort back to a token show of force. Carmichael's account also conveyed that state troopers allowed vehicles on the march route to "veer over, speed up, and zoom by, inches from where our people were walking." One evening state troopers intervened to discourage a few carloads of White hooligans who had driven dangerously close to the marchers' campsite only after the Deacons confronted the marauders.

The march became a venue for the debate between nonviolence and armed resistance. One White nonviolent protestor, Reverend Theodore Seamans, argued that "the movement is no place for guns." Seamans's comments occurred after he observed a .45 handgun in a vehicle driven by one of the Deacons. Responding to Seamans's criticism, Ernest Thomas, the Deacons' spokesperson and national organizer, retorted that it was dangerous to tell Blacks not to fight back in such a violent and hostile situation. The debate between Seamans and Thomas sparked a vigorous exchange between nonviolent advocates and supporters of armed resistance. The debate caught the attention of media observers. CORE field secretary Bruce Baines intervened, saying, "[I]f you want to discuss violence and nonviolence, don't talk around the press. This march is too important." CORE chairman Floyd McKissick maintained a deceptive and conciliatory posture with the press concerning armed security. McKissick told the press he was not aware of arms around the campsite and insisted on telling all marchers, including the Deacons, "[T]he march must remain nonviolent. . . . I don't believe in no damn war."

A growing number of activists appreciated the presence of the Deacons. SNCC members openly praised the Deacons' security efforts and role in the Movement. "Everyone realized that without [the Deacons], our lives would have been much less secure," declared Cleve Sellers. Willie Ricks proclaimed to an audience in Belzoni, "We don't have enough Deacons." The Deacons gave some marchers a feeling of security and confidence that they could prevent White terrorism. SNCC executive committee member Jesse Harris sensed, "Along the march we had no problems because all the white folks, Klansman and everybody, they knew if they came in with a threat, if a church got bombed along the way, boom . . . the Deacons were going to find you." The Deacons' presence and posture provided confidence and confirmed to some that Blacks needed to rely on their own resources for protection.

All of the spokespersons, including Thomas, insisted that the march was nonviolent. However, while the Deacons' leader acknowledged the march as nonviolent, he openly advocated armed self-defense. In a masculinist appeal, Thomas told a rally in Belzoni, "It's time for Black men to start taking care of their Black women and children."

The debate within the ranks of the march represented a developing trend of the Movement toward open advocacy of armed self-defense. Seventy-one-year-old Bishop Charles Tucker of the African Methodist Episcopal Zion Church expressed a patriarchal perspective on the issue, stating, "Any Negro or white has the right to defend himself with arms. Any man who didn't ought to take off his pants and wear a skirt." Other marchers considered abandoning the pledge for the march to be nonviolent. Carmichael stated that harassment from local White supremacists, provocation from local police, and lack of serious protection from state troopers had activists discussing the need for "bringing out their pieces." King and others committed to passive resistance encouraged participants to maintain vigilance and the march to remain nonviolent. King stated, "If anyone can't live with it [the discipline of nonviolence] we'll give him bus fare and let him go his merry way."

Mainstream media was obsessed with and seriously concerned about the Deacons and the significance of their presence. Unlike in marches of the past, where Blacks covertly secured their comrades, observers noticed "disciplined" Black men communicating with "two-way" radios. Probably more troubling were the "bulges" detected "beneath the clothing" of young men patrolling the march. While often speaking in conciliatory terms, Deacons leader Thomas was frank with the press about the presence and purpose of the organization at the march. Thomas told the press that the Deacons were guarding the campsite "with pistols, rifles, and shotguns. . . . But we don't take guns with us when the people are marching. . . . The march is nonviolent." The Memphis *Commercial Appeal* reported that the "[a]ppearance of the 'Deacons' in the Mississippi marching column marked a significant, and to many a frightening shift in tactics of Negroes who for 10 years had been lulled and led by the non-violent oratory of Dr. Martin Luther King, Jr."

A common theme in national coverage of the march emphasized contradictions between King and those embracing armed resistance. A dichotomy was constructed pitting the nonviolent King against the "violent" Deacons and Black Power militants. On June 22nd, a *New York Times* article titled "Dr. King Scores 'Deacons,'" stated that King publicly lashed out at the "Black Power" advocates SNCC and the Deacons. Close examination reveals that King's words were directed not to the protection provided by the Deacons but to the retaliatory violence advocated by other elements of the Movement. King argued,

> Some people are telling us to be like our oppressor, who has a history of using Molotov cocktails, who has a history of using the atomic bomb, who has a history of lynching Negroes. . . . Now people are telling me to stoop to that level. . . . I'm sick and tired of violence. I'm tired of the war in Vietnam. I'm tired of Molotov cocktails.

While King deplored all violence, he made the distinction between "self defense involving defensive violence and retaliatory violence." A growing number of Black Power militants embraced the spontaneous urban rebellions that were becoming common occurrences in the middle and late 1960s. One factor in their support of urban rebellions was their growing fascination with the work of Frantz Fanon and other anticolonial national liberation movements. Fanon, who had become popular among the youth of the Movement, argued that the coercive force of the oppressed was necessary and psychologically liberating. King was concerned about the advocacy of armed resistance, the embracing of Fanon's concepts on violence within the Black Freedom Struggle (particularly within SNCC), and the growing occurrence of spontaneous rebellion in Black communities inside the United States. While King may have critically examined different forms of armed resistance, mainstream media made no distinction.

It is clear that King's consent to allow the Deacons in the march did not mean that he abandoned his allegiance to nonviolence. On the contrary, King was disturbed by the public advocacy of armed self-defense by the Deacons and also a growing number of young activists who had rejected nonviolence. Concerning the growing support of armed resistance, one Black publication quoted him as saying, "I'm worried about this climate." King believed a violent confrontation during the march was potentially "impractical and disastrous." He not only morally supported nonviolence but also believed that it was tactically viable. King argued that since Black people were a minority, it was impossible for them to achieve a strategic victory against a hostile majority through armed resistance. While King was not opposed to self-defense in the face of racist or oppressive violence, he believed that demonstrations utilizing nonviolence assisted activists in achieving a moral high ground from which they could expose injustice rather than be perceived as aggressive antagonists. In spite of his concerns, King respected the Deacons and saw them as a viable part of the Movement. King's associate Andrew Young commented, "[King] would never resort to violence, even in defense of his life, but he would not and could not demand that of others. . . . He saw the Deacons as a defensive presence not a retaliatory one."

PART 6

Contemporary Perspectives on Race and Racial Violence

CHAD WILLIAMS

Kendrick Lamar, in the opening bridge of his song "Blacker the Berry," invokes an image of late 1960s urban unrest and black rage. As the civil rights movement reached its apogee with the 1965 Voting Rights Act, the neglect of inner-city black America and the myriad issues facing its residents, such as unemployment and police brutality, exploded to the surface. From Watts to Newark and Baltimore, African Americans rebelled against their conditions and the devaluation of their lives, whether by the police officer administering "law and order" or the sniper who murdered Martin Luther King Jr. on the balcony of the Lorraine Motel in Memphis, Tennessee.

In "Blacker the Berry," Kendrick Lamar does not offer a retrospective of the late 1960s but instead speaks of the meaning of blackness in 2015, the year of the Charleston, South Carolina, Emmanuel AME shooting. Irrespective of time and place, the massacre of nine men and women inside a church during bible study would have registered as significant. The tragedy of Charleston, however, was compounded by the historical moment and national racial climate in which it took place.

Beginning with the 1968 presidential election of Richard M. Nixon, national politicians pivoted to a "post–civil rights" approach to race relations and inequality. As Thomas Sugrue outlines, shifting government priorities combined with other social and economic forces to devastate urban African American communities. Well-paying jobs with benefits vanished as a result of deindustrialization. Urban renewal projects decimated working-class neighborhoods, replacing single-family homes with housing projects that quickly became overcrowded and poorly maintained. Crucial social and political resources departed with the flight of whites and middle-class African Americans to the suburbs, contributing to eroding tax bases and underfunded schools. These socioeconomic developments were accompanied by a pernicious discourse that blamed the problems African Americans confronted on their own familial behavior and cultural deficiencies.

Arguably no other phenomenon did more to ravage African American communities and families than mass incarceration. President Ronald Reagan's launch of a so-called War on Drugs marked a new stage in a long history of criminalizing blackness and, as Kali Gross illuminates, destroying the right of black women in particular to protect themselves. Police, empowered by harsh sentencing laws and military-style weapons and tactics, specifically targeted predominately African American and Latino neighborhoods. Throughout the 1980s the percentage of black people imprisoned for nonviolent drug offenses skyrocketed. Policies that disproportionately impacted poor African Americans continued under President George H. W. Bush and were strengthened by his successor, President Bill Clinton, who went to great lengths to prove that he and the Democratic Party were tough on crime.

The very meaning of racial progress in the 1980s and early 1990s proved confounding. African Americans could point to important political achievements, such as the presidential campaigns of Jesse Jackson and elections of black mayors in major cities across the country, the steady growth of the black middle class, or the ubiquitous presence of black faces in every realm of American popular culture—Michael Jackson on the music stage, Oprah Winfrey on the television set, or Magic Johnson on the basketball court. However, the intractability of racial inequality and racist violence could not be ignored, and it cut across class lines. African Americans moving into white neighborhoods, as Jeannine Bell demonstrates, faced the threat of hate crimes, while African Americans trapped in the inner city remained subjected to police abuse. The 1992 Los Angeles rebellion, sparked by the acquittal of four white police officers caught on video beating black motorist Rodney King, reflected the pent-up rage felt by many African Americans. When Compton native Kendrick Lamar raps in "Blacker the Berry," "You sabotage my community, makin' a killin' / you made me a killer, emancipation of a real nigga," he is speaking to this frustration and desire to be both heard and seen on his own terms.

As the twenty-first century dawned, the problem of the color line still remained. The September 11, 2001, terrorist attacks triggered a wave of hyperpatriotism and demand for 100 percent Americanism. Many African Americans, however, approached this moment and the nation's subsequent "War on Terror" with a different historical sensibility, one informed by a legacy of slavery, lynching, mass slaughters, state-sanctioned violence, and other forms of racial terror. Hurricane Katrina, the August 2005 storm that, together with a failed government response, killed upwards of eighteen hundred people, resulted in over $100 billion in property damage, and destroyed the black neighborhoods of New Orleans, permanently displacing its residents, again challenged African Americans' faith in their country.

The 2008 election of Barack Obama was seen by many Americans not only as the turning of the page on this recent history but also as a move beyond the nation's long and troubled racial past. As the first African American president of the United States, Obama symbolized hope and the ability to transcend even the most unimaginable racial barriers. The dream of the Obama presidency and a "postracial" America quickly collided with the continued existence of racial inequality and the legacies of white supremacy. In many ways the Obama years heightened the expectations of African Americans, especially among a younger generation, who increasingly refused to accept the disconnect between the promise of America as symbolized by President Obama and its cruel reality when it came to the value of black life.

The February 26, 2012, shooting death of African American teenager Trayvon Martin at the hands of George Zimmerman and subsequent trial was a watershed moment in contemporary race relations and struggles for African American civil rights. Dylann Roof credited the incident for awakening his white racial consciousness. In contrast, after Zimmerman's acquittal on grounds of self-defense, a broad youth-based movement for racial justice emerged, sparked by the Twitter declaration #BlackLivesMatter. The #BlackLivesMatter movement draws inspiration from earlier civil rights groups, such as the Student Non-violence Coordinating Committee (SNCC), while creatively employing social media as a means of communication, mobilization, and consciousness raising. As this new movement continues to evolve, historian Barbara Ransby offers crucial perspective and advice for its long-term viability and success.

The Charleston massacre took place during a year-long span in which the #BlackLivesMatter movement focused the nation's attention on the long-standing problem of police violence against African Americans. The suburban St. Louis city of Ferguson, Missouri, became ground zero following the August 9, 2014, death of eighteen-year-old Michael Brown by white police officer Darren Wilson. The protests that followed, marked by alarming displays of militarized force by area law enforcement, compelled the Justice Department to investigate the practices of the Ferguson police department. Their report, an excerpt of which is included in this section, revealed a systemic pattern of violent abuse and economic exploitation directed toward Ferguson's black residents.

In the aftermath of Ferguson, new stories of black men and women being killed by police became almost daily occurrences. The videotaped murder of Walter Scott, shot in the back multiple times by a North Charleston police officer after a seemingly routine traffic stop, was especially shocking and exposed the inadequacy of simple police reform in lieu of fundamental transformation of the nation's criminal-justice system and the moral logic behind it. State senator Rev. Clementa Pinckney, in a May 9 speech before the South Carolina legislature on the Walter Scott shooting, intoned, "Today, the nation looks at South

Carolina and is looking at us to see if we will rise to be the body, and to be the state that we really say that we are."

The following month, on June 17, Pinckney would be killed in his church along with eight other men and women. As details of the massacre unfolded and Dylann Roof's motives became more clear, much of the nation and, indeed, the world looked to see if South Carolina would honestly confront its troublesome racial past and present, symbolized by the Confederate battle flag flying on the grounds of the state capital building, a history Steve Estes recounts. President Barack Obama's eulogy of Rev. Pinckney touched on this issue and many other themes, among them the historic role of the black church and the power of grace and forgiveness. The article by Esther Armah offers a different perspective on black forgiveness of white supremacist terror, placing it within a global context, as does the essay by Brittney Cooper on the faith and feminism of Bree Newsome. Newsome, as she reached the top of the thirty-foot pole that held the Confederate flag and looked down on the capital police officers prepared to arrest her, boldly pronounced, "You come against me with hatred and oppression and violence. I come against you in the name of God. This flag comes down today!"

In "Blacker the Berry," Kendrick Lamar repeatedly declares, "I'm the biggest hypocrite in 2015." Lamar's honest self-reflection speaks to the internal challenges many African Americans and socially conscious individuals face during moments racial crisis. While it may be easy to celebrate a Bree Newsome, not everyone will possess her courage. Lamar pushes us to seriously consider the ways in which our actions, as well as our passivity in the midst of injustice, allow the conditions that contributed to the Charleston shooting to persist. As Lamar's song concludes with him shouting, "Hypocrite!" one final time, we are left to grapple with how learning about, embracing, and protecting blackness and black lives is a matter of both personal accountability and collective responsibility.

BARACK OBAMA

Remarks by the President in Eulogy for the Honorable Reverend Clementa Pinckney, College of Charleston, Charleston, South Carolina

(June 29, 2015)

THE PRESIDENT: Giving all praise and honor to God.

The Bible calls us to hope. To persevere, and have faith in things not seen.

"They were still living by faith when they died," Scripture tells us. "They did not receive the things promised; they only saw them and welcomed them from a distance, admitting that they were foreigners and strangers on Earth."

We are here today to remember a man of God who lived by faith. A man who believed in things not seen. A man who believed there were better days ahead, off in the distance. A man of service who persevered, knowing full well he would not receive all those things he was promised, because he believed his efforts would deliver a better life for those who followed.

To Jennifer, his beloved wife; to Eliana and Malana, his beautiful, wonderful daughters; to the Mother Emanuel family and the people of Charleston, the people of South Carolina.

I cannot claim to have the good fortune to know Reverend Pinckney well. But I did have the pleasure of knowing him and meeting him here in South Carolina, back when we were both a little bit younger. Back when I didn't have visible grey hair. The first thing I noticed was his graciousness, his smile, his reassuring baritone, his deceptive sense of humor all qualities that helped him wear so effortlessly a heavy burden of expectation.

Friends of his remarked this week that when Clementa Pinckney entered a room, it was like the future arrived; that even from a young age, folks knew he was special. Anointed. He was the progeny of a long line of the faithful—a family of preachers who spread God's word, a family of protesters who sowed change to expand voting rights and desegregate the South. Clem heard their instruction, and he did not forsake their teaching.

He was in the pulpit by 13, pastor by 18, public servant by 23. He did not exhibit any of the cockiness of youth, nor youth's insecurities; instead, he set an example worthy of his position, wise beyond his years, in his speech, in his conduct, in his love, faith, and purity.

As a senator, he represented a sprawling swath of the Lowcountry, a place that has long been one of the most neglected in America. A place still wracked by poverty and inadequate schools; a place where children can still go hungry and the sick can go without treatment. A place that needed somebody like Clem.

His position in the minority party meant the odds of winning more resources for his constituents were often long. His calls for greater equity were too often unheeded, the votes he cast were sometimes lonely. But he never gave up. He stayed true to his convictions. He would not grow discouraged. After a full day at the capitol, he'd climb into his car and head to the church to draw sustenance from his family, from his ministry, from the community that loved and needed him. There he would fortify his faith, and imagine what might be.

Reverend Pinckney embodied a politics that was neither mean, nor small. He conducted himself quietly, and kindly, and diligently. He encouraged progress not by pushing his ideas alone, but by seeking out your ideas, partnering with you to make things happen. He was full of empathy and fellow feeling, able to walk in somebody else's shoes and see through their eyes. No wonder one of his senate colleagues remembered Senator Pinckney as "the most gentle of the 46 of us—the best of the 46 of us."

Clem was often asked why he chose to be a pastor and a public servant. But the person who asked probably didn't know the history of the AME church. As our brothers and sisters in the AME church know, we don't make those distinctions. "Our calling," Clem once said, "is not just within the walls of the congregation, but . . . the life and community in which our congregation resides."

He embodied the idea that our Christian faith demands deeds and not just words; that the "sweet hour of prayer" actually lasts the whole week long; that to put our faith in action is more than individual salvation, it's about our collective salvation; that to feed the hungry and clothe the naked and house the homeless is not just a call for isolated charity but the imperative of a just society.

What a good man. Sometimes I think that's the best thing to hope for when you're eulogized—after all the words and recitations and resumes are read, to just say someone was a good man.

You don't have to be of high station to be a good man. Preacher by 13. Pastor by 18. Public servant by 23. What a life Clementa Pinckney lived. What an example he set. What a model for his faith. And then to lose him at 41—slain in his sanctuary with eight wonderful members of his flock, each at different stages in life but bound together by a common commitment to God.

Cynthia Hurd. Susie Jackson. Ethel Lance. DePayne Middleton-Doctor. Tywanza Sanders. Daniel L. Simmons. Sharonda Coleman-Singleton. Myra Thompson. Good people. Decent people. God-fearing people. People so full of life and so full of kindness. People who ran the race, who persevered. People of great faith.

To the families of the fallen, the nation shares in your grief. Our pain cuts that much deeper because it happened in a church. The church is and always has been the center of African-American life—a place to call our own in a too often hostile world, a sanctuary from so many hardships.

Over the course of centuries, black churches served as "hush harbors" where slaves could worship in safety; praise houses where their free descendants could gather and shout hallelujah; rest stops for the weary along the Underground Railroad; bunkers for the foot soldiers of the Civil Rights Movement. They have been, and continue to be, community centers where we organize for jobs and justice; places of scholarship and network; places where children are loved and fed and kept out of harm's way, and told that they are beautiful and smart—and taught that they matter. That's what happens in church.

That's what the black church means. Our beating heart. The place where our dignity as a people is inviolate. When there's no better example of this tradition than Mother Emanuel—a church built by blacks seeking liberty, burned to the ground because its founder sought to end slavery, only to rise up again, a Phoenix from these ashes.

When there were laws banning all-black church gatherings, services happened here anyway, in defiance of unjust laws. When there was a righteous movement to dismantle Jim Crow, Dr. Martin Luther King, Jr. preached from its pulpit, and marches began from its steps. A sacred place, this church. Not just for blacks, not just for Christians, but for every American who cares about the steady expansion—of human rights and human dignity in this country; a foundation stone for liberty and justice for all. That's what the church meant.

We do not know whether the killer of Reverend Pinckney and eight others knew all of this history. But he surely sensed the meaning of his violent act. It was an act that drew on a long history of bombs and arson and shots fired at churches, not random, but as a means of control, a way to terrorize and oppress. An act that he imagined would incite fear and recrimination; violence and suspicion. An act that he presumed would deepen divisions that trace back to our nation's original sin.

Oh, but God works in mysterious ways. God has different ideas.

He didn't know he was being used by God. Blinded by hatred, the alleged killer could not see the grace surrounding Reverend Pinckney and that Bible study group—the light of love that shone as they opened the church doors and invited a stranger to join in their prayer circle. The alleged killer could have never anticipated the way the families of the fallen would respond when they saw him in court—in the midst of unspeakable grief, with words of forgiveness. He couldn't imagine that.

The alleged killer could not imagine how the city of Charleston, under the good and wise leadership of Mayor Riley—how the state of South Carolina, how the United States of America would respond—not merely with revulsion at his evil act, but with big-hearted generosity and, more importantly, with a thoughtful introspection and self-examination that we so rarely see in public life.

Blinded by hatred, he failed to comprehend what Reverend Pinckney so well understood—the power of God's grace.

This whole week, I've been reflecting on this idea of grace. The grace of the families who lost loved ones. The grace that Reverend Pinckney would preach about in his sermons. The grace described in one of my favorite hymns—the one we all know: Amazing grace, how sweet the sound that saved a wretch like me. I once was lost, but now I'm found; was blind but now I see.

According to the Christian tradition, grace is not earned. Grace is not merited. It's not something we deserve. Rather, grace is the free and benevolent favor of God—as manifested in the salvation of sinners and the bestowal of blessings. Grace.

As a nation, out of this terrible tragedy, God has visited grace upon us, for he has allowed us to see where we've been blind. He has given us the chance, where we've been lost, to find our best selves. We may not have earned it, this grace, with our rancor and complacency, and short-sightedness and fear of each other—but we got it all the same. He gave it to us anyway. He's once more given us grace. But it is up to us now to make the most of it, to receive it with gratitude, and to prove ourselves worthy of this gift.

For too long, we were blind to the pain that the Confederate flag stirred in too many of our citizens. It's true, a flag did not cause these murders. But as people from all walks of life, Republicans and Democrats, now acknowledge—including Governor Haley, whose recent eloquence on the subject is worthy of praise—as we all have to acknowledge, the flag has always represented more than just ancestral pride. For many, black and white, that flag was a reminder of systemic oppression and racial subjugation. We see that now.

Removing the flag from this state's capitol would not be an act of political correctness; it would not be an insult to the valor of Confederate soldiers. It would simply be an acknowledgment that the cause for which they fought—the cause of slavery—was wrong—the imposition of Jim Crow after the Civil War, the resistance to civil rights for all people was wrong. It would be one step in an honest accounting of America's history; a modest but meaningful balm for so many unhealed wounds. It would be an expression of the amazing changes that have transformed this state and this country for the better, because of the work of so many people of goodwill, people of all races striving to form a more perfect union. By taking down that flag, we express God's grace.

But I don't think God wants us to stop there. For too long, we've been blind to the way past injustices continue to shape the present. Perhaps we see that now. Perhaps this tragedy causes us to ask some tough questions about how we can permit so many of our children to languish in poverty, or attend dilapidated schools, or grow up without prospects for a job or for a career.

Perhaps it causes us to examine what we're doing to cause some of our children to hate. Perhaps it softens hearts towards those lost young men, tens and tens of thousands caught up in the criminal justice system—and leads us to make sure that that system is not infected with bias; that we embrace changes in how we train and equip our police so that the bonds of trust between law enforcement and the communities they serve make us all safer and more secure.

Maybe we now realize the way racial bias can infect us even when we don't realize it, so that we're guarding against not just racial slurs, but we're also guarding against the subtle impulse to call Johnny back for a job interview but not Jamal. So that we search our hearts when we consider laws to make it harder for some of our fellow citizens to vote. By recognizing our common humanity by treating every child as important, regardless of the color of their skin or the station into which they were born, and to do what's necessary to make opportunity real for every American—by doing that, we express God's grace.

For too long—

AUDIENCE: For too long!

THE PRESIDENT: For too long, we've been blind to the unique mayhem that gun violence inflicts upon this nation. Sporadically, our eyes are open: When eight of our brothers and sisters are cut down in a church basement, 12 in a movie theater, 26 in an elementary school. But I hope we also see the 30 precious lives cut short by gun violence in this country every single day; the countless more whose lives are forever changed—the survivors crippled, the children traumatized and fearful every day as they walk to school, the husband who will never feel his wife's warm touch, the entire communities whose grief overflows every time they have to watch what happened to them happen to some other place.

The vast majority of Americans—the majority of gun owners—want to do something about this. We see that now. And I'm convinced that by acknowledging the pain and loss of others, even as we respect the traditions and ways of life that make up this beloved country—by making the moral choice to change, we express God's grace.

We don't earn grace. We're all sinners. We don't deserve it. But God gives it to us anyway. And we choose how to receive it. It's our decision how to honor it.

None of us can or should expect a transformation in race relations overnight. Every time something like this happens, somebody says we have to have a conversation about race. We talk a lot about race. There's no shortcut. And we don't need more talk. None of us should believe that a handful of gun safety measures will prevent every tragedy. It will not. People of goodwill will continue to debate the merits of various policies, as our democracy requires—this is a big, raucous place, America is. And there are good people on both sides of these debates. Whatever solutions we find will necessarily be incomplete.

But it would be a betrayal of everything Reverend Pinckney stood for, I believe, if we allowed ourselves to slip into a comfortable silence again. Once the eulogies have been delivered, once the TV cameras move on, to go back to business as usual—that's what we so often do to avoid uncomfortable truths about the prejudice that still infects our society. To settle for symbolic gestures without following up with the hard work of more lasting change—that's how we lose our way again.

It would be a refutation of the forgiveness expressed by those families if we merely slipped into old habits, whereby those who disagree with us are not merely wrong but bad; where we shout instead of listen; where we barricade ourselves behind preconceived notions or well-practiced cynicism.

Reverend Pinckney once said, "Across the South, we have a deep appreciation of history—we haven't always had a deep appreciation of each other's history." What is true in the South is true for America. Clem understood that justice grows out of recognition of ourselves in each other. That my liberty depends on you being free, too. That history can't be a sword to justify injustice, or a shield against progress, but must be a manual for how to avoid repeating the mistakes of the past—how to break the cycle. A roadway toward a better world. He knew that the path of grace involves an open mind—but, more importantly, an open heart.

That's what I've felt this week—an open heart. That, more than any particular policy or analysis, is what's called upon right now, I think—what a friend of mine, the writer Marilyn Robinson, calls "that reservoir of goodness, beyond, and of another kind, that we are able to do each other in the ordinary cause of things."

That reservoir of goodness. If we can find that grace, anything is possible. If we can tap that grace, everything can change.

Amazing grace. Amazing grace.

(Begins to sing)—Amazing grace, how sweet the sound, that saved a wretch like me; I once was lost, but now I'm found; was blind but now I see.

Clementa Pinckney found that grace.

Cynthia Hurd found that grace.

Susie Jackson found that grace.

Ethel Lance found that grace.

DePayne Middleton-Doctor found that grace.

Tywanza Sanders found that grace.

Daniel L. Simmons, Sr. found that grace.

Sharonda Coleman-Singleton found that grace.

Myra Thompson found that grace.

Through the example of their lives, they've now passed it on to us. May we find ourselves worthy of that precious and extraordinary gift, as long as our lives endure. May grace now lead them home. May God continue to shed His grace on the United States of America.

The Blacker the Berry

(2015)

Everything black, I don't want black (They want us to bow)
I want everything black, I ain't need black (Down to our knees)
Some white, some black, I ain't mean black (And pray to a God)
I want everything black (That we don't believe)
Everything black, want all things black
I don't need black, want everything black
Don't need black, our eyes ain't black
I own black, own everything black

Bridge

Six in the morn', fire in the street
Burn, baby, burn, that's all I wanna see
And sometimes I get off watchin' you die in vain
It's such a shame they may call me crazy
They may say I suffer from schizophrenia or somethin'
But homie, you made me
Black don't crack, my nigga

Verse 1

I'm the biggest hypocrite of 2015
Once I finish this, witnesses will convey just what I mean
Been feeling this way since I was 16, came to my senses
You never liked us anyway, fuck your friendship, I meant it
I'm African-American, I'm African
I'm black as the moon, heritage of a small village
Pardon my residence
Came from the bottom of mankind
My hair is nappy, my dick is big, my nose is round and wide
You hate me don't you?
You hate my people, your plan is to terminate my culture
You're fucking evil I want you to recognize that I'm a proud monkey

You vandalize my perception but can't take style from me
And this is more than confession
I mean I might press the button just so you know my discretion
I'm guardin' my feelings, I know that you feel it
You sabotage my community, makin' a killin'
You made me a killer, emancipation of a real nigga

Pre-Hook

The blacker the berry, the sweeter the juice
The blacker the berry, the sweeter the juice
The blacker the berry, the sweeter the juice
The blacker the berry, the bigger I shoot

[Hook: Assassin]

I said they treat me like a slave, cah' me black
Woi, we feel a whole heap of pain, cah' we black
And man a say they put me inna chains, cah' we black
Imagine now, big gold chains full of rocks
How you no see the whip, left scars pon' me back
But now we have a big whip parked pon' the block
All them say we doomed from the start, cah' we black
Remember this, every race start from the block, jus 'member dat

Verse 2

I'm the biggest hypocrite of 2015
Once I finish this, witnesses will convey just what I mean
I mean, it's evident that I'm irrelevant to society
That's what you're telling me, penitentiary would only hire me
Curse me till I'm dead
Church me with your fake prophesizing that I'mma be just another slave in my head
Institutionalized manipulation and lies
Reciprocation of freedom only live in your eyes
You hate me don't you?
I know you hate me just as much as you hate yourself
Jealous of my wisdom and cards I dealt
Watchin' me as I pull up, fill up my tank, then peel out
Muscle cars like pull ups, show you what these big wheels 'bout, ah
Black and successful, this black man meant to be special
Katzkins on my radar, bitch, how can I help you?

How can I tell you I'm making a killin'?
You made me a killer, emancipation of a real nigga

[Pre-Hook]

[Hook]

Verse 3

I'm the biggest hypocrite of 2015
When I finish this if you listenin' then sure you will agree
This plot is bigger than me, it's generational hatred
It's genocism, it's grimy, little justification
I'm African-American, I'm African
I'm black as the heart of a fucking Aryan
I'm black as the name of Tyrone and Darius
Excuse my French but fuck you—no, fuck y'all
That's as blunt as it gets, I know you hate me, don't you?
You hate my people, I can tell cause it's threats when I see you
I can tell cause your ways deceitful
Know I can tell because you're in love with that Desert Eagle
Thinkin' maliciously, he get a chain then you gone bleed him
It's funny how Zulu and Xhosa might go to war
Two tribal armies that want to build and destroy
Remind me of these Compton Crip gangs that live next door
Beefin' with Pirus, only death settle the score
So don't matter how much I say I like to preach with the Panthers
Or tell Georgia State "Marcus Garvey got all the answers"
Or try to celebrate February like it's my B-Day
Or eat watermelon, chicken, and Kool-Aid on weekdays
Or jump high enough to get Michael Jordan endorsements
Or watch BET cause urban support is important
So why did I weep when Trayvon Martin was in the street
When gang banging make me kill a nigga blacker than me?
Hypocrite!

UNITED STATES DEPARTMENT OF JUSTICE
CIVIL RIGHTS DIVISION

From "Investigation of the Ferguson Police Department"

(March 14, 2015)

IV. Ferguson Law Enforcement Practices Violate the Law and Undermine Community Trust, Especially among African Americans

Ferguson's strategy of revenue generation through policing has fostered practices in the two central parts of Ferguson's law enforcement system—policing and the courts—that are themselves unconstitutional or that contribute to constitutional violations. In both parts of the system, these practices disproportionately harm African Americans. Further, the evidence indicates that this harm to African Americans stems, at least in part, from racial bias, including racial stereotyping. Ultimately, unlawful and harmful practices in policing and in the municipal court system erode police legitimacy and community trust, making policing in Ferguson less fair, less effective at promoting public safety, and less safe.

A. FERGUSON'S POLICE PRACTICES

FPD's approach to law enforcement, shaped by the City's pressure to raise revenue, has resulted in a pattern and practice of constitutional violations. Officers violate the Fourth Amendment in stopping people without reasonable suspicion, arresting them without probable cause, and using unreasonable force. Officers frequently infringe on residents' First Amendment rights, interfering with their right to record police activities and making enforcement decisions based on the content of individuals' expression.

FPD's lack of systems to detect and hold officers responsible for misconduct reflects the department's focus on revenue generation at the expense of lawful policing and helps perpetuate the patterns of unconstitutional conduct we found. FPD fails to adequately supervise officers or review their enforcement actions. While FPD collects vehicle-stop data because it is required to do so by state law, it collects no reliable or consistent data regarding pedestrian stops, even though it has the technology to do so.[1] In Ferguson, officers will sometimes make an arrest without writing a report or even obtaining an incident number, and hundreds of reports can pile up for months without supervisors reviewing them. Officers' uses of force frequently go unreported, and are reviewed only laxly when reviewed at all. As a result of these deficient practices, stops, arrests, and uses of force that violate the law or FPD policy are rarely detected and often ignored when they are discovered. . . .

FPD's approach to law enforcement has led officers to conduct stops and arrests that violate the Constitution. We identified several elements to this pattern of misconduct. Frequently, officers stop people without reasonable suspicion or arrest them without probable cause. Officers rely heavily on the municipal "Failure to Comply" charge, which appears to be facially unconstitutional in part, and is frequently abused in practice. FPD also relies on a system of officer-generated arrest orders called "wanteds" that circumvents the warrant system and poses a significant risk of abuse. The data show, moreover, that FPD misconduct in the area of stops and arrests disproportionately impacts African Americans. . . .

The Fourth Amendment protects individuals from unreasonable searches and seizures. Generally, a search or seizure is unreasonable "in the absence of individualized suspicion of wrongdoing. . . ." The Fourth Amendment permits law enforcement officers to briefly detain individuals for investigative purposes if the officers possess reasonable suspicion that criminal activity is afoot. . . . Reasonable suspicion exists when an "officer is aware of particularized, objective facts which, taken together with rational inferences from those facts, reasonably warrant suspicion that a crime is being committed." . . . In addition, if the officer reasonably believes the person with whom he or she is dealing is armed and dangerous, the officer may conduct a protective search or frisk of the person's outer clothing. . . . Such a search is not justified on the basis of "inchoate and unparticularized suspicion;" rather, the "issue is whether a reasonably prudent man in the circumstances would be warranted in the belief that his safety or that of others was in danger." . . . For an arrest to constitute a reasonable seizure under the Fourth Amendment, it must be supported by probable cause, which

1. FPD policy states that "[o]fficers should document" all field contacts and field interrogation "relevant to criminal activity and identification of criminal suspects on the appropriate Department approved computer entry forms." FPD General Order 407.00. Policy requires that a "Field Investigation Report" be completed for persons and vehicles "in all instances when an officer feels" that the subject "may be in the area for a questionable or suspicious purpose." FPD General Order 422.01. In practice, however, FPD officers do not reliably document field contacts, particularly of pedestrians, and the department does not evaluate such field contacts.

exists only if "the totality of facts based on reasonably trustworthy information would justify a prudent person in believing the individual arrested had committed an offense at the time of the arrest." . . .

Under Missouri law, when making an arrest, "[t]he officer must inform the defendant by what authority he acts, and must also show the warrant if required." . . . In reviewing FPD records, we found numerous incidents in which—based on the officer's own description of the detention—an officer detained an individual without articulable reasonable suspicion of criminal activity or arrested a person without probable cause. In none of these cases did the officer explain or justify his conduct.

For example, in July 2013 police encountered an African-American man in a parking lot while on their way to arrest someone else at an apartment building. Police knew that the encountered man was not the person they had come to arrest. Nonetheless, without even reasonable suspicion, they handcuffed the man, placed him in the back of a patrol car, and ran his record. It turned out he was the intended arrestee's landlord. The landlord went on to help the police enter the person's unit to effect the arrest, but he later filed a complaint alleging racial discrimination and unlawful detention. Ignoring the central fact that they had handcuffed a man and put him in a police car despite having no reason to believe he had done anything wrong, a sergeant vigorously defended FPD's actions, characterizing the detention as "minimal" and pointing out that the car was air conditioned. Even temporary detention, however, constitutes a deprivation of liberty and must be justified under the Fourth Amendment. . . .

Many of the unlawful stops we found appear to have been driven, in part, by an officer's desire to check whether the subject had a municipal arrest warrant pending. Several incidents suggest that officers are more concerned with issuing citations and generating charges than with addressing community needs. In October 2012, police officers pulled over an African-American man who had lived in Ferguson for 16 years, claiming that his passenger-side brake light was broken. The driver happened to have replaced the light recently and knew it to be functioning properly. Nonetheless, according to the man's written complaint, one officer stated, "let's see how many tickets you're going to get," while a second officer tapped his Electronic Control Weapon ("ECW") on the roof of the man's car. The officers wrote the man a citation for "tail light/reflector/license plate light out." They refused to let the man show them that his car's equipment was in order, warning him, "don't you get out of that car until you get to your house." The man, who believed he had been racially profiled, was so upset that he went to the police station that night to show a sergeant that his brakes and license plate light worked.

At times, the constitutional violations are even more blatant. An African-American man recounted to us an experience he had while sitting at a bus stop near Canfield Drive. According to the man, an FPD patrol car abruptly pulled up in front of him. The officer inside, a patrol lieutenant, rolled down his window and addressed the man:

LIEUTENANT: Get over here.
BUS PATRON: Me?
LIEUTENANT: Get the f*** over here. Yeah, you.
BUS PATRON: Why? What did I do?
LIEUTENANT: Give me your ID.
BUS PATRON: Why?
LIEUTENANT: Stop being a smart ass and give me your ID.

The lieutenant ran the man's name for warrants. Finding none, he returned the ID and said, "get the hell out of my face." These allegations are consistent with other, independent allegations of misconduct that we heard about this particular lieutenant, and reflect the routinely disrespectful treatment many African Americans say they have come to expect from Ferguson police. That a lieutenant with supervisory responsibilities allegedly engaged in this conduct is further cause for concern.

This incident is also consistent with a pattern of suspicionless, legally unsupportable stops we found documented in FPD's records, described by FPD as "ped checks" or "pedestrian checks." Though at times officers use the term to refer to reasonable-suspicion-based pedestrian stops, or "*Terry* stops," they often use it when stopping a person with no objective, articulable suspicion. For example, one night in December 2013, officers went out and "ped. checked those wandering around" in Ferguson's apartment complexes. In another case, officers responded to a call about a man selling drugs by stopping a group of six African-American youths who, due to their numbers, did not match the facts of the call. The youths were "detained and ped checked." Officers invoke the term "ped check" as though it has some unique constitutional legitimacy. It does not. Officers may not detain a person, even briefly, without articulable reasonable suspicion. . . . To the extent that the words "ped check" suggest otherwise, the terminology alone is dangerous because it threatens to confuse officers' understanding of the law. Moreover, because FPD does not track or analyze pedestrian *Terry* stops—whether termed "ped checks" or something else—in any reliable way, they are especially susceptible to discriminatory or otherwise unlawful use.

As with its pattern of unconstitutional stops, FPD routinely makes arrests without probable cause. Frequently, officers arrest people for conduct that plainly does not meet the elements of the cited offense. For example, in November 2013, an officer approached five African-American young people listening to music in a car. Claiming to have smelled marijuana, the officer placed them under arrest for disorderly conduct based on their "gathering in a group for the purposes of committing illegal activity." The young people were detained and charged—some taken to jail, others delivered to their parents—despite the officer finding no marijuana, even after conducting an inventory search of the car. Similarly, in February 2012, an officer wrote an arrest notification ticket for Peace Disturbance for "loud music" coming from a car. The arrest ticket appears unlawful as the officer did not assert, and there is no other indication, that a third party was disturbed by the music—an element of the offense. . . . Nonetheless, a supervisor approved it. These warrantless arrests violated the Fourth Amendment because they were not based on probable cause. . . .

While the record demonstrates a pattern of stops that are improper from the beginning, it also exposes encounters that start as constitutionally defensible but quickly cross the line. For example, in the summer of 2012, an officer detained a 32-year-old African American man who was sitting in his car cooling off after playing basketball. The officer arguably had grounds to stop and question the man, since his windows appeared more deeply tinted than permitted under Ferguson's code. Without cause, the officer went on to accuse the man of being a pedophile, prohibit the man from using his cell phone, order the man out of his car for a pat-down despite having no reason to believe he was armed, and ask to search his car. When the man refused, citing his constitutional rights, the officer reportedly pointed a gun at his head, and arrested him. The officer charged the man with eight different counts, including making a false declaration for initially providing the short form of his first name (e.g., "Mike" instead of "Michael") and an address that, although legitimate, differed from the one on his license. The officer also charged the man both with having an expired operator's license, and with having no operator's license in possession. The man told us he lost his job as a contractor with the federal government as a result of the charges.

Speech on Walter Scott Shooting

(April 14, 2015)

. . . [A]s I stand here today I am reminded of one of our former colleagues. Though he is small in stature, he stood tall in moments in which the soul of the State, and in particular the soul of the Senate, were called into question. He always challenged us to rise to a higher level. I am referring to the great Senator Patterson, who from time to time would rise and remind us of the greatness of this august body. Today the nation looks at South Carolina to see if we will rise to be the body and the State that we say that we really are. Over the past week many of us have seen on the television and read in newspapers reports about Walter Scott, who in my words was murdered in North Charleston. It has really created a heartache and a yearning for justice. Not just in the African American community, but for all people. Not just in the Charleston area or in South Carolina, but across our country. . . .

As we are in the Christian season of Easter we are reminded of the story of Jesus gathering his disciplines in Galilee in the upper room. In that week following Easter, every disciple was there except Thomas. . . . Jesus walks through a locked door and the disciples see something that amazed them. They saw the living Jesus. They were able to see the nails in his hands and they were able to put their hand in his sides. Jesus allowed them to see this as proof, so that they would have no doubt. But one person was missing, and that was Thomas. When Thomas heard the news, he said he did not believe it. He said there was no way, it had to be impossible. He said that Jesus was dead and there was no way that he came and visited. But the next week Thomas was there. Jesus walked in, he said, "I will not believe until I see the nails. I will not believe until I can put my hand in your side." And it was only when he was able to do that; he said, "I believe, my Lord and my God."

Ladies and gentlemen of the Senate, when we first heard on the television that a police officer had gunned down an unarmed African American in North Charleston by the name of Walter Scott, there were some who said "Wow! The national story has come home to South Carolina." But there are many who said that there was no way that a police officer would ever shoot somebody in the back six, seven, or eight times. Like Thomas, when we were able to see the video and we were able to see the gun shots, and we then saw him fall to the ground

. . . And when we saw the police officer come over and hand cuff him on the ground; without even trying to resuscitate him—without even seeing if he was really alive, without calling an ambulance, without calling for help . . . We saw him die face down on the ground as if he were gunned down like game. I believe we all were like Thomas and said, "I believe." What if Mr. Santiago was not there to record what happened? I'm sure that many of us would still say like Thomas, we do not believe. I believe that as a legislature—that as a State—we have a great opportunity to allow sunshine into this process, to at least give us new eyes for seeing so that we [are] able to make sure that our proud and great law enforcement officers and every citizen that we represent [are] able to at least know that they would be seen and heard and that their rights will be protected. . . . It is my hope as South Carolina Senators that we will stand up for what is best and good about our State and really adopt this legislation in an effort to find a way to have body cameras utilized in South Carolina. Our hearts go out to the Scott family. Our hearts go out to the [Slager] family because the Lord teaches us to love all. We pray that over time that justice will be done. Thank you.

ESTHER ARMAH

Black Bodies, White Terrorism: A Global Reimagining of Forgiveness

(July 4, 2015)

My mama is seventy-nine. Wednesday night is her bible study. Just like Ms. Ethel Lee Lance, mama has her circle of churchgoing elders—black women in their sixties, seventies, and eighties for whom church is home. Maybe even safer than home. Their pain was safe in the hands of this particular Jesus. Unshed tears from the Middle Passage were here. Friendships decades deep were here. Sanctuary was here. Comfort, too. Prayers unheard by a black community too often deaf to the pain of black girls and women were heard here, by this Jesus. Or so they thought.

Mama goes to Roman Ridge Church in Accra, Ghana, is proudly Ashanti and deeply Christian. Ms. Ethel went to AME in Charleston, South Carolina. She was one of six black women, two of them elders, killed by a white terrorist doing the work of white supremacy: attack, destroy, bury black bodies, dreams, and lives.

"I forgive you"; "We forgive you"; "My family forgives you"; we heard these pardons again and again as family members of the massacred lined up and spoke during the first court hearing of Dylann Roof. That outpouring prompted swift reaction. Their words of forgiveness were both praised and criticized. The last time I heard that kind of outpouring on forgiveness was during my trip to South Africa in 1997. It was at the height of the Truth and Reconciliation Commission Hearings led by Archbishop Desmond Tutu. A global white media watched in awe, relief, and approval as Nelson Mandela said, speaking to the black South African majority of the white minority, "Let us forgive them."

Mandela turned into a global hero. His heroism was rooted in that moment, rooted in those words. He became a leader by which the rest of Africa should follow. Forgive white atrocities. Forgive white supremacy. Tutu held press conferences, face wet with tears telling the assorted camera, mics, and print journalists that black South Africans just wanted to know who to forgive. They just needed the killers of their children, the torturers of their bodies, the executioners of their dignity, to tell the truth. Some told it. Others didn't. Still, Tutu asked that black South Africans continue to forgive.

I traveled to Alexandria, South Africa's second biggest township, and sat with black South African women. These women spoke of rage, pain, and powerlessness. They spoke of this soil, grave to their children, and still home to unspoken and unspeakable horrors. One woman, a Xhosa woman, who was mother to a girl not yet twelve, talked about her daughter going to protests with her father. She was mad, scared, and proud of her daughter. "I raised her that way," she told me. "Why would I forgive them? I am here, my child is not. She is dead, buried by their hate. Forgive them? Who are they? I cannot forgive my husband. He let her leave that morning. She was in school uniform. And still they brought the dogs, the sticks, the guns. I wasn't there. I wasn't there."

Women and men, one after another, shared moments of Apartheid atrocity. This was, they said, a calculated cruelty, a designed destruction legislated by a white government and supported by global corporations and governments. One woman spoke of the morning raids. Those family moments were interrupted, desecrated by the boots, truncheons, and shouting voices of police breaking down doors and dragging women in headscarves and nightdresses from bed. All this to be interrogated and assaulted. Why? Reasonable suspicion. *Forgive them?* "I want them to suffer as we have," she told me. "But no, they tell us to forgive them."

I thought about them as I was ushered into Desmond Tutu's office in Cape Town days later during that same trip. This man led the TRC. His demeanor, language, speeches, and tone spoke only of forgiveness. The global media was still here, seeking and telling stories of white atrocities, white terrorism, and black South Africans offering forgiveness for the most heinous of acts. I sat opposite the architect of this white economy of black forgiveness. I shared my interview time with a white Swiss journalist. Archbishop Tutu told us that "South Africa would be a Mecca for whites, as Kenya was." I asked why he was so worried about how white people felt, since they were not the targets, but the beneficiaries of Apartheid. I asked how many of their children had been buried, and why South Africa was so focused on *their* feelings and fears.

I asked why he could support and direct the black majority of this nation to forgive legislated hate, the killing of black children, and the torture of the innocent, but was unwilling to forgive Winnie Mandela, a black woman, an activist, a mama who like the women in Alexandria was subject to morning raids where police constantly terrorized the community. They would not and did not forgive Winnie. They castigated, humiliated, exposed, denied, and rejected her. My interview was over.

Tutu invoked Kenya as a Mecca for whites, an example South Africa wanted to follow. I traveled to Kenya in 2003. It is the birthplace of President Obama's father and his father's people, the Luo tribe. The president's grandfather had been accused of supporting the Mau Mau, and been tortured by the British.

The Mau Mau were a group of Kikuyu-tribe-dominated Kenyans, described by British colonialists as "rebellious." They were freedom fighters; demanding, organizing, and fighting for Kenya's independence. The height of the conflict was known as the Mau Mau Uprising and the Kenyan Emergency, from 1952 to 1960, which was the same time the civil rights movement was gaining momentum in the United States. President Obama's paternal grandfather—Hussein Onyango Obama—was a cook for a British army officer. He was arrested and tortured, his testicles crushed by the British in a high security prison. Kenyan freedom fighters spoke of being castrated, raped, and whipped while imprisoned by the British colonial authority. The treatment of the Mau Mau by the British was similar to the violence enslaved Africans endured in the antebellum South. The obsession with black bodies mirrored that of plantation overseers. Onyango Obama denied he had done anything wrong when he was arrested. The British media sought the perspective of a British historian about Onyango Obama's detention. Reasonable suspicion, the Brit historian confirmed.

Reasonable suspicion. First South Africa, then Kenya. It is a term known by black boys who are stopped and frisked by police on New York City streets. The British media downplayed the violence suffered by Kenyans in those prisons. In 2013, the British government paid fourteen million pounds as a settlement to Mau Mau veterans after eight thousand documents from thirty-seven former British colonies were released, revealing details of torture, castration, and rape. In one memo sent out during the height of these atrocities, Kenya's then attorney general Eric Griffith-Jones wrote: "If we are going to sin, we must sin quietly."

Tutu told me this country, with this history, was a Mecca for whites.

Tribe is to Africa, what race is to America. It is complicated. We are complicated. Tutu's celebration at the hands of the white media didn't stop him from telling me during that same interview how "whites are beginning to take this offer of forgiveness for granted." Under that forgiving smile, he was angry. I was shocked. I think about Tutu wanting to get chosen by white South Africa, but his unwillingness to forgive Winnie Mandela—a black South African woman— for an alleged crime for which she was eventually acquitted. Worse, the willingness to use Winnie's black woman body, to lay it out at the feet of white South Africa and stand on it, in order to achieve that choosing.

Debate continues about Charleston, that moment in court, forgiveness, black folk, white terrorism, and white supremacy. White America, so much of Black America, applauded this forgiveness outpouring, was soothed and calmed by it. As white South Africa was soothed and calmed by Mandela and Tutu's call for forgiveness, and the outpouring that followed.

Charleston, Ghana, South Africa, Kenya: we have a global black inheritance of white supremacist terrorism. It has left a legacy of untreated trauma. That inheritance has trained us to pour our pain into our own bodies. And then turn away when that pain manifests. Particularly when it comes to black girls and women. Our bodies are vehicles for rage, rejection, resentment, and denial to acknowledge the depth of our hurt. Instead, we are judgmental of each other in our pain. We are unkind, we replace empathy with analysis and invite an audience to engage the strength of our intellect. Our pain goes unheard and so instead it finds sanctuary in the intimate violence we subject ourselves and our bodies to. What, now, can we do with our pain? What forgiveness process might we create for ourselves, for all the ways we hurt and harm each other? Will we ever be able to trust each other with our pain?

Black folk are globally committed to notions of justice, due to our intimate relationships with injustice. Our emotionality must be part of that justice project. Emotional justice is crucial to our collective and individual healing. How is our emotionality not profoundly fucked up when every part of our history, the pain inflicted on us still requires that you centralize whiteness? How do we heal when there is no respite from the violence? Who do we become when white supremacy's manufactured fear matters more than our bruised, battered, and bloodied black bodies?

Apartheid was white terrorism. What the British did during the Kenyan Mau Mau was white terrorism. Dylann Roof was a white terrorist, supported by state-sanctioned institutions of white terrorism. We do not negotiate with terrorists. That's what America teaches. Except white terrorism. Then we don't negotiate; we privilege; we prioritize; we centralize. Then we spit up that privilege via white Jesus, heart disease, fibroids, violence, obesity, and a soft, slow, sure killing. White supremacy does not worship our God. It prays at the altar of coffins filled with black bodies. It tithes in the blood of black folks. Its hymn is the sound of our tears and screams. Its amen is the stillness of our stolen breath.

BARBARA RANSBY

Ella Taught Me

Shattering the Myth of the Leaderless Movement

(June 12, 2015)

Who gets to tell the story? This is a question implicit in the work I do as a historian. But the question I have been wrestling with lately is more immediate: *Who gets to shape the narrative, define the history-makers, and capture the words and images of the current black-led, antistate violence movement evolving in the United States right now?*

Even the act of naming a movement like this has its power. Last month the *New York Times Magazine* bestowed part of the defining privilege on a young former sportswriter, Jay Caspian Kang. Kang reduced the growing movement to the personal story lines of two young, earnest, and committed social media activists, DeRay Mckesson and Johnetta "Netta" Elzie. While their work has made a critical contribution, Kang frames that work in a way that misrepresents the larger movement. With a narrow range of sources, Kang's piece concluded that "Twitter is the revolution," that "our demand is simple: stop killing us," and that the emergent movement is "leaderless."

The *New York Times Magazine* profile was problematic on each of these points. Borrowing from my research on Baker and my own participation in social movements, I want to refute the notion that this movement is leaderless. As some contemporary youth activists such as #BlackLivesMatter cofounder and Dignity and Power Now founder Patrisse Cullors have asserted, their movement is not leaderless, it is leader-*full*.

The Revolution Will Not Be Tweeted

Many of our sisters and brothers are masterful users, but social media does not have magical powers. Twitter, Facebook, and Instagram are tools like any other invention. The printing press revolutionized movement building and revolution making. So did the radio, telephone, television, personal computer, cell phone, and a whole variety of media.

Social media tools can lend themselves to many different—and contradictory—purposes. They can bring attention to injustice, communicate the logistics of demonstrations—and they can sell you just about any worthless new commodity on the planet. And while Twitter is a uniquely open platform to exchange ideas, argue, celebrate, commiserate, and mobilize, a Twitter following does not take the place of an organization.

Twitter is personality driven, anonymous when convenient, and an opportunity for spectatorship as much as engagement. We don't know how many of our followers are actually supporters, just as we don't know if all our Facebook friends actually like us. And even retweeting frequently comes with the caveat, "retweet does not constitute agreement." Moreover, these recent technologies are also the site for ever more sinister and sophisticated forms of government surveillance.

This is why leadership and organizing cannot be simply tweeted into existence. Movement building is forged in struggle, through people building relationships within organizations and collectives. Social media is only one part of a much larger effort.

While the mainstream media is all abuzz about social media as if it were a stand-alone entity, it tends to ignore or render invisible the critical work of leader-organizers who are more focused on street action than virtual action. This bias toward social media work woefully distorts not only how we understand this evolving movement but also how we see social movements in general.

Ella Taught Me

Those who romanticize the concept of leaderless movements often misleadingly deploy Ella Baker's words "Strong people don't need [a] strong leader." Baker delivered this message in various iterations over her fifty-year career working in the trenches of racial-justice struggles, but what she meant was specific and contextual. She was calling for people to disinvest from the notion of the messianic, charismatic leader who promises political salvation in exchange for deference. Baker also did not mean that movements would naturally emerge without collective analysis, serious strategizing, organizing, mobilizing, and consensus building.

Baker, a lead organizer in multiple groups dating back to 1930, a colleague and critic of Dr. Martin Luther King Jr., and the impetus for the 1960 formation of the Student Non-Violent Coordinating Committee (SNCC), knew this better than anyone. Although she objected to the top-down, predominately male leadership structures that were typical of groups like the Southern Christian Leadership Council (SCLC) and the NAACP in the 1950s and '60s, she realized the necessity for grounded, community-based leader-organizers such as sharecropper Fannie Lou Hamer and Cleveland, Mississippi-based local organizer

Amzie Moore. Baker was not against leadership. She was opposed to hierarchical leadership that disempowered the masses and further privileged the already privileged.

When Oprah Winfrey complained that recent protests against police violence lack leadership, she was describing the King style of leading, or at least the way in which the King legacy has been most widely branded: the reverend as the strong, all-knowing, slightly imperfect but still not-like-us type of leader.

Baker represented a different leadership tradition altogether. She combined the generic concept of leadership—"A process of social influence in which a person can enlist the aid and support of others in the accomplishment of a common task"—and a confidence in the wisdom of ordinary people to define their problems and imagine solution. Baker helped everyday people channel and congeal their collective power to resist oppression and fight for sustainable, transformative change. Her method is not often recognized, celebrated, or even seen except by many who are steeped in the muck of movement-building work. Yet Baker and her hardworking political progenies were essential.

I underscore this because while some forms of resistance might be reflexive and simple—that is, when pushed too hard, most of us push back, even if we don't have a plan or a hope of winning—organizing a movement is different. It is not organic, instinctive, or ever easy. If we think we can all "get free" through individual or uncoordinated small-group resistance, we are kidding ourselves.

This is not a news flash to serious organizers, past or present. The veterans from the 1960s and '70s (SNCC and the Black Panther Party as two of the best-known examples), held meetings, workshops, debates, strategy sessions, and reading groups to forge the consensus that enabled thousands of people to work under the same rubric and, more or less, operate out of the same playbook, splits and differences notwithstanding.

That collective effort required leaders who were accountable to one another and were not singular. There were many organizers in groups such as SNCC who modeled Baker's brand of what sociologist Charles Payne has called "group-centered leadership."

Rather than someone with a fancy title standing at a podium speaking for or to the people, group-centered leaders are at the center of many concentric circles. They strengthen the group, forge consensus, and negotiate a way forward. That kind of leadership is impactful, democratic, and, I would argue, more radical and sustainable, than the alternatives.

Who's Up Next

We see many examples of group-centered leadership among today's young organizers. They combine their own vision and experience with respect for the collective will. For example, in contrast to the amorphousness, transience and sometimes-awkward anonymity of social media, if you join Black Youth Project 100 (BYP100) you know what you are signing up for. You know that the fast-growing group of eighteen-to-thirty-five-year-olds has been leading anti-police violence protests from the Bay Area to New York.

You know it embraces a black feminist approach that seeks to build transformative leadership, employs nonviolent direct action, and operates through a black queer lens.

Thus, through organizational process, BYP100 has staked its claim on a set of ideas, politics, and tactics. It has a leadership philosophy, structure, and specific requirements for membership. At the same time it is open, democratic, accessible, and collaborative with other organizations. Groups like BYP100 are playing a critical role in movement building, yet they are often invisible to the mainstream and even alternative media.

Another example of the work of leader-organizers being erased from current movement-building narratives is the crude appropriation of the #BlackLivesMatter (BLM) banner. Three black women immersed in labor, immigrants' rights, and social justice organizing conceived of the term in 2012 in the wake of the Trayvon Martin murder case. The term became ubiquitous in 2014 after a series of high profile, racist police, and extrajudicial killings.

Unrelated groups and social media users then changed the phrase to "All Lives Matter," diminishing the originators' intent. In the whole process the slogan was lifted and reappropriated as if it had dropped from the sky. The initiators had no identity, no context, no grounding. Fortunately, one of those initiators, Alicia Garza, an organizer with Domestic Workers Alliance, wrote a powerful piece pushing back against the revisionist narrative that would delete her role and that of her two cocreators, Cullors and Opal Tometi. They did not make this statement to claim authorship in an individualistic way but rather to locate the roots of BLM in a place, community, and lived experience.

About two months ago I had the privilege of cohosting a Chicago gathering of about fifty young, antipolice violence organizers from around the country, including the three BLM creators. Those gathered were a serious, eclectic, savvy collection of eighteen-to-thirty-five-year-olds (and a few of us older supporters) from twelve states. They embodied the kind of grassroots, unapologetically radical leadership that would have made Ella Baker very proud.

Turning Theory into Practice

In my thirty years of working in many different groups, campaigns, and movements, I have been a part of efforts, not always successful, to strike the balance between mass mobilizing and organization building; between inclusivity and accountability; and between strategic actions and spontaneous ones. Groups I've worked with have formed rotating steering and coordinating committees instead of electing officers. They've met regularly and devised ways for there to be lots of talking, learning, processing, and thinking out loud together. Communication was always key and accountability has been crucial.

I have found that without organizations, coalitions, and leadership teams, there is no collective strategy or accountability. An independent or freelance activist may share their opinion, and it may be an informed one, but if these words are not spoken in consultation or conversation with people on the ground, they are limited as a representation of a movement's thinking and work.

When a leader-organizer puts him, her, or themselves on record as being a part of a larger whole, that group can say, "You can or cannot speak for us. We agreed to X and you did Y. We were were counting on you and you opted out just when we needed you." That is accountability.

In turn, the collective can support those who act as representatives or spokespersons at any given moment. This rough formula gets complicated the larger and more diverse a movement gets. Still, the fundamental idea works.

We Need Structure

In 1970, in reference to the predominantly white Second Wave feminist movement that was just getting off the ground, feminist activist Jo Freeman wrote "The Tyranny of Structurelessness." In this essay she argues that the notion of a movement without either structure or leaders obscures and privileges in corrosive ways. In a leaderless movement anyone can name, negotiate, convene, and demand while simultaneously eschewing the label and responsibilities of leadership. At the end of the day these people are beholden to no one.

In order for activists to craft specific goals and demands wedded to a solid justice agenda built on the needs and aspirations of the most oppressed sectors of our communities, leadership, accountability, and organization are necessary ingredients.

That said, let me also caution against the tyranny of leadership to offset Jo Freeman's "tyranny of structurelessness." One should not have to formally join an organization, pay dues, or be subject to group mandates to play a respected role in social struggles.

In fact, it is the job of radically democratic organizations and leaders to make sure that entry points and creative spaces remain open. Groups can become closed, defensive, and even conservative if they don't remain inclusive and pliable. The democratic centralist models of the Old and New U.S. Left offer cautionary examples of organizations that were far more centralist than they were democratic.

In addition to the "leaderless" misnomer, there have been a number of skewed characterizations of the current movement in news and social media. There is not rigid ideological agreement among the half dozen or so black-led groups that have powered antistate violence work since officer Darren Wilson killed Michael Brown in Ferguson in August 2014. There is, however, coherence to the debates and a consistent political framework within which these organizers are operating.

For example, while no one would argue that cops should continue to be allowed to kill unarmed civilians with impunity, some of the most savvy young leaders realize that jailing individual cops does not solve all our problems. Moreover, the "one rogue cop" mantra, repeatedly asserted by mainstream media, betrays the deeper analysis that many movement leaders share, which is that the problem is wider and systemic.

Beyond Police Violence

Not only do the black-led antiracist/antistate violence activists define systemic problems in U.S. law enforcement, they see problems in the laws themselves, especially those that have created our current economic crisis of joblessness, underemployment, and the obscene concentration wealth at the top. The choice of some of these organizers to link antipolice violence to the "Fight for 15" labor movement for a fifteen-dollar minimum wage is brilliant because it foregrounds the economic grievances at the core of black anger, from Ferguson to New York to Baltimore. As the title of one news article proclaimed and a study by the Brookings Institute documents, the Ferguson uprising was "a story of black poverty and white supremacy."

Let's remember also that Eric Garner was harassed and then killed by Staten Island police because of his participation in the informal economy. His crime was selling single cigarettes, a retail enterprise crafted to secure a very modest margin of profit for the struggling father of four. Underlying the overwhelming majority of police killings of black people is a story of poverty, underemployment, illegal economic activity, class vulnerability, and struggling communities. When protest leaders have chanted "black lives matter," the real power in their collective voice is that they are insisting that the lives of the Mike Browns and Eric Garners of the world matter, as distinct from the better-protected and less-vulnerable black political and commercial elites.

If we listen closely, the message of some of the sharpest leaders of this generation reflects not only a class and racial analysis but an intersectional gender analysis as well. On May 21 several groups called for a National Day of Action to End State Violence Against Black Women and Girls to counter the erroneous notion that only black males are victims of police and state violence.

And in the wake of the Trayvon Martin killing, black feminist organizers actively supported the protests around Martin while simultaneously spearheading a defense campaign to draw attention to the case of Marissa Alexander. Project NIA in Chicago and the Crunk Feminist Collective were two important sites for this effort.

More recently activists have publicized and rallied around the case of Rekia Boyd, a young unarmed Chicago woman killed by an off-duty police officer. The black feminist analysis that undergirds these campaigns and is articulated by organizers such as Charlene Carruthers, Angie Rollins, Brittney Cooper, Jasson Perez, and others standing in defiant opposition to the biased logic of male-centered programs and to the reactionary and the ill-informed pronouncements of Fox News's Juan Williams, who sought to link the Baltimore protests to the supposed breakdown of the patriarchal black family.

If one is paying attention, one knows the myriad of problems that oppressed people, specifically poor black folk, are experiencing every day. Solutions, however, are harder to come by.

When we chant "We want our freedom!" that demand can mean many different things, especially as demonstrations become bigger and more diverse. That is why the title of Jay Kang's *New York Times Magazine* article—"Our Demand is Simple: Stop Killing Us"—is so problematic. The demands organizations including BYP100, Dream Defenders, Justice League, Black Lives Matter, Malcolm X Grassroots Movement, We Charge Genocide, Critical Resistance, BlackOUT Collective, Ferguson Action, Organization for Black Struggle, and Hands Up United are making are not simple at all.

Organizers who are grounded in collective work know that we could indeed witness a reduction in police killings but still feel repression, poverty, and violence in so many other ways. People are demanding jobs with a living wage, more funding for schools, access to college, social programs, food justice, and a reversal of the multilayered process of mass incarceration. Moreover, the newer organizations are in advance of previous movements by including the language of antisexism *and* anti-hetero-patriarchy in their political statements and, in some cases, their mission statements.

Some young activists are visionary abolitionists who want to push for a society without prisons. So while reducing and eliminating police killings of black civilians is certainly a goal, freedom has a much higher bar. As Dream Defenders' organizer Phillip Agnew puts it, "This is part of a progression of resistance to economic systems and social systems that stamp out people who are black, brown, oppressed [and] poor."

Decoded

While problems confronting black youth in the era of neoliberalism and postindustrial cities are complicated, they are not undecipherable.

The postindustrial era and the age of global neoliberal policies means cities and neighborhoods have been abandoned. Some of the areas where police have recently killed black civilians are reeling from more than 30 percent unemployment. They're challenged by a booming underground economy that puts participants and bystanders at greater risk of being jailed or killed.

In Chicago's North Lawndale, in West Baltimore, or almost any neighborhood in my hometown of Detroit, there simply are no jobs and no real grocery stores. There is dilapidated and abandoned housing and dramatically dwindling services. The one problem, from a crude capitalist standpoint, is that there are still people in these posteconomic areas but their labor is no longer needed in the steel mills, factories, or private homes. These superfluous, redundant bodies are the dilemma of twenty-first-century racial capitalism.

As Barbara Ehrenreich writes in her recent review of Martin Ford's new book, *Rise of the Robots*, "[T]here should be no doubt that technology is advancing in the direction of full unemployment."

Ford makes this point by quoting a cofounder of a startup dedicated to automating gourmet hamburger production: "Our device isn't meant to make employees more efficient. It's meant to completely obviate them."

So, jobs are being pushed out of neighborhoods, out of the United States, and out of existence. Those at the bottom of the economic pyramid, which has been a racialized hierarchy in the United States since slavery, are bearing the brunt of this economic trajectory. So I ask, *How do we turn it around?*

There are answers. It will be a fight. We need multiple tools and tactics. And we need leaders of the Ella Baker variety to make it happen. I am confident that they are on the rise.

BRITTNEY COOPER

On the Pole for Freedom

Bree Newsome's Politics, Theory,
and Theology of Resistance

(*June 29, 2015*)

Bree Newsome is my shero. And my new favorite theorist and theologian of resistance. On Saturday, she scaled a flagpole in Columbia, South Carolina, to take down the Confederate Flag, which has felt acutely offensive in the less than fourteen days since a vile, misguided, millennial neoconfederate walked into Black sacred space and murdered nine of our people.

I woke to the news of the massacre of nine faithful souls at Mother Emanuel AME Church on a trip abroad for work and play. Startled and devastated, I lay in bed wondering whether to wake my homegirl sleeping next to me, because like me, I knew she was tired of waking up each morning to structural devastation and systemic heartbreak. That's what these times have felt like—like no time to catch one's breath between blows. Undone and outdone, I jostled her awake anyway, as the tears started to leak from the edges of my eyes.

I'm a church girl. My ardent feminism hasn't yet been able to overcome that. Believe me I've tried. But I know that I am here today because of many a Wednesday night spent communing with God and the saints at Wednesday night Bible Study and Prayer Meeting. This isn't so much my spiritual practice anymore, but it remains the practice of so many Christian folk I love. Dylann Storm Roof could have murdered any one of them. Any one of us.

In the aftermath of these killings, we've turned once again to debating the merits of the confederate flag. I despise the stars and bars. I resent having grown up in a place where my classmates and their parents flew that flag freely, pasted it on car bumpers, with the disingenuous tag line, "it's heritage not hate," and reveled in their nostalgia for rebellion. They expected Black folks to be silent and unoffended, expected us to ignore that the celebration of that flag essentially communicated the sentiment, "We wish y'all were still slaves."

Bree Newsome offered the holiest of "fuck thats" to such foolery and went up the pole and took that shit down.

My heart still swells for her courage. But I also think we would do well to see all the ways in which her act of resistance opens up space and possibility for us in the realms of faith and feminism.

As she took down the flag, she spoke to it: "You come against me with hatred and oppression and violence. I come against you in the name of God. This flag comes down today." On the way down, and as she was arrested, she recited the first verse of the twenty-seventh Psalm: "The Lord is my light and my salvation. Whom shall I fear? The Lord is the strength of my life: of whom shall I be afraid?"

The clear Christian framing of her act of civil disobedience matters for a number of reasons. As the families of the nine slain offered their forgiveness to Roof for his heinous acts, I was incensed at what felt like a premature move to forgiveness. While I feel compelled to honor the right of these families to grieve and process this loss in the way that makes most sense for them—after all this is first and foremost *their* loss—I also wonder about whether churches have done a disservice in making Black people feel in particular that forgiveness must show up on pretty much the same day as our grief and trauma and demand a hearing.

If God is indeed "Emmanuel"—translated "God with us"—then how could this God demand that we forgive, and forgive, and forgive again, while we are being led like so many lambs to the slaughter? How about we leave the forgiving to Jesus and the grieving to human beings, assuming that Black people are in fact human, and not superhuman? But here's the thing—this isn't a referendum on forgiveness. I'm clear that forgiveness does a particular kind of spiritual work, a work of healing, a work of freedom, that we need. My problem is that however important forgiveness may be as a personal act, forgiveness does not make for sound and effective politics. Maybe I've finally found an area in feminism that I want to remain personal and not political.

I don't forgive Dylann Roof. I don't forgive white supremacy. I don't forgive white supremacists. I don't forgive patriarchy. I don't forgive capitalism. I don't forgive these systems or their propagators (complicit though I also am) because we have not reckoned with the magnitude of their devastations, deaths, and traumas. I don't forgive those who still have a knife at my throat. I'm not Jesus. Black women are not Jesus.

So Bree Newsome was a reminder to me that forgiveness is not the only thing faith can look like in public. Faith in public can look like a demand—for justice, for recognition, for grace. Faith in public can look like calling white supremacist evil exactly what it is and "coming against it." Faith can look like a Black girl climbing a pole. Faith can look like that Black girl looking into the face of power and telling those come to arrest her that she ain't "neva scared" in the name of God.

And because I'm me, and this is we, let me loop back to that penultimate line. "Faith can look like a Black girl climbing a pole."

We wouldn't be connoisseurs of Crunk in these parts if we did not point you to the hilarity of those law enforcement officers yelling at Bree, "Ma'am. Ma'am. Come down off that pole." . . .

Bree's nonviolent direct action against the state of South Carolina places her in the best traditions of the civil rights movement. There's no denying that.

But Black people have been staring at that rebel flag forever. What is new and important is that Black women, largely because of a heady mashup of hip-hop and Black feminism, now have a different relationship to the pole. I'm only being slightly flippant.

I mean, let's not trip: Discourse about Black girls on poles is ubiquitous these days. Stripper culture made that flagpole a circumstance rather than an obstacle. T-Pain fell in love a few years back. Today Usher "don't mind." And despite how far we've come in pro-sex feminism, most bougie Black girls I know have as a goal the keeping of their daughters, if not themselves, off the pole.

So I'mma say that the pole here—flagpole though it were—still marks a liminal space of possibility for what Black resistance beyond respectability looks like. Bree Newsome's Black girl body climbed a pole, quoting scripture, to take down a flag that is emblematic of so much violence enacted on the Black body by the U.S. nation-state. Her act exploded every simple discourse we are currently having about what faith demands, about what decorum dictates that we should accept, about what are acceptable forms of resistance for (cis) Black women's bodies.

Bree Newsome has challenged and enriched my faith and my feminism. She has reminded me that how Black girls move through space always changes the terms of engagement. She has reminded me on this week when we celebrate marriage equality and the bible thumpers abound, that the only good use of scripture in public is to help us get free.

(If scripture got you spiritually and rhetorically beating the shit out of gay people, women, and Black folks, rather than Bible thumping the shit out of capitalism, white supremacy, and heteropatriarchy, you're using it wrong. God ain't on your side and you might have the devil on your team.)

I still don't know where God was in that Charleston Church on June 17. But I do believe God used a Black girl to serve notice on principalities and powers that be that a change is coming. The flag is back on the pole. But it flies somehow with significantly less swag. And indelibly imprinted on my memory is Bree Newsome's body, fully in possession of the rebel flag, now untethered from its hinges. A Black girl with the trophy of white supremacy in her clutches is the only sermon on freedom I'll ever need.

JEANNINE BELL

From *Hate Thy Neighbor:*
Move-In Violence and the Persistence
of Racial Segregation in Housing

(2013)

The 1990s: Move-In Violence Becomes "Hate Crime"

The 1986 Southern Poverty Law Center report on move-in violence noted the absence of nationwide systematic record keeping in the area of what they termed "hate violence activity." The 1990s began with the advent of a new way of thinking about racial violence in the creation of the category "hate" or "bias" crime. These crimes are crimes motivated by bias on the basis of race, religion, ethnicity, sexual orientation, and a number of other categories prohibited by law. In 1990, Congress passed the Hate Crime Statistics Act (HCSA), which requires the Justice Department to conduct annual nationwide surveys of law enforcement agencies to obtain data on "crimes that manifest evidence of prejudice based on race, religion, disability, sexual orientation, or ethnicity, including where appropriate the crimes of murder, non-negligent manslaughter, forcible rape, aggravated assault, simple assault, intimidation, arson and destruction, damage or vandalism of property."

While the HCSA did not itself provide any type of additional legal remedy for bias-motivated crimes, the legislation was designed to help by encouraging local law enforcement to pay more attention to these types of crimes. The FBI created a series of publications, including *Hate Crime Data Collection Guidelines* and *Training Guide for Hate Crime Data Collection*, which could be used by law enforcement officers for training and for the development of procedures to aid in identifying hate crimes. The HCSA also required the U.S. attorney general to publish a yearly summary of the data collected from different law enforcement agencies around the country. This report, *Hate Crime Statistics*, has appeared each year since 1993 and provides data regarding incidents, offenses, victims, and offenders in crimes motivated in whole or in part by bias against the victims' perceived race/ethnicity, religion, sexual orientation, or disability.

When combined with census figures, *Hate Crime Statistics* can allow some evaluation of the level of anti-integrationist violence. Analyses of hate crime numbers and census data from 2000 reveal links between increases in hate crimes and the migration of minorities to white neighborhoods. One study compared census data to the FBI's nationwide hate crime statistics for 1998, 1999, and 2000. The segregation levels in U.S. cities with more than 95,000 residents were measured using a dissimilarity index score, which in this case described how many blacks would have to change residence in order for the city to be perfectly integrated. This analysis found that cities with higher rates of antiblack hate crime also had higher levels of black-white dissimilarity. In other words, more antiblack hate crimes occurred in cities that were more segregated.

Despite its comprehensiveness—there is no other nationwide measure of hate crime—*Hate Crime Statistics* is not the most *reliable* source of data. This is true for a variety of reasons, the most important of which is the source of the data. The data that make up the annual *Hate Crime Statistics* are submitted by different law enforcement agencies around the count[r]y. The police agencies submitting these reports vary widely in their training, data collection methods, reporting practices, and investigative procedures regarding hate crime. Thus, in some jurisdictions there may be no reports or inaccurate reports at best. For instance, in 2008, even though 13,690 agencies participated in data collection, 11,545 agencies (some 84 percent of all agencies reporting) reported that *not one* bias-motivated incident occurred in their jurisdiction in 2008. Agencies reporting no bias-motivated incidents were unlikely to have dedicated personnel charged with identifying and investigating bias-motivated crime.

A far more accurate yet less comprehensive way of measuring the relationship between housing segregation and the number of hate crimes occurring in a city is to use individual hate crime reports and compare them to segregation levels in a particular city. Examination of data on hate crimes in New York City in the 1990s and Boston in the mid-1980s . . . suggests that race based hate crimes were strongly linked to the migration of minorities to white neighborhoods. For instance, Jack Levin and Jack McDevitt analyzed all the hate crimes identified by the Boston police over a three-year period in the 1980s, and "moving into a neighborhood" was the third most likely cause of hate crime.

The passage of the HCSA in 1990 brought significant national attention to bias-motivated violence. As a result, many jurisdictions passed special statutes criminalizing bias crime. . . . Regardless of the statutory arrangement, bias crime provided a new and sorely needed legal remedy for anti-integrationist violence. The majority of bias crimes are "low-level" crimes—vandalism and assault—from a criminal law perspective. Low-level crimes are frequently not even investigated by the police. Because of this, the new category of bias crime brought much-needed attention to incidents that might not have been investigated by the police, let alone prosecuted. In fact, to deal with the rigors of investigation of this new type of crime, police departments around the country established specialized units. The prosecution of such crimes . . . is also a challenge, requiring special resources and skills.

The increased attention created by hate crime legislation and prosecutors' offices did not put an end to bias-motivated violence occurring as a result of minorities moving to white neighborhoods. One analysis of hate crime data collected by the police and census data from 1990 and 2000 in California revealed a correlation between increases in hate crimes and the migration of minorities to white neighborhoods. In addition to this research, news accounts drawn from newspapers around the country suggest that minorities living in or moving to white neighborhoods continue to be attacked. In 2007 alone, from the East Coast (New York and Philadelphia) to the West (California), in the South and Midwest, minority families experienced cross burnings, graffiti, arson, and verbal harassment committed by their neighbors upon their move to white neighborhoods. The violence of the 1940s and 1950s is eerily similar to incidents occurring since 2000. For instance, in one of several incidents that took place in Philadelphia, Sean Jenkins, a black construction worker, and his girlfriend made plans to rent a house in a quiet, predominately white neighborhood in December 2007. Immediately prior to their taking occupancy, white vandals broke first-floor windows in the house and wrote on a wall, "All n[igger]s should be hung." Later, when Jenkins's girlfriend went to clean the house, a young white man yelled at her, "all n[igger]s taking over the neighborhood!" After these events, the couple changed their mind about the house.

In some cities, like Chicago, crimes directed at minorities who moved to white neighborhoods were part of a continuous battle over housing integration. The struggles over housing integration that Chicago experienced in the 1950s . . . continued as minorities moved to white neighborhoods in the city and also in the suburbs. In 1998 the *Chicago Reporter* compared hate crime statistics with population change in 265 suburbs in the metropolitan area between 1990 and 1997. The results suggested that hate crimes were more likely to strike in areas undergoing demographic change. Suburbs with a white population of between 70 percent and 90 percent that experienced a significant change in their minority population accounted for more than half of all suburban hate crimes in the metropolitan area.

Newspaper accounts from the 1990s show Chicago to be littered with incidents of anti-integrationist violence. Incidents involving attacks on African Americans who had moved to white neighborhoods in and around the Chicago area occurred in Elwood Park (1992, 1998), Berwyn (1992), Portage Park (1998), Glenwood (1994), Ashburn (1996), and Mount Greenwood (1996, 1999). Most of the victims were black, but Hispanics were also targeted. One such incident involved hate graffiti placed on the property of three Hispanic families who had moved to Portage Park in 1998. Though some neighbors were not happy with the graffiti, others viewed their new neighbors as criminals, and felt the treatment was appropriate. One neighbor told a reporter, "They deserve it. This was a nice neighborhood until *they* [the Hispanic families] moved in. People want them out of here."

A similar lack of sympathy for targets and support for perpetrators of move-in violence were offered by neighbors of the Campbells, new black residents of Berwyn, another Chicago suburb. When Clifton Campbell, a Jamaican immigrant, his wife, and three children moved to Berwyn in March 1992, the suburb was 98 percent white. The day after the Campbells moved in, someone threw a brick through a window in the family's house. The following day someone set fire to the Campbells' porch. Though one neighbor quoted seemed dismayed by the crime and felt that the family should not move, several others seemed more supportive of the perpetrator. One neighbor, who declined to be identified, told a reporter, "I feel bad their house got burned . . . but real estate people should have told him that this is an all-white neighborhood, and they should've expected it. I want them to leave. I don't want my property value to go down." The Campbells subsequently put their house up for sale.

Another incident in suburban Chicago involved Andre Bailey and Sharon Henderson, a black couple who moved to Blue Island, Illinois, in the summer of 1996. They moved from south suburban Harvey, and like that of many minorities moving to white neighborhoods, the Bailey-Hendersons' relocation was a move up the social ladder, prompted by their wish to live in a better neighborhood. Soon after the Bailey-Hendersons moved in, someone set fire to a pile of leaves in their front yard and the tires on their car were slashed. The family's dog Bingo was shot with a pellet gun. Then, on June 12, 1996, their neighbor Thomas Budlove burned a six-foot cross on their lawn. Charged with a hate crime, Budlove eventually pled guilty and was sentenced to two hundred hours of community service. Bailey said that after the crime, the children were worried about leaving the house. "I'd give them a look, telling them it's okay to go outside." Nearly three years after the crime, the Bailey-Hendersons testified that they lived in fear of another racially motivated attack.

TABLE 2.1. News Accounts of Anti-Integrationist Violence, 1990–2010

Type of Incident	Number of Incidents
Arson/firebombing	44
Cross burning	96
Harassment & verbal threats	102
Homicide	3
Physical attack	28
Racially motivated shooting	20
Vandalism	162
TOTAL	455

STEVE ESTES

From *Charleston in Black and White: Race and Power in the South after the Civil Rights Movement*

(2015)

When Democrats initially voted to fly the Confederate battle flag above the South Carolina statehouse in the early 1960s, the measure was so uncontroversial that Peter McGee, who joined the legislature just after it went up, nearly forgot that it was there. In hindsight, he wished that he had pushed to bring it down, but McGee and other white Democrats never mustered the votes to do so, even when they held supermajorities in the legislature during the 1960s and 70s. Although black Democrats lobbied to bring down the flag throughout the 1970s and 80s, they got no traction on the issue with their white colleagues. After Republican Governor Carroll Campbell recognized the symbolic power of the issue for white voters in the 1980s, the Republican Party joined black South Carolinians in keeping the issue alive. Pro-flag advocates, including Glenn Mc-Connell and other Republican leaders, raised funds for television and print ads, arguing that outsiders and radical civil rights groups led opposition to the flag. In their 1994 primary, Republicans asked voters a series of questions about taxes, the Confederate flag, and other issues. Seventy-two percent of Republicans wanted to eliminate property taxes, while seventy-four percent wanted to keep the flag flying above the statehouse.

Despite the strong support for the Confederate flag among the Republican rank and file, the flag issue proved to be a double-edged sword for the GOP, just as it cut both ways for the Democrats. South Carolina Democrats officially opposed flying the flag, although white conservatives rejected the party line and moderates recognized that the issue could divide the party's interracial coalition. In the GOP, Governor Carroll Campbell toned down his support for the flag, fearing that it would hurt his chances of joining a Republican administration in Washington during the early 1990s. His successor, David Beasley, stumbled dramatically on the flag issue. A former Democrat who switched parties in 1991, Beasley defeated Arthur Ravenel Jr. for the Republican gubernatorial nomination in 1994. Beasley won the general election that year, vowing to defend the

Confederate flag. Then in 1996, the Republican governor had a change of heart. Worried about worsening race relations, Beasley said that he prayed about what to do. The governor called for removing the flag from the capitol dome and raising it over a Confederate monument on the statehouse grounds. A tsunami of negative responses swept into Columbia. The governor was a "traitor" and a "scalawag," according to one fax from the "Dixie Defenders." Rank-and-file Republicans wrote angry letters to GOP leaders, withdrawing their financial support for fear that some of their money "might fall into Gov. Beasley's pocket to support his liberal sway." Yet for all of the populist anger that Beasley's proposal stirred, there was also quiet support for a compromise from some GOP backers. The Palmetto Business Forum and the South Carolina Chamber of Commerce—traditional GOP allies—worked behind the scenes to take down the flag, fearing that it was limiting outside investment in the state. With fiscal conservatives pushing for a compromise and cultural conservatives willing to defend the flag to the last, the Republicans seemed just as flummoxed on the flag issues as the Democrats. The split within the GOP helped a Democrat win the governor's mansion in 1998, but it did not bring down the flag. If anything, the battle lines were even more starkly drawn.

At the suggestion of local civil rights activists, the NAACP called for a national boycott of South Carolina, discouraging all business and personal travel to the state until the legislature removed the Confederate banner from the statehouse. With tourism a huge part of the state's economy, particularly in the Lowcountry, the boycott could ultimately cost the state millions of dollars in revenue. Reverend Joe Darby, who drafted the original NAACP sanctions, described the flag as a symbol of a dead country and racism. Growing up in Columbia, the AME minister recalled watching Klansman display the rebel flag in demonstrations at the capitol on Confederate Memorial Day. By the 1990s, when Darby took a position at Morris Brown AME in Charleston, his opposition to the flag was resolute. "Until South Carolina lays that flag aside," he said, "we're gonna have a problem."

The NAACP boycott brought additional resources and national attention to the fight against the flag, but it also hardened resistance to bringing the banner down. Though he had originally considered a compromise, State Senator Glenn McConnell was offended by the implication of the boycott. The flag was a source of pride to McConnell, not embarrassment. "I'm not going to surrender it now to a reputation of shame," the Republican legislator said in response to the NAACP sanctions. "If there's one thing we learned at Gettysburg," he concluded, "it's to occupy the high ground and don't leave it." Not everyone occupied the high ground in the pro-flag camp, however. Members of the Klan were quite visible at pro-flag rallies at the capitol in 1999 and 2000. McConnell distanced himself from such extremists, but it was harder to disavow enthusiastic GOP leaders and friends like Arthur Ravenel. Returning to the state senate after an unsuccessful run for governor in the mid-1990s, Ravenel spoke to a rally of 6,000 flag supporters in early 2000. "Can you believe that there are those who think the General Assembly of South Carolina is going to . . . roll over and do the bidding of the National Association of Retarded People?" Ravenel said, mixing up the black civil rights organization and an advocacy group for the mentally disabled. Ravenel, the father of a son with Down syndrome, fueled further controversy by apologizing "to the retarded folks of the world for equating them to the national NAACP."

Mayor Joe Riley and other liberal Charlestonians were appalled by Ravenel's comments. After speaking out against flying the Confederate flag over the statehouse throughout the 1990s, Mayor Riley led a final push to lower the banner in 2000, organizing a protest march from Charleston to Columbia. "The important thing," Riley said, "was to show that South Carolina wasn't a racially polarized state." Still, there were South Carolinians who opposed the famously liberal mayor. "You bring those niggers marching through Calhoun County," one man wrote, "and you will be in the sights of my gun." Charleston Police Chief Reuben Greenberg loaned Riley a bulletproof vest. His wife made him wear it. The fifty-seven-year old mayor marched twelve hours a day for nearly a week to traverse the 120 miles to Columbia. "Every religious denomination, every business organization, every civil rights organization, college boards of trustees and athletic directors, and average citizens, rank and file, have said: remove the Confederate battle flag," Riley told a few thousand people at the state capitol. "And our legislature . . . hasn't even begun to debate the bill. They are out of step with the people of South Carolina." Meanwhile, 300 flag supporters demonstrated on the north side of the capitol, waving hundreds of battle flags. One flag supporter wore a replica of a Confederate uniform, and another held a sign that read "God Save the South." A third blamed Yankees who had moved down from the North for trying to destroy the southern heritage. As impassioned as both sides were, legislators inside the statehouse held out hope for a compromise. If Republican Senator Glenn McConnell agreed to take the flag down, one Democratic senator noted, "It'll be over."

Once again, the compromise would hinge on an alliance of white Republicans and black Democrats. Senator Glenn McConnell did not relish the idea of taking down the battle flag in the face of the NAACP boycott, but he left a small opening for compromise. "I was rigid that that flag should be preserved, and it should not be removed except with honor," McConnell later recalled. "It could not be settled on the basis of power, because we had the power on our side to keep the flag on the dome." But the Republican senator also came to see the Confederate struggle in a longer history of South Carolinians fighting for rights that stretched back to the American Revolution and forward to the civil rights movement. Working with Robert Ford and other African American legislators as well as white Democrats, McConnell crafted a compromise to take the battle flag off the statehouse and place it on a monument to Confederate soldiers in front of the capitol. The state would also commission an African American history monument on the capitol grounds, something that black legislators had long sought. Ironically, the Confederate battle flag would actually be *more* visible to capitol visitors in its new location. NAACP activists were not pleased. It was a "sellout," according to Reverend Joe Darby, that only "got the flag halfway down." Despite the continuing opposition of the NAACP, the legislature passed the flag compromise. On a warm Saturday in the summer of 2000, two Citadel cadets in dress uniforms lowered the Confederate battle flag from the capitol dome. A color guard of Civil War reenactors raised a new flag above the monument to Confederate soldiers.

When the dust settled from the flag fight, Glenn McConnell and Robert Ford continued their unlikely political alliance, one that reflected the complicated relationship between white Republicans and black Democrats in the South of the post–civil rights era. The two men worked together on resolutions to establish state holidays for Confederate Memorial Day and for Martin Luther King Day. McConnell supported Ford's efforts to nominate more African American judges, and Ford brought a Confederate flag back into the statehouse to make a point about the importance of celebrating the Civil War's sesquicentennial. Not everyone believed that the partnership between these two Charleston politicians was an equal one. Former state representative Lucille Whipper thought Ford supported McConnell because the Republican was both personable and a political power broker. "He became friendly with Glenn," she recalled of Ford's change of heart about McConnell. "Now, whether that is a mutual friendship or not, I question that." For his part, McConnell was proud to call Ford a friend. Friendship was one thing, however, political power another. In one legislative session after the flag controversy was settled, only two of the sixty- six bills Ford authored passed into law. By contrast, McConnell saw forty-six of the 106 bills he authored become law. Five years after the Confederate flag fight, McConnell led a Republican majority in the Senate. The GOP controlled the governor's mansion, house of representatives, both U.S. Senate seats, and most of the congressional delegation. Black Democrats like Robert Ford continued to win elections in majority- minority districts, but the Republicans won nearly everywhere else. A fierce critic of the alliance between black Democrats and white Republicans, NAACP activist Joe Darby observed, "In the process of getting a couple more members of the Black Caucus, they actually set the stage for the Republican Party to become pretty much invincible in South Carolina."

All of this had been made possible by the passage and evolution of the Voting Rights Act. A signature accomplishment of the civil rights movement, the act reenfranchised and empowered African Americans throughout the South. Conservative critics continued to challenge the law as unnecessary, unfair, and unconstitutional. This was particularly true, critics argued, of the section of the law that let the Justice Department review changes to state and local voting regulations, including redistricting. One such challenge to the Voting Rights Act reached the Supreme Court in 2009. In oral arguments, Chief Justice John Roberts asked how the Justice Department could support its claim that the preclearance process was still necessary when they rejected only 0.05 percent of changes to state and local voting laws. The government's attorney replied that the threat of rejection kept states from passing discriminatory voting laws. Chief Justice Roberts called this line of reasoning silly, comparing DOJ review to the fabled "elephant whistle." "Well, there are no elephants," he joked, "so it must work." Four years later, the chief justice authored a majority opinion that struck down the section of the Voting Rights Act requiring southern states and other localities with a history of voter discrimination to preclear their electoral changes with the Justice Department.

Chief Justice Roberts may not have seen any elephants, but they were clearly there. The received wisdom on the Republican revolution in the American South holds that the white backlash against civil rights legislation, particularly to Democratic support for laws like the Voting Rights Act, led to the rise of southern Republicans. Certainly, southern whites began to vote for Republican presidential candidates in the late 1960s and continued to do so in increasing numbers through the 2000s. . . .

This set the stage for a battle over Confederate memory in South Carolina and other Deep South states. Confederate memory had welded southern whites together with a shared culture, even when they might have been divided on a host of other issues, including geography, religion, and economics. With black politicians pushing to furl the Confederate flag in the wake of the civil rights movement, white Republican candidates could weld together diverse white constituencies by defending the flag and southern heritage. By the 1990s, however, it became clear that the Confederate flag could divide whites as much as it had once united them. Some Republicans, especially business leaders, feared that public celebration of Confederate memory hurt outside investment; other Republicans warned that such investment was not worth selling out southern heritage. Ultimately, a second coalition between white Republicans and black Democrats ended the standoff on the Confederate flag issue in South Carolina, Georgia, and other southern states. Once again, interests converged to maintain the status quo of political empowerment for a black Democratic minority and a white Republican majority.

THOMAS SUGRUE

From *Not Even Past: Barack Obama and the Burden of Race*

(2010)

In the fall of 2006, around the time that Obama began to lay the groundwork for his presidential campaign, William Julius Wilson and University of Chicago sociologist Richard Taub published a study of race and ethnicity in Chicago, entitled *There Goes the Neighborhood*. In it, they offer a sobering view of a city where ethnic groups look with suspicion across the invisible boundaries that mark urban turf. Wilson and Taub conclude that "neighborhoods in urban America, especially in large metropolitan areas like Chicago, are likely to remain divided, racially and culturally." It is a depressing prognosis that reflects the distance Wilson has traveled from his once strongly held position that racial distinctions were waning in post–civil rights era America. But it also corresponds with the findings of social scientific researchers—and increasingly historians—about the complex relationship of post-1964 immigration to the questions of race and identity in the modern United States.

The book's most important and troubling finding is that when it comes to their perceptions of African Americans, whites and Latinos are more alike than different. Mexican newcomers in Chicago, for example, quickly learned to view blacks as shiftless and prone to crime. In one Chicago neighborhood, Hispanic and white residents formed an alliance to prevent the busing of their children from the neighborhood's overcrowded schools to nearby, mostly black schools. In another, Mexican American residents, many of them recent arrivals, expressed their contempt for blacks, whom they saw as competitors for scarce resources. As a consequence, Chicago has the highest rate of black-Hispanic segregation in the United States.

Chicago is not unique. The nation's largest and most ethnically diverse metropolitan areas, New York and Los Angeles, have experienced similar patterns of interracial hostility and segregation. In Los Angeles, Harvard political scientist Lawrence Bobo and University of Pennsylvania demographer Camille Charles found that newly arriving Asian and Latin American immigrants—while they have a complicated relationship with the white majority—quickly define themselves as "not black." They are attracted to predominantly white neighborhoods and, like whites, view the presence of even a modest number of blacks as a sign that a neighborhood is troubled or in decline.

The new immigration has—despite an outburst of nativism unparalleled since the anti-immigrant crusades of the early twentieth century—destabilized racial categories, though unevenly. The most pronounced reshuffling of the racial deck involves those new Americans of Latino and Asian descent; change has been slowest for Americans of African descent, even those new immigrants from places as diverse as Liberia, Senegal, Haiti, and the Dominican Republic. The Latin American immigrant experience is instructive. For the last thirty years, as tens of millions of Spanish-speaking immigrants from Central and South America and the Caribbean have flooded into the United States, anti-immigrant commentators have fretted about the Latinization of the United States and the emergence of an unassimilable minority. But such fears have proved ungrounded. Despite their incorporation under antidiscrimination and affirmative action laws as a racial minority beginning in the 1970s, and the ongoing efforts of civil rights advocates to protect the rights based on that status, ordinary Latinos have resisted efforts to organize as a racial group because of the diversity of Latino national origins, the incommensurability of racial categories between Latin America and the United States, and the embrace of the category "white" by a majority of Latin American immigrants and their children.

When the U.S. Census Bureau introduced the category "multiracial" in the 2000 census, most observers expected it to reflect the growing number of black-white marriages. Instead, the vast majority of those who checked more than one box selected some Latin American identity and "white." By contrast only 2 percent of self-identified whites and 4 percent of self-identified blacks considered themselves as being of more than one race. By nearly every measure, Latinos of non-African descent (a crucial distinction) have amalgamated to a degree comparable to that of southern and eastern European immigrants in the early twentieth century. Rates of intermarriage between Americans of Hispanic and non-Hispanic European descent are up to one-third in aggregate; and they rise in each generation removed from the first wave of entrance to the United States. And despite such publicized comments as George H. W. Bush's reference to his grandchildren (whose mother is Mexican American) as "little brown ones," data show that mixed-race children of Latin American descent, with no visible African heritage, are regularly viewed as "white."

The instability of racial classification is even more striking when it comes to the groups that are broadly labeled Asian American. There are variants within and between groups, but overall the experience of Asian immigrants since the 1960s inverts the racial order that prevailed as late as the 1940s, when Chinese and Japanese were forbidden to emigrate to the United States, when public health authorities advocated their quarantine, and when many (especially the Japanese) were even prevented from owning property. It is impossible to generalize about Americans of Asian descent: Hmong, Laotian, and Filipino immigrants, for example, have faced greater obstacles than have Indian, Chinese, and Korean newcomers; many of the former groups come from impoverished backgrounds, while many of the latter arrive in the United States with capital and relatively high levels of educational attainment. But even accounting for variations between ethnic groups and the fact that most Asians are new arrivals to the United States, more than one-quarter of all married people of Asian descent in the United States have a non-Asian partner (87 percent of these partners are white). For married people of Japanese American descent, up to 70 percent have a partner who is not Asian.

Immigration patterns have also transformed urban and metropolitan geographies in ways that confound traditional racial categories. Most big cities have Chinatowns, and many have Mexican Villages or their equivalent. Smaller groups are clustered in Japantowns, Little Koreas, and Filipino neighborhoods, especially in older western cities. But more than half of new immigrants to the United States since the 1990s live in suburbs; the result is an extraordinary diversification of what had been, fifty years ago, some of the whitest places in America. And patterns of segregation vary widely from group to group. Asian communities—especially those that are portals for the newest immigrants—remain somewhat concentrated (and those patterns vary by group), but overall less so than those of Latinos. Latino segregation varies by group as well—South American immigrants are the least segregated; Afro-Hispanics (such as immigrants from the Dominican Republic) the most segregated. But overall, the pattern tends toward residential amalgamation, with the noteworthy exception of African-descended immigrants.

By nearly every measure, African Americans stand alone. The most persistent manifestation of racial inequality in the modern United States has been racial segregation in housing and education. From 1920 through 1990, patterns of black-white segregation hardened in most of the United States, despite shifts in white attitudes about black neighbors, and despite the passage of local and state antidiscrimination laws and the enactment of Title VIII of the Civil Rights Act (1968) which prohibited housing discrimination nationwide. There was slight improvement in the last decade of the twentieth century, mostly in and around military bases, college towns, and new exurbs in the Sun Belt with no extensive history of racial hostility, and with metropolitan or regional governments. That those places desegregated to some degree was a reminder of the powerful role that government policy and the structure of local governments could play in undermining racial segregation: the military is the largest substantially racially mixed institution in the United States; colleges and universities institutionalized diversity through affirmative action; and metropolitan governance discouraged segregation because whites lacked the opportunity to jump across municipal boundaries for towns with better schools and public services, while leaving minorities behind.

By contrast, in metropolitan areas with fragmented governments and school districts, overwhelmingly in the Northeast and Midwest, racial segregation rates have remained particularly high. The reasons are varied, but they reflect the long-term effects of discriminatory patterns that date to the early twentieth century. Before that, in most places—North and South—blacks and whites lived in relatively close proximity. Real estate brokers refused to rent or sell houses to blacks in white neighborhoods, actuaries determined that a neighborhood's racial composition was the most important factor in measuring property values, and whites began to resist black incursion, sometimes with violence. And federal pro-homeownership programs, beginning in the New Deal, wrote discriminatory provisions into public policies. The result was that during the mid-twentieth century, expectations about the racial composition of neighborhoods were established that proved extraordinarily resistant to change.

After the 1968 Fair Housing Act, real estate agents developed more furtive tactics to preserve the racial homogeneity of neighborhoods. The most significant was "steering," that is, the practice of directing white home buyers to all-white communities and black home buyers to predominantly black or racially transitional neighborhoods. Real estate brokers catered to what they believed were the prejudices of their white customers. Audit studies of housing discrimination conducted by the Department of Housing and Urban Development and by local housing and nonprofit agencies, where matched pairs of black and white "testers" are sent to randomly selected real estate offices, consistently show the persistence of discriminatory treatment of black home seekers and renters. And more recently, studies have shown stark racial differences in access to mortgages and loans—leaving minority neighborhoods especially devastated by the collapse of the real estate market that began in 2006 and accelerated rapidly during the "Great Recession" that began in 2008. Discrimination continues to play a significant role in dividing housing markets by race. When house hunting or loan shopping, blacks simply do not have the same degree of choice as do whites.

Persistent residential segregation compounded educational disparities. Beginning in the late 1970s, when courts began a thirty-year process of abandoning the mandate of Brown v. Board of Education, school districts around the country resegregated by race, especially by black and white. In the North—where Brown was never wholly enforced, and where white mobility thwarted integration—

blacks witnessed some educational gains in the 1960s and 1970s, notably a narrowing of test-score gaps with whites. But schools resegregated in the period between the 1980s and the early twenty-first century and the test-score gap leveled off. The process of educational resegregation has accelerated most recently in the South, where the Civil Rights Act of 1964, Department of Education intervention, and court-ordered busing led to enormous shifts in racial patterns in the late 1960s. Since the late 1990s, however, metropolitan-wide school desegregation plans have been rolled back by federal courts that have declared districts "unitary"—that is, racially balanced. A good example is Charlotte, North Carolina, where a 1972 Supreme Court ruling led to a metropolitan-wide busing plan. By the 1980s, Charlotte had one of the most integrated school districts in the country, and racial gaps in achievement narrowed. That experiment in integration ended in 2001, and considerable resegregation followed. Most recently, in the 2007 *Parents Involved* case, the conservative majority on the Supreme Court struck down as unconstitutional (using the color-blind rationale) voluntary school desegregation programs in Louisville, Kentucky, and Seattle, Washington, and threatened similar programs elsewhere. Education research has shown consistently that majority-minority schools face one of several problems: they are underfunded by comparison to schools in nearby majority-white districts; they face high teacher turnover; they are more likely to have outdated facilities and classroom materials; and, most significantly, their students tend to be disproportionately poor, lacking the familial resources and the cultural capital to do well in the classroom.

It is important to note that black-white residential segregation by race is not—and has not been—a natural consequence of disparities in income between blacks and whites. Middle-class and wealthy blacks are only slightly more likely to live near whites than are poor blacks. In an examination of the thirty metropolitan areas with the largest black populations in the United States, sociologists Douglas Massey and Nancy Denton found no significant difference in the segregation rates of poor, middle-class, and well-to-do African Americans. "Even if black incomes continued to rise," write Massey and Denton, "segregation would not have declined: no matter how much blacks earned, they remained racially separated from whites." The most recent census data reaffirm that regardless of income, African Americans, in the aggregate, remain residentially segregated, and that the differences in rates of segregation between blacks of high and low socioeconomic status remain modest.

African Americans are far more likely than whites to be economically insecure. The statistics are grim. In 2006, the median household income of blacks was only 62 percent of that of whites. Blacks were much more likely than whites to be unemployed (black unemployment rates have remained one and a half to two times those of whites since the 1950s), in part because of workplace discrimination. Data from the Russell Sage Foundation's Multi-City study of Urban Inequality show that in Detroit, Boston, Atlanta, and Los Angeles, many employers make hiring decisions on the basis of stereotypes about minorities, and use race or ethnicity as "signals" of desirable or undesirable work characteristics. Social scientists have documented employers discriminating against job applicants with comparable credentials when one has a "black" name or has a place of residence in a known "black" neighborhood. Even more significant, blacks are still most likely to live in areas that have been left behind by the profound restructuring of the national and international economy, notably in major cities in the Northeast and Midwest. The suburbanization of employment—but not of minority housing and transportation—has further hindered black job opportunities. As a result, nearly one-quarter of all American blacks, but only one in ten whites, live beneath the poverty line.

The starkest racial disparities in the United States are in wealth (a category that includes such assets as savings accounts, stocks, bonds, and especially real estate). In 2003, the U.S. Census Bureau calculated that white households had a median net worth of $74,900, whereas black households had a median net worth of only $7,500. It is here that the burden of history is the greatest. Census surveys and social scientific studies have documented an enormous gap in asset holdings between blacks and whites, largely because of differences in holdings in real estate, the only significant asset that most Americans own. Blacks are still less likely to own their own homes. Even in 2005, at the peak of the most recent real estate bubble, only 49 percent of blacks owned their own homes, compared to 74 percent of whites. And because of persistent racial segregation, the value of homes that blacks own is significantly lower than that of white-owned homes. Racial differences in homeownership rates and disparities in real estate values and household assets have devastating long term effects. Whereas many whites can expect financial support at crucial junctures in their lives (going to college, getting married, buying a home, paying for a medical emergency), the vast wealth gap means that blacks cannot. The wealth gap also affects intergenerational transfers. A majority of whites can expect at least modest inheritances as the result of their parents' accumulated wealth, but few blacks can expect such good fortune.

Not surprisingly, blacks have been disproportionately affected by market failures in home financing and personal credit from the New Deal through the early twenty-first century. From the 1930s through the late 1960s, blacks seldom had access to federally backed mortgages and loans; in that period and beyond, they were more likely to buy properties using expensive nonmortgage instruments like land contracts; and beginning in the 1980s and 1990s, as the Reagan,

Bush, and Clinton administrations deregulated the financial, personal loan, and mortgage markets, predatory lenders (from pawnshops to payday loan agencies to subprime mortgage brokers) found their most lucrative markets among minorities. In 2006, more than half of subprime loans went to African Americans, who comprise only 13 percent of the population. And a recent study of data from the Home Mortgage Disclosure Act found that 32.1 percent of blacks, but only 10.5 percent of whites, got higher-priced mortgages—that is, mortgages with an annual percentage rate three or more points higher than the rate of a Treasury security of the same length. The result has been growing economic insecurity among African Americans, even those of middle-class status.

KALI NICOLE GROSS

From "African American Women, Mass Incarceration, and the Politics of Protection"

(2015)

On November 28, 2013, Marissa Alexander was freed from a Florida prison after serving three years of her twenty-year sentence. Her crime: firing a warning shot during a confrontation with her estranged abusive husband—a man against whom she had a restraining order. Even after her release, however, Alexander was not out of the woods. While Judge James H. Daniel found the original jury instructions flawed and overturned her conviction, he denied her request for a new hearing under Florida's stand-your-ground law, which had been amended to include warning shots in its allowance of force in the face of imminent threat. On July 21, 2014, Judge Daniel found that the amended statute "could not be applied retroactively." Alexander's experience brings into high relief the persistent biases in American justice, particularly given her case's stark contrast to the George Zimmerman acquittal in 2013. Whereas Zimmerman successfully used the stand-your-ground defense after taking the life of the unarmed black teenager Trayvon Martin in 2012, Alexander was unable to invoke the same protections. No one died and no one was hurt at the hands of the battered black woman, yet she received a twenty-year sentence. Alexander's new trial was originally scheduled for December 2014, however in November of that year she accepted a plea deal that sent her to the Duval County Jail to serve an additional sixty-five days. The plea also included two years of probation for Alexander under "house detention and wearing a surveillance monitor." She agreed to these terms rather than face the new charges filed against her—charges that could have amounted to a maximum of sixty years in prison. Alexander's calamity is rooted in a tangled set of circumstances that ensnare black women when race, gender, violence, and criminal justice collide.

Alexander's case reflects the legacies of an exclusionary politics of protection whereby black women were not entitled to the law's protection, though they could not escape its punishment. Structured by colonial and antebellum judiciaries, laws representing the priorities of enslavers effectively negated and criminalized black womanhood by subjecting black women to brutality and exploitation and by barring them from lawful avenues for redress. Without institutional safeguards, black women seeking security or justice would have to create those circumstances for themselves, which often placed them on the receiving end of harsh sentences from the same legal system that failed them.

This history is rarely brought to bear on black women's current overrepresentation in the U.S. prison system. If the issue of black female incarceration is raised, it is usually as a tangential afterthought in discussions about the carceral experiences of black men—and even then the role of intraracial gender violence is rarely discussed. This essay will provide a brief overview of the early foundations of racialized, gendered notions of protection. It will also examine how these phenomena contributed to black women's disproportionate incarceration in the late nineteenth and early twentieth centuries. And it will analyze how these legacies influence the relationship among black womanhood, violence, and mass incarceration.

The Fundamentals of Exclusionary Protection

Black womanhood in the United States is framed by the politics of protection—not simply with respect to the legal system but because of it. Roughly twenty-one years after the arrival of nineteen Africans in Jamestown in 1619, the colonies began to sanction and codify slavery; included among the statutes were laws directly responsible for the denigration of black womanhood. Virginia's December 1662 decree (part of the Virginia Slave Laws) that the children of enslaved Africans and Englishmen would be "held bond or free according to the condition of the mother" did not just counter traditional English practices. The decree also mapped enslaved women's sexual exploitation and, in effect, monetarily incentivized the acts, as their offspring would swell planters' coffers—a prospect boon to countless rapes and instances of forced breeding. Colonial rape laws compounded black women's subjugation by excluding their sexual assault. As Steve Wilf makes plain, "the rape of black women was not acknowledged by early American law." Mainstream attitudes further negated their victimization with ruinous myths about black women's libidinous sexual proclivities.

Slave labor and practices governing it further eroded black womanhood. Virginia's legislature distinguished black female labor from white female labor by treating black women as "tithable"—classifying them "as field laborers with a productive capacity equivalent to that of men." Planters meted out harsh corporal punishments, often without regard to gender. Countless slave narratives describe the humiliation—including forced stripping—that accompanied whippings. Frederick Douglass's account of his aunt Hester's experience at the hands of her master exposes the carnage as well as the consequences of agency: the master, who desired Hester, caught her returning from a visit to an enslaved man; he hung her from a ceiling joist, stripped her, and beat her bloody. Hester's defiance, and that of scores of others, also evidences resistance—which ranged from exercising spatial mobility to petitioning courts for freedom to taking flight. Black women also violently lashed out against their captors, but punishment for these infractions did not always end on plantations or at the hands of overseers. Rather, they would be punished by the system responsible for their subjection—with the antebellum case of Celia, an enslaved black woman who was executed for killing her rapist-owner in 1855 Missouri, serving as a potent example. Such instances mark the cruel hypocrisies of American justice: black women would be denied protection under the law, only to be fatally condemned by it.

After emancipation, black women's bodies would be the terrain upon which white men aimed to reinscribe old racial hierarchies. Sexual violence visited upon black women took the form of rapes organized by the Ku Klux Klan as well as daily assaults on black domestics. As before, such encounters "were considered consensual, even coerced by the seductions of black women's lascivious nature." Barriers to protection remained firmly in place, and in those instances when black women deigned to fight back they faced severe punishment, and the violence that was brought to bear tarnished their womanhood that much more. Criminal anthropologists assessed female deviance, in part, by subjects' proximity to, or distance from, Western ideals of femininity, morality, and virtue—standards against which black women failed to measure up. Proponents such as Cesare Lombroso and Guglielmo Ferrero masculinized black women, claiming that their physical "correspondence with the male is very strong"—an aberration reputedly indicative of congenital criminality. These abstractions held multiple consequences for black women, particularly as they entered the criminal justice system.

Black Women and Disproportionate Incarceration

Black women's exclusion from notions of protection cast a pall over their experiences in the criminal justice system during the late nineteenth and early twentieth centuries. Most black women lived in poverty, due in large part to being limited almost exclusively to domestic service and agricultural work. Domestic service in particular imperiled black women because they were vulnerable to sexual harassment in white homes and also profoundly susceptible to white employers' accusations of theft—whether real or imagined. Although officers routinely arrested black women for sex work and domestic disputes, larceny constituted the lion's share of black women's criminal arrests; and white judges and juries more often trusted the testimony of white employers and other white authority figures over the word of black women. Notwithstanding blatant bias,

African American women also battled a general presumption of their guilt, owing to commonly held notions of their low character and lack of morality, as well as to the popularity of racialized caricatures depicting their purported fiendish, criminal ways.

These dynamics, together with an increased emphasis on punishing crimes against property, resulted in black women enduring some of the harshest outcomes in early criminal courts. Between 1794 and 1835 in Philadelphia, roughly 72 percent of black women who went before juries were convicted. They also had fewer of their cases dismissed than any other group and were more starkly overrepresented in prison than black men. For example, black women were approximately 47.5 percent of female prisoners, whereas black men accounted for only 29 percent of imprisoned men—both were disproportionately represented however, as African Americans were far less than one-quarter of the city's population. These trends occurred in the North and South. In Tennessee in 1868, 60 percent of male prisoners were black as opposed to 100 percent of the women prisoners. Moreover, the disparities lasted well into the twentieth century, as black men in the South accounted for 72.4 percent of male prisoners in 1880, while black women accounted for 85.8 percent; those numbers grew to 73 percent and 90.2 percent, respectively, by 1904, but dropped to 59.6 percent and 79.6 percent, respectively, in 1923. . . .

Social attitudes undergirding exclusionary notions of protection also influenced the kind of time black women served in prison. In places such as Philadelphia in the late nineteenth century, black women served longer prison sentences: 14.1 months on average, while white women served 8.5 months for comparable offenses. Moreover, young white women and girls found themselves shipped off to newly constructed reformatories in the early twentieth century—institutions built with a cottage design and staffed by white matrons aiming to restore white womanhood. Because reformers believed that black women and girls were innately licentious due to "stigmas associated with their African ancestry and legacy of American enslavement," blacks typically served their sentences at custodial institutions. White middle-class prison reformers "ignored altogether the serious problems faced by young African American women." If black women were admitted to reformatories, they often languished in segregated units. In custodial prisons, reform was ignored, and black women existed as prey for unscrupulous prison officials. . . .

Against this backdrop, Marissa Alexander's experience not only summons the history of the politics of protection in criminal justice but also calls attention to the way that politicized protection has engendered the violence for which black women are often criminalized. The Alexander case also points to the more troubling aspects of the relationship between black womanhood, intraracial gendered violence, and mass incarceration. . . .

Black Womanhood, Gendered Violence, and Mass Incarceration

Beth Richie's book on black women and incarceration notes that the second most common cause of death for black women and girls between the ages of 15 and 25 was homicide, primarily caused by intimate-partner violence. Given the ominous statistics about black men and violent death, black women's equally stark numbers should come as no surprise. . . .

Structural and systematic impediments to protection have placed black women at a greater risk for violence and abuse—conditions related to increased instances of incarceration. In 1999, for example, 57 percent of female state prisoners were victims of abuse prior to their confinement, 46.5 percent had been physically abused, and 39 percent had been sexually assaulted. By 2011, when upward of 1 million women were either "incarcerated or otherwise under the control of the justice system," between 85 percent and 90 percent of those women reported a history of domestic and sexual violence as opposed to 22.3 percent of women nationally. Given black women's representation in the criminal-justice system and their historic and ongoing vulnerability, there can be little doubt that gender violence is a key factor in their disproportionate representation. Indeed, 68 percent of incarcerated black women had been victimized by intimate-partner violence, and, compared to white women, black women are twice as likely to be killed by a spouse. . . .

Further, exclusionary notions of protection have created a need for black women to trade in extralegal violence for personal security. Historical accounts are replete with examples of otherwise-law-abiding black women found carrying small knives and other weapons to guard against daily assaults and violations at home and in the workplace—behaviors gesturing toward their often-overlooked vulnerability. African American women experience domestic violence at a rate 35 percent higher than the rate for white women and roughly 2.5 percent higher than the rate for other races, suggesting that little has changed. These facts are not hidden, yet they rarely seem to be at the forefront of discussions surrounding race, gender, and justice. A similar dynamic seems to be at work in the discourses surrounding the Alexander case. While many have railed against the blatantly racist double standard of her twenty-year sentence vis á vis George Zimmerman's acquittal, there appears to be far less protest about the fact that Alexander had been beaten by a black man, and so terrified of another beating that she discharged a firearm in the family home—actions that spotlight her desperation and fear. Based on the numbers that Richie cites, that fear was more than justified. Save pulling that pistol, the scenario in which Alexander found herself is exactly how [black] women [like her] die and have been dying for decades.

APPENDIX

This is the actual #Charlestonsyllabus list as it appears on the website of the African American Intellectual History Society. For additional resources, please visit the official #Charlestonsyllabus website: http://www.thecharlestonsyllabus.com/

#Charlestonsyllabus

Here is a list of readings that educators can use to broach conversations in the classroom about the horrendous events that unfolded in Charleston, South Carolina, on the evening of June 17, 2015. These readings provide valuable information about the history of racial violence in this country and contextualize the history of race relations in South Carolina and the United States in general. They also offer insights on race, racial identities, global white supremacy, and black resistance. Readings are arranged by date of publication, except for sections for op-eds and editorials and websites, which are arranged alphabetically because of lack of publication data or the relatively small span of time in which the works were published. This list is not meant to be exhaustive—you will find omissions. Please check out the Twitter tag at #Charlestonsyllabus and the Goodreads List (https://www.goodreads.com/list/show/89150._CharlestonSyllabus?page=1) for additional reading suggestions.

#Charlestonsyllabus was conceived by Chad Williams (@Dr_ChadWilliams), associate professor of African and Afro-American studies at Brandeis University. With the help of Kidada Williams (@KidadaEWilliams), the hashtag started trending on Twitter on the evening of June 19, 2015. The following list was compiled and organized by AAIHS blogger Keisha N. Blain (@KeishaBlain) with the assistance of Melissa Morrone (@InfAgit), Ryan P. Randall (@foureyedsoul), and Cecily Walker (@skeskali). *Special thanks to everyone who contributed suggestions via Twitter.*

"#Charlestonsyllabus is more than a list. It is a community of people committed to critical thinking, truth telling, and social transformation."
—CHAD WILLIAMS

General Historical Overviews

- Vincent Harding, *There Is a River: The Black Struggle for Freedom in America* (1981)
- Robin D. G. Kelley, *Freedom Dreams: The Black Radical Imagination* (2002)
- Steven Hahn, *A Nation under Our Feet: Black Political Struggles in the Rural South from Slavery to the Great Migration* (2003)
- Manning Marable, *Living Black History: How Reimagining the African American Past Can Remake America's Racial Future* (2005)
- Tom Holt, *Children of Fire: A History of African Americans* (2010)
- Robin Bernstein, *Racial Innocence: Performing American Childhood from Slavery to Civil Rights* (2011)
- Pero Gaglo Dagbovie, *What Is African American History?* (2015)

Op-eds and Editorials

- Yoni Applebaum, "Why Is the Flag Still There?," 21 June 2015, *Atlantic.* http://www.theatlantic.com/politics/archive/2015/06/why-is-the-flag-still-there/396431/
- Ta-Nehisi Coates, "Take Down the Confederate Flag–Now," 18 June 2015, *Atlantic.* http://www.theatlantic.com/politics/archive/2015/06/take-down-the-confederate-flag-now/396290/
- Jelani Cobb, "Terrorism in Charleston," 29 June 2015, *New Yorker.* http://www.newyorker.com/magazine/2015/06/29/terrorism-in-charleston
- Heather Cox Richardson, "Reconstructing the American Tradition of Domestic Terrorism," 18 June 2015, *Werehistory.org.* http://werehistory.org/american-domestic-terrorism/
- Michael Eric Dyson, "Love and Terror in the Black Church," 20 June 2015, *New York Times.* http://www.nytimes.com/2015/06/21/opinion/michael-eric-dyson-love-and-terror-in-the-black-church.html?_r=0
- Douglas R. Egerton, "Before Charleston's Church Shooting, a Long History of Attacks," 18 June 2015, *New York Times.* http://www.nytimes.com/2015/06/18/magazine/before-charlestons-church-shooting-a-long-history-of-attacks.html
- Benjamin Foldy, "Rhodesian Flag, Confederate Flag: Roof & the Legacies of Racial Hate," 20 June 2015, *Juan Cole at Informed Comment.* http://www.juancole.com/2015/06/rhodesian-confederate-legacies.html
- Robert Greene II, "Racism Can't Destroy This Charleston Church," 19 June 2015, *Politico.com.* http://www.politico.com/magazine/story/2015/06/charleston-shooting-emanuel-african-methodist-episcopal-church-119205#.VYcKdE3JDIW
- Libby Nelson, "The Confederate Flag Symbolizes White Supremacy—and it Always Has," 20 June 2015, *Vox.* http://www.vox.com/2015/6/20/8818093/confederate-flag-south-carolina-charleston-shooting
- Nell Irvin Painter, "What Is Whiteness?," 20 June 2015, *New York Times.* http://www.nytimes.com/2015/06/21/opinion/sunday/what-is-whiteness.html?_r=0

- Charles P. Pierce, "Charleston Shooting: Speaking the Unspeakable, Thinking the Unthinkable," 18 June 2015, *Esquire*. http://www.esquire.com/news-politics /politics/news/a35793/charleston-shooting-discussion/
- David Remnick, "Charleston and the Age of Obama," 19 June 2015, *New Yorker*. http://www.newyorker.com/news/daily-comment /charleston-and-the-age-of-obama
- Manisha Sinha, "The Long and Proud History of Charleston's AME Church," 19 June 2015, *Huffington Post*. http://www.huffingtonpost.com/manisha-sinha /the-long-and-proud-history-of-charlestons-ame-church_b_7620910.html?utm _hp_ref=black-voices&ir=Black%20Voices
- Rebecca Traister, "Our Racist History Isn't Back to Haunt Us. It Never Left Us," 18 June 2015, *New Republic*. http://www.newrepublic.com/article/122073 /our-racial-history-isnt-back-haunt-us-it-never-left-us
- Kidada Williams, "Centuries of Violence," 19 June 2015, *Slate*. http://www.slate .com/articles/news_and_politics/history/2015/06/charleston_church_shooting _for_black_americans_dylann_storm_s_attack_is.html

Readings on South Carolina

- William W. Freehling, *Prelude to Civil War: The Nullification Controversy in South Carolina, 1816–1836* (1966)
- Stephen Channing, *Crisis of Fear: Secession in South Carolina* (1970)
- Gerda Lerner, *The Grimké Sisters from South Carolina: Pioneers for Women's Rights and Abolition* (1971)
- Peter Wood, *Black Majority: Negroes in Colonial South Carolina from 1670 through the Stono Rebellion* (1974)
- Thomas Holt, *Black over White: Negro Political Leadership in South Carolina during Reconstruction* (1977)
- Daniel Littlefield, *Rice and Slaves: Ethnicity and the Slave Trade in Colonial South Carolina* (1981)
- Charles Joyner, *Down by the Riverside: A South Carolina Slave Community* (1984)
- Margaret Washington Creel, *A Peculiar People: Slave Religion and Community Culture among the Gullah* (1988)
- Julie Saville, *The Work of Reconstruction: From Slave to Wage Laborer in South Carolina, 1860–1870* (1994)
- Stephanie McCurry, *Masters of Small World: Yeoman Households, Gender Relations, and the Political Culture of the Antebellum South Carolina Low Country* (1995)
- Richard Zuczek, *Reconstruction in South Carolina* (1996)
- Leslie Schwalm, *A Hard Fight for We: Women's Transition from Slavery to Freedom in South Carolina* (1997)
- Douglas Egerton, *He Shall Go Out Free: The Lives of Denmark Vesey* (1999)
- David M. Robertson, *Denmark Vesey: The Buried History of America's Largest Slave Rebellion and the Man Who Led It* (1999)

- Manisha Sinha, *Counterrevolution of Slavery: Politics and Ideology in Antebellum South Carolina* (2000)
- Judith Carney, *Black Rice: The African Origins of Rice Cultivation in the Americas* (2001)
- Michael Johnson, "Denmark Vesey and his Co-conspirators," *William and Mary Quarterly* 58, no. 4 (2001): 915–76. http://www.jstor.org/stable/2674506?seq= 1#page_scan_tab_contents
- Charles J. Holden, *In the Great Maelstrom: Conservatives in Post–Civil War South Carolina* (2002)
- John Hammond Moore, *Carnival of Blood: Dueling, Lynching, and Murder in South Carolina, 1880–1920* (2006)
- Peter Lau, *Democracy Rising: South Carolina and the Fight for Black Equality since 1865* (2006)
- Andrew Billingsley, *Yearning to Breathe Free: Robert Smalls of South Carolina and His Families* (2007)
- Orville Vernon Burton and Winifred B. Moore, eds., *Toward the Meeting of the Waters: Currents in the Civil Rights Movement of South Carolina during the Twentieth Century* (2008)
- Katherine Mellen Charron, *Freedom's Teacher: The Life of Septima Clark* (2009)
- Orville Vernon Burton, Emory Campbell, and Wilbur Cross, *Penn Center: A History Preserved* (2014)
- LeRhonda S. Manigault-Bryant, *Talking to the Dead: Religion, Music, and Lived Memory among Gullah-Geechee Women* (2014)
- Charlotte S. Riley, *A Mysterious Life and Calling: From Slavery to Ministry in South Carolina* (2016)

ON CHARLESTON, SOUTH CAROLINA

- Bernard Powers, *Black Charlestonians: A Social History, 1822–1885* (1999)
- David Blight, "The First Decoration Day" (2001). http://zinnedproject.org/materials/the-first-decoration-day/
- Harlan Greene, Harry Hutchins Jr., and Brian E. Hutchins, *Slave Badges and the Slave-Hire System in Charleston, South Carolina, 1783–1865* (2004)
- Stephanie Yuhl, *A Golden Haze of Memory: The Making of Historic Charleston* (2005)
- Edmund Drago, *Charleston's Avery Center: From Education and Civil Rights to Preserving the African American Experience* (2006)
- R. Scott Baker, *Paradoxes of Desegregation: African American Struggles for Educational Equity in Charleston, South Carolina, 1926–1972* (2006)
- Amrita Myers, *Forging Freedom: Black Women and the Pursuit of Liberty in Antebellum Charleston* (2011)
- Blain Roberts and Ethan J. Kytle, "Looking the Thing in the Face: Slavery, Race, and the Commemorative Landscape in Charleston, South Carolina, 1865–2010," *Journal of Southern History* 78, no. 3 (2012): 639–68.
- Ethan J. Kytle and Blain Roberts, "'Is It Okay to Talk about Slaves?': Segregating

the Past in Historic Charleston," in Karen L. Cox, ed., *Destination Dixie: Tourism and Southern History* (2012), 137–59.

- Blain Roberts, "Uncovering the Confederacy of the Mind: Or, How I Became a Belle of the Ball in Denmark Vesey's Church," *Southern Cultures* 19, no. 3 (2013): 6–25.
- Stephanie Yuhl, "Hidden in Plain Sight: Centering the Domestic Slave Trade in American Public History," *Journal of Southern History* 79, no. 3 (2013): 593–624. https://jsh.rice.edu/uploadedFiles/Yuhl%20JSH79%20Aug13.pdf
- Steve Estes, *Charleston in Black and White: Race and Power in the South after the Civil Rights Movement* (2015)
- Jeff Strickland, *Unequal Freedoms: Ethnicity, Race, and White Supremacy in Civil War–Era Charleston* (2015)

Readings on Slavery

GENERAL OVERVIEWS

- Benjamin Quarles, *The Negro in the American Revolution* (1961)
- Sylvia Frey, *Water from the Rock: Black Resistance in a Revolutionary Age* (1991)
- Ira Berlin, *Many Thousands Gone: The First Two Centuries of Slavery in North America* (1998)
- Philip D. Morgan, *Slave Counterpoint: Black Culture in the Eighteenth-Century Chesapeake and Lowcountry* (1998)
- Linda M. Heywood and John K. Thornton, *Central Africans, Atlantic Creoles, and the Foundation of the Americas* (2007)
- Edward E. Baptist, *The Half Has Never Been Told: Slavery and the Making of American Capitalism* (2014)
- Sylviane Diouf, *Slavery's Exiles: The Story of the American Maroons* (2014)
- Gerald Horne, *The Counter-Revolution of 1776: Slave Resistance and the Origins of the United States of America* (2014)

ON SLAVERY IN THE U.S. SOUTH

- John Hope Franklin, *The Militant South, 1800–1861* (1956)
- John W. Blassingame, *The Slave Community: Plantation Life in the Antebellum South* (1972)
- Eugene Genovese, *Roll, Jordan, Roll: The World the Slaves Made* (1974)
- T. H. Breen, *Myne Owne Ground: Race and Freedom on Virginia's Eastern Shore, 1640–1676* (1980)
- Deborah Gray White, *Ar'n't I a Woman?: Female Slaves in the Plantation South* (1985)
- William Dusinberre, *Them Dark Days: Slavery in the American Rice Swamps* (1996)
- Brenda Stevenson, *Life in Black and White: Family and Community in the Slave South* (1996)
- Edward Ball, *Slaves in the Family* (1998)

- Michael Angelo Gomez, *Exchanging Our Country Marks: The Transformation of African Identities in the Colonial and Antebellum South* (1998)
- Noralee Frankel, *Freedom's Women: Black Women and Families in Civil War Era Mississippi* (1999)
- Walter Johnson, *Soul by Soul: Life inside the Antebellum Slave Market* (1999)
- Sally Hadden, *Slave Patrols: Law and Violence in Virginia and the Carolinas* (2001)
- Sharla M. Fett, *Working Cures: Healing, Health, and Power on Southern Slave Plantations* (2002)
- Gwendolyn Midlo Hall, *Africans in Colonial Louisiana: The Development of Afro-Creole Culture in the Eighteenth Century* (2002)
- Dylan C. Penningroth, *The Claims of Kinfolk: African American Property and Community in the Nineteenth-Century South* (2003)
- Stephanie Camp, *Closer to Freedom: Enslaved Women and Everyday Resistance in the Plantation South* (2004)
- David Brion Davis, *Inhuman Bondage: The Rise and Fall of Slavery in the New World* (2006)
- Daina Ramey Berry, *Swing the Sickle for the Harvest Is Ripe: Gender and Slavery in Antebellum Georgia* (2007)
- Thavolia Glymph, *Out of the House of Bondage: The Transformation of the Plantation Household* (2009)
- Adam Rothman, *Beyond Freedom's Reach: A Kidnapping in the Twilight of Slavery* (2015)

ON SLAVERY IN THE U.S. NORTH

- Lorenzo J. Greene, *The Negro in Colonial New England, 1620–1776* (1942)
- Gary B. Nash, *Forging Freedom: The Formation of Philadelphia's Black Community, 1720–1840* (1988)
- James Oliver Horton and Lois E. Horton, *In Hope of Liberty: Culture, Community, and Protest among Northern Free Blacks, 1700–1860* (1997)
- Joanne Pope Melish, *Disowning Slavery: Gradual Emancipation and "Race" in New England, 1780–1860* (1998)
- Leslie M. Harris, *In the Shadow of Slavery: African Americans in New York City, 1626–1863* (2003)
- Erica Armstrong Dunbar, *A Fragile Freedom: African American Women and Emancipation in the Antebellum City* (2008)

ON SLAVERY IN THE ATLANTIC WORLD

- John Thorton, *Africa and Africans in the Making of the Atlantic World, 1400–1800* (1998)
- Hilary Beckles and Verene Shepherd, eds., *Caribbean Slavery in the Atlantic World* (2000)
- Peter Linebaugh and Marcus Rediker, *The Many-Headed Hyrda: Sailors, Slaves, Commoners, and the Hidden History of the Revolutionary Atlantic* (2000)

- Verene Shepherd, *Working Slavery, Pricing Freedom: Perspectives from the Caribbean, Africa, and the African Diaspora* (2002)
- Jennifer Morgan, *Laboring Women: Reproduction and Gender in New World Slavery* (2004)
- Pamela Scully and Diana Paton, eds., *Gender and Slave Emancipation in the Atlantic World* (2005)
- Stephanie E. Smallwood, *Saltwater Slavery: A Middle Passage from Africa to American Diaspora* (2007)
- Edda L. Fields-Black, *Deep Roots: Rice Farmers in West Africa and the African Diaspora* (2008)

Readings on the Civil War and Reconstruction

- Booker T. Washington, *Up from Slavery* (1901)
- W. E. B. Du Bois, *Black Reconstruction* (1935)
- Hortense Powdermaker, *After Freedom: A Cultural Study in the Deep South* (1939)
- Leon Litwack, *Been in the Storm So Long: The Aftermath of Slavery* (1979)
- Michael P. Johnson and James Roark, *Free Family of Color in the Old South* (1984)
- George Rable, *But There Was No Peace: The Role of Violence in the Politics of Reconstruction* (1984)
- Eric Foner, *Reconstruction: America's Unfinished Revolution, 1863–1877* (1988)
- James M. McPherson, *Battle Cry of Freedom: The Civil War Era* (1988)
- Ira Berlin, *Slaves No More: Three Essays on Emancipation and the Civil War* (1992)
- Elsa Barkley, "Negotiating and Transforming the Public Sphere: African American Political Life in the Transition from Slavery to Freedom," *Public Culture* 7 (1994): 107–46. http://drum.lib.umd.edu/bitstream/handle/1903/13704/barkleybrown_negotiatingandtransforming.pdf;jsessionid=E87BA2FFAF0A163FE-338A69063B3FA72?sequence=1
- Martha Hodes, *White Women, Black Men: Illicit Sex in the Nineteenth-Century South* (1997)
- Tera W. Hunter, *To 'Joy My Freedom: Southern Black Women's Lives and Labors after the Civil War* (1997)
- Tony Horwitz, *Confederates in the Attic: Dispatches from the Unfinished Civil War* (1998)
- David Blight, *Race and Reunion: The Civil War in American Memory* (2001)
- Charles Dew, *Apostles of Disunion: Southern Secession Commissioners and the Causes of the Civil War* (2001)
- Alfred Brophy, *Reconstructing the Dreamland: The Tulsa Riot of 1921: Race, Reparations, and Reconciliation* (2003)
- Douglas Blackmon, *Slavery by Another Name* (2008)
- Carole Emberton, *Beyond Redemption: Race, Violence, and the American South after the Civil War* (2009)
- Stephanie McCurry, *Confederate Reckoning: Power and Politics in the Civil War South* (2010)

- Doug Egerton, *The Wars of Reconstruction: The Brief, Violent History of America's Most Progressive Era* (2013)

READINGS ON THE CONFEDERATE FLAG

- George Schedler, *Racist Symbols and Reparations: Philosophical Reflections on Vestiges of the American Civil War* (1998)
- Robert Bonner, *Colors and Blood: Flag Passions of the Confederate South* (2002)
- K. Michael Prince, *Rally 'Round the Flag, Boys! South Carolina and the Confederate Flag* (2004)
- John Coski, *The Confederate Battle Flag: America's Most Embattled Emblem* (2005)

Readings on Post-Reconstruction and Jim Crow

- W. E. B. Du Bois, *The Souls of Black Folk* (1903)
- C. Vann Woodward, *The Strange Career of Jim Crow* (1974)
- Nell Irvin Painter, *Exodusters: Black Migration to Kansas after Reconstruction* (1977)
- Wilson Jeremiah Moses, *The Golden Age of Black Nationalism, 1850–1925* (1978)
- Howard N. Rabinowitz, *Race Relations in the Urban South, 1865–1890* (1978)
- Neil R. McMillen, *Dark Journey: Black Mississippians in the Age of Jim Crow* (1989)
- Robin D. G. Kelley, "We Are Not What We Seem: Rethinking Black Working-Class Opposition in the Jim Crow South," *Journal of American History* (1993): 75–112. http://www.sscnet.ucla.edu/polisci/faculty/chwe/austen/kelley.pdf
- Glenda Gilmore, *Gender and Jim Crow: Women and the Politics of White Supremacy in North Carolina, 1896–1920* (1996)
- Grace Elizabeth Hale, *Making Whiteness: The Culture of Segregation in the South, 1890–1940* (1998)
- Leon F. Litwack, *Trouble in Mind: Black Southerners in the Age of Jim Crow* (1998)
- Deborah Gray White, *Too Heavy a Load: Black Women in Defense of Themselves, 1894–1994* (1999)
- Nell Irvin Painter, *Southern History across the Color Line* (2002)
- Manning Marable, *The Great Wells of Democracy: The Meaning of Race in American Life* (2002)
- Michele Mitchell, *Righteous Propagation: African Americans and the Politics of Racial Destiny after Reconstruction* (2004)
- W. Fitzhugh Brundage, *The Southern Past: A Clash of Race and Memory* (2005)
- James C. Cobb, *Away Down South: A History of Southern Identity* (2005)
- James W. Loewen, *Sundown Towns: A Hidden Dimension of American Racism* (2005)
- Mark Smith, *How Race Is Made: Slavery, Segregation, and the Senses* (2006)
- Bruce E. Baker, *What Reconstruction Meant: Historical Memory in the American South* (2007)

- Kate Dossett, *Bridging Race Divides: Black Nationalism, Feminism, and Integration, 1896–1935* (2008)
- Blair L. M. Kelley, *Right to Ride: Streetcar Boycotts and African-American Citizenship in the Era of Plessy v. Ferguson* (2010)
- Isabel Wilkerson, *The Warmth of Other Suns: The Epic Story of America's Great Migration* (2010)
- Michelle Alexander, *The New Jim Crow: Mass Incarceration in the Age of Colorblindness,* (2011)
- Andrew W. Kahrl, *The Land Was Ours: African American Beaches from Jim Crow to the Sunbelt South* (2012)

READINGS ON RACIAL VIOLENCE

- Frantz Fanon, *The Wretched of the Earth* (1961)
- Nancy MacLean, *Behind the Mask of Chivalry: The Making of the Second Ku Klux Klan* (1994)
- Saidiya V. Hartman, *Scenes of Subjection: Terror, Slavery, and Self-Making in Nineteenth-Century America* (1997)
- David Grimsted, *American Mobbing: Toward Civil War* (1998)
- Sheila Smith McKoy, *When Whites Riot: Writing Race and Violence in American and South African Culture* (2001)
- Christopher Waldrep, *Lynching in America: A History in Documents* (2006)
- Rebecca Nell Hill, *Men, Mobs, and Law: Anti-lynching and Labor Defense in U.S. Radical History* (2008)
- Crystal Feimster, *Southern Horrors: Women and the Politics of Rape and Lynching* (2009)
- Hannah Rosen, *Terror in the Heart of Freedom: Citizenship, Sexual Violence, and the Meaning of Race in the Post-emancipation South* (2009)
- Amy Louise Wood, *Lynching and Spectacle: Witnessing Racial Violence in America, 1890–1940* (2009)
- Danielle McGuire, *At the Dark End of the Street: Black Women, Rape, and Resistance* (2010)
- Kidada Williams, *They Left Great Marks on Me: African American Testimonies of Racial Violence from Emancipation to World War I* (2012)
- Michael J. Pfeifer, *Lynching beyond Dixie: American Mob Violence outside the South* (2013)
- Brenda E. Stevenson, *The Contested Murder of Latasha Harlins: Justice, Gender, and the Origins of the L.A. Riots* (2013)

READINGS ON WHITE RACIAL IDENTITY

- Ian Haney-López, *White by Law: The Legal Construction of Race* (1996)
- George Lipsitz, *The Possessive Investment in Whiteness: How White People Profit from Identity Politics* (1998)
- David R. Roediger, *Colored White: Transcending the Racial Past* (2002)

- Thomas Guglielmo, *White on Arrival: Italians, Race, Color, and Power in Chicago, 1890–1945* (2004)
- David R. Roediger, *Working toward Whiteness: How America's Immigrants Became White* (2005)
- Shannon Sullivan, *Revealing Whiteness: The Unconscious Habits of Racial Privilege* (2006)
- Nell Irvin Painter, *The History of White People* (2010)

READINGS ON WHITE SUPREMACY IN THE INITED STATES AND ABROAD

- Reg Austin, *Racism and Apartheid in Southern Africa* (1975)
- George M. Frederickson, *White Supremacy: A Comparative Study* (1981)
- John Cell, *The Highest Stage of White Supremacy: The Origins of Segregation in South Africa and the American South* (1982)
- Thomas J. Noer, *Cold War and Black Liberation: The United States and White Rule in Africa, 1948–1968* (1985)
- David Theo Goldberg, *Racist Culture: Philosophy and the Politics of Meaning* (1993)
- Michel-Rolph Trouillot, *Silencing the Past: Power and the Production of History* (1995)
- Brenda Gayle Plummer, *Rising Wind: Black Americans and U.S. Foreign Affairs, 1935–1960* (1996)
- Jessie Daniels, *White Lies: Race, Class, Gender, and Sexuality in White Supremacist Discourse* (1997)
- Penny Von Eschen, *Race against Empire: Black Americans and Anticolonialism, 1937–1957* (1997)
- Stephen David Kantrowitz, *Ben Tillman and the Reconstruction of White Supremacy* (2000)
- Thomas Borstelmann, *The Cold War and the Color Line: American Race Relations in the Global Arena* (2001)
- Howard Winant, *The World Is a Ghetto: Race and Democracy since World War II* (2001)
- James Meriwether, *Proudly We Can Be Africans: Black Americans and Africa, 1935–1961* (2002)
- Eduardo Bonilla-Silva, *Racism without Racists: Color-Blind Racism and the Persistence of Racial Inequality in America* (2003)
- Joe R. Feagin, *Systemic Racism: A Theory of Oppression* (2006)
- Marilyn Lake and Henry Reynolds, *Drawing the Global Color Line: White Men's Countries and the International Challenge of Racial Equality* (2008)
- Carl Nightingale, *Segregation: A Global History of Divided Cities* (2012)

Readings on Race and Religion

- Gayraud S. Wilmore, *Black Religion and Black Radicalism: An Interpretation of the Religious History of African Americans* (1963)

- Marcus Garvey and Amy Jacques Garvey, *The Philosophy and Opinions of Marcus Garvey* (1967)
- Charles Wesley, *Richard Allen: Apostle of Freedom* (1969)
- Carol V. R. George, *Segregated Sabbaths: Richard Allen and the Emergence of Independent Black Churches, 1760–1840* (1973)
- William R. Jones, *Is God a White Racist?: A Preamble to Black Theology* (1973)
- Albert Raboteau, *Slave Religion: The Invisible Institution in the Antebellum South* (1978)
- Leonardo Boff and Clodovis Boff, *Introducing Liberation Theology* (1987)
- James Campbell, *Songs of Zion: The African Methodist Church in the United States and South Africa* (1995)
- Howard Thurman, *Jesus and the Disinherited* (1996)
- Allan D. Austin, *African Muslims in Antebellum America: Transatlantic Stories and Spiritual Struggles* (1997)
- Paul Harvey, *Redeeming the South: Religious Cultures and Racial Identities among Southern Baptists, 1865–1925* (1997)
- Eddie Glaude Jr., *Exodus! Religion, Race, and Nation in Early Nineteenth-Century Black America* (2000)
- Albert Raboteau, *Canaan Land: A Religious History of African Americans* (2001)
- Karla Holloway, *Passed On: African American Mourning Stories* (2002)
- Jason R. Young, *Rituals of Resistance: African Atlantic Religion in Kongo and the Lowcountry South in the Era of Slavery* (2007)
- J. Kameron Carter, *Race: A Theological Account* (2008)
- Charles Irons, *Origins of Proslavery Christianity: White and Black Evangelicals in Colonial and Antebellum Virginia* (2008)
- Richard Newman, *Freedom's Prophet: Bishop Richard Allen, the AME Church, and the Black Founding Fathers* (2008)
- Charles Reagan Wilson, *Baptized in Blood: The Religion of the Lost Cause, 1865–1920* (2009)
- Willie James Jennings, *The Christian Imagination: Theology and the Origins of Race* (2010)
- George C. Rable, *God's Almost Chosen Peoples: A Religious History of the American Civil War* (2010)
- James H. Cone, *The Cross and the Lynching Tree* (2011)
- Rebecca Anne Goetz, *The Baptism of Early Virginia: How Christianity Created Race* (2012)
- Edward J. Blum, *The Color of Christ: The Son of God and the Saga of Race in America* (2012)

READINGS ON AFRICAN AMERICAN WOMEN'S RELIGIOUS HISTORY

- Evelyn Brooks Higginbotham, *Righteous Discontent: The Women's Movement in the Black Baptist Church, 1880–1920* (1993)
- Delores S. Williams, *Sisters in the Wilderness: The Challenge of Womanist God-Talk* (1993)

- Katie G. Cannon, *Katie's Cannon: Womanism and the Soul of the Black Community* (1995)
- Marcia Riggs, *Can I Get a Witness?: Prophetic Religious Voices of African American Women* (1997)
- Judith Weisenfeld, *African American Women and Christian Activism: New York's Black YWCA, 1905–1945* (1997)
- Cheryl Gilkes, *If It Wasn't for the Women: Black Women's Experience and Womanist Culture in Church and Community* (2001)
- Jualynne E. Dodson, *Engendering Church: Women, Power and the AME Church* (2002)
- Marla Faye Frederick, *Between Sundays: Black Women and Everyday Struggles of Faith* (2003)
- Joycelyn Moody, *Sentimental Confessions: Spiritual Narratives of Nineteenth-Century African American Women* (2003)
- Carolyn Moxley Rouse, *Engaged Surrender: African American Women and Islam* (2004)
- Anthea D. Butler, *Women in the Church of God in Christ: Making a Sanctified World* (2007)
- Bettye Collier-Thomas, *Jesus, Jobs, and Justice: African American Women and Religion* (2010)

Readings on the Civil Rights–Black Power Era

- James Baldwin, *The Fire Next Time* (1963)
- James Cone, *Black Theology and Black Power* (1969)
- Howell Raines, *My Soul Is Rested: Movement Days in the Deep South Remembered* (1977)
- Clayborne Carson, *In Struggle: SNCC and the Black Awakening of the 1960s* (1981)
- Aldon D. Morris, *The Origins of the Civil Rights Movement: Black Communities Organizing for Change* (1984)
- Adam Fairclough, *To Redeem the Soul of America: The Southern Christian Leadership Conference and Martin Luther King, Jr.* (1987)
- David J. Garrow, *Bearing the Cross: Martin Luther King, Jr., and the Southern Christian Leadership Conference* (1986)
- David J. Garrow, "Martin Luther King, Jr., and the Spirit of Leadership," *Journal of American History* 74 (1987): 438–47. http://vi.uh.edu/pages/buzzmat/articles/garrow%20mlk%20roundtable.pdf
- Jo Ann Gibson Robinson and David J. Garrow, *The Montgomery Bus Boycott and the Women Who Started It: The Memoir of Jo Ann Gibson Robinson* (1987)
- Taylor Branch, *Parting the Waters: America in the King Years, 1954–63* (1988)
- Clayborne Carson, *The Eyes on the Prize: Civil Rights Reader* (1991)
- William Van Deburg, *New Day in Babylon: The Black Power Movement and American Culture, 1965–1975* (1992)

- David L. Chappell, *Inside Agitators: White Southerners in the Civil Rights Movement* (1994)
- John Dittmer, *Local People: the Struggle for Civil Rights in Mississippi* (1994)
- Charles Payne, *I've Got the Light of Freedom: The Organizing Tradition and the Mississippi Freedom Struggle* (1995)
- Gerald Horne, *Fire This Time: The Watts Uprising and the 1960s* (1995)
- Robert F. Williams, *Negroes with Guns* (1998)
- Chana Kai Lee, *For Freedom's Sake: The Life of Fannie Lou Hamer* (1999)
- Jennifer Smith, *An International History of the Black Panther Party* (1999)
- Komozi Woodard, *A Nation within a Nation: Amiri Baraka (LeRoi Jones) and Black Power Politics* (1999)
- Bettye Collier-Thomas and V. P. Franklin, eds., *Sisters in the Struggle: African American Women in the Civil Rights Black Power Movement* (2001)
- Bruce Nelson, *Divided We Stand: American Workers and the Struggle for Black Equality* (2001)
- Martha Biondi, *To Stand and Fight: The Struggle for Civil Rights in Postwar New York City* (2003)
- Barbara Ransby, *Ella Baker and the Black Freedom Movement: A Radical Democratic Vision* (2003)
- Lance Hill, *The Deacons for Defense: Armed Resistance and the Civil Rights Movement* (2004)
- Matthew Countryman, *Up South: Civil Rights and Black Power in Philadelphia* (2005)
- Clive Webb, *Massive Resistance: Southern Opposition to the Second Reconstruction* (2005)
- Peniel E. Joseph, *Waiting 'til the Midnight Hour: A Narrative History of Black Power in America* (2006)
- Thomas Jackson, *From Civil Rights to Human Rights: Martin Luther King, Jr., and the Struggle for Economic Justice* (2007)
- Glenda Elizabeth Gilmore, *Defying Dixie: The Radical Roots of Civil Rights, 1919–1950* (2008)
- Thomas Sugrue, *Sweet Land of Liberty: The Forgotten Struggle for Civil Rights in the North* (2008)
- Hasan Kwame Jeffries, *Bloody Lowndes: Civil Rights and Black Power in Alabama's Black Belt* (2009)
- Joshua Bloom and Waldo Martin, *Black against Empire: The History and Politics of the Black Panther Party* (2013)
- Akinyele Umoja, *We Will Shoot Back: Armed Resistance in the Mississippi Freedom Movement* (2013)
- Rhonda Williams, *Concrete Demands: The Search for Black Power in the 20th Century* (2015)

African American Literature

- Charles W. Chestnutt, *The House behind the Cedars* (1900)
- James Weldon Johnson, *The Autobiography of an Ex-Colored Man* (1912)
- Nella Larson, *Quicksand* (1928)
- Nella Larson, *Passing* (1929)
- Zora Neale Hurston, *Their Eyes Were Watching God* (1937)
- Richard Wright, *Black Boy* (1945)
- Ralph Ellison, *Invisible Man* (1952)
- James Baldwin, *Go Tell It on the Mountain* (1953)
- Lorraine Hansberry, *A Raisin in the Sun* (1959)
- Charles W. Chesnutt, *The Marrow of Tradition* (1969)
- Toni Morrison, *The Bluest Eye* (1970)
- Ernest J. Gaines, *The Autobiography of Miss Jane Pittman* (1971)
- Toni Cade Bambara, *Gorilla, My Love* (1972)
- Richard Wright, *American Hunger* (1977)
- Octavia E. Butler, *Kindred* (1979)
- Alice Walker, *You Can't Keep a Good Woman Down* (1981)
- John Edgar Wideman, *Brothers and Keepers* (1984)
- Toni Morrison, *Beloved* (1987)
- Charles Johnson, *Middle Passage* (1990)
- Walter Mosley, *Devil in a Blue Dress* (1990)
- Edward P. Jones, *Lost in the City* (1992)
- Ernest J. Gaines, *A Lesson before Dying* (1993)
- Rita Dove, *The Darker Face of the Earth* (1994)
- Tananarive Due, *The Between* (1996)
- Charles W. Chestnut, *Conjure Tales and Stories of the Color Line* (2000)
- Lalita Tademy, *Cane River* (2001)
- Edward P. Jones, *The Known World* (2003)
- Percival Everett, *Damned If I Do: Stories* (2004)
- Toni Morrison, *A Mercy* (2008)
- Danielle Evans, *Before You Suffocate Your Own Fool Self* (2010)
- Ntozake Shange, *Some Sing, Some Cry* (2010)
- Lorene Cary, *If Sons, Then Heirs* (2011)
- Jesmyn Ward, *Men We Reaped* (2013)
- Jeffery Renard Allen, *Song of the Shank* (2014)
- Kekla Magoon, *How It Went Down* (2014)
- Jina Ortiz and Rochelle Spencer, eds., *All about Skin: Short Fiction by Women of Color* (2014)
- Alysia Burton Steele, *Delta Jewels: In Search of My Grandmother's Wisdom* (2015)

POETRY

- Poetry by Gwendolyn Brooks. http://www.poetryfoundation.org/bio/gwendolyn-brooks
- Poetry by Lucille Clifton. http://www.poetryfoundation.org/bio/lucille-clifton

- Poetry by Rita Dove. http://www.poetryfoundation.org/bio/rita-dove
- Poetry by Nikky Finney. http://www.poetryfoundation.org/bio/nikky-finney
- Poetry by Vievee Francis. http://www.poetryfoundation.org/bio/vievee-francis
- Poetry by Nikki Giovanni. http://www.poetryfoundation.org/bio/nikki-giovanni
- Poetry of Robert Hayden. http://www.poetryfoundation.org/bio/robert-hayden
- Poetry by Langston Hughes. http://www.poetryfoundation.org/bio /langston-hughes
- Poetry by James Weldon Johnson. http://www.poetryfoundation.org/bio /james-weldon-johnson
- Poetry by Claude McKay. http://www.poetryfoundation.org/bio/claude-mckay
- Poetry by Claudia Rankine. http://www.poetryfoundation.org/bio /claudia-rankine
- Poetry by Natasha Tretheway. http://www.poetryfoundation.org/bio /natasha-trethewey
- Poetry by Kevin Young. http://www.poetryfoundation.org/bio/kevin-young

Selected Primary Sources

- Absalom Jones, "A Thanksgiving Sermon" (1808). http://anglicanhistory.org/usa/ ajones/thanksgiving1808.html
- David Walker, "Appeal to the Coloured Citizens of the World" (1829). http:// docsouth.unc.edu/nc/walker/walker.html
- Mary Prince, *The History of Mary Prince, A West Indian Slave* (1831). http:// docsouth.unc.edu/neh/prince/prince.html
- Richard Allen, *The Life, Experience, and Gospel Labours of the Rt. Rev. Richard Allen* (1833). http://docsouth.unc.edu/neh/allen/menu.html
- Charles Ball, *A Narrative of the Life of Charles Ball* (1837). http://docsouth.unc .edu/neh/ballslavery/ball.html
- Henry Highland Garnet, "An Address to the Slaves of the United States" (1843). http://www.blackpast.org/1843-henry-highland-garnet-address-slaves-united-states
- Frederick Douglass, *Narrative of the Life of Frederick Douglass, an American Slave* (1845)
- Frederick Douglass, "Slaveholding Religion and the Christianity of Christ" (1845). http://declaringamerica.com /douglass-slaveholding-religion-and-the-christianity-of-christ-1845/
- Jarena Lee, *Religious Experience and Journal of Mrs. Jarena Lee* (1849). https:// archive.org/details/religiousexperi00leegoog
- Frederick Douglass, "What to the Slave Is the Fourth Of July?" (1852). http:// teachingamericanhistory.org/library/document /what-to-the-slave-is-the-fourth-of-july/
- Benjamin Morgan Palmer, "Thanksgiving Sermon" (1860). http://civilwarcauses .org/palmer.htm
- Ida B. Wells-Barnett, *A Red Record: Alleged Causes of Lynching* (1895). http:// www.gutenberg.org/ebooks/14977?msg=welcome_stranger

- Mark Smith, ed., *Stono: Documenting and Interpreting a Southern Slave Revolt*
- *WPA Slave Narratives* (1930s). http://memory.loc.gov/ammem/snhtml/
- Martin Luther King Jr., "Letter from a Birmingham Jail" (1963). http://www .uscrossier.org/pullias/wp-content/uploads/2012/06/king.pdf
- Charles Morgan, "A Time to Speak" (1963). https://www.youtube.com /watch?v=7KCP8yZgxW4
- Malcolm X and Alex Haley, *The Autobiography of Malcolm X* (1965)
- Anne Moody, *Coming of Age in Mississippi* (1968)
- John Lewis, *Walking with the Wind: A Memoir of the Movement* (1998)
- David Halberstam, *The Children* (1998)
- Manning Marable and Leith Mullings, eds., *Let Nobody Turn Us Around: Voices of Resistance, Reform, and Renewal* (2000)
- Jane Dailey, *The Age of Jim Crow: A Norton Casebook in History* (2009)
- James W. Loewen and Edward H. Sebesta, eds., *The Confederate and Neo-Confederate Reader* (2010)

Multimedia Resources

FILMS

- Spike Lee, *Do the Right Thing* (1989)
- William Elwood, *The Road to Brown* (1990)
- Julie Dash, *Daughters of the Dust* (1991)
- Terrence Francis, *Black Sci-Fi* (1992). https://www.youtube.com/playlist?list =PL_3kaNQwRbyDM-dJ_rDw7UTbSWx992S8L
- Haile Gerima, *Sankofa* (1993)
- Toni Morrison, *Beloved* (1999)
- Zora Neale Hurston, *Their Eyes Were Watching God* (2005)
- Harry Moore, Michael Carter et al., *Black Wall Street, Tulsa* (2007)
- Bestor Cram and Judy Richardson, *Scarred Justice: the Orangeburg Massacre 1968* (2009)
- Göran Hugo Olsson, *The Black Power Mixtape 1967–1975* (2011)
- Douglas Blackmon, *Slavery by Another Name* (2012). http://www .slaverybyanothername.com/pbs-film/?doing_wp_cron=1434811700.27593398094 17724609375
- Ryan Coogler, *Fruitvale Station* (2013)
- Dawn Porter, *Spies of Mississippi* (2014)

MUSIC

- "Oh Freedom" (approx. 1865). https://www.youtube.com/watch?v=veiJLhXdwn8
- Paul Robeson's version of "No More Auction Block" (Gustavus D. Pike, 1873). https://www.youtube.com/watch?v=3rE-Ljcw8ro
- Bessie Smith, "Preachin' the Blues" (1927). https://www.youtube.com/watch?v= iUVdm4jUEwk&list=PLguB2-0S9Kmt57-9-gojkdtosMsuPGBTM&index=15

- Louis Armstrong, "Black and Blue" (1929). https://www.youtube.com /watch?v=YGiUi2oir3I
- Bessie Smith, "Long Old Road" (1931). https://www.youtube.com/watch?v= RNg4E55EDfQ&list=PLguB2-oS9Kmt57-9-gojkdtosMsuPGBTM&index=12
- Billie Holiday, "Strange Fruit" (1939). https://www.youtube.com /watch?v=h4ZyuULy9zs
- Big Maybelle, "Gabbin' Blues" (1952). https://www.youtube.com/watch?v= 2oPKJzlT5NM
- Odetta, "Spiritual Trilogy: Oh, Freedom; Come and Go with Us; I'm on My Way" (1956). https://www.youtube.com/watch?v=GEsSABmWKu8
- Theolonius Monk, "Blue Monk" (1958). https://www.youtube.com /watch?v=_40V2lcxM7k
- Nina Simone, "Chilly Winds Don't Blow" (1959). https://www.youtube.com /watch?v=JZwXzpcuSIc
- *We Insist! Max Roach's Freedom Now Suite* (1960). https://www.youtube.com /watch?v=UsvFzXr-0-8&feature=youtu.be
- John Coltrane, "Alabama" (1963). https://www.youtube.com/watch?v= saN1BwlxJxA
- Sam Cooke, "A Change Is Gonna Come" (1964). https://www.youtube.com /watch?v=nEM4VlnGNXU
- Bob Dylan, "Only a Pawn in Their Game" (1964). https://www.youtube.com /watch?v=Wvz23ET5ARM&feature=youtu.be
- The Impressions, "Keep on Pushing" (1964). https://www.youtube.com /watch?v=HU-mEsCk3D8
- Nina Simone, "Mississippi Goddamn" (1964). https://www.youtube.com /watch?v=fVQjGGJVSXc
- Gil Scott-Heron, "The Revolution Will Not Be Televised" (1970). https://www .youtube.com/watch?v=qGaoXAwl9kw
- The Temptations, "Ball of Confusion" (1970). https://www.youtube.com /watch?v=Gy_aahkIdEI
- Marvin Gaye, "Inner City Blues / Makes Me Wanna Holler" (1971). https://www .youtube.com/watch?v=57Ykv1DoqEE
- Donny Hathaway, "Someday We'll All Be Free" (1973). https://www.youtube.com /watch?v=cv1BoejhFVE
- The McIntosh County Shouters, "Wade the Water to My Knees" (1984). https:// www.youtube.com/watch?v=YjXbgrsgiFE
- The Specials, "Racist Friend" (1984). https://www.youtube.com/watch?v= gqH_oLPVoho
- The Freedom Singers, "In the Mississippi River" (1997). https://www.youtube .com/watch?v=g_HIof3irKo
- Wynton Marsalis, "Blood on the Fields" (1997). https://www.youtube.com /watch?v=3UH8qpvLDt4
- Stephen Said, "The Ballad of Abner Louima" (1997). https://www.youtube.com /watch?v=51ZqqthQars

- Sweet Honey in the Rock, "Ella's Song" (1998). https://www.youtube.com/watch?v=U6Uus—gFrc
- J. B. Lenoir, "Alabama Blues" (2004). https://www.youtube.com/watch?v=kKecJVJ493g&feature=youtu.be
- Wynton Marsalis, "From the Plantation to the Penitentiary" (2007). https://www.youtube.com/watch?v=yQAgrzc8hXw
- Mavis Staples, "Down in Mississippi"(2007). https://www.youtube.com/watch?v=FeZmZ1Pt6C0
- Kendrick Lamar, "Alright" (2015) *Explicit content*. https://www.youtube.com/watch?v=Z-48u_uWMHY
- Kendrick Lamar, "The Blacker the Berry" (2015) *Explicit content*. https://www.youtube.com/watch?v=rMxNYQ71LOk
- John Legend featuring Common, "Glory" (2015). https://www.youtube.com/watch?v=ZzbKaDPMoDU
- Vince Staples, "Lift Me Up" (2015) *Explicit content*. https://www.youtube.com/watch?v=CRjpYAsY-DE

WEBSITES

- *After Slavery: Race, Labor, and Politics in the Post-Emancipation Carolinas.* http://ldhi.library.cofc.edu/exhibits/show/after_slavery
- *Charleston Hospital Workers Movement, 1968–1969.* http://ldhi.library.cofc.edu/exhibits/show/charleston_hospital_workers_mo/civil_rights_unionism
- *The Color Line—on the History of Racism in the United States.* https://zinnedproject.org/materials/the-color-line-colonial-laws/
- *Facing History and Ourselves' List of Resources on Teaching Reconstruction.* https://www.facinghistory.org/reconstruction-era?utm_campaign=Charleston&utm_source=ReconstructionEraTwitter
- *Hudson River Valley Heritage Digital Collection of Primary Sources.* http://www.hrvh.org/cdm/search/searchterm/African%20Americans/field/hrvh/mode/exact/page/1
- *RACE: A Public Education Project through the American Anthropological Association.* http://www.aaanet.org/resources/A-Public-Education-Program.cfm
- *Voices from the Days of Slavery (Library of Congress).* http://memory.loc.gov/ammem/collections/voices/
- *Wabash Center for Teaching and Learning in Theology and Religion.* http://wabashcenter.typepad.com/antiracism_pedagogy/
- *Without Sanctuary: Photographs and Postcards of Lynching in America.* http://withoutsanctuary.org/main.html
- *Zinn Education Project—Teaching a People's History.* https://zinnedproject.org/

COURSE HANDOUTS AND OTHER TEACHING SOURCES

- Black History Resources for Children. http://guides.mysapl.org/print_content.php?pid=417841&sid=3415431&mode=g

- Caleb McDaniel's "The American Civil War Era" Rice University Course Hand-outs. https://github.com/wcaleb/civil-war-reader
- Quotes, Videos, and Various Sources on Antiblackness. http://antiblacknessisatheory.tumblr.com/
- Selected Historical Newspapers (courtesy of the Library of Congress). http://chroniclingamerica.loc.gov/
- State Sanctioned: Sample Curricula and Lesson Plans on Racial Violence. http://statesanctioned.com/sample-curricula-and-lesson-plans/#race
- William Buckley Debates James Baldwin at Cambridge. https://www.youtube.com/watch?v=oFeoS41xe7w

For Young Readers

- Joy Hakim, *Reconstruction and Reform* (1994)
- Zak Mettger, *Reconstruction: America after the Civil War* (1994)
- Marybeth Lorbieck, *Sister Anne's Hands* (1998)
- Karen Katz, *The Colors of Us* (1999)
- Joyce Hansen, *Bury Me Not in the Land of Slaves: African-Americans in the Time of Reconstruction* (2000)
- Patricia McKissack, *Goin' Someplace Special* (2001)
- Deborah Wiles, *Freedom Summer* (2001)
- Meg Greene, *Into the Land of Freedom: African Americans in Reconstruction* (2004)
- Doreen Rappaport and Shane Evans, *Free At Last! Stories and Songs of Emancipation* (2004)
- Tonya Bolden, *Cause: Reconstruction America, 1863–1877* (2005)
- Michael Tyler, *The Skin You Live In* (2005)
- James M. McPherson, *Into the West: From Reconstruction to the Final Days of the American Frontier* (2006)
- Adriane Ruggiero, *Reconstruction* (2007)
- Linda Barrett Osborne, *Traveling the Freedom Road from Slavery & the Civil War through Reconstruction* (2009)
- Deborah Wiles, *Revolution* (2014)
- Chris Barton and Don Tate, *The Amazing Age of John Roy Lynch* (2015)

CREDITS

Benjamin Foldy, "Rhodesian Flag, Confederate Flag: Roof and the Legacies of Racial Hate," from *Informed Comment*, June 20, 2015. Courtesy of the publisher.

Crystal N. Feimster, From *Southern Horrors: Women and the Politics of Rape and Lynching*, pp. 212–15, 215–16, 219–20, 221–22, 223, 231–32, 232–33. Copyright © 2009 by the President and Fellows of Harvard College.

Robin D. G. Kelley, From "'We Are Not What We Seem': Rethinking Black Working-Class Opposition in the Jim Crow South," pp. 75–78, 89, 95, 96, 97–98, 102, from *Journal of American History* 80, no. 1 (June 1993): 75–112. Courtesy of the author.

Cherisse Jones-Branch, From "'To Speak When and Where I Can': African American Women's Political Activism in South Carolina in the 1940s and 1950s," pp. 204–7, 208, 209–11, 211–12, 216, 223–24, from *South Carolina Historical Magazine* 107, no. 3 (July 2006): 204–24. Courtesy of the South Carolina Historical Society.

George Lipsitz, From *The Possessive Investment in Whiteness: How White People Profit from Identity Politics*, pp. 1–2, 2–5, 7, 12–13, 23 (Philadelphia: Temple University Press, 1998). Courtesy of the publisher.

Manning Marable, "'Blackness beyond Boundaries': Navigating the Political Economies of Global Inequality," pp. 1–7, introduction to *Transnational Blackness: Navigating the Global Color Line*, edited by Manning Marable and Vanessa Agard-Jones (New York: Palgrave Macmillan, 2008). Courtesy of the estate of Manning Marable.

Robin Blake, "Is It Time to Reevaluate the Church's Role in the Civil Rights Movement?" from *Afropunk.com*, July 13, 2015. Courtesy of the author.

Danielle McGuire, "More Than a Seat on the Bus," from *We're History* website, December 1, 2015. Courtesy of the author. McGuire is associate professor of history at Wayne State University and author of *At the Dark End of the Street: Black Women, Rape, and Resistance—a New History of the Civil Rights Movement from Rosa Parks to the Rise of Black Power* (Knopf, 2010).

Genna Rae McNeil, From "'Joanne Is You and Joanne Is Me': A Consideration of African American Women and the 'Free Joan Little' Movement, 1974–75," pp. 259–61, 261–63, 263–64, 266–67, 270–71, 273–74, 274–75, chapter 14 of *Sisters in the Struggle: African American Women in the Civil Rights–Black Power Movement*, edited by B. P. Franklin and B. Collier-Thomas (New York: New York University Press, 2001). Courtesy of the publisher.